E-Procurement Management for Successful Electronic Government Systems

Patricia Ordóñez de Pablos
University of Oviedo, Spain

Juan Manuel Cueva Lovelle
University of Oviedo, Spain

Jose Emilio Labra Gayo
University of Oviedo, Spain

Robert D. Tennyson
University of Minnesota, USA

Information Science
REFERENCE

Managing Director: Lindsay Johnston
Editorial Director: Joel Gamon
Book Production Manager: Jennifer Romanchak
Publishing Systems Analyst: Adrienne Freeland
Development Editor: Myla Merkel
Assistant Acquisitions Editor: Kayla Wolfe
Typesetter: Nicole Sparano
Cover Design: Nick Newcomer

Published in the United States of America by
Information Science Reference (an imprint of IGI Global)
701 E. Chocolate Avenue
Hershey PA 17033
Tel: 717-533-8845
Fax: 717-533-8661
E-mail: cust@igi-global.com
Web site: http://www.igi-global.com

Library of Congress Cataloging-in-Publication Data

E-procurement management for successful electronic government systems / Patricia Ordonez de Pablos ... [et al.], editors.
p. cm.
Includes bibliographical references and index.
Summary: "This book enhances the understanding and collaboration in e-government and the role of information technologies in supporting the development of improved services for citizens"--Provided by publisher.
ISBN 978-1-4666-2119-0 (hardcover) -- ISBN 978-1-4666-2120-6 (ebook) -- ISBN 978-1-4666-2121-3 (print & perpetual access) 1. Government purchasing. 2. Internet in public administration. I. Ordsqez de Pablos, Patricia, 1975-
JF1525.P85E69 2012
352.5'302854678--dc23
2012015950

British Cataloguing in Publication Data
A Cataloguing in Publication record for this book is available from the British Library.

Editorial Advisory Board

Table of Contents

Detailed Table of Contents

Union standards and began to develop an e-procurement system within the scope of e-transformation Turkey project. As a result of the works carried out under the leadership of the Public Procurement Authority, which is an independent administrative authority, the e-procurement system started to be used in some stages of the procurement process. Four public hospitals were determined as pilot administrations in order to improve the implementation and it was aimed to make the implementation common in all sectors according to the experiences gained in this field. The objective of this chapter is to reveal benefits gained and barriers faced during the development process of the e-procurement by focusing on the above mentioned pilot implementation field. In order to attain this objective, the method of case study was adopted in this research, and guiding experiences were tried to be gained for the e-procurement implementations in the future.

Governments are seeking to benefit from information technology by incorporating various government services online for the benefits of the citizen. The Malaysian government as part of its Multimedia Super Corridor (MSC) project introduced e-filing in 2006, which is the process of filing taxes using the Internet as one of the e-government services. This is an exploratory study to model the determinants of intention to use an Internet tax filing system. The authors used 4 variables as predictors or intention to use which were perceived usefulness, perceived ease of use, perceived risk, and facilitating condition. Data was collected from 100 respondents using non probability purposive sampling via a structured questionnaire. As hypothesized, perceived ease of use, perceived usefulness, and facilitating condition were positively related to intention to use. The findings show that perceived usefulness has the strongest influence on intention to use ($\beta = 0.341$), followed by perceived ease of use ($\beta = 0.278$) and facilitating condition ($\beta = 0.234$). As hypothesized, perceived risk was negatively related ($\beta = -0.223$) to intention to use indicating that users are concerned by the risk involved in filing taxes online. The regression results show that the four variables can explain 52.2% of the variation in intention to use which indicates good explanatory power. Understanding these factors can extend the knowledge, which can lead to better planning and implementation of e-Filing in Malaysia.

E-government can provide citizen with better and/or more convenient services as oppose to traditional government services. Using electronic approach in completing a procurement process opens up a lot of issues regarding security. Transparent nature of the process at hand is requiring a sophisticated security system. Unauthorized access or different intrusion types are presenting a legitimate threat. On the other hand, developing such system in a developing country as Serbia bears many difficulties. Some of them are legal obstacles, technical weaknesses, as well as human resistance towards change. The focus of this chapter lies on methods used to overcome those difficulties as well as provide a strong security system that will guarantee the protection of sensitive data.

Preface

INTRODUCTION

Essentially, e-government is about using the tools and systems made possible by information and communication technologies to provide better public services to citizens and businesses. However, e-government involves much more than just the tools. Effective e-government also involves rethinking organizations and processes, and changing behavior so that public services are delivered more efficiently to the people who need to use them. When it is well implemented, e-government will enable all citizens, enterprises and organizations to carry out their business with government more easily, more quickly and at lower cost (European Commission, Information Society).

Governments seek to remodel and restyle their services and the field of E-Government attracts continuous interest and attention from public administrations, politicians, academics and citizens. New dynamic topics such as e-democracy, e-citizenship, e-identity, e-procurement and e-voting have become core elements in the development of public sector delivery

Additionally the implementation of e-procurement systems helps companies and institutions to organize their interactions with their strategic suppliers. It provides those who use it with a set of built-in monitoring tools to help control costs and assure maximum supplier performance. It offers an organized way to keep an open line of communication with potential suppliers during a business process. And finally e-procurement helps with the decision-making process by keeping relevant information neatly organized and time-stamped.

The book *E-Procurement Management for Successful Electronic Government Systems* aims to bridge academia, industry, and government with new ideas and fresh research in the broad area of E-Government.

The subject area is a combination of e-government, e-democracy, e-identity, e-procurement management, information systems, public services, web semantics, and web services.

OBJECTIVE OF THE BOOK

In the Ministerial Declaration of E-Government on November 18, 2009, it was declared that "E-Government has not only become mainstream in national policies but has also reached beyond national boundaries to become an important enabler to deliver European-wide policy goals across different sectors, from justice to social security, to trading business services and beyond. [...] better public services need to be delivered with fewer resources, and that the potential of E-Government can be increased by promoting a common culture of collaboration and by improving the conditions for interoperability of our administrations" (p. 1).

Another interesting topic is e-procurement. The concept is more than just a system for making purchases online as it encompasses the management of correspondence, bids, questions and answers, previous pricing, and multiple emails sent to multiple participants.

Therefore, information and communication technology systems are now at the heart of government processes, but efforts are still needed to ensure they continue to improve the delivery of government services.

The aims and scope of this book is to be an international platform to bring together academics, researchers, lecturers, and persons in decision making positions, policy makers and practitioners from different backgrounds to share new theories, research findings, and case studies, enhancing understanding and collaboration in e-government and the role of information technologies in supporting the development of better services for citizens. The book analyzes recent developments in theory and practice.

TOPICS COVERED IN THE BOOK

Chapter 1 introduces the construction of a generic platform and open secure voting and multipurpose for the realm of the Internet. This platform will allow the collection of signatures and support multiple contexts through the use of electronic IDs and digital certificates. Potential applications of this platform are almost endless, but some of the most significant may be: Voting at shareholders meetings, voting in communities of neighbors, collecting signatures, collecting signatures for nominations, developing proposals for ILP (popular legislative initiatives), any activity needing a platform for a reliable vote, meetings of parents, collegiate, et cetera. Currently the use of e-government for the identification of people through digital documents is on the increase, and the possibilities it presents are endless. That is why solutions are provided to allow these uses; it is of general interest for the present society.

Chapter 2 explores government procurement practices, and more specifically, how they influence large volumes of spending in communities and how further procurement can be influenced through legislative efforts. Through these mechanisms, government bodies carry significant influence on the way in which procurement spending occurs and they have the ability to influence the direction that the procurement may take. Carefully constructed parameters in public-private partnerships (PPP) can shift the focus of procurement activities towards engaging with the local businesses and communities. This represents an approach for government bodies to increase supplier diversity so that, in alignment with UN Millennium goals of poverty reduction, local suppliers can be provided with business opportunities and methods to reduce poverty. A two-focus approach is adopted; first, government drivers and policies are examined in the context of social engagement. Second, the roles and challenges faced by small firms in the local communities are highlighted. This demonstrates the way in which e-government procurement systems play a pivotal role in supporting local sourcing initiatives.

Chapter 3 delves into the area of public electronic procurement. The chapter discusses how e-procurement provides a new means of communication between contracting authorities and economic operators, as well as being one of the most important areas in the development in the business-to-business (B2B) e-commerce like buyers and suppliers entities respectively. European Union (EU) has been working hard for the adoption of e-procurement in the governments of member states, over all action plans for the development of e-government occurred during the new millennium. However, this transition, from the traditional model of procurement management procedure to electronic means, is very complicated, on one side by the impact of any new technology brings and the required regulatory policies, both within the EU and in member states. This study presents the e-procurement from the e-government regulatory contexts in EU. Then, it outlines the basic pillars of both the public e-procurement process and the management systems, and finally, introduces large-scale pilot projects by the European Commission (EC) that provide technology solutions for many of the stages of the procurement process.

Chapter 4 identifies benefits achieved by the Caixa Economica Federal (Caixa) with regard to improvements in efficiency and to deploy of its e-procurement solution associated with MRO (Maintenance, Repair, and Operation). Through simple case study, the chapter seeks to analyze the strategic importance of deploying shopping site Caixa, investigating how the dimensions of technological, organizational, and cultural influence the efficiency of their production processes. Although the results are significant in relation to the recovery time of investment, and promising for the potential to reduce administrative costs of the company, factors linked to participation and willingness to adopt a new sales model and the investment capacity and flexibility to adopt models were extremely important from the perspective of suppliers.

Chapter 5 discusses E-Government, particularly its effectiveness with rethinking organizations and processes, and changing behavior so that public services are delivered more efficiently to the people who need to use them. But the nature of the public sector is not a simple one. Lots of variables have to be considered: the number of entities involved in public sector procurement, the complexity of relationships among them, historical events that impact on the public sector, and different tensions between central and local parts of the public sector. In general, the most striking feature is the sheer complexity of the public sector. In the authors' opinion, it required a reconceptualisation of market exchange, evolving the procurement scenario from competition to collaboration. Public e-procurement is still an under-researched area. Therefore the aim of the chapter is to conduct a reflection to identify the features of purchasing and supply in the public sector and its further developments toward forms of collaboration and group purchasing.

Chapter 6 looks at the current interest in understanding main issues involved in implementing e-auction events, especially in a Business to Business (B2B) environment. This chapter offers clear classifications and systematizes the numerous variables directly or indirectly affecting e-auction suitability. Final performance determination is evident also from previous conceptual literature contributions. Nevertheless, a lack of empirical work in this field is evident. This chapter provides a contribution to the body of knowledge on critical factors impacting on e-Reverse Auctions (e-RA) performance in a B2B context. Based on an explorative factor analysis addressed to a panel of academic experts and practitioners, it aims at identifying the main factors affecting price and process performance in B2B e-RA.

Chapter 7 describes *re-use* in the field of public procurement within the European Union (EU). It describes how the lack of a pan-European information platform, providing one single access point to EU public procurement notices, hampers the access for companies to this market, especially for SMEs. To bring one possible solution to this significant issue, Euroalert.net (a company powered by open data), is currently developing commercial services fuelled by the re-use of public sector information (PSI) related to public procurement. The chapter also describes *10ders information Services* (*10ders IS*), a

Euroalert.net R&D project aimed at building a pan-European platform to aggregate public procurement information data generated by hundreds of thousands of contracting authorities in the EU.

Chapter 8 recognizes that in almost every country, public procurements are the primary issue which citizens are the most sensitive to in terms of how public money is spent. It is seen that electronic procurement systems in the public sector has been adopted as a solution in order to respond to the sensitivity of citizens because of the benefits it promises. The objective of this chapter is to reveal benefits gained and barriers faced during the development process of the e-procurement by focusing on a pilot implementation field. In order to attain this objective, the method of case study was adopted in this research and guiding experiences tried to be gained for the e-procurement implementations in the future.

Chapter 9 aims its focus at governments that are seeking to benefit from information technology by incorporating various government services online for the benefits of the citizen. The Malaysian government as part of its Multimedia Super Corridor (MSC) project introduced e-Filing in 2006, which is the process of filing taxes using the Internet as one of the e-government services. This is an exploratory study to model the determinants of intention to use an Internet tax filing system. The authors used four variables as predictors or intention to use which were perceived usefulness, perceived ease of use, perceived risk and facilitating condition. Data was collected from 100 respondents using non probability purposive sampling via a structured questionnaire. As hypothesized, perceived ease of use, perceived usefulness, and facilitating condition were positively related to intention to use. The findings show that perceived usefulness has the strongest influence on intention to use ($\beta = 0.341$), followed by perceived ease of use ($\beta = 0.278$) and facilitating condition ($\beta = 0.234$). As hypothesized, perceived risk was negatively related ($\beta =-0.223$) to intention to use indicating that users are concerned by the risk involved in filing taxes online. The regression results show that the four variables can explain 52.2% of the variation in intention to use which indicates good explanatory power. Understanding these factors can extend the knowledge which can lead to better planning and implementation of e-filing in Malaysia.

Chapter 10 explores how e-government can provide citizens with better and/or more convenient services as opposed to traditional government services. Using electronic approaches in completing a procurement process opens up issues regarding security. Transparent nature of the process at hand is requiring a sophisticated security system. Unauthorized access or different intrusion types are presenting a legitimate threat. On the other hand, developing such systems in a developing country as Serbia bears many difficulties. Some of them are legal obstacles, technical weaknesses, as well as human resistance towards change. The focus of this chapter lies on methods used to overcome those difficulties as well as provide a strong security system that will guarantee the protection of sensitive data.

Chapter 11 notes that in almost every country, government agencies are making their services available online. The success of E-Government initiatives is contingent upon citizen's willingness to use these Web-enabled services. This chapter investigates and examines the intention to use E-Government services among students in Universiti Sains Malaysia (USM), Penang. A survey involving a total of 145 university students was conducted. The results reveal that relative advantage and ease of use are the significant drivers of intention to use e-government, whereas image and compatibility were not important. The implications for research and practice are also explored.

Chapter 12 discusses that within the last decade, the Small and Medium Enterprises (SME) market has been enormously raised and the major vendors are trying to adapt their software to suit it. One important factor to be taken into consideration in such context is the support of internal and external business process integration. Service-oriented systems are offering reasonable business process integration support. However, they lack semantic definition of their service interfaces. The research presented in this chapter tries to solve this issue by proposing a semantic-enabled enterprise service-oriented framework where services can be semantically grouped based on the domains to which they belong. The proposed framework is merging both business processes and service orientation concepts to provide an agile and flexible enterprise solution that utilizes reusability, better quality, and faster time-to-market factors. This chapter illustrates this framework, its goals and outcomes, together with demonstration of a business case built on top of it.

Chapter 13 focuses on the relationship of e-procurement and government, within the context of a larger whole, namely e-government. E-Procurement and e-government are very important tools for the government to act in this rapidly changing society. But as for must business, the tools may be important, but the vision and the strategy to use these tools are much more important. Therefore we will discuss e-government and e-procurement in their strategic contexts, in which intelligence (contextual integrated information) is a key factor to survive. The reason why is because the government is a Complex Adaptive System (CAS). Without intelligence and the agility of its structure and processes, the government will not survive, or at least it will be less efficient and effective in developing strategies and in executing these strategies. Game theory is discussed to show that flexibility and agility of an e-procurement system (together with a good strategy) are key factors for a successful system; otherwise, e-procurement is more of weakness in the government's value chain of procurement of goods and services. In the last part of the discussion on Cloud Computing and E-Procurement, the authors argue that ERP systems (so called best practices) are not well adapted to other contexts than the simple context of the Cynefin Framework. Service Oriented Architecture solutions can provide better (adapted) solutions for E-Procurement. Cloud computing in combination with SOA may be the next generation solution.

Chapter 14 addresses how local authorities or municipalities have different organizational structure and goals and as such implementing a customized information systems project requires a separate evaluation that would fit their needs. In the case of an electronic procurement system, the implementation of this project at the central government level is not without challenges. Similarly, at the local government level, issues prevailed. Thus, this chapter highlights the issues encountered by twelve local authorities in the state of Selangor, Malaysia. The issues are broken down into four themes, namely, political, economic, social, and technological. It is important to note that local authorities fall within the jurisdiction of the state government, thus, more issues are abound particularly with regards to political interference. Nonetheless, the ultimate goal of having an online public procurement system is a win-win situation for both the local authority concerned and the vendors or suppliers. Hence, identifying the issues and learning from them will limit project failures or extended scheduling. Inherently, the implications of lessons learned from others who have implemented an online public procurement system will provide valuable guidelines for other lagging municipalities, yet at the same time, the late implementers will benefit more as they are able to avoid the pitfalls made by their counterparts that embarked earlier. In fact, the late-comers tend to achieve better success rate and report a significant return of investment.

Chapter 15 details how Supply Chain Management (SCM) is a strategy that has allowed the organizations that have established this system in their business models have a competitive advantage. The supply chain is a network of elements, where different key process such as: procurement, manufacturing, distribution, inventory, customer services, and information should be managed and controlled to meet customer requirements. To achieve this goal, different tools have been developed to help to the key processes of the supply chain, one of these tools is the e-procurement system, which helps an organization to controlled the interactions with the most crucial suppliers.

The Editors

Patricia Ordóñez de Pablos
University of Oviedo, Spain

Juan Manuel Cueva Lovelle
University of Oviedo, Spain

Jose Emilio Labra Gayo
University of Oviedo, Spain

Robert Tennyson
University of Minnesota, USA

REFERENCES

European Union. (2009). *Ministerial declaration of e-government* (p. 1). Retrieved from http://www.egov2009.se/2009/11/19/an-open-europe-with-accessible-public-administration/

Acknowledgment

We would like to thank all authors for the participation in this book as well as IGI Global staff for their continuous support during the development of the book.

Chapter 1
Design of an Open Platform for Collective Voting through EDNI on the Internet

Rubén González Crespo
Pontifical University of Salamanca, Spain

Oscar Sanjuán Martínez
Carlos III University, Spain

José Manuel Saiz Alvarez
Nebrija University, Spain

Juan Manuel Cueva Lovelle
University of Oviedo, Spain

B. Cristina Pelayo García-Bustelo
University of Oviedo, Spain

Patricia Ordoñez de Pablos
University of Oviedo, Spain

ABSTRACT

The present chapter aims to introduce the construction of a generic platform and open secure voting and multipurpose for the realm of the Internet. This platform will allow for collecting signatures and supporting multiple contexts through the use of electronic IDs and digital certificates. Potential applications of this platform are almost endless but some of the most significant may be: Voting at shareholders meetings, and votes in communities of neighbors, collect signatures, collect signatures for nominations, proposals for ILP (Popular Legislative initiatives), any activity susceptible to need a platform for reliable vote, meetings of parents, collegiate, et cetera. Currently the use of e-government for the identification of persons through digital documents is on rise, and the possibilities it presents are endless. That is why this chapter provides solutions for allowing these uses; it is of general interest for the present society.

INTRODUCTION

An electronic ID emerges as an opportunity to accelerate the implementation of the Information Society in Spain. Through its use, we can ensure our identity through Internet for shopping signed, secure transactions with banks, complete formalities in Public Administration, etc. In addition, we make sure that nobody would supplant our identity. The ID card it is a bet for the security, being the engine of social change that we are positioned between the first posts in the list of the leading countries in the information and communication society (Peña-López, 2011). Today there are many

DOI: 10.4018/978-1-4666-2119-0.ch001

routine procedures that still require the physical presence of a person or group of persons to verify your identity in Spain: voting in communities of neighbors, associations, etc. This solution aims to create a tool to facilitate all these procedures, and reduce costs (UNPAN, 2010), providing a means for citizens to be able to use in their daily procedures. To do this, the solution will allow the introduction and the specification of surveys, as well as the corresponding respondents who are deemed timely. These surveys will be made available to interested parties in the same automatically. Each user may exercise their right to vote in the same, keep in safe their data securely.

The cost of the infrastructure necessary for the functioning of the platform might be insurmountable for an individual user. Therefore, with this solution we intend to give support and advice to users that require a service such as ours. The client user of our tool will be duly with all existing legislation to close to the Organic Law for Data Protection and other applicable laws. In addition, this correct compliance will be completely transparent for the. In this way, we will achieve that users understand the use of the electronic ID as a simple tool that provides advantages such as the acceleration of procedures and security in the same, and no complications.

In addition this idea pursues give a response to the European Directive on the development of the "e-government". On the internal market of the European Union, the people are able to move freely either for work or for personal reasons, and therefore have to be able to cope with public services outside their country of origin increasingly.

If the e-government services are to provide a significant added value to citizens and businesses, then it is essential that different governmental bodies, both within a country and in different countries in the EU, are able to easily share information and cooperate in the service to citizens (Adeces & Internet Users Association, 2009).

There are various initiatives underway to achieve these objectives, but to give the possibility to citizens to use these resources (such as the electronic ID) for the largest number of possible activities, promotes its use and dissemination.

It is intended in the same way to give a response to the need to eliminate the digital divide and help to digital literacy. The gap in technological development among those nations more visionary and the rest begin to consolidate slowly but inexorably (Figure 1) (Cáceres, 2004). Internet is a technological infrastructure for short life; however, the speed of its development in some nations has led to extend its application beyond the computers and spaces associated with them. This solution will help to increase the use of the technologies associated with internet.

Finally we presume to give an answer to the improvement of the use and development of the Internet as a key strategy for Spain. Access to the Internet by improved in Europe in a spectacular way, both in use and the possibilities of connectivity (Dutton, 2010) (Fernández-i-Marin, 2010).

In spite of this, as you can see in Figure 2, Spain is still far away from the head of Internet at European level (eEspaña, 2011). For this reason this solution has a strategic interest from the point of view to be a dynamic mechanism and capable of strengthening to Spain on the head of the projects for the implantation of the e-government and in this case use of the electronic ID.

A NEW ERA CHARACTERIZED BY THE PREFIX "E"

This new information age is characterized by the prefix "e", the e-business, e-commerce, e-government, e-society, the relationship between government-society has also been transformed, and the benefits are substantial, communication is essential to know the social needs, and the receivers can see that the public services are doing to cover their expectations, both sides recognized (Parycek, 2010). The relationship is always in two directions, the government, local, autonomous

Figure 1. Development of ICT at the global level

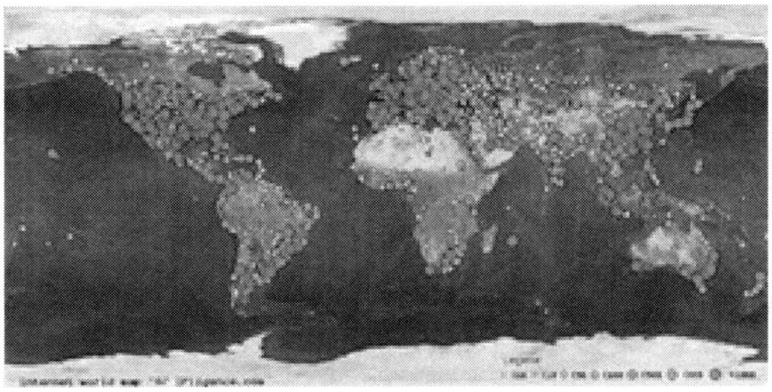

Figure 2. Situation of Spain in front of the rest of the EU on the use of ICT (©eEspaña 2011)

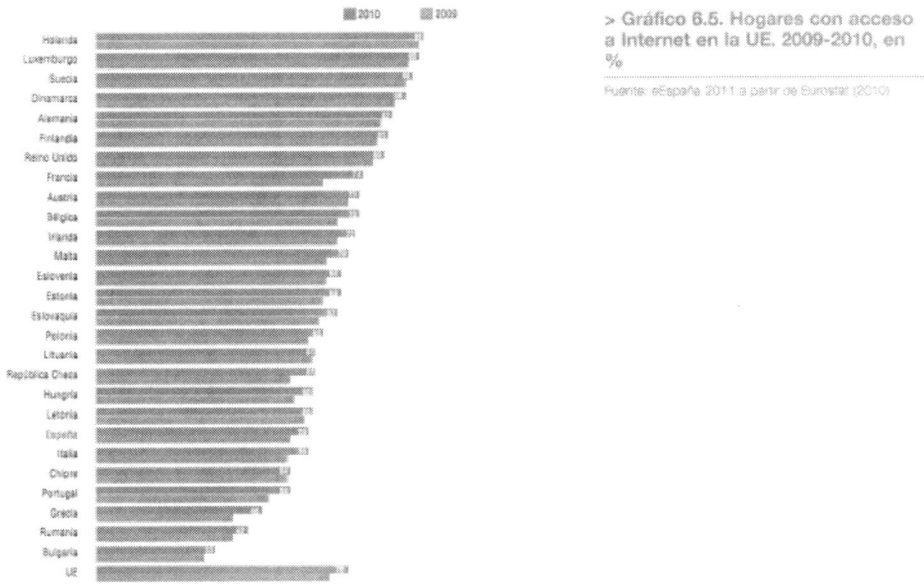

region, of the nation, reports and supply services, and society receives and proposes improvements. It is obtained as a result the knowledge. There is no clear consensus about what is meant by each of these terms, although they could be defined as well (Cerrillo, 2008):

- **E-Administration (E-Government):** Are all electronic mechanisms that allow the provision of public services in the Administration, to the citizens and businesses.
- **E-Democracy (Electronic Democracy):** Electronic processes that allow the participation of citizens in political life, either directly or through their representatives.
- **E-Government (E-Government):** Form of relationship between citizens and public administrations, and among the latter, carried out through information technologies and telecommunications. E.g.: the declaration of taxes through the Internet, or the information services and processing offered through the web sites of Public Administrations.

The e-government is an opportunity to advance to a "better government" of public administrations, where technology is a means and not an end in itself. The way to provide the services is transformed, and this requires coordination between departments and the most important thing a cultural change in the public officials.

The e-administration is applicable to all levels of administration, both the central government, as to the Autonomous Communities and to the municipalities. Until now the files are handled manually, in a number of considerable human and material resources by becoming a long and tedious process.

With the e-administration the situation changed, making administrative processes will not be long, there are no delays in its resolutions and that users do not have to go around several windows to achieve management. In the implementation of e-administration involved three main parts: Public Administrations, citizens and businesses.

Within the objectives presented to global way each of the parties we have (ICTC, 2009):

- **Public Administrations:**
    - Internal processes via the web
    - Relationships between different administrations through telematic means
    - Centralized Access to the databases of administrative information
- **Citizens:**
    - Fast Internet Access
    - Multimedia content (video-conferencing ...)
    - Communities of interest.
    o E-voting
- **Enterprise:**
    - Internal processes via the web (information, training ...)
    - Corporate Intranets
    - e-commerce platforms B2B

Of the relationship between each of these parts we get the following benefits:

- **Relationship Management - Citizens:**
    - Resolution of procedures and consultations via the web
    - Resolution of procedures via the web
    - E-procurement platforms
- **Relationship citizens - Companies:**
    - Shopping on-line
    - Channel customer care via the Internet.

Within the e-democracy where falls this solution, that give a solution to the current needs (van der Hof, 2011).

EVOLUTION OF THE E-ADMINISTRATION

The European Council held in Lisbon 2000, established as objective to make Europe the most competitive economy, and for this bet the opportunities offered by new technologies (Torrejón, 2005).

As a result at the Feira European Council adopted the Plan of Action e-Europe2002, with three clear objectives:

- Get an intranet quickly and cheaply.
- Investing in people and training.
- Stimulate the use of the Internet.

The Action Plan Info XXI, with a force from 2001 to 2003, was approved by the Spanish government to promote the development of the Information Society in Spain. This action plan was formed by three main axs:

- The momentum of the telecommunications sector and the technologies of the information provided, by completing the liberalization and by promoting competition.

- The empowerment of the e-government.
- Access for all to the Information Society.

In regard to compliance with the Lisbon Agenda 2004, according to a comparative whose index is based on the valuation on seven of the proceedings of each country (the Information Society, innovation and R&D, liberalization, network industries, Financial Services, Entrepreneurship, Social Inclusion, Sustainable Development), placed in Spain in 12TH place of the 16 countries compared.

Later, it was approved in Seville the Plan of Action e-Europe 2005, with the following objectives:

- On-line public services: advanced electronic Administrations interconnected with broadband networks, education services on-line, on-line health services.
- Creation of a dynamic environment that favors the e-business.
- Greater availability to broadband access at competitive prices.
- Infrastructure for secure communications.

Also in this Plan, the European Commission established the 20 basic services that measure the degree of development of the Administrations. These services are:

- From the point of view of public services to citizens:
    - Birth and marriage certificates.
    - Notification of changes of address.
    - Personal documents.
    - Health-related services.
    - Registration of cars.
    - Social Security.
    - Job search services.
    - Registration in institutions of higher education.
    - Access to the catalogs of the libraries.
    - Statement of income.
    - Statements to the police.
- From the point of view of public services for companies:
    - Request and authorisations of customs duties.
    - Social Contribution to employees.
    - Registration of new companies.
    - Public requests.
    - Declaration and notification of the value added tax.
    - Sending data to statistical offices.
    - Statements from customs duties.

The key aspects that were considered essential in the implementation of Electronic Administration in Spain were:

- It requires a cultural change that affects all the agents involved.
- The citizen must become the main shaft.
- Technology is a means not an end.
- You need a horizontal strategy for the achievement of the objectives.
- The reorganization processes becomes priority.
- Political leadership continued over time.
- Bet on the modernization of processes.
- Development of the "back office".
- Training of public service employees.
- Universal Access.
- The need for compatible standards.

Within the Plan Connects (2004-2007), encompass five key projects:

- **Certifies:** Which he claimed that the 80% of the certificates in role of administrations, should perform with exchanges of secure data.
- **eID:** Is the new ID card that will allow us to identify us in the network. eID.
- **Citizens.es:** It is intended to organize new spaces for attention and communication with the citizens via the internet, to make

more rapid the relationship between citizen and administration.

- **Simplifies:** Simplification of procedures obtaining savings in time and facilitating the connection between administrations.
- **MAP on Network Programs:** MAP for the relationship with officials and citizens.

Within the framework of the Plan Avanza 2006-2010 approved by the Council of Ministers, the government has allocated 785.6 million euros to promote the development of the information society and the use of the Internet, in homes, SMES and Administrations.

It is currently in force on the Plan Avanza 2 that will be completed in 2015. This includes the initiatives aimed at the promotion of the Information Society. Its objetives are (eEspaña, 2011)

- Promote innovative processes ICT.
- Extend the ICTS in the health and social welfare.
- Enhance the application of ICT to the education and training system.
- To improve the capacity and the extension of telecommunications networks.
- Extend the culture of safety among the citizens and businesses.
- Increase the use of advanced digital services by the public.
- Extend the use of ICT solutions for business in the company.
- Develop the technological capabilities of the ICT sector.
- Strengthen the digital content sector.
- Develop ICT greens.

Although there have been major advances in the implementation of Electronic Administration, and some followed by Autonomous Communities and Local Administrations, as may be the AEAT or census, there are still many areas with a very low level of development. Additionally, Spain continues to occupy the last positions of the countries of the European Union, in terms of access for all to the Information Society, distanced itself from Austria or Sweden that are at the forefront (Capgemini Consulting, 2011).

THE ELECTRONIC ID AND DIGITAL SIGNATURE

The electronic ID is part of the citizenship digital, where it pursues the treatment of personal data with full respect for the human rights of their owners; require the explicit consent of the owner for the treatment of personal data:

- Especially protected: ideology, unionization, religion, belief, racial, sexual health and life.
- Identifiers: name, ID, dirección, teléfono.
- Personal characteristics: marital status, birth date, nationality.
- Academics and labour: Diploma, experience, post work.
- Economic: income, assets, loans, credit cards.

That is why you need the use of the digital signature for that access to all of this information through the web can be made. The digital signature authenticates the identity of citizens and entities involved in the exchange of information; maintains the integrity of the information exchanged, thus ensuring that there will be no handling and finally guarantee non-repudiation, may not deny the ownership of the messages that have been signed.

The digital signature as you can see in Figure 3 is developed through a robust mechanism to ensure the safety (CERES, 2012).

Although the use of digital certificates and the electronic ID will gradually extended between the citizens, the growth, dissemination, and implementation of its use is far from being massive, this proposal seeks to increase its use, and in particular offer a voting mechanism robust and reliable to assist in providing more functionality to the eID.

The new electronic ID has two certificates (DNIElectronico, 2012):

- **Authentication Certificate:** Aims to ensure electronically the identity of the citizen to perform a transaction telematics. The Authentication Certificate (Digital Signature) ensures that electronic communication is done with the person that says it is. The holder may through its certificate prove his identity in the face of any already that he is in possession of the certificate of identity and of the private key associated with the same.
- **Signature Certificate:** This certificate is which we will use for the signature of documents by ensuring the integrity of the document and non-repudiation of origin. It is a certificate X509v3 standard, which has assets in the Key Usage bit of ContentCommitment (non-repudiation) and that is associated with a couple of public and private keys, generated in the interior of the CHIP of the DNI (Figure 4)

It is this certificate issued as a qualified certificate and created on a Device Secure signature creation, which converts the advanced electronic signature in recognized electronic signature, allowing its legal matching with the handwritten signature (Law 59/2003 and Directive 1999/93/EC).

The tenure of the eID evolves gradually as you can see in the graph (Figure 5), not the functionality that you can provide.

DESCRIPTION OF THE STATE OF TECHNOLOGY

Actually, the voting systems existing in Spain operate rather as systems pollsters that as systems whose purpose is to collect the legal opinion of a person: collects often the name and e-mail address. The problem with these systems is, moreover, that are not safe: anyone could supplant our identity in this type of voting systems.

Figure 3. Operation of the digital signature

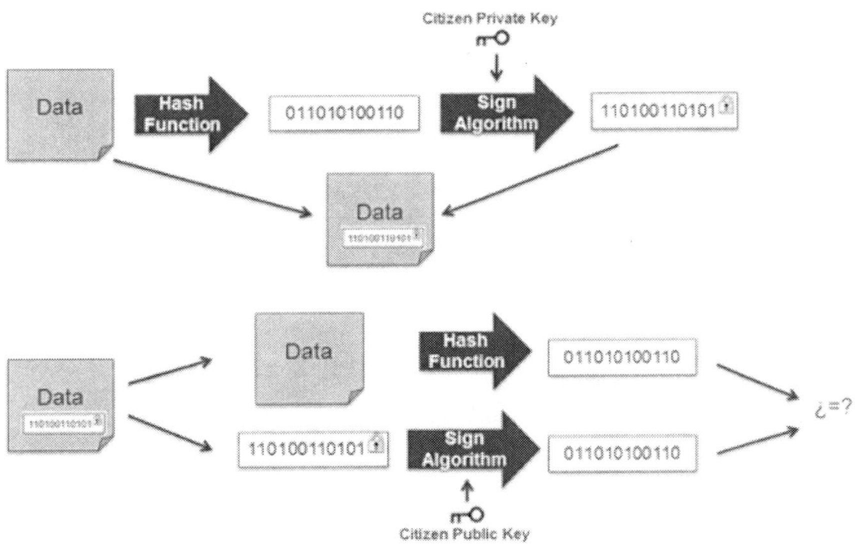

Figure 4. Electronic ID

Recent studies on the electronic voting systems, like one made in United States "Electronic Voting Offers Opportunities and Presents Challenges ", provide a set of good practices to carry out security, test and maintenance activities required by this kind of systems.

Initiatives such as eParticipa have already been implemented in other countries of the world. In this section, we will analyze some of them in a very brief manner:

- Change.org (Figure 6) (CAMBIO, 2012): this is a web-based platform, which offers a service of vote for causes of various types. These causes are divided into two groups: human rights, justice, education, environment, etc. Participation is open to all users to register on the portal, and allows these votes in the causes as they deem appropriate. The purpose of this platform is to promote initiatives for social change, launching and promoting causes through its site.
- Simply Voting (Figure 7) (SIMPLY, 2012) is a tool for payment, which allows the creation of surveys and supports the electoral process. You can access the site that supports it from the web page: http://www.simplyvoting.com. Among its most outstanding features, provides encrypted communication and mechanisms to prevent fraud in the voting. Although it provides a certain level of security, this tool is not adequate to the eID spanish.
- Spotme (Figure 8) (SPOTME, 2012) provides a different approach to other, existing systems: this is a system of voting directly on events that you are attending. In this way, it manages to get a feedback of the users who are leading certain information. One of their main disadvantages is that it requires a physical tool that provides support to all its services. In addition, being a product international, nor supports authentication through an electronic ID.

Figure 5. Growth in Spain of eID (©eEspaña 2011)

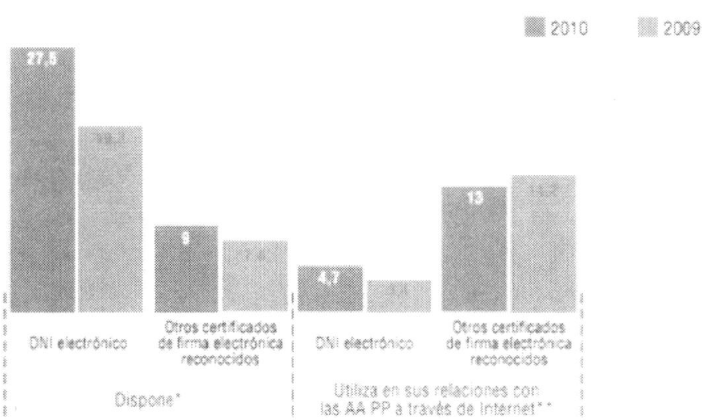

Figure 6. Change.org©

Figure 7. Simply Voting©

- Everyone Counts (Figure 9) (EVERY, 2012) It is a software platform secure, which provides the necessary infrastructure for the custody of the votes. Under the project Everyone Counts, they have created several tools, building architecture by layers with specific products according to the needs of the votes. A remarkable feature is that some of the products it offers, as eLect Today, with Open Source license. eLect Today Provides the final votes on a physical medium (paper) to be presented in the legislative body relevant.

APPROXIMATION TO THE SOLUTION OF ePARTICIPA

The proposal eParticipa represents the technological challenge that it goes on to describe below in response to each of the three fundamental components of the idea.

- Web-based platform generic and open for voting. Consists a web site that works by way of social network of proposals (campaigns) and votes, which are organized into groups and thematic. Provides a search engine and the possibility to register as a user to be able to participate actively in the social network and comment on the campaigns, the news, other comments, etc.
- Secure Platform for the vote through certificates and eID. When a user wants to sign or vote on a proposal, in case it is required (not all queries may require signature, some can be informal consultations), the user can sign it legally with the use of an electronic identity card or your digital certificate.
- Platform for storage of personal data and sensitive from electronic voting: The data to be stored are of a personal nature and in many cases also be sensitive, this implies that it has been necessary to develop a specific platform for storage that takes into

Figure 8. Spotme©

Figure 9. Everyone Counts©

account all the necessary guarantees (see Figure 10).

To achieve the practical development of the idea is necessary the use of technologies such as:

- **MDE (Engineering Headed by models) and MDA (Architectures Led by Models):** Architecture directed by models (Model-Driven Architecture or MDA) is an approach to software design, proposed and sponsored by the Object Managemente Group (OMG). MDA has been designed to support the engineering directed to models of the software systems. MDA is an architecture that provides a set of guidelines for structuring specifications expressed as models. MOU refers to the set of techniques of a general nature and independent of GMOS that support the construction of systems through models.
- **Orchestration of Services:** The orchestration of Web services is based on a model that centralizes the interactions between Web services, in many cases with the aim of producing new services.
- **SOA (architectures based on Services)**: SOA is an acronym for service-oriented

Figure 10. Elements of the platform eParticipa

Arquitectures (Service oriented architectures), a term that tries to describe an architecture that allows new applications are not developed from scratch but as an integration of a set of services that are already published, described and developed for that purpose.

- **Web Services:** Web services (in english Web Service) are a set of protocols and standards that serve to exchange data between applications. Various software applications developed in different programming languages, and executed on any platform. This interoperability is achieved through the adoption of open standards, organizations OASIS and W3C are the committees responsible for the architecture and regulation of Web services.
- **XML:** To facilitate the exchange of structured information. The acronym for Extensible Markup Language, is a tensile labels metalanguage developed by the World Wide Web Consortium (W3C). It comes from a simplification and adaptation of SGML and allows you to define the grammar of specific languages (in the same way that HTML is to turn a language defined by SGML). Therefore XML is not really a language in particular, but a way of defining languages for different needs.
- **Cloud Computing:** Cloud computing is a technology that allows it to offer computing services via the Internet. In this type of computing everything that can offer a computer system is offered as a service, so that users can access the services available "in the Internet cloud" without knowledge (or, at least without being experts) in the management of the resources they use. According to the IEEE Computer Society is a paradigm in which the information is stored permanently in servers on the Internet and is sent to temporary caches of the client, which includes desktop equipment, leisure centers, laptops, etc.
- **Semantic Web:** The semantic Web is the "data Web". It is based on the idea of adding semantic metadata and ontology to the World Wide Web. This additional information, which describes the content, meaning and the relationship of the data, you must provide in a formal manner, so that it is possible to assess them automatically by processing machines. The aim is to improve Internet expanding interoperability between computer systems and reduce the necessary mediation of human operators. The precursor of the idea, Tim Berners-Lee, attempt since the principle include semantic information in its creation, the World Wide Web, but for different reasons it was not possible. For that reason he introduced the concept of semantics with the intention of recovering the omission.

CONCLUSION AND FUTURE WORK

The recent introduction of the electronic ID makes that there are still a wide range of possibilities in computer applications that make use of the same. This solution has as main objective is to promote the use of the electronic ID as a tool that, in the future, in the short term, it would be useful and simple for Spanish citizens. The rapprochement of applications that use electronic ID to the citizens, it is essential to do this. With this project, we intend to achieve this approach by providing tools in the service of the user in their activities of the day to day. Access to the Internet has improved in Spain of dramatically, both in use and the possibilities of connectivity in the last few years. In spite of this, Spain is still far away from the introduction leader of Internet at European level. For this reason this solution has a strategic interest from the point of view to be a dynamic mechanism and able to put Spain at the head of the projects of the Internet of the future, taking inspiration similar initiatives in other countries such as Germany or the United States.

Through the incorporation of the use of technology in everyday formalities, we hope that the dissemination of the eID, reaches a wide range of users, of different ages and backgrounds.

Finally eParticipa aims to develop plugins for the voting can be published in some of the social networks more known, as for example Facebook. The reason for this is not another that the massive use of these networks on the part of the population. This usage, far from sag rising increasingly. Therefore, the future development of plugin for a social network will allow you to submit to the user in a interface well known by the surveys of this invited to participate, by facilitating collaboration in them.

REFERENCES

Adeces & Asociación de Internautas. (2009). *E-administración autonómica. Se buscan ciudadanos que usen los servicios electrónicos*. Madrid, Spain: Adeces. Retrieved February 4, 2012, from http://www.adeces.org/administracion%20electronica%202009.pdf

Cáceres, S. (2004). *Observatorio de la sociedad de la información. Un mundo de brechas y puentes digitales*. Retrieved February 5, 2012, from http://fundacionorange.es/areas/28_observatorio/pdfs/DEF_20.pdf

Capgemini Consulting. (2011). *Estudio comparativo 2011 de los servicios públicos online en las comunidades autónomas*. Resultados 5ª Medición, Abril 2011. Madrid, Spain: Fundación Orange. Retrieved February 7, 2012, from http://www.informeeespana.es/docs/Estudio_Comparativo_2011_Servicios_on_line.pdf

CERES. (2012). *Entidad pública de certificación que permite autentificar y garantizar la confidencialidad de las comunicaciones*. Retrieved February 8, 2012, from http://www.cert.fnmt.es

Cerrillo, A. (2008). *E-administración*. Barcelona, Spain: UOC.

CHANGE. (2012). *Change.org*. Retrieved February 5, 2012, from http://www.change.org

CTIC. (2009). *Polílticas de uso de servicios de participación ciudadana en el contexto de las administraciones públicas*. Gijón, Spain: CTIC Centro Tecnológico. Retrieved January 25, 2012, from http://ct.ctic.es/web/export/sites/default/es/documentos/864-2009.pdf

DNIElectronico. (2012). *Portal oficial sobre el DNI electrónico*. Retrieved January 20, 2012, from http:// http://www.dnielectronico.es/

Drapeau, M. (2009). Government 2.0: The rise of the Goverati. Retrieved January 31, 2012, from http://www.readwriteweb.com/archives/government_20_rise_of_the_goverati.php

Dutton, W. H., & Eynon, R. (2010). Networked individuals and institutions: A cross-sector comparative perspective on patterns and strategies in government and research. *The Information Society*, *25*(3), 207.

eEspaña. (2011). *Informe anual sobre el desarrollo de la sociedad de la información en España*. Fundación Orange. Retrieved February 10, 2012, from http://www.informeeespana.es/docs/eE2011.pdf

EVERY. (2012). *Everyone counts*. Retrieved February 5, 2012, from http://www.everyone-counts.com

Fernández-i-Marín, X. (2010). *The impact of e-government promotion in Europe: Internet dependence and critical mass*. Communication at the Internet, Politics, Policy 2010: An Impact Assessment Conference, 16-17 September 2010. Oxford, UK: Oxford Internet Institute. Retrieved February 13, 2012, from http://fundacionorange.es/areas/28_observatorio/pdfs/DEF_26.pdf

Parycek, P., & Prosser, A. (Eds.). (2010). *EDem2010, Proceedings of the 4th International Conference on E-Democracy.* Wien, Austria: Österreichische Computer Gesellschaft.

Peña-López, I. (2011). *Empowerment and governance in the information society*. Position paper for the Democracy and the power of the individual conference, The Ditchley Foundation, 03-05 February 2011, Enstone. Retrieved February 14, 2012, from http://ictlogy.net/articles/20110204_ismael_pena-lopez_-_empowerment_governance_information_society.pdf

SIMPLY. (2012). *Simply voting online election system*. Retrieved February 5, 2012, from http://www.simplyvoting.com

SPOTME. (2012). *Make your meetings matter – SpotMe*. Retrieved February 5, 2012, from http://www.spotme.com

Torrejón, A. (2005). *Algunas reflexiones sobre las ciudades del siglo XXII*. Observatorio de la Sociedad de la Información. Retrieved February 5, 2012, from http://microsites.oii.ox.ac.uk/ipp2010/system/files/IPP2010_Fernandez-i-Marin_Paper.pdf

UNPAN. (2010). *UN e-government survey 2010: Leveraging e-government at a time of financial and economic crisis*. New York, NY: UNPAN. Retrieved January 30, 2012, from http://unpan1.un.org/intradoc/groups/public/documents/un-dpadm/unpan038851.pdf

van der Hof, S., & Groothuis, M. (Eds.). (2011). *Innovating government: Normative, policy and technological dimensions of modern government*. The Hague, The Netherlands: TMC Asser Press.

Chapter 2
Poverty Reduction Strategies via Public-Private Partnerships:
The Role of E-Government Solutions in Supporting Supplier Diversity Programmes

Ananda S. Jeeva
Curtin University, Australia

Lincoln C. Wood
Curtin University, Australia

ABSTRACT

Government procurement practices influence large volumes of spending in communities and further procurement can be influenced through legislative efforts. Through these mechanisms government bodies carry significant influence on the way in which procurement spend occurs and they have the ability to influence the direction that the procurement may take. Carefully constructed parameters in public-private partnerships (PPP) can shift the focus of procurement activities towards engaging with the local businesses and communities. This represents an approach for government bodies to increase supplier diversity so that, in alignment with UN Millennium goals of poverty reduction, local suppliers can be provided with business opportunities and methods to reduce poverty. A two-focus approach is adopted; first, government drivers and policies are examined in the context of social engagement. Second, the roles and challenges faced by small firms in the local communities are highlighted. This demonstrates the way in which e-government procurement systems play a pivotal role in supporting local sourcing initiatives.

INTRODUCTION

Poverty remains a wide-spread challenge in many developing countries. Since the 1960's there have been significant resources devoted to alleviating the challenge, yet both governments and non-government organizations (NGOs) experience variable successes in reducing poverty. This chapter outlines how government policy, coupled with effective use of public-private partnerships (PPPs) may be used to reduce poverty in local communities.

DOI: 10.4018/978-1-4666-2119-0.ch002

Sourcing of raw materials and other inputs for government-directed projects can be supplied and sourced from most developing or under-developed countries to produce final products or services for consumption. Such a programme is able to reduce trade deficits, improve monetary circulation in the local economies, and improve the socio-economic conditions of families locally. Thus, strategic procurement using e-government systems are able to assist in poverty reduction through generating self-sustaining and renewing systems.

The United Nations Resolution of Millennium Declaration 55/2/III focuses on economic development and poverty reduction and outlines several approaches which our concept supplements. The UN Resolution promotes the role of local government and MNC in targeted assistance of economic growth in lower socio-economic areas in developing countries, frequently through developing, or instituting changes to, procurement policies and strategies.

Commitments were made to eradicate poverty (amongst other objectives) as part of the United Nations Millennium Development Goals (MDG). The intention was for sustained, broad-based, economic growth in impoverished regions to lift the welfare of residents and thus eliminate poverty. The MDGs also identified priority areas that needed to be addressed as part of this process, including alleviating hunger, policy development and implementation for food security, improving access to clean water, strengthening local capabilities, improving capability building, increasing vocational training, improving health, improving gender equality, youth unemployment, increasing trade, and improving development of domestic resources. These objectives are hardly new or novel, as aid organisations, governments, and NGOs have, for the last fifty years, been attempting to improve economic outcomes in all societies, frequently with limited success. Most of the world's population still survives below the 'poverty line'. In 1980 it was estimated that there were 1.9 billion people living below this poverty line. Over a 25-year period that has been little change: in 2005 it was estimated that there were still 1.4 billion people, or one quarter of the developing world, that lived below the international poverty line of $1.25 US per day (Chen & Ravallion, 2008).

Eight important goals were established during the 2000 UN Millennium Summit: ending hunger, achieving gender equality, improving the health of children, improving maternal health, combatting HIV/AIDs, creating global partnership, improving environmental sustainability, and providing universal education.

This chapter discusses poverty and procurement using e-government systems, focusing on the role of supplier diversity (SD) and procurement policies in meeting MDG objectives of reducing poverty. Poverty is examined in more detail, as well as the links between local governments, MNCs, aid organisations, and supplier diversity programmes implemented through procurement policies. Competitive advantages from SD programmes are outlined, along with the risks and challenges of implementation. As a solution, e-government systems and their role in promoting PPP relationships are discussed, demonstrating how SD programmes can be incorporated using e-government systems. Potential future challenges are discussed to provide future research directions.

SUPPLIER DIVERSITY AND POVERTY

First we define poverty and procurement to aid in following discussions.

Poverty Definition

Poverty is frequently a slippery term, as the acceptable standard of living in different regions of the world can be perceived as being vastly different. Frequently definitions are based on income distributions within the society or the level of incomes achieved. Other national governments will set local criteria for the level of poverty, based on a regional concept of poverty, which may be out of alignment with commonly accepted international standards.

However, a qualitative definition of poverty that has been widely accepted has been provided by the World Summit on Social Development in Copenhagen (1995), where absolute poverty was defined as “a condition characterised by severe deprivation of basic human needs, including food, safe drinking water, sanitation facilities, health, shelter, education and information as well as services.” Six years later another key definition emerged from the United Nations Committee on Social, Economic and Cultural Rights, where in 2001 poverty was defined as “a human condition characterized by sustained or chronic deprivation of the resources, capabilities, choices, security and power necessary for the enjoyment of an adequate standard of living and other civil, cultural, economic, political and social rights” – an expansion of the earlier definition to include a wider range of specific rights that poverty impinges upon.

Procurement Definition

While procurement has always been present in all public and private endeavours throughout history, a clear definition has not always been forthcoming. A recent important definition of procurement is that it is “the function of purchasing inputs used in the firm’s value chain, including raw materials, supplies and other consumables as well as machinery and equipment” (van Weele, 2005, p. 10). Other authors have noted that this is a restrictive and narrow definition, and have instead suggested that procurement is merely a wider term than purchasing, implying “the acquisition of goods or services in return for a payment of money, which may include borrowing or leasing” (Lysons & Farrington, 2006, p. 6). More recently, there has been increasing focus on the role of procurement within organisations, taking a process-orientated perspective, highlighting the criticality of the function within successful contemporary organisations. The role therefore includes a range of activities and processes, such as “searching and qualifying suitable suppliers, negotiating terms, purchase orders, invoicing, shipping and remittance payment” (Laudon & Traver, 2007, p. 689). With this perspective, procurement is not an isolated function within an organisation, and instead involves multiple inter-functional linkages within an organisation.

While many of these activities remain internal to an organisation, there are also important procurement activities that are externally-focused. Key amongst these is activities that emphasise a diverse range of suppliers, which may frequently include non-traditional, or regional, suppliers. Such suppliers may frequently have a lower level of professionalism and require additional effort through engagement to also provide coaching, than traditional procurement practices may indicate.

This chapter proposes that SD initiatives cannot be isolated or occur spontaneously within a procurement function. They must instead be nurtured through organisational vision and carefully designed strategies that encompass the entire organisation, and the links to the procurement department, to ensure success.

Supplier Diversity

The key element of supplier diversity (SD) programmes includes widening the supply base to include a greater breadth of non-traditional suppliers. The SD concept originated in the United States of America where the government began to pay attention to the role of small businesses in the 1950s. The Small Business Administration (SBA) was initially established as a federal agency with the mandate to assist the initiation and growth of small businesses (www.sba.gov/aboutsba/). Soon after, during the 1960s, the burgeoning civil rights movement in the USA was generating greater attention and awareness of the relatively poor socio-economic status of minority groups within the USA (Shah & Ram, 2006). These developments occurred in parallel before combining in 1972 when the National Minority Supplier Development Council was formed with the intention of developing and nurturing linkages between large corporates and (smaller) minority-owned business enterprises (MBEs), with the intention of improving the business opportunities for the smaller organisations. This was envisaged as occurring through changing the sourcing approaches used by corporates to include greater minority-owned business contributions. The concept of 'diversity' in SD therefore emphasises not a range of suppliers, or a widening supply base, but increasing 'diversity' through the inclusion of non-traditional, or non-corporate, suppliers.

Another recurring challenge, also acknowledged in the MDG, is gender inequality – still a significant social feature of many societies throughout the world. While a national population may consist of approximately 50% women, such numeric equality is rarely mirrored in other aspects of life. The exploitation, subjugation, and marginalisation of women in contemporary economic activities reduce the potential for a nation to fully develop their economic potential. As a result, only half of a nation's population is frequently engaged in reducing poverty through improving living standards.

In all of these cases, a minority group can be enfranchised through the development and deployment of SD programmes, which can be formulated to encourage engagement with these groups and foster entrepreneurship. This can align effectively with other, more established, programmes run by other agencies or NGOs that have been formed to break the established cycles of discrimination and oppression. Thus, SD models may include a range of suppliers from various groups that may include not only minority-owned businesses, but also suppliers including businesses run by other disadvantaged groups, such as women or war veterans. While many large corporates have yet to establish efforts in this area, there are sterling examples, such as Apple Inc., which established a SD programme in 1993. Other large firms, such as Caterpillar, have also implemented supplier diversity programmes and found that not only are sourcing costs lowered, quality can be enhanced, providing additional competitive advantage, but the process may require careful planning (Min, 2009). This trend towards SD initiatives may continue as other larger corporates begin to acknowledge economic support for communities can translate into improved purchasing power, and thus greater demand, creating new, localised, business opportunities for the firms (Jeeva, 2011).

GOVERNMENT AND POVERTY IN THE COMMUNITY

Local Governments are powerful change agents within their regional communities (Edmondson, Suh, & Munchus, 2008) through changing the intentions, societal behaviours, and operations within the communities of the society. Governmental organisations have the capability to generate increasingly large opportunities for minority groups throughout the region, through encouraging ownership, providing education, and improving linkages to multinational corporations (MNC) and global aid organisations.

Relationships between globalised aid organisations and Global organisations require local partnerships to create effective change and thus the global aid organisations contract and fund their local organisations so that they can jointly create successful projects. Success and long-term effectiveness of projects for the organisations rely on these local collaborators. This can be particularly important as global staff rarely have adequate interaction with recipients of aid locally (Satterthwaite, 2001). The two parties, therefore, lack suitable connections and the challenge of sustained project success.

Local governments make ideal partners as they are embedded within their communities and have a commitment to local improvements and serving their citizens. Through their mechanisms local government officers should spearhead change and ensure that strategies implemented within their communities are sustainable. This is part of their responsibility to encourage economic development within the region. With a significant input of resources, local governments have the ability to create significant change through their sourcing, where a local focus can improve engagement with communities and strengthen the local economy while also improving regional employment.

Both federal and local government bodies may need appropriate legislation in place to encourage or nurture organisations – including government bodies and their agencies – to modify procurement policies to support the local communities. The steps can be enhanced through the compilation of guidelines to promote 'buying locally produced products and services first'. The approach can be spearheaded by local government agencies, providing impetus to other organisations to replicate the concept, while providing immediate equitable results for their communities.

When the approach is first implemented there will be a shortage of suppliers that meet the requirements and are capable of sustained effective supply. The shortage will force the creation of many new suppliers to meet the procurement objectives outlined by the procuring agency and this creation of new suppliers provides the opportunity for minority groups to become involved. The opportunity provides the potential for significant benefit for the community and the greater economic structure in such a way that the poverty can be reduced in the community through the provision of greater employment.

The role of procurement is important in contemporary environments and so this approach must be carefully considered and executed. Strategic procurement strategies have been recognised as essential in the age of global competitiveness (Baier, Hartmann, & Moser, 2008), yet most procurement research and the extant literature tends to promote the concept that economic gain, through cost reductions, provides suitable impetus for new policies. The contention of this chapter is sharply different: carefully designed strategic procurement policies can promote local sourcing, expanding local customer bases, and increasing market opportunities locally. Thus, sourcing locally provides support to the communities, the members of which consume services and outputs from government organisations. Such an approach presents a cyclic vision of a local, community-focused, supply system, where suppliers of materials into a government agency may be consumers of products or services which their materials contributed to. It is a like a close economic system, such as found in small, isolated, communities, where all production is consumed within the community.

Such a system is unlikely to occur spontaneously and may need to be encouraged through the implementation of new SD programmes and related procurement policies, which may rely on suitable support by government legislation or requirements. PPPs can be influenced by governments, which may provide governments with a method to influence significant procurement that they do not directly engage in. SD programmes can therefore be implemented in such a way to benefit local users of services. Additional efforts may be required to support SD programmes through the implementation of infrastructure improvements that may help smaller, newer, suppliers to gain the capabilities to engage with businesses, through training, education, and e-government systems.

Designing Policies to Influence Supplier Diversity through Procurement

The rational and requirement for SD programmes is heterogeneous globally. In some countries, such as the USA, there are adequate incentives for organisations to introduce these programmes, while in others, such as Australia, the minority population is smaller and the programmes need additional support (Blake, 2007). Such a programme, however, does have significant advantages for a country such as Australia, allowing indigenous Australians the opportunity to break free from the welfare cycle (Jeeva, 2011). Such differences in business climates and society mean that incentives may be required to help encourage the introduction of SD programmes, such as the opportunity for organisations to engage with their local community and provide development opportunities. Such an approach creates jobs and increases local capabilities, yet the challenges may require significant leadership capabilities and may require support from governments through financial incentives, legislation, or ground-breaking practices that may be emulated by other organisations.

Many organisations will also find new challenges in SD programmes as they change the focus from rationalisation of the supply base, running counter to conventional procurement wisdom. Additionally, the concept requires greater thought, planning, and creativity in the management of procurement and purchasing.

Outcome and Motivation for SD

The overall outcomes and rationale for moving towards SD programmes is important to understand, as the concept can provide significant competitive advantage.

Effective operations are often predicated by effective supplier relationships and strong supply networks, providing a solid foundation for supply chain management and sustained competitiveness. Yet, many organisations find that supplier development and relationship management can be challenging and time-consuming in traditional business environments. This is frequently due to a lack of trust between parties and power imbalances in the supply chain. Contrastingly, minority or disadvantaged groups are more likely to provide a motivated partner for a buying organisation, a partner that is keen to cooperate and comply with set requirements, whether they are quality standards, lead times, or other critical factors. In this way, a more cooperative spirit in the supply chain may be achieved through engaging SD programmes.

There are three key influences of SD programmes: ethical, economic opportunities, and stakeholder expectations.

Particularly in the UK, the concept of corporate social responsibility (CSR) has been heavily influenced through the promotion of 'think small first' campaign, which has promoted the inclusion and engagement with small businesses including MBEs. Overwhelmingly, ethical concerns have been the key driving force behind the adoption of most CSR strategies, including SD programmes. While the origins in the UK for CSR programmes may have been swayed by social issues, this is changing as more firms realise that enhancing their reputation is critical as this has long been recognised as being linked to strategic advantage (Bharadwaj, Varadarajan, & Fahy, 1993). Public relations work can enhance the public perception of these strategies, increasing business legitimacy (Suchman, 1995) in the public sector, providing for competitive advantages, and recognising that the suppliers also represent a market and potential workforce.

Localised economic impacts and new economic opportunities also influence CSR. With a domino effect, MBEs that secure contracts with large buying organisations are able to influence their local communities and other businesses. They may also invest resources into combating economic inequality where other organisations have failed. Overall, this can lead to societal groups where there is reduced crime and improved quality of life, while the rising wealth can lead to increased demand for the output from the original buying organisation. SD programmes can therefore provide further competitive advantage.

The expectations and legitimation secured in the local communities can be an important motivating factor in the establishment of CSR programmes. Engagement with a range of stakeholders, such as potential customers, lobby groups, new business partners, employees and other agencies can be seen as a positive reflection of SD on the community. Here, SD is a mechanism to enhance stakeholder satisfaction with the buying organisations, thereby providing competitive advantage to the organisation (Shah & Ram, 2006)

Competitive Advantage through SD

Despite the apparent additional complexity that should arise from working with a supply base of diverse suppliers, Kerr (2006) asserts that firms successfully implementing SD programmes are more successful due to the increase in minority business. Recent research by the Hackett Group also finds significant benefits, stating that organisation with diverse suppliers tended to outperform average firms, with 133% greater return on costs of procurement operations. The indication is that rapidly the additional costs relating to increased procurement complexity may be balanced by improved revenue. Firms sourcing from effective MBEs, by sourcing competitively, encourage growth in the sector and, thereby, improve their reputation and gain new markets and customers. A multi-sourcing strategy using SD policies may rapidly become more cost-effective than single-sourcing policies – which should provide significant encouragement for organisations seeking to use this approach.

While rapid cost benefits are possible, other procurement-related benefits can also be realised with a SD-based multi-sourcing strategy. Working with a wider range of organisations also exposes a buying organisation to greater possibilities of being exposed to innovative solutions to their own problems (Carter, Auskalnis, & Ketchum, 1999). Exposure to new ideas and approaches may lead to adoption of cutting edge concepts in the buying organisation to provide significant strategic advantage.

Benefits may accrue in the future, providing further compelling reasons to adopt SD programmes. As an example, in the USA it has been projected that at current rates of demographic change, by 2045 minority groups may represent 46% of the total US population (Worthington, Ram, Boyal, & Shah, 2008) – representing a significant market share in the world's largest economy. Early engagement with these communities may allow an organisation to establish strong links with groups that may prove to be powerful markets in the near future. Having a strong first-mover advantage may also enable sustainable competitive advantage and deter new entrants. Furthermore, the use of business intelligence gained from the SD implementation can also provide additional insights and understanding of new market segments, helping marketers to derive the needs of a diverse new customer base (Slater, Weigand, & Zwirlein, 2008).

The ability to react to volatile markets can provide significant benefits to firms (Christopher, Lowson, & Peck, 2004) and organisational agility may be enhanced through SD programmes. Small MBEs may have increased flexibility to change to economic challenges, or even the requirements of a buying organisation, largely due to their smaller organisation structure (Golder, 2004). Smaller size firms are also more likely to be owner-operated, providing greater likelihood of being dynamic and responsive to new requirements. This flexibility can also translate into being able to provide more customised solutions for clients than larger, single, suppliers may be able to achieve (Ram & Smallbone, 2003). Procurement can, therefore, provide support for agility throughout the organisation by working with these more agile suppliers.

Many developing regions may benefit and are ripe for the innovation of SD. As an example, in regional Thailand regions, which are agrarian-based economies, many farmers have eschewed relying solely on traditional farm activities for various reason and have created a portfolio of economic activities (Rigg & Nattapoolwat, 2001). A core farming activity in the region is rice cultivation. Many fathers are now involved part-time manufacture of artificial flowers, an activity that provides similar incomes to their main employment, while providing more direct compensation while being more fun and less physically demanding than farming. Other regions have also seen similar changes, particularly involving women as an important demographic group. Many aid organisations have attempted to raise the profile of women as this group is rapidly becoming better educated, increasing their buying power and decision-making capabilities within their communities.

Strategic and Supplier Diversity Risks and Challenges

The implementation of SD programmes is not without challenge or difficulty, particularly due to the relatively poor management and technological capabilities of the new potential suppliers, and the difficulty of finding qualified suppliers.

Previous studies have indicated that it is critical to proactively address the capabilities of potential MBE suppliers (Shah & Ram, 2006). While some forms of engagement may be virtual, relying on technology, in developing countries it is more critical for information to be provided on a face-to-face basis. Typical engagement with new suppliers may include business fairs, presentations, 'meet the buyer' sessions, or trade shows; other outreach activities may raise the general awareness of the community.

Many MBEs will not be technologically savvy and may lack the appropriate technology or equipment to engage with a large buying organisation as a large supplier would. This requires adjustment on the part of the buying organisation, which must be more flexible and provide appropriate inter-organisational interfaces when dealing with these suppliers. Long-term relationships with key suppliers and a mentoring programme may need to be established, as the larger buyers may need to provide a nurturing environment (Bates, 2001). Such a programme can also help overcome a scarcity of suppliers or a lack of specific capabilities.

While cost is always a consideration during procurement, other important factors include stability of supply, quality, and lead-times (Lysons & Farrington, 2006). These additional requirements must be clearly communicated with MBE suppliers, as disruptions in supply, quality problems, or long lead times may negatively impact on the ability to supply a buying organisation's own customers. Initial articulation of requirements and on-going management of these factors is critical in the SD programme and will require more than just a champion; practices must be codified and recorded to enable effective monitoring.

Senior management support and commitment to the programme is critical for success. SD programmes must be supported by all staff in the buying organisation (Whitfield & Landeros, 2006). Several important internal requirements must be considered, particularly the initial costs of resourcing required to undertake an effective SD programme. Work must be undertaken to generate a potential pool of adequate suppliers while guidelines and requirements must be carefully codified to align with corporate requirements. Policies relating to procurement must also incorporate elements that are deemed important in the vision and mission statements as marketed to the public. Staff allocations should be undertaken with the consideration that not all members will be equally committed to SD programmes; appropriate staff should be further empowered and enabled to understand their KPIs. Finally, external factors should be evaluated, particularly the ability for the organisation to undertake public awareness campaigns, highlighting their CSR objectives and their community relationships.

Perhaps a key challenge to implementation of SD programmes is the drive for shareholder value and the concomitant move towards rationalisation of the supply base, which appear, initially, to provide significant roadblocks. Contemporary procurement practices favour the consolidation and optimisation of the supplier base during supplier rationalisation programmes (Lysons & Farrington, 2006). This change in the supply base is an attempt to achieve competitive advantage with fewer relationships that are more carefully managed and are longer-term (Pearson, Fawcett, & Cooper, 1993). Similarly, Adobor and McMullen (2007) have suggested that modern production approaches, such as Just in Time (JIT), have resulted in a greater reliance on fewer preferred suppliers, representing a natural contraction of the supply base. Initially, SD may seem to run counter to these concepts.

Locating qualified suppliers that have the requisite capabilities and available capacity is perceived by larger organisations as a significant barrier to SD adoption. Such suppliers do tend to cluster infrequently in particular industries and may lack skills, capital, and technology. Moreover, small and medium enterprises (SMEs) may also represent their capabilities (either intentionally or otherwise) to win corporate contracts (Dollinger, Enz, & Daily, 1991). Krause et al. (1999) confirm that these problems of access to capital, the conflict between supplier rationalisation and SD adoption, and a lack of qualified staff in potential suppliers negatively impacts the ability of the diverse suppliers to secure adequate business.

One method to overcome the challenge of rationalisation and qualification of suppliers is the use of supply cooperatives. MBEs can form cooperatives to increase their own purchasing power, negotiation power with buying organisations, and creating a consolidated and pseudo-consolidated supply base for corporations. The cooperative structure can act as a 'buffer' and improve supplier relationship management, and ensure that appropriately qualified suppliers are selected and used for work, while providing buying organisations with confidence in the stability and long-term prospects of suppliers. The cooperative can undertake some of the work that may otherwise be undertaken by the buying organisation.

Alignment of SD objectives with corporate objectives is also important. Existing culture and strategies will have influenced the current procurement and supply management practices. Separate and novel objectives relating to CSR, incorporating elements of the SD programme, will need to be introduced separately, rather than trying to align the programme with existing strategies and extant culture. This is particularly true as many extant approaches will promote a focus on cost-reduction and efficiency through supply rationalisation (Baily, Farmer, Jessop, & Jones, 2008). While SD may initially be believed to increase risks and complications in terms of SRM, long-term benefits in CSR should outweigh these considerations and be moderated through the implementation of supply-side solutions.

Possible Supply-Side Solutions

Many of the challenges that have been discussed may be mitigated by diverse suppliers or MBEs forming a business cooperative. This will present a single, unified façade, to the buying organisation and it is recognised as being able to prevent the incidence of power imbalances in the relationship (Kelliher, 2007).

Globally there are several cottage industries where production occurs in a home-based environment as opposed to in a factory. The items tend to be unique or created on a small-scale and are not mass-produced. The output may, however, be components for use in larger-scale production. However, the volumes required for a manufacturer to compete in a traditional retail supply chain will likely outstrip the capacity of a single supplier. In addition there may be other disadvantages that cottage industries face as they compete with factory-based production, such as the fact that they are not part of established supplier networks and require additional commitment to include them in the supply base.

The presence of a supplier cooperative alone may not, however, be adequate. Changes inside of the buying organisation must also occur. The commitment to SD practices must be cultivated carefully and embodied within the emerging culture to ensure that all behaviours are appropriate. There is required to be deep commitment which may be improved through demonstration of the value of diversity to success, the provision of clear targets and appropriate metrics, emphasis on fairness and a clear rationale, crafting appropriate SD strategies aligned with senior executive expectations, the identification of diverse suppliers, and the implementation of methods to avoid conflicts between the parties (Slater, et al., 2008).

E-GOVERNMENT SOLUTIONS IN PPP ARRANGEMENTS

A more modern approach to SD, able to overcome many of the challenges, is the use of e-government solutions. In a nutshell e-government means "governance through the use of information and communication technology (ICT)" (Sharma & Loh, 2009, p. 204), providing the ability for efficient and transparent interaction between a government body (or agency) and other stakeholders in society, using ICT. These systems allow the bundling and simplification of business processes to provide "simplified procedures and shorter lead times, making the system more approachable for smaller, less well-resourced, enterprises" (Panayiotou, Gayialis, & Tatsiopoulos, 2004, p. 100); in procurement such a system may encompass tenders, workflow, electronic marketplaces, electronic catalogues, and exchange and auctions. The use of ICT to improve government may have connotations of a standardised government approach, removing the alibility or opportunity for flexibility through improved autonomy. Yet, e-government has been promoted strongly as a key platform for government reform and appears as a natural match to the improved engagement with community as "digital government must reposition itself to become an engaged and constructive partner in shaping the new governance patterns" (Allen, Juillet, Paquet, & Roy, 2001, p. 103), presenting a natural alignment of constructs and philosophies.

Policies relating to public procurement can be utilised as a tool to bring about desired changes (Rolfstam, 2009). They can provide a method for local and federal governments to make small investments in infrastructure and finances (like co-operatives) to assist marginalised groups to start-up businesses, or create incubators to develop specialised cottage industries, acting in an incubatory role. Not only can financial investments be made in a community, but there can be improved exchange of knowledge and information, inciting greater technological development in the wider community (Phillips, Knight, Caldwell, & Warrington, 2007).

The potential benefits of e-government to developing regions are substantial; however there are significant shortfalls in the funding and capabilities or skills available in the public sectors that may make the concept impractical. One method that may help address this is the PPP, which is "an agreement between government and businesses or NGOs for the provision of services by sharing of risks and rewards of the venture" (Sharma & Loh, 2009, p. 205).

Through the use of the PPP model, suitable amounts of talent and funding may be utilised in e-government projects. The model seeks to overcome the barrier of 'lack' in the government, providing greater speed, efficiency, and service in government provision of services. Partners may be suitable organisations from industry or other groups within society such as non-profits (Lawther, 2003), which leverage their capabilities so that they can complement the government agency strengths. The approach is critical as it has proven to be a "viable business model for e-Government implementation, to impart economic sustainability and provide necessary soft-skills [. . .] where there is a lack of critical resources such as finances and technical skills" (Sharma & Loh, 2009, p. 210).

PPP Use with Governments

PPPs may be advantageous where there is a higher level of complexity, as mechanisms are instituted to ensure that participants interact as equals, changing the relationships. The model is particularly useful in situations where there is a high level of risk, trust, commitment, coordination, complexity or uncertainty, and cost-sharing that is required (Lawther, 2003, p. 208). The implementation needs to be carefully considered, particularly concerning risk allocation and conversations between parties before the contract is awarded (Li, Akintoye, Edwards, & Hardcastle, 2005a).

Three key success factors for the implementation of PPPs include the presence of a strong private consortium, appropriate risk allocation models between the parties, and the availability of financial support and financial markets (Li, Akintoye, Edwards, & Hardcastle, 2005b) p. 496. It has also been suggested that there are important underlying legal elements, such as legal values, democratic participation, particularly as the modern governments act to facilitate and support the provision of services that are being more frequently supplied by other parties using PPP arrangements (Lienhard, 2006, p. 558). Strong internal integration is important to maintain cost-effectiveness, while integration with suppliers will vastly improve the supply reliability (Lee, Kwon, & Severance, 2007).

Through the ability to open a portal to governments, government agencies, and partners, e-government systems and the incorporation of e-procurement systems within PPPs provide significant opportunities – all of which can be influenced through the introduction of appropriate procurement policy. Their use offsets some of the technological and managerial challenges that diverse suppliers face, helping to reduce the challenges of implementing SD programmes in PPPs, providing that suitable cultural and managerial changes can be made internally.

CONCLUSION

Supplier diversity is business process that seeks to provide suppliers equal access to supply management opportunities and it may be enhanced through appropriate procurement policies that influence e-government and PPP structures. There are multiple examples that provide strong business cases for the adoption of SD initiatives, particularly as minority groups represent significant future growth markets in many societies globally, both in developed and developing nations. SD programmes can also offer implementing organisations certain strategic benefits including:

- Increased returns on procurement activities
- Improved stakeholder satisfaction
- Greater engagement in the local communities
- Economic opportunities in local communities through a domino effect
- Improved corporate image through application of CSR models
- Improved agility, flexibility, and resilience to change in the buying organisation.

While SD initiatives were taken to support minority groups and other disadvantaged society groups in developed countries, we have demonstrated that the concept can be applied in other regions to improve standards of living. This chapter has asserted that procurement policies, particularly those of governmental agencies, represent a key lever in the battle with poverty – particularly where PPPs are concerned.

A strategy for buying companies wishing to implement a SD programme must have multiple facets. Firstly Government bodies and MNCs must establish CSR policies. Second, Local governments should actively identify communities or disadvantaged groups that may benefit from SD involvement. Third, CSR policies should be translated into appropriate and aligned procurement policies that promote SD programmes and management. Fourth, local governments must support the development of capacity and capability within communities, which may be aided by the implementation of e-government and e-procurement systems within PPP programmes.

Such ventures may also be aided through supply-side initiatives, such as the formation of cooperatives. Such cooperatives may also require government support, particularly in developing improved infrastructure and management capabilities.

E-government and e-procurement programmes can support the development of effective PPPs that can be influenced through government policy to source from the local community. This can provide an important boost to local communities and economies, and may be supplemented with the development of supply-side cooperatives, enabling effective engagement with diverse suppliers.

We suggest that that:

- Corporate Social Responsibility should be aligned with organisation mission statements and objectives
- Organisation performance may be improved through SD initiatives
- Procurement policies, and CSR initiatives such as SD, can provide advantage to organisations
- Careful evaluation of diverse suppliers is required and support and a long-term relationship may be required to enable effective supplier development
- Procurement policies of government agencies can influence e-government systems and PPPs to encourage development of SD programmes.

Governments can influence their own procurement, and that of other organisations using PPPs, to encourage greater engagement with local communities using SD programmes. These may allow governments to transform local communities and may provide a method for governments to move towards objectives established in the UN Millennium Declaration Goals.

REFERENCES

Adobor, H., & McMullen, R. (2007). Supplier diversity and supply chain management: A strategic approach. *Business Horizons*, *50*(3), 219–229. doi:10.1016/j.bushor.2006.10.003

Allen, B. A., Juillet, L., Paquet, G., & Roy, J. (2001). E-Governance & government on-line in Canada: Partnerships, people & prospects. *Government Information Quarterly*, *18*(2), 93–104. doi:10.1016/S0740-624X(01)00063-6

Baier, C., Hartmann, E., & Moser, R. (2008). Strategic alignment and purchasing efficacy: An exploratory analysis of their impact on financial performance. *Journal of Supply Chain Management*, *44*(4), 36–52. doi:10.1111/j.1745-493X.2008.00071.x

Baily, P., Farmer, D., Jessop, D., & Jones, D. (2008). *Procurement principles and management* (10th ed.). London, UK: Prentice Hall.

Bates, T. (2001). Minority business access to mainstream markets. *Journal of Urban Affairs*, *23*(1), 41–56. doi:10.1111/0735-2166.00074

Bharadwaj, S. G., Varadarajan, P. R., & Fahy, J. (1993). Sustainable competitive advantage in service industries: A conceptual model and research propositions. *Journal of Marketing*, *57*(4), 83–99. doi:10.2307/1252221

Blake, J. (2007). Caring for the bottom line. *Human Resource Planning*, *30*(1), 36–44.

Carter, C. R., Auskalnis, R. J., & Ketchum, C. L. (1999). Purchasing from minority business enterprises: Key success factors. *Journal of Supply Chain Management*, *35*(1), 28–32. doi:10.1111/j.1745-493X.1999.tb00053.x

Chen, S., & Ravallion, M. (2008). The developing world is poorer than we thought, but no less successful in the fight against poverty. *The World Bank Development Research Group*. Retrieved from http://elibrary.worldbank.org/docserver/download/4703.pdf?expires=1328136769&id=id&accname=guest&checksum=13842B7AFFC09192E20FCFBA7D547269

Christopher, M., Lowson, R., & Peck, H. (2004). Creating agile supply chains in the fashion industry. *International Journal of Retail & Distribution Management*, *32*(8), 367–376. doi:10.1108/09590550410546188

Dollinger, M. J., Enz, C. A., & Daily, C. M. (1991). Purchasing from minority small businesses. *International Journal of Purchasing and Materials Management*, *27*(2), 9–14.

Edmondson, V. C., Suh, W. S., & Munchus, G. (2008). Exceeding government-mandated social programs: Minority supplier development programs. *Management Research News*, *31*(2), 111–124. doi:10.1108/01409170810846830

Golder, A. (2004). Buyers prefer web to find suppliers. *Supply Management*, *9*(10), 8–10.

Jeeva, A. (2011). *Poverty reduction strategies via procurement policies*. Paper presented at the The 20th Annual IPSERA Conference International Purchasing and Supply Education and Research Association, Maastricht, The Netherlands: Maastricht University.

Kelliher, F. (2007). Small firm cooperative constructs: Addressing industry power relationships. *Journal of Small Business and Enterprise Development*, *14*(3), 501–513. doi:10.1108/14626000710773574

Kerr, J. (2006). The changing complexion of supplier diversity. *Supply Chain Management Review*, *10*(2), 38–45.

Krause, D. R., Ragatz, G. L., & Hughley, S. (1999). Supplier development from the minority supplier's perspective. *Journal of Supply Chain Management*, *35*(4), 33–41. doi:10.1111/j.1745-493X.1999.tb00242.x

Laudon, K. C., & Traver, C. G. (2007). *E-commerce: Business, technology, society* (3rd ed.). Upper Saddle River, NJ: Prentice Hall.

Lawther, W. C. (2003). Contracting for the 21st century: A partnership model. In Abramson, M. A., & Harris, R. S. III, (Eds.), *The procurement revolution* (pp. 167–216). Lanham, MD: Rowan and Littlefield.

Lee, C. W., Kwon, I.-W. G., & Severance, D. (2007). Relationship between supply chain performance and degree of linkage among supplier, internal integration, and customer. *Supply Chain Management*, *12*(6), 444–452. doi:10.1108/13598540710826371

Li, B., Akintoye, A., Edwards, P. J., & Hardcastle, C. (2005a). The allocation of risk in PPP/PFI construction projects in the UK. *International Journal of Project Management*, *23*(1), 25–35. doi:10.1016/j.ijproman.2004.04.006

Li, B., Akintoye, A., Edwards, P. J., & Hardcastle, C. (2005b). Critical success factors for PPP/PFI projects in the UK construction industry. *Construction Management and Economics*, *23*(5), 459–471. doi:10.1080/01446190500041537

Lienhard, A. (2006). Public private partnerships (PPPs) in Switzerland: Experiences—risks—potentials. *International Review of Administrative Sciences*, *72*(4), 547–563. doi:10.1177/0020852306070083

Lysons, K., & Farrington, B. (2006). *Purchasing and supply chain management* (7th ed.). Essex, UK: Pearson Education.

Min, H. (2009). The best-practice supplier diversity program at Caterpillar. *Supply Chain Management*, *14*(3), 167–170. doi:10.1108/13598540910954502

Panayiotou, N. A., Gayialis, S. P., & Tatsiopoulos, I. P. (2004). An e-procurement system for governmental purchasing. *International Journal of Production Economics*, *90*(1), 79–102. doi:10.1016/S0925-5273(03)00103-8

Pearson, J. N., Fawcett, S. E., & Cooper, A. (1993). Challenges and approaches to purchasing from minority-owned firms: A longitudinal examination. *Entrepreneurship: Theory & Practice*, *18*(2), 71–88.

Phillips, W., Knight, L., Caldwell, N., & Warrington, J. (2007). Policy through procurement - The introduction of digital signal process (DSP) hearing aids into the English NHS. *Health Policy (Amsterdam)*, *80*(1), 77–85. doi:10.1016/j.healthpol.2006.03.008

Ram, M., & Smallbone, D. (2003). Supplier diversity initiatives and the diversification of ethnic minority businesses in the UK. *Policy Studies*, *24*(4), 187–204. doi:10.1080/0144287042000216117

Rigg, J., & Nattapoolwat, S. (2001). Embracing the global in Thailand: Activism and pragmatism in an era of deagrarianization. *World Development*, *29*(6), 945–960. doi:10.1016/S0305-750X(01)00021-3

Rolfstam, M. (2009). Public procurement as an innovation policy tool: The role of institutions. *Science & Public Policy*, *36*(5), 349–360. doi:10.3152/030234209X442025

Satterthwaite, D. (2001). Reducing urban poverty: Constraints on the effectiveness of aid agencies and development banks and some suggestions for change. *Environment and Urbanization*, *13*(1), 137–157. doi:10.1177/095624780101300111

Shah, M., & Ram, M. (2006). Supplier diversity and minority business enterprise development: Case study experience of three US multinationals. *Supply Chain Management*, *11*(1), 75–81. doi:10.1108/13598540610642493

Sharma, A., & Loh, P. (2009). Emerging trends in sourcing of business services. *Business Process Management Journal*, *15*(2), 149–165. doi:10.1108/14637150910949425

Slater, S. F., Weigand, R. A., & Zwirlein, T. J. (2008). The business case for commitment to diversity. *Business Horizons*, *51*(3), 201–209. doi:10.1016/j.bushor.2008.01.003

Suchman, M. C. (1995). Managing legitimacy: Strategic and institutional approaches. *Academy of Management Review*, *20*(3), 571–610.

van Weele, A. J. (2005). *Purchasing & supply chain management: Analysis, strategy, planning and practice* (4th ed.). Australia: Thomson.

Whitfield, G., & Landeros, R. (2006). Supplier diversity effectiveness: Does organizational culture really matter? *Journal of Supply Chain Management*, *42*(4), 16–28. doi:10.1111/j.1745-493X.2006.00019.x

Worthington, I., Ram, M., Boyal, H., & Shah, M. (2008). Researching the drivers of socially responsible purchasing: A cross-national study of supplier diversity initiatives. *Journal of Business Ethics*, *79*(3), 319–331. doi:10.1007/s10551-007-9400-x

Chapter 3
Electronic Government Systems for E-Procurement Procedure in the EU

Sergio Bravo Martín
University of Salamanca, Spain

Francisco J. García Peñalvo
University of Salamanca, Spain

ABSTRACT

Public Electronic Procurement provides a new means of communication between contracting authorities and economic operators, as well as being one of the most important areas in the development in the business-to-business (B2B) e-commerce like buyers and suppliers entities respectively. European Union (EU) has been working hard for the adoption of e-Procurement in the governments of member states; overall action plans for the development of e-government occurred during the new millennium. However, this transition, from the traditional model of procurement management procedure to electronic means is very complicated; the impact of any new technology brings much change and the required regulatory policies, both within the EU and in Member States. This study presents the e-procurement from the e-government regulatory contexts in EU. Then, it outlines the basic pillars of both the public e-procurement process and the management systems, and finally, introduces large-scale pilot projects by the European Commission (EC) that provide technology solutions for many of the stages of the procurement process.

1. THE PUBLIC E-PROCUREMENT ON THE E-GOVERNMENT CONTEXT

The Information Society is part of the policies of the European Union that promotes open and competitive society with a focus on e-Government. The development of these policies was marked for the period 2000-2010 through the Lisbon Strategy (EC, 2000) and the Action Plans: e-Europe 2002 (EC, 2002), e-Europe 2005 (EC, 2005) and the i2010 Strategy (EC, 2010). However, the global economic crisis has significantly affected the results, very different than expected. This is the reason that has prompted a redesign of the political strategy of the European Union and which results in Europe 2020 (EC, 2011), a strategy for smart growth, sustainable and inclusive.

DOI: 10.4018/978-1-4666-2119-0.ch003

Europe 2020 makes again a commitment to the development of the Information Society as a cornerstone of an inclusive, intelligent and sustainable. This has led to the inclusion among the seven key initiatives[1] in Europe 2020, "A Digital Agenda for Europe", adopted by the Commission during the Spanish Presidency of the European Union in the first half of 2010 (EC, 2010, August 26). The purpose of the Digital Agenda is to achieve the sustainable economic and social benefits to be derived from a digital single market based on ultrafast Internet and interoperable applications.

The implementation of e-Procurement should be based on a gradual enrolled in the plan of development of e-Government in the field of public administration. Such is the importance of e-Procurement that the European Digital Agenda foresees the adoption of a White Paper which will outline the measures the Commission intends to take to establish an infrastructure of networked electronic public procurement.

An acceptable definition of the public electronic procurement, may be found in the *Green Paper on expanding the use of e-Procurement in the EU* (2010, October 18), referring to the term as: "use of electronic communications and transaction processing by government institutions and other public sector organizations when buying supplies and services or tendering public works". It is not simply a conversion of a system on paper to electronic form. Electronic Procurement, as mentioned in the various European Digital Agendas and Action Plans, can contribute substantial improvements in contracting goods and services, public management and operation of public procurement internal markets in the field of national contracts.

The development of e-Government in the European Union particularly arises from a consensus reached by Member States in the Ministerial Declarations occurred since 2001 in Brussels, and especially from Manchester (Ministers of EU, 2005), with the creation of the i2010 e-Government Action Plan (EC, 2006). This action plan focused on five major objectives[2] for e-Government with specific objectives, three of which related directly to e-Procurement:

1. Deploying high-impact e-Government services like e-Procurement can save billions of Euros for European public administrations, which means more taxpayers money available for essential services[3]. Member States committed themselves to the goal that, by i2010 Action Plan, 100% of public procurement will be available electronically and 50% of actual use of procurement procedures above the legal European Union thresholds (from 50.000 Euros for simple services and 6 million for public works).
2. Turning efficiency and effectiveness in fact, contributing significantly to greater satisfaction, greater transparency and responsibility, reduced administrative burden and increased efficiency.
3. Developing essential tools, enabling citizens and businesses benefit from an authenticated access, comfortable, secure and interoperable public services across Europe.

The Action Plan i2010 highlights the importance to expedite the establishment of the electronic administration in Europe, in order to answer to a series of challenges and requirements:

1. Modernizing and doing more effective public services.
2. Offering services of higher quality and more insurance to the population.
3. Responding to demand from companies who desire minus bureaucracy and more efficiency.
4. Ensuring the continued cross-border services.

All of these Ministerial Declarations agree on the idea of promoting e-Government and identify it as a key tool, available to citizens and entities from public and private sector, which allow the construction of a single market and the arrival of more sustainable government.

However, EC, by the Lisbon strategy evaluation document (2010, February 2), suggests more research, development and innovation. The system of standards remains fragmented and too slow given fast technological developments. The use of demand driven instruments such as public procurement has brought some improvements although the system has not developed to its full potential

Today, after the Malmö Ministerial Declaration (2009, November 18), there is a new e-Government Action Plan in Europe (2010, December 15) for the period 2011-2015 based on the experience gained in the Action Plan 2006, and subtitled "Harnessing ICT to promote smart, sustainable & innovative Government". In accordance with this subtitle, e-Government goes from being seen as a key tool for supporting to an element to promote the public administration. It is a large scale Action Plan, even with a major presence of e-Procurement, although some of its actions are included in the Digital Agenda for Europe[4]. This Action Plan aims to support the transition to a new generation of open, flexible and seamless e-Government services at local, regional, national and EU levels. More specifically, the Plan aims to make services work as well in other EU Member States as they do at home and to open the way to allowing users actively to shape the online public services which suit their needs best.

Regarding electronic procurement on 2010, October 18, EC was published the *Green Paper on expanding the use of e-Procurement in the EU*, which provides among other things, that the effective implementation of public electronic procurement, in most countries individually and in the European Union as a whole remains low and is estimated at less than 5% in value of total public procurement. Portugal is the exception in this respect because in that Member State from November 1, 2009, is required the use of electronic means to develop all phases of procurement process, including the award for most government contracts.

Public procurement is still a relatively untapped area of e-Government. Given the promise it holds to generate new business and innovation opportunities – with all this implies in terms of economic growth and job creation – e-Procurement is a priority under the e-Government action plan. Such systems open up the possibilities for companies to sell their goods and services to public agencies and governments, thanks to better publicizing opportunities and reducing the costs of bidding. The five-year e-Government Action Plan 2011-2015 outlines a list of measures stands to benefit citizens and businesses (EU, 2010a). Specially, in the field of business, the aim of the new Action Plan is that 80% of enterprises will be using online public services by 2015. Businesses should be able to sell goods and services to public administrations all across the EU, through easy electronic public procurement. By 2015, a number of key cross-border services, such as e-Tendering, should be available online and enable entrepreneurs to set up and run a business anywhere in Europe more quickly and easily, independent of their original location.

This section has introduced the concept of public electronic procurement and has surveyed the state of it in the context of e-Government. The following section discusses the basic legal framework in the context of the European Union. A third section explores the key elements of a public procurement system by electronic means from the viewpoint of the contracting authorities and from economic operators. The fourth section presents the electronic systems of publicizing notices in the Official Journals of the EU. The fifth section discusses the problems of cross-border e-Procurement systems, to continue in the next section with the large scale European projects, which have efficient operational solutions to other phases of e-Procurement management in the public sector and in the context of an internal market and networked. The chapter ends with some reflections about the technological solutions presented in previous sections and ways to forward effective and efficient extension of them.

2. LEGAL FRAMEWORK FOR PUBLIC E-PROCUREMENT IN THE EU

Public procurement is the knowledge base that regulates the procedures that public and private organizations must continue to manage the needs of public goods and services with a commitment to ensure compliance with the principles of free access to tenders, publicity and transparency of procedures and, non-discrimination and equal treatment of candidates. Public procurement is a key sector in the European economy, as recalls the Digital Agenda for Europe when it says that this service represents 19.4% of GDP in the European Union.

Studies from consulting firms have been shown that proper use of e-Procurement helps reduce costs, improve efficiency and destroy barriers that ultimately result in savings for the taxpayer, which could provide between 2 and 5% decrease offers and between 40 and 60% improvement in resources and time spent in management. It would also allow a better fiscal policy since the saving of between 2 and 5% of the budget is a useful increase in spending for the administration, and also could be used between 40 and 60% of the resources now devoted to too bureaucratic management. Hence, the modernization and opening of electronic border is sufficiently justified and crucial for European competitiveness and for creating new business opportunities, particularly on the side of SMEs. The traditional procurement process is long and protracted, as well as resource-intensive. For this reason, the various action plans that have occurred have reinforced the use of ICT in achieving the public e-Procurement. Furthermore, conducting public procurement by electronic means would be an orderly and expeditious progress towards e-commerce between the government and its suppliers, and even within their own public authorities (systemic interaction or Business-to-business, B2B). The effort to create standards that ensure full interoperability between different procurement systems of the member states is postulated as one of the highlights of the current Action Plan in achieving an internal market. Do not forget that associated with the B2B e-Procurement, encompasses not only the relationship between public authorities and suppliers of goods and services, but also to other authorities in their various fields of action (national, regional and local) with each other, and between authorities of different Member States.

The creation of the legislative package of procurement directives by the European Commission, 2004/17/EC (European Parliament, 2004a) and 2004/18/EC (European Parliament, 2004b) provides a legal framework for open electronic procurement, transparent and non discriminatory, that states for electronic bid and the conditions of new purchasing techniques based on electronic means. Member States, based on article 80 of Directive 2004/18/EC, undertake to bring into force the laws, regulations and administrative provisions, necessary to provide its management with the necessary means for implementing e-Procurement, advantage new technologies and adapting legal frameworks as necessary[5].

2.1. Directives 2004/17/EC and 2004/18/EC

Article 1.13 of Directive 2004/18/EC defines the electronic means as those using electronic equipment for processing (including digital compression) and storage of data and those use the media, sending and reception cable, radio, by optical or other electromagnetic means. The introduction of electronic means in public procurement incorporates a number of legal issues relating mostly to the electronic organization of the procedures originally designed for processing in paper format. Public procurement bases its regulatory framework primarily on selection procedures and award of tenders. The transition to electronic public procurement should not change any phase of the existing procurement procedures. Simply it is intended that any economic operator in the European Union can participate, with one simple electronic equipment, in a procurement procedure to be performed wholly or partly by electronic means.

The advantages of the incorporation of electronic means on public procurement process are notable; however one of the most remarkable is the speed in the publication of notices by contracting authorities and the reduction of procedural deadlines. Not only because of the nature of the electronic means itself but also by the the articulated policies. According to articles 38.6 of Directive 2004/18/EC (corresponding provision, Article 45.6 of Directive 2004/17/EC), will be a reduction of five days of the deadline for receipt of tenders, provided that the contracting authority offers a full access, direct an unrestricted by electronic means to the contract documents an additional documents (the text of the notice should specify the internet address at which this documentation). According to this approach, define the buyer profiles as a set of data on procurement activities of contracting authority, and the option to include notices and any other pertinent information such general, for example, contact points (point 2.b) of Annex VIII of Directive 2004/18/EC and point 2.b) of Annex XX to Directive 2004/17/EC.

On the other hand, some of these procedures (for example, receipt of tender), by including the electronic media in its regular process, are forced to incorporate an advanced electronic signature, as stated in Articles 42.5.b) and 48.5.b) of Directives 2004/18/EC and 2004/17/EC respectively, to guarantee the authenticity and integrity of the information provided.

In turn, these policies have optionally, two new electronic procurement procedures leaving Member States the decision to implement them. These are the dynamic purchasing systems (Article 1.6 of Directive 2004/18/EC and Article 1.5 of the 2004/17/EC) and electronic auctions (Article 1.7 of Directive 2004/18/EC and Article 1.6 of the 2004/17/EC). First, dynamic purchasing system is a completely electronic process for making commonly used purchases, limited in time (the duration shall not exceed four years, with some exceptions) and open throughout its validity to any economic operator which satisfies the selection criteria and has submitted an indicative tender that complies with the specification. Meanwhile, electronic auction is a repetitive process involving an electronic device for presentation of new prices, revised downwards, and/or new values concerning certain elements of tenders, which occurs after the initial full evaluation of the tenders and has an impact on their classification using automatic evaluation methods. The auction may be based either solely on prices when the contract is awarded to the low (current auction) or on prices and / or values of the elements of tenders indicated in the specification, awarded to the most economically advantageous tender (actual competition).

The electronic catalogues are another key point of these policies (Articles 12 and 20 Directives 18 and 17 respectively). These e-Catalogues are defined as instruments that facilitate the procurement, specifically as a way to participate in tenders with framework agreements or when a dynamic purchasing system is being used in order to rules applicable to communication (Articles 42 and 48 Directives 18 and 17 respectively).

Finally, electronic notification is another key (Articles 36.2, 36.3 and 36.6 of Directive 2004/18/EC and Articles 44.2 and 44.3 in 2004/17/EC), to be conducted using standard forms but not necessarily by electronics means; in accelerated procedures, notices should be sent by fax or electronic means. The electronic notification allows abbreviated publication and increases the permitted extent of advertisements.

Given that these directives do not include the standards "detail" of electronic procedures, the Commission adopted in July 2005, a working paper on the requirements of using electronic means in public procurement, in order to clarify the rules on electronic contracting. This paper presents the practical application of the principles of accessibility, availability, non-discrimination and interoperability in the different phases and types of procedures (interpretation of Articles 42.4 and 48.4).

The document clarifies that entities may choose to provide that all communications are done electronically or live with the paper medium, possibly with a relationship in parallel or in stages. However, the right of choice of the contracting authority is limited under the Directive. Such is the case of electronic auctions procedures and dynamic purchasing systems in which the processing is limited only by electronic means. Also, the directive includes in its Articles 42.3 and 48.3, the conditions of integrity and information security aspects that are not derived from electronic procurement, but the traditional. These aspects may require ad-hoc solutions to meet them in a purely electronic mean. Do not forget also to ensure traceability aspects in the procurement process and the publication of notices.

3. KEY ELEMENTS FOR PUBLIC E-PROCUREMENT SYSTEMS

Manage the all phases of procurement process is an important and complicated work. First, because almost all services involved are vertical and cross services for a public organization, and also requires them to adapt the legal framework of the European Union and the particulars provided by contracting authorities in the Member States (local level, regional, national, supranational or even dependent organisms).

In this sense, it is crucial that procurement procedure management solutions covering entire life cycle associated with the procurement process, from the need for an acquisition of a good or service arises, or (from the contracting unit or from the proponent department which is origin of the need), through publication in the buyer profile and the final award and ending in electronic archiving and document custody.

There are several different procedures available for public authorities. These include the open, restricted, negotiated and competitive dialogue procedures. Each of these procedures sets its own limitations on the contracting authority, which must be considered when choosing the appropriate procedure. The procedure of public procurement is intended to be fully transparent with the intention of creating a free and competitive Europe-wide market. So, projects above a certain financial threshold must publish in the Official Journal of the European Union (OJEU) a contract notice. Buyer can advertise the contract more widely, but cannot do so before it has dispatched a notice for publication in the OJEU, and is forbidden from including information that isn't given there. After the prescribed date, the bids are opened and assessed, and either the "lowest cost" or "most economically advantageous tender" is chosen. The contract award must also be reported in the OJEU.

However, beyond the reduction of administrative costs of contracting entities and economic operators, it is the opportunity to rationalize, review and streamline (where possible) the hiring process and do not make the transition to electronic form a simple copy of the traditional paper-based procedures (EC, 2010, October 18).

Once the basic process of e-Procurement is clear the following phases can be identified:

1. **E-Sourcing**: Preparatory activities conducted by the contracting authority to collect and reuse information for the preparation on a need.
2. **E-Noticing**: Advertisement of calls for tenders through the publication of contract notices in electronic format in the relevant

Official Journal of the European Union and in the buyer profile of the contracting authority.

3. **E-Tendering**: Bidding stage developed on the side of tenderers covering the e-Access and e-Submission phases:
   a. **E-Access**: Electronic access in a non-discriminatory way to tender documents and specifications for the preparation of an offer, e.g. clarifications, questions and answers.
   b. **E-Submission**: Submission of offers in electronic format to the contracting authority (i.e. through e-Register).
4. **E-Awarding**: Opening and evaluation of the electronic tenders received, and award of the contract to the best offer in terms of the lowest price or economically most advantageous bid. Once awarded another e-Noticing phase is necessary.
5. **E-Contract**: Conclusion, enactment and monitoring of a contract (or agreement) through electronic means between the contracting authority and the winning tenderer.
6. **E-Orders**: Preparation and issuing of an electronic order by the contracting authority and its acceptance by the contractor.
7. **E-Invoicing**: Preparation and delivery of an invoice in electronic format.
8. **E-Payment**: Electronic payment of the ordered goods, services or works.

Figure 1 shows the features or phases in the electronic procurement process, from the viewpoints of contracting authorities and economic operators. According to these phases, it is important that procurement management solutions include mechanisms to following:

1. Automate the processing of procurement procedures with at least the following features:
   a. Generation official documents from default and customizable templates (for example: resolutions, proposals, communications, letters and so on).
   b. Control data entry forms in accordance with current legal framework at European level and state level (for example: classifications, CPV codes, guarantees, deadlines, award amounts and so on).
   c. Generation many kinds of reports about procurements (for example, global reports of records, global reports of bidders, reports by procurement, dates, amounts and so on).

Figure 1. Functionalities covered in the public e-procurement process

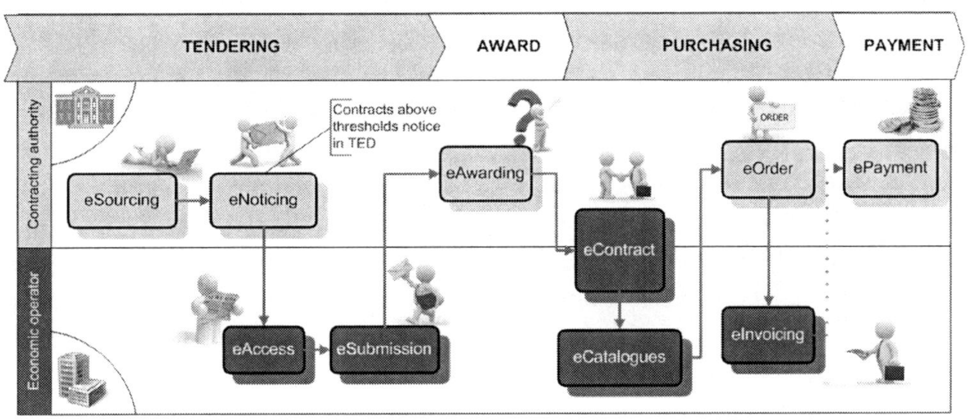

2. Define the steps of the workflow associated with each type of contract.
3. Guide the staff processing the procedure throughout its life cycle, regardless of the nature of the procurement process (including the water, energy, transport and postal services).
4. Notify the procedure owner or supervisor, through a system of alarms triggered by proximity or expiration of the defined time period on procedures, and for the supervisor to allow access to tracking and condition monitoring of files in progress.

Similarly, a system for processing procurement procedures must be able to interact with other additional external modules (for example, the buyer profile and the contracting registry), to provide greater automation and optimization for the process to obtain a global, efficient and inclusive solution.

Therefore, to make legally valid and operational electronic management of procurement procedures across borders, e-Procurement systems relay on the following elements:

1. An electronic office of the public authority justified by the need to clearly define the electronic administrative office with which relationships are established, promoting a regime of identification, authentication, minimum content, legal protection, accessibility, availability and responsibility.
2. A buyer profile[6] that allows electronic access, to tender documents and specifications as well as additional related documents, in a non-discriminatory way, included in the electronic office of the public authority (or the link/integration to the State or Region Procurement Platform under current regulations of the Member State), to publish information and documents associated with the public offering procurement. The buyer profile gives legal effect to the publications (i.e. pending and final awards) as well as ensuring a reliable way to establish the date of the publication of information on procurement notices contained.
    a. All information and contractual documents published must be time stamped by a certification service provider[7] that must irrefutably prove the start time for public internet publication relating to the procurement notices.
    b. Means of identification, authentication and integrity of the contract documents will be displayed with the electronic signature.
3. A tenderer's website to present and consult all the documentation associated with an electronic procurement procedure by any provider (suitably qualified).
4. A system for electronic procurement management and integrated with the electronic services available in its own e-Government, and the ability to electronically manage a portion of the procedures (dynamic purchasing system) or all of them (electronic auctions).

Other key enablers for effective electronic procurement systems (shown in Figure 2) are the following:

1. **E-Signature**: As an electronic mean to ensure the electronic identity of bidders (electronic identity) and integrity of information received.
2. **E-Register**: To receive offers and get a receipt proving the presentation.
3. **E-Attestations**: To prove compliance with the selection and exclusion criteria of a procurement procedure[8]. Tenderers and contracting authorities access to special websites in the manner as "Single Point of Contact" solution for Business Certificates and attestations required in the procurement process.

Figure 2. Knowledge base of e-procurement

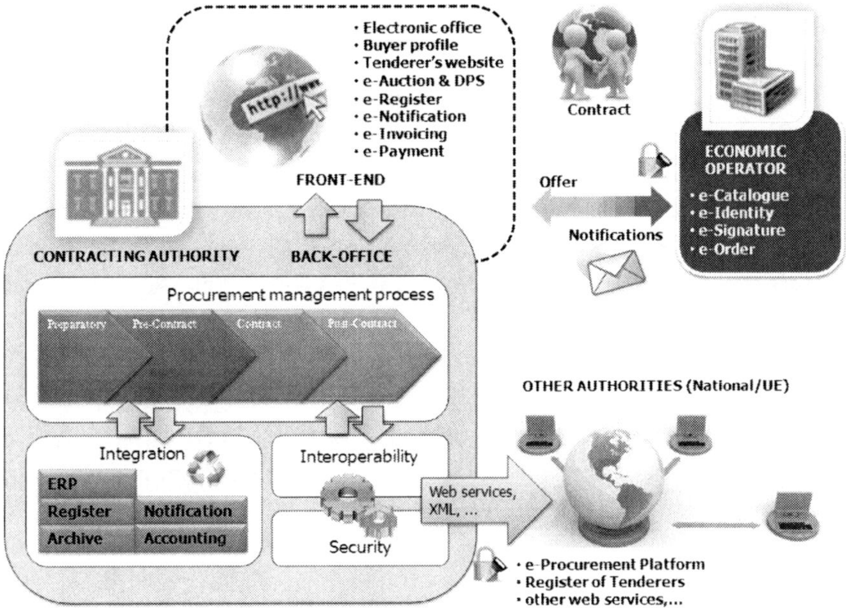

4. **E-Catalogues**: Used to prepare and submit offers or parts of them.
5. **E-Archiving and Custody:** As an electronic mean for long-term preservations of documents in digitalized format, ensuring that they can be easily retrieved without conversions.

All these elements, shown on Figure 5, represent the knowledge base of e-Procurement and should be based in open technological standards, modular approach, scale, open and based on integrations, functional standards (EC, 2005, January) and really knowledge of the environment.

To face the issue of the public procurement process, from the viewpoint of economic operators, is also a set of activities from which we can identify the following:

1. Access to Information Of Tenders[9] published in Official Journals (for example TED in UE), as well as the additional documentation in buyer profile,
2. Study the selected procurement process (both preparation and evaluation),
3. Prepare documents (and envelopes) adapted for the type of offer and indications of the specifications,
4. Prepare the requested attestations[10], documents and payment of taxes,
5. submit the bid and additional documentation (if required later) by any available means (preferably by electronic means),
6. In case of be the winner, sign the contract, perform the requirements to deliver successfully the goods or services required, issue and submit the invoice (preferably by e-Invoice).

There are many issues that vary depending on the contracting authority involved, and the ways of approaching the process also vary considerably too, depending on whether the size of the business is big or small.

4. ADVANCES USING INTERNET TO ADVERTISE PROCUREMENT NOTICES

The information system for European public procurement is based on three web services (see Figure 3): eNotices, SIMAP and TED.

First, tender notices are published on TED[11] (Tenders Electronic Daily), the website of the Supplement to the Official Journal of the European Union. TED is the single official source for timely information on public procurement opportunities in the European Union, the European Economic Area and beyond. The contracting authorities for tenders can be central governments, local or regional authorities, bodies governed by public law, or associations consisting of authorities or bodies governed by public law. In compliance with EU directives and international agreements, notices for public works, services and supply contracts above certain thresholds[12] must be published in the Supplement to the Official Journal of the European Union.

Second, eNotices[13] (formerly SIMAP on-line forms) is a web-based tool for preparing public procurement notices and sending them for publication in the Supplement to the Official Journal of the European Union. This tool is a free service that simplifies and speeds up preparation and publication of tender notices. eNotices also helps to check for possible errors in notices and for the compliance with the EU directives regulating public procurement procedures. Other available publication mechanism is a service named eSenders that allows qualified organizations to submit public procurement notices directly as XML files.

Finally, SIMAP[14] provides access to information about public procurement in Europe, for buyers (the public purchasers) as well as for suppliers. The SIMAP project has developed the buyer profile that allows contracting authorities to facilitate, by electronic means of communication, technical specifications and other necessary documents for preparing the contract notices. These buyer profiles provide more information on procurement procedures of buyer entities, responsible for procurement, pending bids and the economic (and/or technical) specification documents among others.

TED provides free access to business opportunities by a multilingual search interface and browse and sort procurement notices by country, region (NUTS), business sector (CPV), RSS and other interactive tools. Figure 4 shows a typical session in TED filtering search results by NUTS (e.g. the NUTS code for Salamanca, Spain is ES415). Information about every procurement document is published in the 23 official EU languages. It is updated five times a week with approximately 1.500 new public procurement notices from the European Union, the European Economic Area and beyond.

Figure 3. Information system for European public procurement

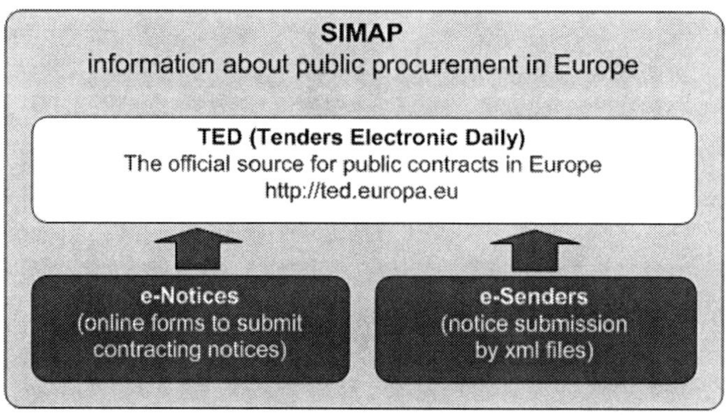

Figure 4. TED search interface

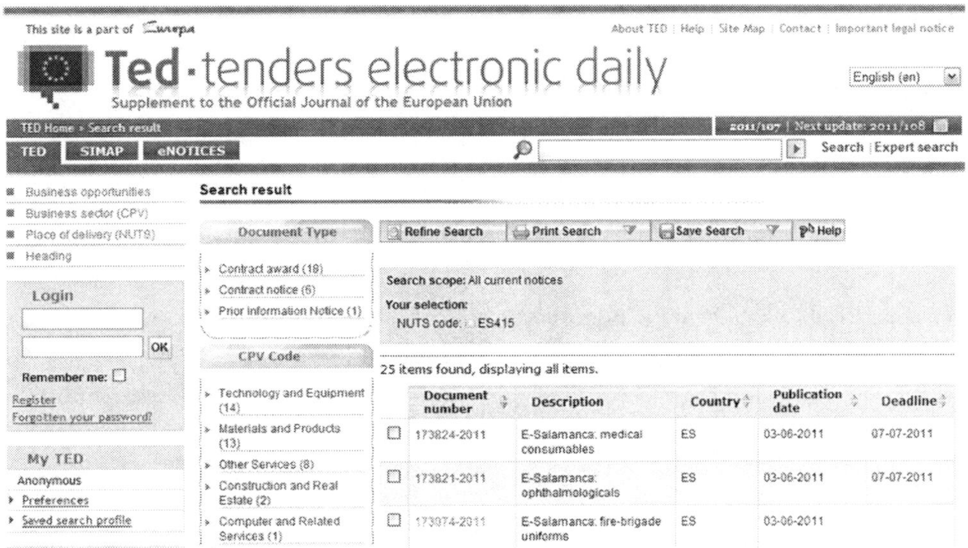

The documents published on TED are about the following topics:

1. Contracts from all EU Member States and candidate countries.
    a. Public contract notices for works, supplies and services.
    b. Utilities contract services (water, energy, transport and postal services).
2. Contract notices from the European institutions:
    a. Public works, supplies and services.
    b. External aid and European Development Fund contract notices.
    c. Phare, Tacis and other contracts in central and eastern Europe.
3. European Economic Area contract notices. The contracting parties to the EEA Agreement are three of the four EFTA States (Norway, Liechtenstein and Iceland) and the 27 EU Member States.
4. Contract notices from Switzerland pursuant to the Government Procurement Agreement (GPA), concluded within the framework of the GATT/World Trade Organization (WTO).
5. Projects financed by the European Investment Bank, the European Central Bank and the European Bank for Reconstruction and Development.
6. Notices concerning European economic interest groupings (EEIGs), European groupings for territorial cooperation (EGTCs), European companies (SEs), European cooperative societies (SCEs).
7. Public contract notices for air services.

4.1. CPV (Common Procurement Vocabulary)

The CPV establishes a single classification system for public procurement aimed at standardizing the references used by contracting authorities and entities to describe the subject of procurement contracts.

The CPV consists of a main vocabulary for defining the subject of a contract, and a supplementary vocabulary for adding further qualitative information. The main vocabulary is based on a tree structure comprising codes of up to 9 digits (an 8 digit code plus a check digit) associated with a wording that describes the type of supplies, works or services forming the subject of the contract:

1. The first two digits identify the divisions (XX000000-Y).
2. The first three digits identify the groups (XXX00000-Y).
3. The first four digits identify the classes (XXXX0000-Y).
4. The first five digits identify the categories (XXXXX000-Y).
5. Each of the last three digits gives a greater degree of precision within each category.
6. A ninth digit serves to verify the previous digits.

Figure 5, shows and expanded view of a typical contract award notice: section I shows information about contracting authority (e.g. the address of the buyer profile), section II describes the object of the contract (e.g. CPV codes assigned to the current notice: 35811100 code means "Fire-brigade uniforms" and 35811200 means "Police uniforms") and finally the section V, the award of contract with the tendering winner.

The supplementary vocabulary may be used to expand the description of the subject of a contract. The items are made up of an alphanumeric code with a corresponding wording allowing further details to be added regarding the specific nature or destination of the goods to be purchased.

The alphanumeric code is made up of:

1. A first level comprising a letter corresponding to a section,
2. A second level comprising four digits, the first three of which denote a subdivision and the last one being for verification purposes.

The use of the CPV is mandatory in the European Union as from 1 February 2006 and the version 2008 is the current CPV version[15].

Figure 5. Expanded view of a contract award notice

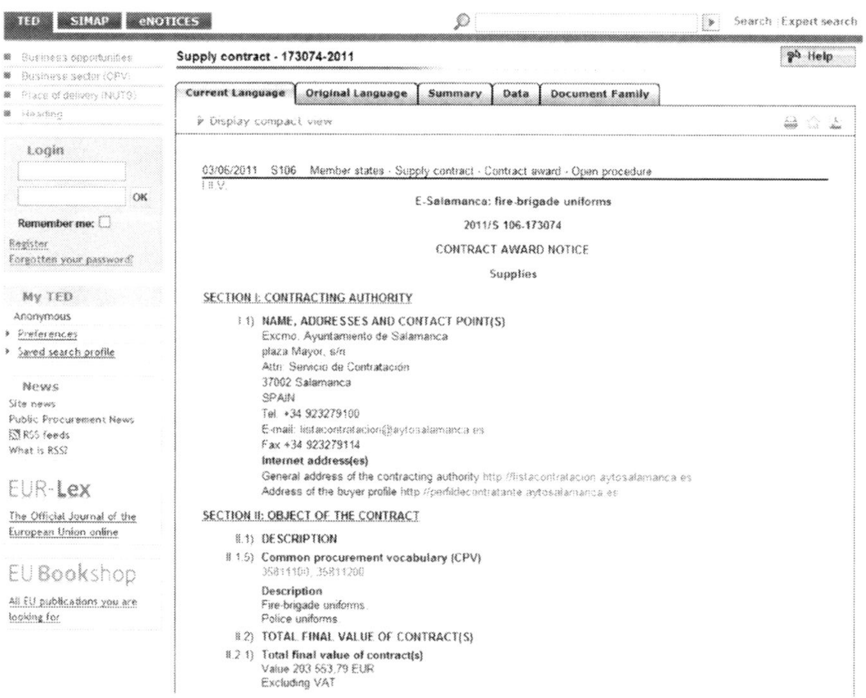

4.2. NUTS (Nomenclature of Territorial Units for Statistics)

The Nomenclature of Territorial Units for Statistics (NUTS) was established by Eurostat[16] in order to provide a single uniform breakdown of territorial units for the production of regional statistics for European Union.

The NUTS classification[17] is a hierarchical system for dividing up the economic territory of EU for the purpose of:

1. The collection, development and harmonization of EU regional statistics.
2. Socio-economic analyses of the regions (major, basic and small socio-economic regions for specific diagnoses).
3. Framing of EU regional policies.

5. PROBLEMS OF CROSS-BORDER ELECTRONIC PUBLIC PROCUREMENT

Electronic public procurement has an enormous potential for the integration of procurement markets in the EU. Potentially, electronic contracting has the advantage of shorter distances, saving gaps in information and encourages greater participation by increasing the number of potential suppliers and the possible expansion of the markets. While e-procurement does not allow minimizing the importance of factors such as proximity or distance in the effective implementation of business activity covered by the contract clearly provides the opportunity to reduce the costs of geographical distance in order to participate in the recruitment process (EC, 2010, October 18). Furthermore, the benefits of this transparency becomes even more within the borders of a country, because the providers in a region can take advantage of business opportunities that arise in other regions. Although there are certain structural factors and costs may discourage companies to participate in the procurement, other services can be provided wholly or partly at a distance[18].

Achieving a single market in the European Union implies generalize fully electronic public procurement. This generalization requires some guidelines that allow, first to the government and then the companies make the right decisions about IT for the transformation of this business system (the public procurement) to electronic form (Caño et al., 2011). The challenges for extending e-Procurement at national and supranational levels are interoperability and generalization.

5.1. Interoperability

Interoperability between information systems appears to be reduced to the area of technological support for the exchange of information. However, the processes, content and systems can not operate together in supranational markets, without identifying other expressions of interoperability: semantic and organizational (CEPAL, 2007).

On one hand, organizational interoperability refers to the coordination and alignment of business objectives and processes involved in contracting activities that are considered common both within the government and its public entities, as compared to other procurement systems of other nations. In this sense, the EU has made a major effort through the signing of treaties and international cooperation agreements to eliminate trade barriers before facing interoperability between national electronic public procurement.

In addition, semantic interoperability means, among other things:

1. Use a common vocabulary, precise and unambiguous about what is being contracted and under what conditions,
2. Identify ways to label the cross-phases and stages of the procurement process and,
3. Identify the types of existing procurement processes.

Technical interoperability refers to the development of technological solutions that enable connection and data transfer between systems and services, including key areas such as open communication interfaces, middleware, accessibility and security services. In this sense, the technical challenge faced by the European Commission is already delivering results, through standards (CEN BII[19]), pilot projects (STORK and SPOCs), reusable components (ePRIOR and eCERTIS) and a public network, secure and affordable recruitment (PEPPOL).

An e-Procurement system cannot be a separate island to achieve its objectives alone. This translates into the need to further develop methodologies to create interoperable procurement systems, that is, enjoying the "ability to exchange data and enable sharing of information and knowledge". This type of interaction, also named systemic interaction, technically interconnect information systems of contracting authorities in the nation with the Official Platform for Procurement (local, regional, national or supranational) to exchange electronic documents involved in the procurement, through standards and web services supported by an infrastructure with stable and secure communications[20].

5.2. Generalization

Generalization is an adaptive challenge to be faced for all Member States, and it requires an understanding and governance of those technologies that implement public e-Procurement and, in some cases, exceeds the capacity of governments have to develop the implementation plans themselves. This is a task of leadership with conceptual and technical support, to be primarily driven by the European Commission and then by the central and regional administrations of Member States. To achieve this task is necessary to develop guidelines with the heads of each government and public authorities in ensuring e-Government projects within the stipulated periods[21].

In any case, the transition to electronic procurement from all Member States, takes place at different speeds. The clearest example is shown in Portugal, where the legal framework requires the use of electronic means in public procurement procedures, in whole or in part, in all matters relating to purchases.

6. CROSS-BORDER PILOT PROJECTS

Electronic procurement starts to become an operational reality. Today there is hardly a single technology or tool that supports all phases of the procurement process. In this sense, the European Commission has launched several pilot projects at European level that provide effective solutions for very specific stages. Some of these projects are currently in operation and are being used by various countries. Others, however, are still under development and some others are very difficult to face up because of the inherent limitations of the electronic mean[22].

Some Member States, through its central and regional governments have also made great efforts and developments with significant results. For example, Spain includes the State Procurement Platform in the general Government levels (all Ministries), and at regional levels, there are many other platforms that are gaining strength and support in smaller areas (e. g. the Government Procurement platform from Euskadi, awards finalist for European e-Government Awards 2009).

Following sections present some large-scale pilot projects from 2006 European e-Government Action Plan, centre on the needs of citizens and businesses making life easier through better access to more efficient and cost effective public services. These pilot projects provide the foundation of the new e-Government Action Plan 2011-2015 (EU, 2010b).

6.1. PEPPOL and e-PRIOR

First PEPPOL[23] is a major cross-border e-Procurement project intended to provide large-scale, standards-based IT infrastructure and services to set up and run on-line pan-european public procurement operations. PEPPOL runs by public-sector organizations from various EU countries and co-funded by the European Commission. The project will support practical solutions to the pre-awarding phase of Public e-Procurement by key-enablers like e-Attestation.

Existing national systems of electronic public procurement will be linked so that all participants can enjoy the full benefits of a single European market. PEPPOL is operated under the European Commission's Competitiveness and Innovation Framework Programme's ICT Policy Support Programme.

The broader vision of PEPPOL is that any company in the EU can communicate electronically with any EU governmental institution for pre-award and post-award electronic procurement activities. PEPPOL will allow any supplier in the EU to respond to any European public tender and conduct any resulting purchasing utilizing their existing national infrastructure. The immediate benefits of PEPPOL will allow for businesses to widen their markets and carry out cross-border, easier and more efficient public procurement transactions. There is an important objective to standardize electronic procurement process from e-Catalogue to e-Invoice in order to a more economic and secure interoperability for enterprises and SMEs.

Figure 6 shows the components of PEPPOL that provide support on different activities for pre-award and post-award electronic procurement procedure.

An interesting project in the activities linked to the pre-award phase, is the Virtual Company Dossier (VCD). The objective of the VCD is to replace paper certificates with electronic attestations by a special Single Point of Contact solution. The VCD shall enable suppliers to collect business certificates and attestations from existing registries and to submit those evidences electronically and assembled as information package to any public sector awarding entity in Europe. This is the origin of some voluntary state or regional registry of suppliers[24].

For the post-awarding phase of Public Procurement, there is the IDABC e-Invoicing and e-Ordering project. It started in 2007 by the Directorates-General for Internal Market (DG-MARKT) and for Informatics (DIGIT) of the European Commission. One major accomplishment of this project was the go-live of the e-Procurement platform named e-PRIOR[25] on October 2009. This platform was funded by the ISA Programme of the EC and its goal is to stimulate the implementation of interoperable e-Procurement by public

Figure 6. PEPPOL components

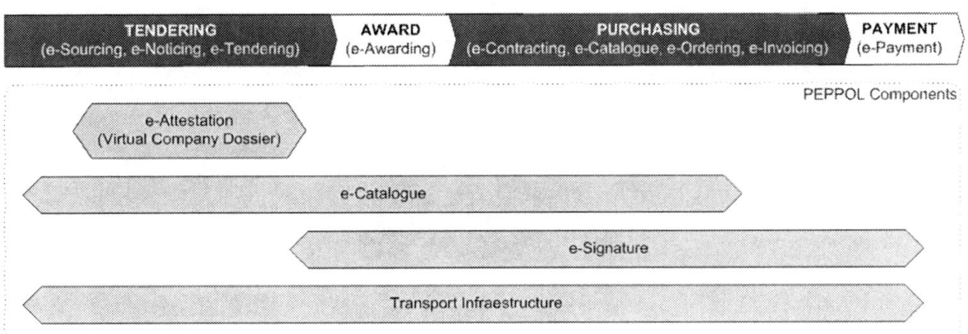

administrations in Europe, including the European Institutions. It is using European standards - based on the CEN/BII business profiles and the data model of UBL2.0, thus enabling interoperability in a cross-border environment. Now, e-PRIOR is being used by the EC to automate procurement processes such as e-Catalogue, e-Ordering and e-Invoicing.

At the same time, there is an open-source version named Open e-PRIOR, with the same functionalities that the abovementioned e-PRIOR platform. It aims at accelerating the implementation of e-Procurement, at lower cost and in less time, by European Member States in general and the participation to the PEPPOL project in particular. It uses European standards based on the CEN/BII business profiles and the data model of UBL2.0 and is connected to PEPPOL. This open-source initiative is currently in production[26] at the European Commission and it is freely available at the website of the Open Source Observatory & Repository of Europe (OSOR Community) on the internet address http://www.osor.eu/projects/openeprior.

Both Open e-PRIOR and e-PRIOR are connected to the PEPPOL (Pan European Public Procurement on Line) network via their own PEPPOL Gateway. Every supplier connected to PEPPOL is thus automatically connected to the EC and to whomever will have Open e-PRIOR implemented.

Figure 7 shows the steps in a typical e-PRIOR scenario (DIGIT, 2010):

1. The Buyer creates the Order in its own system.
2. The Buyer transmits the Order to the Supplier via e-PRIOR and PEPPOL.
3. The Supplier (same/other country that buyer) creates the Invoice in its own system.
4. The Supplier transmits the Invoice to the Buyer via PEPPOL and e-PRIOR. e-PRIOR: Validates the message; Applies business rules; Routes it to the receiver; makes available a human readable version of the invoice and the status of its processing (additionally).

6.2. STORK and e-CERTIS

One of the main challenges identifies in the Green Paper (EC, 2010, October 18) that prevents and blocks the successful transition to e-Procurement is the onerous technical requirements, particularly for bidder authentication and the lack of cross-border interoperability of electronic signatures and recognition of electronic identification. These problems are not specific to the e-Procurement context but arise in any situation where electronic authentication and signatures are required. The main hopes for these challenges are based in two pilot solutions supported by PEPPOL: STORK[27] and e-CERTIS[28].

Figure 7. e-PRIOR scenario

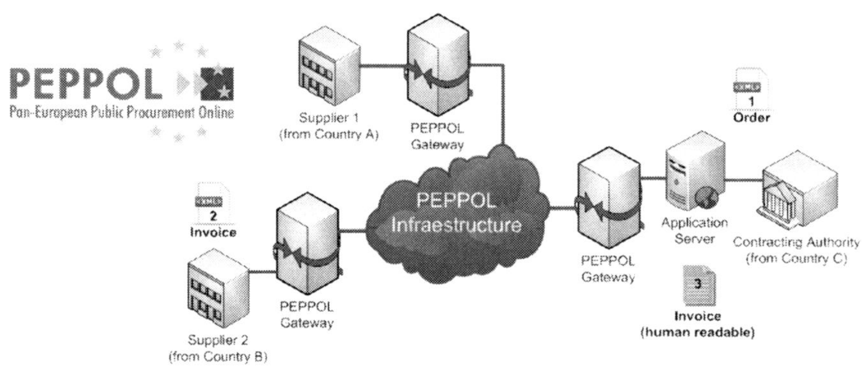

Figure 8. STORK logo

STORK is a competitiveness and innovation framework programme, co-funded by EU. It aims at implementing an EU wide interoperable system for recognition of electronic ID and authentication that will enable businesses, citizens and government employees to use their national electronic identities[29] in any Member State. It will also pilot transborder e-Government identity services and learn from practice on how to roll out such services, and to experience what benefits and challenges an EU wide interoperability system for recognition of e-ID will bring (Figure 8).

The other problem encountered so far relate to the requirement for contracting authorities to assess evidentiary documents submitted by tenders to prove eligibility for selection. This problem is closely related to the Virtual Company Dossier project in order to expedite and facilitate the certifications required by the contracting authority in competitive tendering. These documents are issued at national or local levels in accordance with the relevant conventions, formats and languages.

e-CERTIS is a free, on-line information tool for companies and contracting authorities, developed by the European Commission, to assists on (Figure 9):

1. Different documents required when tendering for a public contract in another country,

Figure 9. e-CERTIS logo

2. Certificate most frequently requested in procurement procedures across the EU[30] to understand what information is being requested / provided and identify mutually acceptable equivalents. It provides details of the different certificates and attestations frequently requested in procurement procedures.

6.3. SPOCS

Finally, other large-scale pilot project named SPOCS[31], aims to build the next generation of online portals (Point of Single Contact or PSC[32]), through the availability of high impact cross-border electronic procedures. The SPOCS pilot project aims to enhance the quality of these procedures, with more interoperable and user-friendly systems, making it easier for businesses to offer their services abroad. This project was launched in May 2009 after the European Parliament and the Council adopted the Directive on services in the Internal Market and will benefit from the results achieved by the STORK (electronic identity) and PEPPOL (electronic procurement) projects. The Services Directive[33] requires the Member States to simplify procedures and formalities that service providers need to comply with. In particular, it requires Member States to remove unjustified and disproportionate burdens and to substantially facilitate:

1. The establishment of a business (for example, cases in which a natural or legal person wants to set up a permanent establishment in a Member State), and

2. The cross-border provision of services (for example, cases in which a business wants to supply services across borders in another Member State, without setting up an establishment there).

7. CONCLUSION

Broadly, the effective implementation of electronic public procurement, in most countries individually and in the European Union as a whole remains low and is estimated at less than 5% in value of public procurement total. Some countries have chosen to force the use of certain support tools on specific phases of the procurement process (for example, e-Noticing), and others, even opted for the mandatory use of electronic means to cover all phases.

From the technological point of view, various systems emerge to provide effective solutions to electronic procurement process. However, these systems show little in common, since they consist of isolated solutions in which business processes, types and formats of documents and forms of communication are not sufficiently standardized. Since no standard and predefined components appear to guarantee an interoperable environment, the generalization of electronic public procurement across borders will be difficult and slow. This is why many economic operators feel apprehensive when participating in e-Procurement procedures in other Member States where the way to face up with the process is very different.

It has been observed as electronic trading has a lot of partners and independent systems to exchange information. It is necessary to apply a common approach to rules and normalized formats, at least for most common procurement procedures, in order to encourage the reuse of technology solutions in this area. So, it is a key moment to assess the current technological solutions in electronic public procurement, and encourage the adoption of certain tendencies to generalize and reuse the use of them in Member States, both in national and regional levels. Adopt a fragmented model where each nation, region or locality has its own electronic procurement platform does not help to cross border interoperability. Actually exacerbates the problem because of the complexity lies in gateways to interconnect each other platforms. Also life becomes very difficult both to economic operator and contracting authorities, (especially employees of hiring authorities). They are forced to understand and use different technological solutions. At least if this normalization only affect the most common procurement procedures, economic operators could take part in procurement procedures of different systems with minimal effort and cost, and with a simple readjustment of the tender offer on course.

European Commission has made great progress on actions related to electronic procurement process particularly in the chapter on infrastructure and interoperability by large-scale projects (PEPPOL is the most relevant). They are also remarkable progress both in the pre-award phase (with the publication and dissemination by electronic means of announcements concerning contracting opportunities at TED) and post-award phase (with pilot projects such as e-PRIOR to the electronic catalog creation, formalization of online orders and sending electronic invoices). In Fact, the EC's Efforts to expand e-Procurement to the Member States are even more important in today's Economic context WHERE cuts in Government Spending are required at all levels (for example, in the liberalization of the Open e-PRIOR platform and a dedicated team providing assistance to Member States, European Institutions and Agencies to help them reuse this technology).

However, less progress has been made in the unification and standardization for the presentation and management of online offerings. As the Green Paper warns about widespread use of electronic procurement in the EU, here is where real benefits (and challenges) of electronic procurement become.

ACKNOWLEDGMENT

We want to thank members of the Group of Research in Interaction and eLearning of the University of Salamanca for their collaboration in the form of critical feedback in the development of this article. This work is partially supported by the Castile and Lion Regional Government through GR47 excellence project.

REFERENCES

Caño, M. J., & Folgueras, A. (2011, May 25). *IT governance for e-procurement. Applicability of the norm ISO/IEC to reach the interoperability and generalization*. Retrieved May 31, 2011, from http://es.scribd.com/doc/56447197/iT-Governance-for-E-Procurement-6

DIGIT. Directorate-General for Informatics. (2010, February 9). *The value of e-PRIOR, the European e-Procurement platform offered by the European Commission*. Retrieve June 10, 2011, from www.epractice.eu/files/e-PRIOR%20 v1.0.ppt

European Commission. (2000). *Lisbon strategy for growth and jobs*. Retrieved May 30, 2011, from http://ec.europa.eu/archives/growthand-jobs_2009/

European Commission. (2002). *e-Europe 2002 action plan*. Retrieved May 30, 2011, from http://ec.europa.eu/information_society/eeurope/2002/index_en.htm

European Commission. (2005, January). *Functional requirements for e-procurement (Volume I, main requirements)*. Retrieved June 8, 2011 from http://ec.europa.eu/idabc/servlets/Doc1ad3.pdf?id=22191

European Commission. (2005). *e-Europe 2005 action plan*. Retrieved May 30, 2011, from http://ec.europa.eu/information_society/eeurope/2005/index_en.htm

European Commission. (2005, July 8). *Requirements for conducting public procurement using electronic means under the new public procurement directives 2007/18/CE and 2004/17/CE*. Retrieved June 3, 2011, from the http://ec.europa.eu/internal_market/publicprocurement/docs/eprocurement/sec2005-959_en.pdf

European Commission. (2006, April 25). *i2010 eGovernment action plan: Accelerating eGovernment in Europe for the benefit of all*. Retrieved May 30, 2011, from http://ec.europa.eu/information_society/activities/egovernment/policy/action_plan/index_en.htm

European Commission. (2009, December 1). *Commission regulation (EC) No 1177/2009, of 30 November 2009, amending Directives 2004/17/EC, 2004/18/EC and 2009/81/EC of the European Parliament and of the Council in respect of their application thresholds for the procedures for the award of contracts*. Retrieved June 4, 2011, from http://eur-lex.europa.eu/LexUriServ/LexUriServ.do?uri=OJ:L:2009:314:0064:0065:EN:PDF

European Commission. (2010). *e-Europe 2010 action plan*. Retrieved May 30, 2011, from http://ec.europa.eu/information_society/eeurope/i2010/index_en.htm

European Commission. (2010, February 2). *Lisbon strategy evaluation document*. Retrieved May 30, 2011, from http://ec.europa.eu/archives/growthandjobs_2009/pdf/lisbon_strategy_evaluation_en.pdf

European Commission. (2010, August 26). *A digital agenda for Europe*. Retrieved 30 May, 2011, from http://eur-lex.europa.eu/LexUriServ/LexUriServ.do?uri=COM:2010:0245:FIN:EN:PDF

European Commission. (2010, October 18). *Green paper on expanding the use of e-Procurement in the EU*. Retrieved June 1, 2011 from http://ec.europa.eu/internal_market/consultations/docs/2010/e-Procurement/green-paper_en.pdf

European Commission. (2010, December 15). *The European eGovernment action plan 2011-2015. Harnessing ICT to promote smart, sustainable & innovative Government*. Retrieved May 30, 2011, from http://ec.europa.eu/information_society/activities/egovernment/action_plan_2011_2015/docs/action_plan_en_act_part1_v2.pdf

European Commission. (2011). *Europe 2020*. Retrieved May 30, 2011, from http://ec.europa.eu/europe2020/index_en.htm

European Parliament. Council. (2004a, March 31). *Directive 2004/17/EC of the European Parliament and of the Council of 31 March 2004 coordinating the procurement procedures of entities operating in the water, energy, transport and postal services sectors*. Retrieved June 2, 2011 from http://eur-lex.europa.eu/LexUriServ/LexUriServ.do?uri=CELEX:32004L0017:EN:NOT

European Parliament. Council. (2004b, March 31). *Directive 2004/18/EC of the European Parliament and of the Council of 31 March 2004 on the co-ordination of procedures for the award of public works contracts, public supply contracts and public service contracts*. Retrieved June 2, 2011 from http://eur-lex.europa.eu/LexUriServ/LexUriServ.do?uri=CELEX:32004L0018:EN:NOT

European Union. (2010a, December 15). *Digital agenda: E-government action plan - What would it do for me?* Retrieved May 31, 2011, from the http://europa.eu/rapid/pressReleasesAction.do?reference=MEMO/10/681

European Union. (2010b, December 15). *Digital agenda: Pilot projects show the way in easy access to online public services across the EU*. Retrieved June 10, 2011, from http://europa.eu/rapid/pressReleasesAction.do?reference=MEMO/10/680

Head of State of Spain. (2007, June 22). *Law 11/2007, of 22 June, on citizen's electronic access to public services*. Retrieved May 31, 2011, from http://www.boe.es/boe/dias/2007/06/23/pdfs/A27150-27166.pdf

Head of State of Spain. (2007, October 30). *Law 30/2007 of 30th October, on public sector contracts*. Retrieved May 31, 2011, from http://www.boe.es/boe/dias/2007/10/31/pdfs/A44336-44436.pdf

Head of State of Spain. (2011, March 4). *Law 2/2011, of March 4, sustainable economy*. Retrieved May 31, 2011, from www.boe.es/boe/dias/2011/03/05/pdfs/BOE-A-2011-4117.pdf

Ministers of European Union (EU) Member States, Accession States and Candidate Countries and Ministers of the European Free Trade Area (EFTA) Countries. (2005, November 24). *Ministerial declaration approved unanimously on 24 November 2005, Manchester, United Kingdom*. Retrieved May 30, 2011, from http://ec.europa.eu/information_society/activities/e-Government/docs/pdf/manchester_declaration.pdf

Ministers responsible for eGovernment policy of the European Union (EU) Member States, the Candidate Countries and the European Free Trade Area (EFTA). (2009, November 18). *Ministerial declaration on eGoverment*. Malmö, Sweden Retrieved May 30, 2011, from http://ec.europa.eu/information_society/activities/e-Government/events/past/malmo_2009/press/ministerial-declaration-on-e-Government.pdf

Official e-Government Website of the Ministry of Territorial Policy and Public Administration of Spain. (n.d.). Retrieved May 31, 2011, from http://administracionelectronica.gob.es

Suarez, G., & Laguado, R. (2007, April). *Public e-procurement manual for Latin America: Conceptual and legal model, indicators, interoperability*. United Nations Publication. Retrieve May 31, 2011 from http://www.eclac.org/publicaciones/xml/8/28648/DocW130.pdf

ENDNOTES

1 These seven initiatives classify in three reinforcing priorities: Smart growth (Digital agenda for Europe, Innovation Union and Youth on the move), Sustainable growth (Resource efficient Europe and An industrial policy for the globalization era) and Inclusive growth (An agenda for new skills and jobs and European platform against poverty).

2 The 5 targets for the EU in 2020: Employment (75% of the 20-64 year-olds to be employed), Research, Development and Innovation (3% of the EU's GDP, public and private combined, to be invested in R&D&i), Climate change and energy (greenhouse gas emissions 20%, or even 30%, if the conditions are right, 20% of energy from renewable, 20% increase in energy efficiency), Education (reducing school drop-out rates below 10% and at least 40% of 30-34–year-olds completing third level education), Poverty and social exclusion (at least 20 million fewer people in or at risk of poverty and social exclusion).

3 Government revenues account for some 45% of GDP and public authorities purchase services and goods to the value of some 15 to 20% of GDP or €1.500 to €2.000 billion in Europe every year. Electronic procurement and invoicing could save 5% in total procurement costs and reduce transaction costs by 10% or more, leading to savings of tens of billions of Euros annually (EC, 2006).

4 Some Member States have created new action plans to relaunch e-Government. Spain, for example, through the Council of Ministers approved on July 16 (2010), the agreement by approving the 2011-2015 Strategy named Plan Avanza 2, which continues the previous Avanza Plan, incorporating the actions implemented and updating its initial objectives to suit the new challenges (http://www.planavanza.es).

5 In the case of Spain, this legislation transposing the EU directives on e-Procurement is reflected in two rules enforced by Law. First, the Law 11/2007, of 22 June, on Citizen's Electronic Access to Public Services (Head of State of Spain, 2007a), establishes the general framework of the E-Government in Spain, and computers to access information and departments of the government by civil society (citizens and businesses) in a virtual environment to access existing traditional far. This Law has been one of the major challenges within the modernization of the Spanish e-Government in recent years. On the other hand, Law 30/2007, of October 30, Public Sector Contracts (Head of State of Spain, 2007b), is the specific rule that sets the general framework for public procurement in Spain, as well as the changes described in the Law 34/2010, of 5 August, and subsequent Royal Decrees for developing it. Both rules apply to the Public Administration of the State and its related agencies and advocates promoting the use of a computer, electronic and data communications in their dealings with citizens and economic operators. More recently, Law 2 / 2011, of March 4, Sustainable Economy (Head of State of Spain, 2011), instigates on Chapter V, the efficiency in public procurement and public-private collaboration as fundamental elements of relationship between public government and the business. In the area of procurement initiatives, like Green Public Procurement (GPP), are postulated in both public and private sector. The GPP offers a process of investment and expenditure based on a sustainable procurement and acquisition (or green procurement) to get their needs for goods, services, works and not by a private cost-benefit analysis, but with a vision to

maximize real benefits for themselves and rest of the world.

6 In Spain, Article 42 of the Law 30/2007, of October 30, Public Sector Contracts (Head of State of Spain, 2007b), regulates the buyer profile, through which the contracting authorities should notice information on the Internet on its contracting activity.

7 In compliance with the obligations of the e-Government some Member States have made available to their respective state, regional and local governments IT platforms for use electronic signatures and time stamping services. Spain, in line with the above, made available to all government a Platform for Validation and Electronic Signature (@ firma). Integrated with this platform is a time stamping authority (TS@) in order to provide sealing services, validation and resealing of time stamps.

8 Member states in compliance with e-Procurement legislation have complementary registers of bidders (i.e.: in Spain, the General Directorate for State Assets, is responsible for Classifying Contractors and keeping the Official Register of Bidders and State Classified Companies and the Register of Public Sector Contract, http://registrodelicitadores.gob.es).

9 There are internet platforms that allow, once registered, receive alerts about new tender notices or updates to existing ones. These alerts are based mainly on internet messaging services (electronic mail) and mobile telephony (short message service).

10 Some member states, at the state level and even regional, have created Registry of bidders, in order to exonerate the companies to present, in certain processes of recruitment, documentation of his personality, ability to act, representation, classification and other certifications provided for in the procurement process. In cases belonging to the record is not sufficient; at least the certificates issued by these records are also supported like electronic evidence of such attestations.

11 TED (Tenders Electronic Daily) is the official source for public contracts in Europe. This service is available on the website http://ted.europa.eu.

12 Depending on the nature of the contract, the thresholds for publication on TED are the following (EC, 2009, December 1): supplies and services for central government authorities: 125.000 €; supplies and services for non-central government authorities: 193.000 €; supplies and services in water, energy, transport and postal services: 387.000 €; works: 4.845.000 €.

13 Service available on the website http://simap.europa.eu/enotices.

14 Service available on the website http://simap.europa.eu.

15 The CPV, adopted by Regulation (EC) No. 213/2008 is in use since 17/09/2008. Available on http://eur-lex.europa.eu/LexUriServ/LexUriServ.do?uri=OJ:L:2008:074:0001:0375:EN:PDF.

16 Service available on the website http://epp.eurostat.ec.europa.eu.

17 The list of current NUTS codes is available on the website http://simap.europa.eu/codes-and-nomenclatures/codes-nuts/codes-nuts-table_en.htm.

18 System and software development, consulting, design or advisory services and online help.

19 Business Interoperability Interfaces for Public procurement by European Committee For Standardization.

20 Spain is an example of unity in the General Administration through the State Procurement Platform (https://contrataciondelestado.es). This technological solution is based on a component architecture and standard electronic documents, called CODICE (Interoperable Components and Documents

for Electronic Procurement), enabled for the development of e-Procurement applications, according to European directives and Spanish legislation procurement. The services offered by this platform is mainly focused on phases of the contracts (and other documents relating to the bid) and receive (and forward) of electronic bids. Notably, the automatic integration with the Official Journal at national/regional (e.g. BOE) and at European level (e.g. TED) as indicated.

21 The strategic Action Plans to promote development of e-Government in general and, in particular e-Procurement, are clearly shown in Spain at the official e-Government website (http://administracionelectronica.gob.es). Almost all Spanish regions have developed their own Strategic Plan. However, some technological solutions deployed resolve electronic procurement effectively, but also a very focused and isolated.

22 See chapter "Automatic evaluation strategies in complex procurement" on Green Paper on expanding the use of e-Procurement in the EU (2010, October 18).

23 PEPPOL, Pan-European Public Procurement OnLine (http://www.peppol.eu).

24 For example, at national level in Spain exists an Official Registry of Tenderers and Classified named ROLECE (http://registrodelicitadores.gob.es), created pursuant to the provisions of articles 301-307 of Law 30/2007 (Head of State of Spain, 2007b). Suppliers can enroll in the data referred to in article 303 of the mentioned Law and their certificates (obtained from the platform) prove them against all the organs of public sector procurement. The Registry has an electronic nature, and both applications for registration and obtaining certificates are in electronic means, credited the applicant's identity through the use of electronic ID.

25 e-PRIOR, electronic PRocurement Invoicing and ORdering (http://www.epractice.eu/cases/ePRIOR).

26 Recently a version of Open e-PRIOR has been deployed in Greece as a test implementation in the context of the PEPPOL initiative.

27 STORK, Secure idenTity acrOss boRders linked (https://www.eid-stork.eu).

28 e-CertIs, electronic Certificates Information System (http://ec.europa.eu/markt/ecertis).

29 This project is the seed for a future to permit the acceptance of digital Spanish certificates, such as electronic DNI in e-government services in other countries, thus facilitating the connection of our citizens and businesses with other European public administrations. Spain is an active member of the STORK project by the initiative: "Pan-European recognition of electronic identities" (retrieved June 8, 2011 from the official e-Government website of Spain http://administracionelectronica.gob.es).

30 e-CERTIS operate across 27 Member States, two Candidate Countries (Turkey and Croatia) and the three EEA countries (Iceland, Liechtenstein and Norway).

31 SPOCS, Simple Procedures Online for Cross- Border Services (http://www.eu-spocs.eu).

32 The Spanish Point of Single Contact (located at http://www.eugo.es), is a project run by the Ministry of Public Administrations and Public Administration of the Government of Spain. This website answers to established obligations for the Services Directive which was incorporated into the Law 17/2009 of November 23 on the free access to and exercise of service activities.

33 Directive 123/2006/EC

Chapter 4
E-Procurement Associated with MRO: The Case of Caixa Econômica Federal

Alexandre Ferreira Oliveira
Brazilian School of Public and Business Administration at Getulio Vargas Foundation, Brazil

Luiz Antonio Joia
Brazilian School of Public and Business Administration at Getulio Vargas Foundation, Brazil

ABSTRACT

The purpose of this chapter is to identify the benefits achieved by the Caixa Economica Federal (Caixa), with regard to improvements in efficiency, to deploy its e-procurement solution associated with MRO (Maintenance, Repair, and Operation). Through a simple case study, this chapter seeks to analyze the strategic importance of deploying shopping site Caixa, investigating how the dimensions of technological, organizational and cultural influence the efficiency of their production processes. Although the results are significant in relation to the recovery time of investment, and promising for the potential to reduce administrative costs of the company, factors linked to participation and willingness to adopt a new sales model and the investment capacity and flexibility to adopt models were extremely important from the perspective of suppliers.

INTRODUCTION

With the passage of time, social changes, economic and technological have occurred, more intense and fast, causing society to constantly adapt and dynamic, seeking new strategies and technology alternatives. This evolutionary scenario requires the state, as co-responsible for the provision of public services, a fitness for this technological acceleration (Baião and Seco, 2000).

Despite the developments, enterprise systems in the federal public administration are centralized, poorly integrated, and focused on the structure and process management functions not.

DOI: 10.4018/978-1-4666-2119-0.ch004

Brazilian legislation has been updated in light of changes in social, economic and technological areas. The organizations have sought to optimize the use of Information Technology (IT), intensifying and expanding this powerful tool, in order to change the basis of competitiveness and business strategies. Organizations began to plan and strategize the main ally of IT (Joia and Zamot, 2002).

A milestone for implementing this new vision was to enhance the Procurement Law, to ensure greater speed in transactions, a wider range of opportunities to suppliers, better quality control of products and services, and effective reduction cost (Joia and Zamot, 2002).

Therefore, this chapter investigates the perceptions of suppliers and employees of a Public Company - Caixa Economica Federal (CAIXA), regarding the process of implementing e-Procurement associated with Maintenance, Repair and Operation (MRO).

This study could be useful, since they contain information and data that can provide support in assessing the implementation of the shopping site, thus increasing the chances of success of similar ventures in the context of public enterprises.

LITERATURE REVIEW

The literature on associated traditional MRO Procurement is not large or diverse in its approach. You can find on Neef (2001), Gebauer & Segev (2001) and Aberdeen Group (1999 and 2001) a good summary of academic and practical approaches on the subject.

Although this theme is not new, only in recent years he has been the focus of attention in academy, due to have assumed strategic importance. This importance arose from the pressures for cost reductions and greater agility in the purchasing process, imposed by global markets.

Increased global competition and pricing pressures have forced companies to continually identify new opportunities to increase productivity and reduce costs. As a result, many companies began to focus its attention on improving the management activities of the supply chain, particularly in cases of corporate Procurement (Aberdeen Group, 1999).

In many organizations, particularly in the manufacturing sector, activities related to Procurement can be categorized into two dimensions. On the one hand, Direct Procurement - products related to production - and another the Indirect Procurement - goods not related to production (Gebauer and Segev, 2001).

The indirect Procurement, in turn, has received little attention over time, both organizationally and in relation to greater use of IT (Gebauer and Segev, 2001).

The MRO (Maintenance Supplies, Repair and Operation) covers products and services routinely used, ordinary, customary, that the organization purchased in their day to day, ie, office supplies, furniture, travel services, computers, Maintenance services, light bulbs, among others. Purchased in large volume, have low price. However, they generate a great expense of energy for their provision (Neef, 2001, p. 26).

IT has been applied to support the exchange of goods, services and information between organizations. With the advent of Procurement systems and Internet-based electronic markets Business to Business (B2B), real opportunities for online transactions have been opened to close the gap and improve performance relative to time (Dai and Kauffman, 2000).

The internet, through its innovative applications, enabling new organizational arrangements that can change the shape of the supply chain. This is due to greater automation of procurement processes, which allows the department greater concentration in their business strategy (Gebauer and Segev, 2001).

Technological advances, including the spread of Internet use by society, have allowed the review of operating procedures and the availability of government services to citizens. Information is the basis for the functioning of Government and of any process of modernization and public sector reform, considering the fundamental role of the use of IT to provide efficiency, effectiveness and be an agent of change (Baião and Seco, 2000).

From the standpoint of logistics, the major impact of the Internet was the modification of the concept of distance and time. The Internet access with the same ease as the main store at the corner of a page or a shop across the world. This creates a sense that both must deliver the goods within the same period. The space on the Internet has no geographical barriers, appropriating the truly global vision. What characterizes this space is only the address of the sites, which have no hierarchy among themselves, says Franco Jr. (2001).

The data transfer and electronic management of information allowed, according to Nazario (2002), reduce logistics costs and improve services through better provision of information to customers.

Electronic commerce is not having a recent practice, however, its reach and effect on network components that integrate technology increased exponentially by the Internet (Mair and Taylor, 1999).

To meet the challenges of electronic commerce the first step is to understand the specifics that generate the need for new logistics solutions. Lack of awareness about the size of these challenges is the main factor that favors the problems faced by virtual commerce companies (Fleury et al., 2000).

According Cavanha Filho (2001), electronic commerce transforms the logistics operations with greater speed than the very new concepts in management, engineering and logistics, producing variations in business processes with its own logic.

The Internet has done much more than just allow the buying and selling online, it led to the creation of a whole new way of structuring the business, where the most effective tools for achieving success in the world of electronic commerce and collaboration are involvement (Bressler and Grantham, 2000).

Although for years the financial institutions have used electronic commerce to transact and transfer of funds, currently, the Internet is seen as a medium that enables organizations to reach millions of businesses and consumers through a single network and form extremely cheap. The rapid growth of Electronic Commerce is stimulating the economy, creating new opportunities and increasing competition. Are expected huge cost savings in some sectors, which predicts that electronic distribution might decrease by 40% the cost of the supply chain (Joia and Zamot, 2001).

To Maira and Taylor (1999) the central point for the deployment of electronic commerce is of cultural origin. People who make up the organization must be connected to structural changes, which hurt the traditional concepts of linear hierarchy and chain of command and control of power - the inheritance of Fayol - by divesting itself of the hierarchy and linking them to processes. These, in turn, consolidated traditionally and historically, are also at odds with the new requirements.

Maira and Taylor (1999) described that the main barriers, by the business side, relate to the security of systems and networks, availability of resources and expertise to adopt e-commerce processes and integrate new technologies with legacy systems.

According Novaes (2001) the evolution of e-commerce business-to-business (B2B) will provide the vertical solutions. Unlike the intermediate horizontal, vertical search agents to focus on the inefficiencies that occur along the supply chain specific. Your goal is to speed transactions for inputs and products along the chain. The trend is to expand the B2B market with the formation of business communities, containing broader spectrum of suppliers and buyers, and bringing greater economic benefits to participants.

E-Procurement: The Use of Internet Technology

As the breadth and complexity of buying swell, the importance of IT as a tool in this evolutionary process grows amazingly. Public enterprises, the quest for efficiency has focused on core activities, outsourcing to other functions that do not directly add value to the business (PricewaterhouseCoopers, 2001).

Another form of e-commerce is e-Procurement used to purchase goods and services using electronic media, aiming at a better control over purchasing processes and cost reduction since the products are procured from different vendors (Lopes and Santos 2006).

Referring to the e-procurement as the Department of virtual shopping, Franco Jr. (2001) states that its function is to find suppliers and quote prices and supply conditions across the board. As functionality of corporate systems, he adds Franco Jr. (2001), e-Procurement is a tool that significantly increases the efficiency of the purchasing department, either by obtaining better terms of purchase, either through the department's productivity.

There are basically two alternative technological infrastructures available for a company to adopt e-Procurement: EDI and Internet.

It was this environment that began to emerge in the mid-90s, the e-Procurement solutions based on Internet, which have proven to be an answer to the problem, since they provide an infrastructure that enables companies to automate their processes shopping, gradually transforming the way they communicate with their suppliers (PricewaterhouseCoopers, 2001).

B2B electronic marketplaces create value for buyers and suppliers through real-time transactions, providing liquidity to support the exchange of demand and supply information and reduced transaction costs. E-Procurement systems can also be used to integrate with corporate enterprise systems (ERPs) and Intranets organizations (Dai and Kauffman, 2000).

Purchase and sale transactions between organizations, through E-commerce, e-procurement has on the most important area and greater potential for development in order to restructure fundamentally the way companies conduct their purchases (Neef, 2001 p. 37).

The biggest benefit of adopting a system of Electronic Procurement is to reduce the costs of research and operation, providing high return on investment (Dai and Kauffman, 2000). According to Neef (2001) the demand for integration of e-Procurement processes directly with the supply chain in pursuit of cost reduction and improving the procurement process, can be found in several areas.

To Neef, a means of analyzing the impact of Procurement spending in perspective is to simply check the percentage of total cost in purchasing non-productive assets. Using this model, the Center for Advanced Purchasing Studies estimates that companies, depending on the industry to which they belong, they tend to spend 40% of resources in purchases of non-productive assets (Neef, 2001, p.15).

According to several studies, according to Neef (2001, p. 19), a 10% reduction in costs for Procurement may result in something around 50% increase in profit of the company.

The biggest advantage offered by e-Procurement is to keep buyers and suppliers in direct, constant and instantly, making the process simpler and more efficient. This advantage can only be achieved because the system turns the traditional processes of communication - based on paper - in new processes - based on electronic exchanges (PricewaterhouseCoopers, 2001).

With electronic catalogs, electronic auctions and other skills supported by the new electronic markets, buyers can analyze, compare the purchase with thousands of suppliers and then select the best, in real time. At the same time, they need not permit a specific infrastructure for the system of

Internet-based Procurement. This is obviously a big draw for many businesses, as it is for other possibilities to reduce costs, which makes it clear why new electronic markets emerge every month (Dai & Kauffman, 2000).

Aberdeen Group (1999) also indicates that organizations can achieve significant benefits in productivity and cost items, by improving the way we manage and control the acquisition of MRO goods and services.

The Internet and Web-based technologies support and automate the tasks of the Procurement of various ways, ranging from provision of access of information prior to the purchase, management support and approval procedures for automatic replenishment, to the payment procedures and monitoring contracts (Gebauer & Segev, 2001).

Auction: Main Types

The first attempts to employ some dynamism to the customizations come with the price of online auctions. It is interesting for the consumer to negotiate directly with the organization to say how much to pay, and that, electronically, to decide who will buy. Auctions are used in the electronics market for years, standing out among them, the pigs in Taiwan and Singapore, the car in Japan and the flowers in the Netherlands, which has been computerized, through local networks, in 1995 (Turban et al., 1999). At first they resembled the traditional off-line auctions, except that it be performed by computer.

The traditional auctions have several limitations, including the time required for each item is sold (Turban et al., 1999). This time can intimidate the small buyer who decides not to bid because there was no time for the decision or even to analyze the product. Thus, the buyer cannot obtain the best prices. In the traditional auction, there are several complicating factors, such as the movement of goods to the local auction, the high commissions, the cost of local advertising and promotion of the event and the remuneration of professionals - The auctioneer and his assistants. Since the electronic auctions, by their very nature, do not have these problems (Turban et al., 1999).

In terms of distribution of digital assets, there is nothing more effective than Internet. The transaction can be made online in its entirety. However, when it comes to physical goods, the impact on the logistics of distribution is very large. The speed of online transaction requires an immediate response of the system of logistics for distribution (Dutta et al. 1997).

The Internet provides an infrastructure for low cost implementation of auctions, involving a large number of buyers and sellers. Individual consumers or businesses can participate in this rapid growth and convenience of this great e-commerce (Turban et al., 1999).

In short, according to Neef (2001, p. 88), the online auction is two big advantages: speed and cost reduction. Paradoxically, there is an accurate understanding of why this practice can still wake up some level of consumer disinterest. Some are not willing to interact so closely with suppliers, and prefer to simply know how much it costs and the well buy it as quickly as possible (Dutta et al., 1997).

According to Guttman and Maes (1998), despite the increasing use of electronic-commerce, online auctions are existing features that make it unrewarding for both buyers and sellers. Although some of the protocols used in online auctions is understanding and using relatively simple, determining the best strategy for bidding is not so simple.

Various types of auctions are available, differing among themselves only in the rules established for participation of stakeholders (Wurman et al., 1998). The reverse auction is characterized by operating in reverse, ie instead of buyers are increasing their offerings are the vendors that offer products at lower prices. In this mode the buyer receives bids from several vendors and submitting the lowest bid will be automatically declared the winner once the auction is closed

(Wyld, 2000). This process, in theory, creates a more efficient market, since both the buyer and the seller are as many interventions as needed. Both the traditional auction and reverse auction portals are used in negotiations Procurement (Giunipero and Sawchuk, 2000). In short, we can say that the reverse auction technology uses the same auction, but with declining prices (Turban et al., 1999).

The category of B2B online auction that has had more development is that of Reverse Auctions (Turban et al., 1999). In this category, companies who make their purchases online can advertise their invitations to a much larger number of potential sellers, who may compete by making bids for the sale of the product sought. Additionally, there is a reduction in purchasing process costs, because there is a quick interaction with market fluctuations, reducing the time for the purchasing company can make the request, the identity and contact suppliers individually (Vigoroso, 1999).

Moreover, through the Internet, it is possible that the buyer organization has at its disposal a large group of potential suppliers. However, that universe of companies includes suppliers efficient and inefficient, being there, the organization, the task of developing strategies for selecting the one that best meets their needs (Turban, 1997).

RESEARCH METHODOLOGY

This chapter is about a contemporary event, which attempts to determine the benefits related to efficiency, since the implementation of the shopping site on the Caixa. We used a strategy of explanatory case study, according to the approach of Yin (2001), to help show how the decisions affected the improvement of the procurement process of the institution.

Three techniques were used in the collection of data: document analysis, semi-structured interview and questionnaire.

The documentary analysis was used to retrieve historical data for performance, growth and organizational structure of the Caixa, as well as assumptions made to implement the shopping site. It was also adopted as a complementary technique to ratify or rectify the information and data obtained through interviews and questionnaires.

The interview is one of the main instruments to collect data that a researcher has at his disposal. According Triviños (1992), semi-structured interviews is that from certain basic questions, supported by theories and hypotheses of interest to research and then offer a wide range of information to the interviewee.

For this study, we interviewed four officeholders who participated Caixa strategic analysis of the previous process and the redesign and implementation of the model through the shopping site.

The questionnaires were applied to two different audiences, composed of an external and an internal suppliers consist of employees both participants in the procurement process earlier - traditional and current procurement process - innovative. For research with suppliers, it was considered a population of 6,050 suppliers with a confidence level of 95% and a margin of error of 5%, adding up to a desired sample of 362 respondents. The sample selection was done through the process of simple random sampling and operationalized through a table of random numbers generated by computer. To search with the workforce, given the size of the population is only 44 individuals, we chose to carry out a census of the workforce Box directly involved with the procurement system.

Thus, the choice of strategy of case study that follows a specific purpose is to investigate "how" and "why", as perceived by suppliers and employees, the process of implementing e-procurement Caixa's website brought benefits in terms efficiency when compared to traditional methods previously adopted by the company to make their purchases and contracts for MRO.

A common criticism of case studies is that the researcher can not develop a sufficiently operational set of measures and that subjective judgments are used to gather data, thereby to increase the construct validity, we used the approach Yin (2001), through the use of multiple sources of evidence, namely - the institution's internal documents, files, interviews, direct observation and questionnaires, and review the draft report by key informants and also by another researcher who also addressed the shopping site Box on your case study, with an attempt to corroborate the facts and evidence presented in the report of a case study.

As for internal validity, according to Yin (2001), the investigator must determine precisely the relationship between the events being studied. For this study, we evaluated, the rate of utilization of the purchasing process, as well as the cost / benefit of the proceedings, proportionate to the Caixa. The rate of use of procedures by the providers was measured from the records of participation in quotes and electronic bidding contests. These access logs were obtained from the management reporting system.

The efficiency of the electronic model was evaluated by its cost, cycle time for procurement and quality offered by the new acquisition model. These factors were compared to traditional processes used to measure the efficiency afforded by this new methodology.

For internal validation, was also carried out a quantitative and qualitative data collected. The statistical treatments (Descriptive Analysis, Frequency Analysis and Factor Analysis by Principal Component Method) were performed using SAS software, complemented by software SPSS for Windows v.10. The quantitative analysis was performed mainly with respect to the factors mentioned by employees and suppliers as the most important in the process of buying the Web The qualitative analysis aimed to complement the previous analysis, since it is based on the level of satisfaction of managers in the process of supplies with different aspects of the electronic procurement process.

Regarding the external validity of Yin (2001) validates the approach of a case study through analytical generalization rather than statistical, such as the research investigation. This case study is proposed to be conducted as an introduction to other studies that may use it as a pilot deployment of a shopping site for other institutions with similar characteristics to Caixa.

THE CAIXA ECONÔMICA FEDERAL CASE

Characterization of the Organization

The object of observation in this study refers to a major company in the financial sector - Caixa - a public financial institution under private law, created to encourage fundraising and implement social policies of the Federal Government, acting as government agent promotion in the areas of housing and urban development, and distribution of public policies.

Caixa seeks to position itself strategically as a popular bank, dedicated to serving the citizens of poor and to micro, small and medium enterprises market segments rather sensitive to the price charged by the service and require a high service capacity. Caixa has faced this challenge seeking to systematically improve the productivity of their resources by investing heavily in information systems and communication networks as well as removing anomalies in the structure of operating costs, reduce staff costs, administrative expenses and costs associated with distribution logistics.

Given the global scenario and the guidelines of the Brazilian government, Caixa also needed to prepare to work intensively with electronic transactions in relations G2G, G2C, G2B, besides the typical B2B and B2C relations. For this, a technological support embodied in a Communication Network of the business, internal and external, should be constantly evolving to support a full range of enterprise bargaining, particularly in access across different virtual channels.

In this context, the Caixa has established its Master Plan for Technology (PDTec) with the basic policies and strategic objectives of their area of technology as a tool to support other business areas.

The Caixa Econômica Federal's E-Procurement Model

A new intelligence has been developed and adapted to law which the company is subject, as regards the implementation of direct purchases (limited to R$ 16,000.00) and electronic trading (through the auction method reverse), which, while they fit the legal limit to be redesigned and B2B technologies.

The Management of National Supplies (GESUP) answered today by hiring, administration and payment of all contracts for goods and services for the bank. The hiring of services cover a spectrum of activities ranging from the negotiation of agreements with taxis, and airlines to transport employees, by bidding on software factories, the development of information systems of the Bank, involving a budget next year from $ 2.45 billion. Supply contracts cover the supply of goods forms and office supplies to leasing of computer processing centers, involving other $350 million / year budget of the Bank.

These contracts and purchases under more immediate delivery, generated in the years 2000 and 2001, a number of annual operations of which amounted to 37,000 cases of outright purchases and 1,300 bids. Due to these operations and administration of contracts, were made approximately 342,000 vendor payments each year.

Whereas much of the efforts of decentralized units are connected to the process of buying, invested in the creation of Shopping Site Caixa, together with the outsourcing strategy of the operations internally, allowed GESUP centralize purchasing activities, hire, manage and pay suppliers. The range of solutions, Site Procurement and outsourcing operations, led to decreases in all structures of branches of the processes of the company's supply area.

The bids for the purchase of common goods and services are conducted primarily in the modality or Electronic Auction Bidding, except for construction and engineering services for real estate leases for sales in general, for goods and services, information technology and automation, or if there is justification enough for use in another manner provided for in the Act.

Both the Auction as the Electronic Auction may be used to purchase common goods and services, regardless of the estimated value of the contract. The process of Electronic Bidding starts with the preparation and subsequent is closure of the bidding documents on the Internet. This process is accomplished without the physical presence of bidders and other interested companies. The bidding company is responsible for all transactions that are made in his name in the electronic system, assuming as true and firm proposals and their bids. The meeting of the Electronic Auction is conducted online, with free access to accredit.

With the purpose of raising the expectations of the process managers supply the Caixa with the deployment of shopping site, interviews were conducted involving four professionals who participated in the process. They said this deployment required a simplification of the process and the establishment of standards. This results in streamlining and reducing the cost of buying, and reduces also the purchase price. According to respondents, the main goal was to expand the market supply of goods and services demanded by Caixa. Thus, we obtain an increase in the competition between the bidders and therefore a price reduction. In the Caixa was a step of lowering the purchase prices of approximately 25% compared to prices of purchases made in the previous model.

The purchase cost was also reduced by automation of manual activities, such as consultation with suppliers, tabulating prices, registration and maintenance search for new suppliers. The respondents did not identify harm in adopting this process. However, they warned that this technology requires a change in the competence of the people operating the process, or the need to upgrade the technological knowledge is the understanding of the new features in the behavior of suppliers. The main change in behavior is the fact that the monitoring process should be in real time. As highlighted the advantages of scale, standardization of applications, effectiveness of control and compliance, reduce person, increased range of activities, the democratization process and transparency in the process. Disadvantages noted the high concentration of manpower and technological limitations as a factor in excluding certain suppliers.

To respondents reducing the cost of purchasing transactions is significant. In Caixa, restricting the assessment to the resources allocated in the process of direct purchases (up to $ 16,000), reached 60%. This however should vary significantly from company to company, depending on the existing structure to effect purchases. Also discussed was the issue of reducing inventory costs, because cost reduction of the purchase process allows the definition of a new batch of purchase, which enables, in most cases, direct delivery at the point of use, eliminating stocks. In this aspect has not been possible to estimate the cost impact of Caixa, as inventories remain above that require the maintenance of the structure. Transaction time is also reduced. However, considering that should be minimum legal deadlines, time gain refers to that which would be added by human intervention in the preparatory phases of the application and research of price.

In the case of Caixa, the interviewees believe that the electronic purchases are not being used at its full potential. The causes are due to two aspects that have been mentioned as being critical factors in the process - the conversion / adaptation of bids and specifications of goods and services to be procured and qualified technicians to be alert to changing the behavior of suppliers, requiring online monitoring of the ongoing process. Another point is associated to technological questions that should ensure smooth operation of the system, ensuring access to all stakeholders.

Supplier's Vision

Trying to identify the vision of providing the application of the questionnaire was made available on the Internet and answered by the suppliers themselves. Through this procedure, 361 questionnaires were collected from a population of 6,050 suppliers registered in the system of procurement. Confidence Level of 95% was reached at a margin of error of 5.0019%, calculated using the software SURVEY.

Each questionnaire represents the vision of a supplier. The questionnaire consisted of closed questions, structured, and without logical sequence in order to avoid bias and conditioning responses. For the questionnaire, we used a technique of scaling non-comparative (Malhotra, 2001, p.252). Applied to Likert scale with five response categories ranging from "strongly disagree" to "strongly agree", and it requires that respondents indicate a degree of agreement or disagreement with each of a series of claims related to stimulus objects (Malhotra, 2001, p.255). For the analysis, was assigned to each statement a numeric score ranging from 1 to 5. The analysis was done by calculating a total score.

Data Analyses

First, we used a frequency analysis, presented by category, for the 23 variables. Table 1 shows the values for each frequency, where a number that corresponds to the "Disagree" category and number five "Agree".

It can be considered, based on the results that, in general, if got a good trial for the characteristics observed in the study. Built up a ranking by calculating the weighted frequency of variables according to each category, as shown in Table 2, the variable f.17, it shows trial closer to the lower limit of the scale, referring to the disclosure

Table 1. Response by category, in the view of suppliers

	Frequencies				
Variables	**1**	**2**	**3**	**4**	**5**
1	12	11	21	133	175
2	16	46	27	150	119
3	11	15	17	125	190
4	11	8	25	111	201
5	4	9	16	112	217
6	37	62	53	146	57
7	15	15	39	144	126
8	15	27	34	119	162
9	23	45	39	154	96
10	20	38	38	149	110
11	45	26	13	84	189
12	15	22	30	95	187
13	14	13	32	125	171
14	21	36	49	129	118
15	35	28	42	126	124
16	69	47	50	93	91
17	53	36	45	78	57
18	16	22	30	115	174
19	37	15	31	95	170
20	13	18	19	90	215
21	19	23	39	112	163
22	22	28	48	126	127
23	21	21	40	114	159
Total	**545**	**613**	**780**	**2,729**	**3,403**

Table 2. Frequency weighted by category, in the view of suppliers

Position	Variable	Frequency Weighted
1	F.17	857
2	F.16	1140
3	F.6	1189
4	F.9	1326
5	F.15	1341
6	F.14	1346
7	F.10	1356
8	F.22	1361
9	F.7	1368
10	F.2	1384
11	F.19	1390
12	F.11	1417
13	F.23	1434
14	F.21	1445
15	F.8	1457
16	F.12	1464
17	F.18	1480
18	F.13	1491
19	F.1	1504
20	F.20	1541
21	F.3	1542
22	F.4	1551
23	F.5	1603

Prior to moving to the procurement system, by the Caixa. That is, most companies that survey respondents did not agree, totally or partially, which has been affirmed by the disclosure Caixa. Second, the variable appears f.16, referring to investment in purchasing management or purchasing management to the customer. This means that most respondents do not agree that your company provides management services purchases or inventory management to customers.

The other variables that have received judgments closer to the lower limit of the range allude to the process of Internet sales for the company, and to adapt to this new business process. The variable with trial closer to the upper limit of the scale, the respondents, is the variable f.5, whose theme is the company's flexibility with respect to changes in technology and competition in the economic environment.

Later he was made a factor analysis to identify, from a larger set, a subset of variables that stand for use in a subsequent multivariate analysis (Malhotra, 2001). The factor analysis presented here follow three basic steps for its preparation are that the calculation of the correlation matrix of variables, extracting the most significant factors

Table 3. Checking the adequacy of the application of factor analysis

KMO Measure of Sampling Adequacy	2786.154
Bartlett Test of Sphericity	0.912
Sig.	0.000

that represent the data and the application of rotation, the factors to facilitate their understanding.

In the correlation matrix of variables studied, it is observed that correlations between variables has a maximum value of 0.625 which is the correlation between variables F.8 and F.9.

Applying the Bartlett test of sphericity and measure of Kaiser-Meyer-Olkin (KMO), presented in Table 3, we conclude that the application of factor analysis is appropriate.

The reliability of this block was measured by Cronbach's alpha, which showed a value of 0.8959, a value considered fully satisfactory.

Applying the principal component analysis to determine the minimum number of factors that account for maximum variance in the data (Malhotra, 2001), we see the eigenvalues in Table 4, for which they identified five factors that account for 55.03% of variance.

After obtaining the matrix of factor loadings. we used the Varimax rotation method. which provided the following matrix of factor loadings rounds (Table 5).

Factor 1 refers to characteristics related to the company's flexibility to adapt their processes to meet your Caixa in new procurement model, which can then be called "supplier's process".

The characteristics that make up the second factor is related to the utility company strategy with regard to its prioritization of investment and the more timely order fulfillment. then. can be called "investment strategy of the supplier ".

Factor 3 can be called the "vision of the supplier against the electronic model".

Factor 4 adds the variables that relate to service requests in any region of the country eliminating geographic barriers. So this factor can be called "area of expertise of the supplier".

Table 4. Initial statistics

Factors	Eigenvalues	% Variance	% Acc
1	7.302	31.749	31.749
2	1.854	8.059	39.808
3	1.286	5.593	45.401
4	1.191	5.178	50.579
5	1.024	4.453	55.032
6	0.942	4.097	59.129
7	0.884	3.844	62.973
8	0.827	3.595	66.568
9	0.757	3.291	69.859
10	0.738	3.207	73.066
11	0.679	2.954	76.020
12	0.650	2.827	78.847
13	0.582	2.533	81.380
14	0.549	2.387	83.767
15	0.520	2.262	86.029
15	0.493	2.145	88.174
16	0.460	1.999	90.173
17	0.450	1.956	92.129
18	0.434	1.886	94.015
19	0.405	1.761	95.776
20	0.358	1.556	97.332
21	0.326	1.417	98.749
22	0.288	1.250	99.999

Each component is related to a factor that explains the way in which the suppliers have noticed the change of the procurement model made by Caixa. being the order of importance the following:

- Process the supplier;
- Investment strategy of the supplier;
- Vision of the supplier against the electronic model;
- Area of expertise of the supplier;
- Flexibility of the supplier before the market.

Table 5. Round component matrix

	Components				
Variables	1	2	3	4	5
f.20	0.669				
f.21	0.645				
f.23	0.630				
f.19	0.613				
f.18	0.610				
f.22	0.608				
f.16	0.578				
f.17	0.543				
f.15	0.513	0.466			
f.9		0.789			
f.8		0.763			
f.14	0.420	0.643			
f.10		0.588			
f.2		0.537			
f.6		0.457			
f.7			0.676		
f.1			0.649		
f.3			0.538		
f.12				0.773	
f.11				0.708	
f.13				0.491	0.439
f.5					0.741
f.4			0.501		0.579

That is companies that provide supplies/ services to the Caixa has adjusted its production process, and prioritized investments to meet this new paradigm of engagement. These companies have increased their area of expertise, seeking to satisfy its domestic market. Additionally, the respondents believed that the reduction in handling time and costs for delivery of orders.

Caixa's Vision

The data, which aimed to identify the views of employees involved in the supply process for the implementation of Caixa's electronic procurement website, were obtained through a questionnaire posted on the company Intranet. Through this procedure 29 questionnaires were collected in a population of 44 possible respondents. Confidence Level of 95% was reached at a margin of error of 10.7481%, calculated using the software SURVEY.

Each questionnaire collected represents the vision of an employee. The questionnaire consisted of closed questions, structured, and without logical sequence in order to avoid bias and conditioning responses. For the questionnaire, we used a technique of scaling non-comparative (Malhotra, 2001). Applied to Likert scale with five response categories ranging from "strongly disagree" to "strongly agree ".

Data Analyses

First we applied the calculation of the weighted frequency for the 51 variables captured in the questionnaire to the employees of Caixa, for which the variables I.42 (The Internet makes the purchasing process more impersonal?) and I.3 (Reduced transaction costs of shopping is an important reason for adopting the Business to Business?) were the most associated with the trial showed the upper limit of the scale.

The variable I.21 which concerns the existence of patterns of control and payments to suppliers who use the site. is the trial that shows most associated with the lower limit of the scale.

In the correlation matrix of variables under study. there was a maximum value of 0.818 between variables I.37 and I.38.

Later the Bartlett test of sphericity provided the value zero for the level of significance. The Cronbach's Alpha was 0.8938 showing the adequacy of the analysis. Initially we extracted factors by the method of principal components where the first 6 factors have the cumulative percentage of variance explained of 64.070%.

After obtaining the matrix of factor loadings we used the varimax rotation method, which provided a new matrix of factor loadings rounds (Table 6).

Factor 1 refers to characteristics related to the activities of the company to make purchases electronically and can be called a "process of EC in Caixa".

Factor 2 adds the variables that relate to "productivity ".

Factor 3 can be called "cost reduction" model of innovative compared to traditional procurement model improving the competitiveness of the company.

Factor 4 can be called "reliability" since according to respondents' opinion there is a greater partnership between the Caixa and the suppliers. As i.2 variable has negative coefficient respondents argue that competition does not use the model of electronic contracting.

The variables that comprise Factor 5 have negative coefficients. Therefore, it is reasonable to assume that employees who responded to the survey disagree with such assertions. This factor can be called "critical aspects of the electronic model".

Factor 6 corresponds to "the attitude of employees towards the new model of procurement".

The deployment of e-procurement model in Caixa, in the view of employees who responded to this survey and who participated in the traditional procurement model of how innovative, it was guided mainly by the following factors by level of importance:

- EC process in Caixa;
- Productivity;
- Cost reduction;
- Reliability;
- Critical aspects of the electronic model;
- Attitude of employees towards the new model of procurement.

In other words employees who responded to the survey believe that there was an increase in the number of suppliers, standardization and control of the production process, greater transparency in procurement and increased training of staff. As consequences of the deployment of electronic model, we have: cost reduction of inventory maintenance, the final price of products and services, transactions and the time of purchase, as well as greater employee productivity, increase the area of performance of suppliers, reliability access to internal data from the Caixa and suppliers. Also, in view of employees, faced the biggest impediment to employee resistance was the shopping area to accept the new model of Internet shopping.

DISCUSSION

With one year and six months of trial operations where there was no campaign to publicize the site, while organized the Central Purchasing and she adapted the specifications of the various goods and services for the preparation of the appropriate notices electronically, the site exceeded the mark of 6,000 registered suppliers, attracted by the demand represented by 8,133 fairs, with an average percentage price reduction for the period was 24%.

According to information managers, obtained through the interviews when there was a reduction of prices obtained in the first purchases made through the site, compared to prices in purchase operations immediately prior to the deployment of this new system, it was at rates of order 60%, when added operating costs and new prices for the contracted goods. It is clear also that the reduction of purchase prices of goods and services was measured in relation to the purchase price of the last performed.

Data analysis showed that companies that provide supplies/services to the Caixa has adjusted its production process and prioritized investments to meet this new paradigm of engagement. These companies have increased their area of expertise, seeking to satisfy its domestic market. Addition-

Table 6. Round component matrix

	Components					
Variables	**1**	**2**	**3**	**4**	**5**	**6**
i.21	.786					
i.50	.781					
i.15	.751					
i.10	.725					
i.30	.711					
i.44	.662					
i.7	.653					
i.32	.641					
i.18	.624		.402			
i.11	.618		.555			
i.47	.570					.444
i.31	.514					
i.29	.504					
i.20						
i.39		.826				
i.36		.823				
i.40		.806				
i.34		.769				
i.6		.767				
i.35		.620				
i.28		.603				
i.43		.526	.452			
i.16	.435	.512	.468			
i.51	.458	.509				
i.49		.481				
i.38			.819			
i.37			.816			
i.1			.768			
i.33			.639			
i.41	.452		.603			
i.17		.426	.462			
i.27				.670		
i.2			.427	-.665		
i.26				.659		
i.48	-.549			.649		
i.19				.612		
i.13				.550		
i.3			.405	-.459		

continued on following page

Table 6. Continued

	Components					
Variables	**1**	**2**	**3**	**4**	**5**	**6**
i.5				-.447		
i.22				.431		
i.46					-.759	
i.14					-.684	
i.25					.576	
i.24					-.529	
i.8					.496	
i.4					-.461	
i.45						.714
i.42						.598
i.9						.576
i.12						.568

ally, the respondents believed that the reduction in handling time and costs for delivery of orders.

In the analysis of data obtained through the research applied to employees who answered the survey and who participated in the traditional procurement model of how innovative it was observed that in their view, there was an increase in the number of suppliers, standardization and control of the production process, greater transparency in procurement and increased training of staff. As a result of the implementation of electronic model, in the view of employees, it found also to reduce maintenance costs of inventory, the final price of products and services, transactions and the time of purchase, as well as greater employee productivity, increase on the scope of suppliers, reliable access to internal data from the Caixa and suppliers. Also in view of employees, faced the biggest impediment to employee resistance was the shopping area to accept the new model of Internet shopping.

Although the results are significant in relation to the payback time and promise in relation to its potential to reduce the costs of Caixa a factor also considered very important is that the site has great potential to add value to the Caixa's results since it is turning into a marketable product and generating revenue by selling services. According to interviews with managers, Caixa already has a portfolio of clients interested in the product, including private companies, ministries and municipal governments.

CONCLUSION

This work indicates that the development of procedures for administrative support Caixa was result of a combination of three factors. The first refers to changes in internal and external environments, which now require constant improvements in quality and productivity of logistics processes. The second, the creation of the technological conditions of the base, through investments directed to support the business of the company, which created a technological environment with excess capacity, dictated by the level of complexity of banking. And, finally, the perception of opportunity created by this technological environment, to create innovative solutions in logistics within the company.

In reviewing the history of purchases during the period, it was found that the company has significantly reduced its internal costs. From the responses given by managers in interviews and the analysis performed on available documentation, we noticed a significant reduction in costs to hire and get quotes from several companies. The search for new suppliers, since the implementation of the new hiring process, also happened to have a very low cost when compared to the cost of traditional shopping method. Cost reduction is also observed with increasing the number of suppliers, because the traditional process had been limited to regional coverage of each branch of supplies. Currently, the suppliers involved in the supply nationwide.

Additionally it was found that after implementing the new procurement model deadlines for the implementation of the procurement process was between 12 hours and 2 days. When assessing the costs to change the model of acquisitions with the projections provided by reducing costs, it is clear that assertiveness of the decisions taken by the company regarding implementation of electronic solution for their purchases.

One can also cite the greater transparency of process buy electronics, once the provider participates in the listing and have immediate access to all information of the procurement process, which are published on the site.

As suggestion for future research is recommended that it is applied to different segments that companies have deployed sites to the acquisition of MRO in order to demonstrate the universality of its applicability and widen the field observations, testing them in larger number organizations.

REFERENCES

Aberdeen Group. (1999). *Internet procurement: The importance of maintenance and repair.* Executive White Paper. Boston, MA: Aberdeen Group, Inc. Retrieved from http://www.aberdeen.com

Aberdeen Group. (2001). *Commerce networks: Extending the value of e-commerce*. Executive White Paper. Boston, MA: Aberdeen Group, Inc. Retrieved from http://www.aberdeen.com

Baião, J., & Seco, A. (2000). *Gestión de los recursos de tecnología de la información en el contexto de la modernización gobernamental*. BID.

Bressler, S., & Grantham, C. (2000). *Communities of commerce: Building internet business communities to accelerate growth, minimize risk, and increase customer loyalty*. New York, NY: McGraw Hill.

Cavanha Filho, A. O. (2001). Logística: Novos modelos. *Qualitymark, 167*.

Dai, Q., & Kauffman, R. J. (2000). *Business models for internet-based e-procurement systems and b2b electronic markets: An exploratory assessment*. Minneapolis, MN: University of Minnesota.

Dutta, S., Kwan, S., & Segev, A. (1997). *Transforming business in the marketspace: Strategic marketing and customer relationships*. Fontainebleau, France: INSEAD.

Fleury, P. F., Wanke, P., & Figueiredo, K. F. (2000). *Logística empresarial: A perspectiva Brasileira. Collection COPPEAD DE Administração*. São Paulo, Brazil: Atlas.

Franco, C. F. Jr. (2001). *E-business: Tecnologia da informação e negócios na Internet*. São Paulo, Brazil: Atlas.

Gebauer, J. & Segev. A. (2001). *Changing shapes of supply chains – How the internet could lead to a more integrated procurement function*. University of California, Berkeley, Haas School of Business. Fisher Center for Information Technology and Marketplace transformation - Working Paper 01 – WP – 1041.

Giunipero, L. G., & Sawchuk, C. (2000). *E-purchasing plus – Changing the way corporations buy*. ShareMax.com.

Godoy, A. S. (1995). Introdução à pesquisa qualitativa e suas possibilidades. *Revista de Administração de Empresas, 35*(3).

Guttman, R. H., & Maes, P. (1998). Agent-mediated integrative negotiation for retail electronic commerce. In *Proceedings of the Workshop on Agent Mediated Electronic Trading* (AMET'98).

Joia, L. A., & Zamot, F. (2002). Reverse auctions in the Brazilian government: A case study. Retrieved December 4, 2008, from www.ebape.fgv.br/academico/asp/dsp_opb_artigos.asp

Lopes, E., & Santos, L. (2006). *Estratégias de e-procurement na administração pública: Uma revisão de literatura. Conferência Ibérica de Sistemas e Tecnologias de Informação*. CISTI.

Maira, A. N., & Taylor, M. R. (1999). *The big picture: An overview of eletronic commerce. Prism. First Quarter. Arthur D.* Little.

Malhotra, N. K. (2001). *Pesquisa de marketing: Uma orientação aplicada*. Porto Alegre, Brazil: Bookman.

Manly, B. F. J. (2000). *Multivariate statistical methods: A primer*. New York, NY: CRC Press.

Marcoulides, G. A., & Hershberger, S. L. (1997). *Multivariate statistical methods: A first course*. Mahwah, NJ: L Erbaum.

Monteiro, J. C. (2002). *Logistica S/A - A logística corporativa auto suficiente*. Monograph at Instituto de Ciências Sociais (ICS) of AEUDF, Brasília.

Nazário, P. (2002). *A importância de sistemas de informação para a competitividade logística*. Centro de Estudos Logística – COPPEAD/UFRJ. Rio de Janeiro. Retrieved December 14, 2008, from http://www.cel.coppead.ufrj.br/fr- bench2.htm

Neef, D. (2001). *E-procurement – From strategy to implementation*. Upper Saddle River, NJ: Prentice Hall.

Novaes, A. G. (2001). *Logística e gerenciamento da cadeia de distribuição: Estratégia, operação e avaliação*. Rio de Janeiro, Brazil: Campus.

PricewaterhouseCoopers. (2001). *Como implanter um E-Procurement na Internet*. Webb Fácil 3. Retrieved December 12, 2008, from http://www.webb.com.br

Triviños, A. N. S. (1992). *Introdução à pesquisa em ciências sociais*. São Paulo, Brazil: Atlas.

Turban, E. (1997). Auctions and bidding on the Internet: An assessment. *EM – Electronic Auctions, EM – Eletronic Markets, 7*(4).

Turban, E., Chung, H. M., Chung, M., & Lee, J. K. (1999). *Electronic commerce: A managerial perspective*. Upper Saddle River, NJ: Prentice Hall.

Vargas, L., & Maldonado, G. (2001). *Guia para a apresentação de trabalhos científicos*. Rio Grande do Sul, Brazil: UFRGS.

Venetianer, T. (1999). *Como vender seu peixe na Internet: Um guia prático de marketing e comércio eletrônicos*. Rio de Janeiro, Brazil: Campus.

Vergara, S. C. (1998). *Projetos e relatórios de pesquisa em administração* (2nd ed.). São Paulo, Brazil: Atlas.

Vigoroso, M. (1999). Are Internet auctions ready to gear up? *Purchasing, 126*(2), 85–86.

Wurman, P. R., et al. (1998). *Flexible double auctions for electronic commerce: Theory and implementation*. University of Michigan, Artificial Intelligence Laboratory. Retrieved April 2, 2011, from http://citeseerx.ist.psu.edu/viewdoc/download?doi=10.1.1.35.1798&rep=rep1&type=pdf

Wyld, D. (2000). *The auction model: How the public sector can leverage the power of e-commerce through dynamic pricing*. Southeastern Louisiana University. Hammond.

Yin, R. E. (2001). *Estudo de caso – Planejamento e métodos* (2nd ed.). Porto Alegre, Brazil: Bookman.

APPENDIX

Questionnaire to CAIXA's Vendors

Use the scale below to determine their agreement or disagreement with the following statements:

		Totally Disagree	Partially Disagree	Agree or Disagree	Partially Agree	Totally Agree	Do not Know
		1	2	3	4	5	
f.1	The senior management of your company has developed strategies to Internet						
f.2	All areas of the company are integrated with strategies for Internet						
f.3	With the migration to the procurement system your company had to adapt systems to continue providing for Caixa						
f.4	With the adoption of the procurement system. the relationship of your company with the CAIXA has become more distant						
f.5	Your company is flexible in the face of rapid changes in competition. technologies and economic environment.						
f.6	Internet Sales component is critical to the success of your company						
f.7	Supply costs have reduced due to the implementation of the procurement system by Caixa						
f.8	The period between the request for supply and delivery of product / service decreased after the implementation of the procurement system Caixa						
f.9	The company gives priority to the implementation of activities related to strategies for the Internet.						
f.10	The company has developed appropriate procedures for marketing of products and services through the Internet.						
f.11	His company serves customers around the country						
f.12	Company's strategies seek to eliminate geographic barriers						
f.13	His company has created opportunities for developing partnerships with other companies						
f.14	The company has made investments in training and employee development aimed at implementing strategies for electronic commerce.						
f.15	The company has developed information systems (from supply chain integration) to adapt to the needs of customers who make electronic purchases.						
f.16	His company provides management services or inventory management to customers						
f.17	BOX issued prior to undertaking the move to electronic procurement system						
f.18	His company regularly conducts market analysis and its business segment.						
f.19	With the adoption of the procurement system by Caixa your company needed to adapt the logistics						

continued on following page

Table. Continued

		Totally Disagree	Partially Disagree	Agree or Disagree	Partially Agree	Totally Agree	Do not Know
		1	2	3	4	5	
f.20	His company works with clients in standardization of products and solving problems						
f.21	His company has a direct communication channel with its customers in order to inform them about their products and services. strategies. partnerships and changes in their processes and partnerships strategies changes in their processes						
f.22	With the adoption of the procurement system by Caixa his company had to adjust prices to make them competitive						
f.23	There was increased volume of business transacted with CAIXA after the adoption of the procurement system						

Questionnaire to CAIXA's Employee

Use the scale below to determine their agreement or disagreement with the following statements:

		Totally Disagree	Partially Disagree	Agree or Disagree	Partially Agree	Totally Agree	Do not Know
		1	2	3	4	5	
i.1	The Electronic Procurement (EP) are crucial for maintaining the competitiveness of the Caixa						
i.2	The competitors use the Internet to make purchases						
i.3	The reduction of transaction costs of shopping is an important reason for adopting the Business to Business (B2B)						
i.4	Concern over security in online transactions has detrimental for the system EP						
i.5	The lack of qualified personnel is a barrier to adoption EP						
i.6	Caixa heavily modified internal procedures during migration to Internet shopping						
i.7	Were trained employees of the shopping before the adoption of EP						
i.8	Training was done and / or dissemination of new procedures Internet shopping for all employees of the Caixa						
i.9	Strategic decisions. such as the adoption of EP. are often made from top to bottom						
i.10	EP processes are centralized						

continued on following page

Table Continued

		Totally Disagree	Partially Disagree	Agree or Disagree	Partially Agree	Totally Agree	Do not Know
		1	2	3	4	5	
i.11	The processes and tools are standardized EP						
i.12	Unanticipated fluctuations occur in demand for materials in various areas of business						
i.13	Caixa has established just-in-time inventory management						
i.14	There is resistance from users in using the system of EP						
i.15	Occurs evaluating results and reporting on the effectiveness of EP						
i.16	There was an increase in productivity in their unit or company due to adoption of Internet shopping						
i.17	The process of shopping online is more efficiently due to the reduction in transaction costs and the price of goods or services						
i.18	Managers have used the EP as a priority in the supply area						
i.19	The current rules governing the procurement and contracting has obstructed the realization of electronic purchases over the Internet						
i.20	The purchasing department makes quotation of prices of products and services from suppliers in the traditional way						
i.21	There are patterns of control over the pace of the EP and payment to suppliers						
i.22	There is quality control standard in the receipt of products or services						
i.23	All stages of the supply chain are automated. from the applicant's request area via the Intranet to the receipt and payment of goods and services purchased						
i.24	Caixa easily change supplier when another supply company has better contract						
i.25	Caixa ensures that your electronic procurement systems are compatible with the systems of suppliers						
i.26	The Caixa allows suppliers to access internal data						
i.27	Vendors allow Caixa has access to its internal data						
i.28	EP allowed a reduction in dependence on its suppliers						
i.29	EP reduced the loyalty of suppliers						
i.30	EP caused an increase in the number of current suppliers						
i.31	The Internet has provided greater agility and efficiency in controlling the quality of products and services						
i.32	Traditional suppliers are resistant to the processes of EC						
i.33	Suppliers have invested in IT in order to adapt to e-commerce						
i.34	Many vendors have the capacity to perform deliveries of its products throughout the country						
i.35	EP offers greater convenience						

continued on following page

Table Continued

		Totally Disagree	Partially Disagree	Agree or Disagree	Partially Agree	Totally Agree	Do not Know
		1	2	3	4	5	
i.36	EP reduces the time purchase orders						
i.37	EP enables reduction in transaction costs on purchases						
i.38	EP allows reduction in the price of final goods and services						
i.39	EP allows reduction in maintenance costs of inventories						
i.40	EP provides an increase in employee productivity						
i.41	EP permits reduction of errors in orders received						
i.42	The Internet makes the purchasing process more impersonal						
i.43	Information management is facilitated by the processes of EP						
i.44	The processes of EP allow greater transparency in negotiations with Caixa's vendors						
i.45	There was resistance from employees in the area accepting new measures for Internet purchases						
i.46	EP processes hamper emergency purchases						
i.47	There was increased competition among suppliers						
i.48	The frequency of requests for purchases increased						
i.49	IT investments are constant and increasing for EP process						
i.50	Top management is committed to the EP system and formulate strategies for using the Internet in various areas						
i.51	Caixa creates opportunities to develop partnerships or provide e-procurement services to private and /or public agencies						

Chapter 5
New Organisational Culture for New Public E-Procurement:
From Competition to Purchasing Groups

Pietro Previtali
University of Pavia, Italy

ABSTRACT

Effective e-government involves rethinking organizations and processes, and changing behavior so that public services are delivered more efficiently to the people who need to use them. But the nature of the public sector is not a simple one. Lots of variables have to be considered: the number of entities involved in public sector procurement, the complexity of relationships among them, historical events that impacted on the public sector and different tensions between central and local parts of the public sector. In general, the most striking feature is the sheer complexity of the public sector. In the author's opinion, it required a reconceptualisation of market exchange, evolving the procurement scenario from competition to collaboration. Nowadays public (e) procurement is still an under-researched area which has not spread out yet. Therefore, the aim of the chapter is to conduct a reflection to identify the features of purchasing and supply in the public sector and its further developments toward forms of collaboration and group purchasing.

INTRODUCTION

There are some fundamental differences between countries in their public sector services which impact on purchasing and supply to support these services. Major reforms have been undertaken in some jurisdictions directly related to changing ideas on the appropriate degree of autonomy of states or regions within a national or federal system. In some cases there are vigorous, current efforts to devolve power to regional level, in others, the states hold power which has only been ceded to a limited extent to federal levels. This has been reflected by the applications of public procurement as these are strictly connected to public sector processes. The extent and quality of engagement

DOI: 10.4018/978-1-4666-2119-0.ch005

of politicians and policy makers with strategic procurement personnel varies significantly in each country. In fact, public procurement has to manage multiple stakeholder objectives which may be contradictory and variable over time. Pressure to act tends to be resisted until the point when it is shown to be the new dominant paradigm, then the system will react in the opposite direction.

Modernization of procurement practices and processes presents Government with a clear opportunity to leverage significantly improved value for money from its total spend on goods and services. It will be necessary to build on this momentum moving forward the following goals:

- **Resourcing the Strategy:** The organizational and budgetary resources needed to support a modernization of public sector procurement arrangements must be clearly acknowledged as an invest-to-save proposition;
- **The E-Tenders Website:** A clear priority should be given to enhancing the functionality of the existing e-tenders website to support online submission of tenders and the deployment of electronic catalogues and framework agreements.
- **Supporting SME Adjustment:** Government needs to develop specific programmes to support adjustment by SMEs to modernization of public sector procurement arrangements.
- **Alternative Co-Operations:** In a climate of budgetary constraints, careful consideration should be given to the potential of alternative partnerships to accelerate implementation of the strategy, including potential cooperation with private sector partners.

In our consideration, to achieve this goals it must be respected an important requirement: the change in culture, process and methods, toward new forms of public sector procurement practices suggest the need to reconceptualise market exchange as a process of social construction, in which actors in self-organizing systems negotiate rules, norms and institutional frameworks, rather than taking the "rules of the market" as given, evolving the setting from competition to collaboration.

Literature Review

The public sector is a very complicated one, and the public sector supply is even more intricate. The framework suggested by Harland et al. (2000) provides a way of making sense of the extreme complexity of descriptive cases of purchasing and supply in public sectors).

Their conceptual model has as its centre the government action to be taken. Decisions to be taken here include the location of where the action should be taken (in central government, in a government department, within an individual government organization, by a team within a public sector organization or by an individual within public sector), the type of action to be taken (policy, strategy, managerial or operational), and the level of authority required for the action. The appropriate government action is decided through consideration of relevant factors relating to the supply market (e.g., product and service characteristics, risk, value), the customer market (e.g., criticality, specificity), prevailing constraints (e.g., capacity, capability), available mechanisms (e.g., purchase cards, electronic shopping malls) and the environment (e.g., political, economic, social and technological environmental factors).

More specifically, Johnson et al. (2003) found that there were significant differences in the roles and responsibilities of purchasing between public and private sector organizations, as indicated through measures such as organizational structure, supply chain responsibilities and reporting line, team working and involvement in major corporate activities. Quayle (1998) and Knight et al. (2003) found that purchasings recognition as a significant function was poor in the public sector, but awareness of the strategic role of purchasing is starting to increase. There were some indications that public procurement internationally was moving towards a policy role, and focused less on transactional procurement (Knight et al., 2003). Similarly, Quayle et al. (2000) found that government purchasing in the UK and Canada was moving from a reactive to proactive model and private sector practices had been adopted where appropriate. A new range of skills and competencies was perceived as crucial for this development. Through a Delphi study to develop an agenda for public procurement research, Harland et al. (2002) suggested the need to promote more active involvement of senior public sector managers in supply management issues. The authors also suggested improved information systems for supply management and developing new collaborative forms of relationship such as public private partnerships or private finance initiatives.

Concerning e-procurement, some literature espouses the benefits of innovative solutions through procurement systems, mostly connected with ICT implementation (Aberdeen Group, 2005; Heywood, Barton and Heywood, 2001; Schoenherr and Tummala, 2007; Tanner et al., 2007). These benefits include the acceleration of the execution times of procedures and reduction in announcement expenses, simplification of processes and the direct and constant monitoring of public spending; the opportunity to spend time out of routine administrative tasks (automated by new tools) through activities with higher added value in terms of function-specific purchases (e.g. marketing intelligence); the improvement in transparency because of the uniformity of access to information without discrimination because the tender documents are online; and the standardisation of procedures, which ensures that the timing and quality of processes can be more easily controlled by external actors (e.g. information asymmetries).

Nevertheless, some studies (Andersen, 2004; Henriksen, Mahnke and Hansen, 2004; Vaidya, Sajeev and Callender, 2006) reveal that these benefits tend to decrease in the public sector, mainly because of the impact of different economic, institutional and social factors (Calista and Melitski, 2007; Gichoya, 2005; Heeks, 2008; Mahadeo, 2009; Maniatopoulos, 2004; Tonkin, 2003). These differences have resulted in a number of specific regulations and standards that have been developed for public e-procurement that require bureaucratic procedures. This bureaucracy, which is also related to the nature of the institutions involved (Kanishka and Hepu, 2010; Somasundaram and Damsgaard, 2005), covers audit, accountability and compliance standards with national and international rules to ensure supply competition and transparency in the awarding of contracts. In particular, certain problems remain crucial, such as inadequate Internet coverage and the digital divide and the inertia of users in change management from an organisational and cultural point of view. Moreover, resistance at the local level in wanting to play and compete within a system tends to increase by bringing into question its own consolidated market components (Liu, Derzsi, Raus and Kipp, 2008; Schwester, 2009; Shackleton and Dawson, 2007; Thomson, 2009).

TOWARD NEW FORMS OF PARTNERSHIP

In spite of many critiques of the move to externalization of services (Walsh and Davis, 1993; Hambleton, 1998) there was a much greater understanding than ever before that the market had a major potential role in supplementing – even sometimes replacing – the role of public sector in-house provision. With this understanding, however, came the realization that the public sector had traditionally misunderstood the range of possible relationships between actors in the "market" (Kettl, 1993; Boyne, 1998). With the dawning appreciation that market relationships were socially constructed in the procurement process, not simply a product of "market conditions", the need became clear for a more proactive role by public sector organizations in market management (Filkin et al., 1999) and greater attention to developing mutually rewarding relationships with external contractors, whether they were in the public, private or voluntary sectors (Erridge and Greer, 2002).

In recent years two important trends spread in public procurement: the move to more collaborative working in public sector organizations (both joined-up working within the public sector and closer working with organizations in other sectors) and the move to more complex forms of co-ordination in the procurement process, with larger numbers of players involved in both the commissioning and providing roles. The combination of these two factors produces the opportunity for a range of different market relationships from those traditionally considered in the "make or buy" decision. However, the relevance of these activities for the organization's performance requires an accurate analysis of what it is outsourced and how (Walker et al., 2001; Kakabadse and Kakabadse, 2005).

Outsourcing can be defined as the "contracting-out" of services that were previously performed in-house. Outsourcing is a supply strategy often chosen as a means of increasing organizational efficiency and effectiveness (Steane and Walker, 2000). Whilst some short-term benefits for organizations can be achieved through outsourcing, there is a growing recognition that there may be longer-term costs not fully assessed by them (Bettis et al., 1992). Outsourcing can impact on the size, structure and competitiveness of purchaser and vendor sectors. Outsourcing also has an effect on employment levels, patterns and conditions (Postner, 1990). Social issues may be affected in respect of growth in earnings inequality since the contracts offered little scope to compete other than by worsening employees' terms and conditions of employment (Patterson and Pinch, 1995). Risks of outsourcing include losing in-house expertise and knowledge, unintentional loss of control, and reductions in quality.

Traditional contracting-out involves a single commissioner of a service placing contracts with a range of providers for its services and is based on an explicit specification of the service and performance criteria that are predetermined. The need to predetermine a specification for what are, typically, complex services in a dynamically changing environment and then to manage subsequent (typically frequent) "contract variations", has made public agencies vulnerable to all the opportunistic behaviours which are associated with "transactional contracting" (Williamson 1975; Walsh 1995). Hence, there is an increasing awareness in management literature that the decision to outsource is a complex one with uncertain outcomes (Hui and Tsang, 2004), and this is the reason why for example since the 1980s the UK public sector has been characterized by continued government emphasis on the need for contracting-out of services, but at the same time the growth in contracting-out has remained patchy, sporadic and contested (Walsh 1995).

Relationships in Public Procurement

In the last decade, there have been a number of important drivers of change in public sector procurement which reflect new strategic directions, new policies and new practices in public service provision. While these trends at least partly mirror similar developments in the private sector, the way they have played out in the public sector has had a number of distinctive aspects.

One of the most important key driver of these different procurement approaches is the nature of the organizational relationships in the procurement process. In the traditional model, it was adversarial, with the principal trying to find ways of procuring services from the agent on beneficial terms by means of contract mechanisms which would curb any opportunistic behaviour on the part of the agent and reduce the agent's inherent advantage that could stem from asymmetric access to information (Williamson 1975). In the new approaches to procurement, the emphasis has switched dramatically to collaborative behaviour whereby each party expects to reap benefits from helping to make the joint working more successful (Lorange and Roos, 1992; Dror and Hamel, 1998) creating a "collaborative advantage" (Kanter, 1994; Huxham, 1995).

A second key driver of these different procurement approaches is the growth in the number of interfaces between service commissioners and service providers. This growth is partly due to the rapid fragmentation of public service commissioners and providers into a larger number of organizations. This is something that has been observed in most services and in most European countries (Rosenau 2004; Skelcher 2005) and is partly due to the unbundling of services which has been noticeable in both public and private services (Drucker 1992; Hagel and Singer, 1999). The result has been greater challenges of coordination in the procurement decision and therefore the need for more systematic procurement procedures (Byatt 2002; Erridge, 2002). So we can delineate four very different scenarios depending on whether service commissioners act alone or as a coordinated group and whether a service provider is treated as a special, one-off provider of a service or as just one of many providers picked out of the marketplace (Boivard, 2007).

Whereas the traditional in-house provision model involves no external parties, and the traditional contracting-out model is one of atomistic competition between many uncoordinated providers which provide services to the commissioning principal, each of the variants involves a significant degree of co-ordination, either of the commissioners or the providers, or of both. What has made for the largest changes, however, is where this coordination has moved further to positive collaboration. We distinguish three types of market relationship where these collaborative relationships have become important:

1. Relational contracting;
2. Partnership procurement;
3. Distributed commissioning.

Relational Contracting: As a conceptual approach, derives from a number of theoretical sources: transaction cost minimization in economics (Walsh, 1995), economies of scope in collaborative networks (Piore and Sabel, 1984), strategic alliances (Lorange and Roos, 1992) and collaborative advantage (Huxham, 1995), relationship marketing (Christopher et al., 1991). Relational contracting first appeared as a major force in the UK public sector (even if in a somewhat unimaginative form), in the block contracts in National Health Service internal market and in the "generalized service agreements" in social services (Kirkpatrick *et al.*, 2001) in the late 1980s. Since then, it has become the new conventional wisdom in public service contracting in UK. This approach demands both an open-minded approach to sharing and a willingness to innovate (Coulson *et al.,* 1998); neither of these are, as yet, common characteristics in public agencies (Allen, 2002). The former often falls foul of the political determination (evident both in national ministries and in individual local authorities) to maintain control over decision making rather than sharing responsibilities (Klijn and Teisman, 2004). In addition, the latter is often sacrificed to "safety-first" procedures because of the penalties attached to failure in public life (Perri *et al.*, 2002). Because public sector service purchasers in such relationships are intrinsically monopsonists (i.e. have market power in purchasing), some analysts are suspicious of the long-term risks to private firms from entering into such long-term partnerships, and argue that the results of such partnerships can be lower payoffs for the final service user (Parker and Hartley, 1997). However these obstacles can be overcome where the parties concerned become convinced that they have a shared interest in doing so (Bovaird, 2007).

Partnership procurement has several manifestations in the public sector:

1. Public Private Partnerships (PPPs), such as Strategic Service Delivery Partnerships (SSDPs), in which there is a genuine partnership between several organizations (often across public, private and voluntary sectors), each of which contributes a particular expertise to some part of the commissioning, purchasing or providing process;
2. Private Finance Initiatives (PFIs), a financially-driven PPP, in which the motive for the partnership is fundamentally the readier access to capital finance enjoyed by private sector partners, whose expertise may otherwise add little or no value to the service (Ball *et al.*, 2001);
3. Purchasing consortia, which normally seek mainly economies of bulk purchasing and lower transaction costs, rather than any synergies in the service delivery process (Byatt, 2002).

Distributed Commissioning: involves a public sector purchaser in the task of enabling many smaller agencies, often geographically defined (as in neighbourhood, parish, electoral ward or district), to determine for themselves the priorities between public services which will be provided for them from the purchaser's budget (Bovaird, 2007). This has been a feature of rural governance in the UK for many years, for example in "community chest" schemes funded by the Rural Development Commission and the Countryside Agency. However, in the 1990s, it also became prominent in many metropolitan areas and has been reinforced recently by the funding arrangements for Local Strategic Partnerships in many local areas (Turner and Martin, 2004) and by EU funding schemes such as URBAN (Bache, 2001).

GROUP PURCHASING

The forming of collaborative purchasing arrangements is suggested to be an increasing trend in purchasing and supply, and in particular over the last years there has been an increasing interest in the stakes related to public purchasing groups and purchasing consortia in countries such as Canada, Finland, Germany, the Netherlands, the UK, and the U.S. (Kivisto et al., 2003, Nollet and Beaulieu, 2003; Kamann et.al., 2004; Schotanus, 2005). Purchasing groups are widely used by health, school and governmental organizations to keep prices low and achieve other organizational objectives (Essig, 2000; Stefan and Santiago, 1989). The evolution of purchasing groups seems necessary and unavoidable.

The notion of a purchasing group is conveyed under at least three other names: joint procurement (DTLR, 2001), purchasing consortium, and cooperative purchasing (Rozemeijer, 2000). These expressions bring forward the idea of an agreement between two or more entities, which is often motivated by the expectations of improved efficiency and better effectiveness due to economies of scale and economies of scope. Nollet and Beaulieu (2003) define purchasing group as a formal or virtual structure which makes the consolidation of purchases for many organizations possible. Consolidation is a procurement practice used by local entities to transfer to a central entity activities such as: bidding, supplier evaluation, negotiation, and contract management. This approach makes it possible for the members of the group to acquire additional suppliers; consequently, they get more favourable conditions than those they would have obtained individually. By the same token, consolidation reduces administrative costs, since the negotiation process is performed by only one organization, instead of all local entities.

The healthcare sector has been a leader in group purchasing. United States are a really good example of the spread of purchasing consortia in this sector; in that country more than 70% of healthcare purchases are made that way (Muse & Associates, 2000). Nollet and Beaulieu (2003) examining the American healthcare purchasing groups (a typical example of joint procurement), notice that these purchasing form have been able to maintain a key role in the supply chain, despite many purchasers would prefer that purchasing groups become more aggressive to get better prices rather than widen the scope of the services provided (Williamson, 2000). More in details, trough the study of the dynamics and evolution of purchasing groups is possible to identify few critical factors impacting the development of purchasing groups: procurement strategy and nature of benefits, payers' intervention, structure, nature of relationship with suppliers and resources.

The strategy of a purchasing group could be more or less extended, depending on the nature of the benefits desired. However, beyond all types of activities performed, the focus is often on savings, since it is quite difficult to justify the use of a purchasing group for other reasons. For example, a survey of 221 American healthcare institutions indicates that the savings due to purchasing groups vary from 10% to 15% (Muse & Associates, 2000). Pedersen (1996) compared the performances of purchasing groups of a few sectors (electronics products, auto manufacturers, and healthcare); his study indicates that the other sectors get savings of 20–35% in comparison with the 10–15% often mentioned in the healthcare sector. It is the variety in the procurement approaches used, not only the consolidation of purchases that provides these additional savings. Consequently, a procurement strategy is used, among other objectives, to identify the areas more likely to generate potential savings, and then to use the approaches making it possible to do so. A procurement strategy should specify the extent of group negotiations. For instance, a group might prefer to limit group negotiations to commodities common to all members of the group. Furthermore, a sound procurement strategy goes beyond simply acquiring goods and services, and contributes significantly to organizations not only by reducing costs, but as well by adding value through better operational links with suppliers, by distancing competitors through better quality inputs, and by shortening lead times (Fung, 1999).

Also Payers' intervention, mostly through government and insurance companies, appears to trigger changes in purchasing groups. The intervention can be direct, when the intent is to define precisely the respective roles of purchasing groups and healthcare centres regarding procurement. It can also be indirect, through decisions made about healthcare: for example, the emphasis could be on a continuous focus on savings, which would stimulate the use of group purchasing.

There are two major types of structures for group purchasing: a superstructure where a separate and autonomous entity manages the group's contracts, and a confederation, where the contracts to be negotiated are shared among members. In addition to its type (superstructure vs. confederation), we believe that there are two other dimensions in a structure. The first one is the geographical scope of the purchasing group, whether it be regional or national. While a regional scope makes it easier to maintain close relationships between the purchasing group and the members, a national scope allows the consolidation of more important volumes, which should provide a purchasing group with more clout for negotiations with suppliers. Aiming for the "optimal structure" of a purchasing group implies that an equilibrium should be reached between a size sufficient to offset the suppliers' negotiating power, but still small enough so that its administrative costs don't exceed the savings generated.

Another dimension is the nature of the relations between the purchasing group and its members. For example, in last 1980s in the United States, national groups could not guarantee a firm quantity to the suppliers, and were promoting the agreed-upon products to their members. At the beginning of the 1990s, some groups added a clause to their contract: in order to be a member of the group, the healthcare centre had to support the negotiated contract. Such clauses limit the flexibility that healthcare centres have in managing their procurement activities.

Finally there is another critical factor which is important to consider: the resources invested in the group's structure. Resources are human (competencies) as well as technological (for example information systems making transactions with and among members easier). The quantity and quality of these resources have not only a financial impact, but as well an impact on the development of a purchasing group.

Procurement and E-government development requires collaboration among government agencies and private partners to ensure interoperability, avoid duplication, ensure coherent action in a range of crucial areas such as security and privacy, and provide the framework and capacity for seamless services. E-government must be built on a fluid, constantly adapting collaborative governance system that responds to several challenges in the public sector: (1) new opportunities to link agencies through online applications; (2) policy challenges demanding a growing level of coordination across all levels of government and sectors; and 3) an emphasis on performance requiring external alignment and internal integration and cooperation. In order to develop e-government, government agencies that traditionally focus on their own missions and narrowly defined publics must now cooperate to enhance services across government agencies and levels.

CONCLUSION

The organizational culture of a public agency often can resist dramatic change within a short amount of time. In addition to organizational factors, the technology field changes very quickly creating a challenges for the public sector to keep pace with innovations. Hence, public agencies are sometimes reluctant to change course and alter their way of doing things.

It is easy to conclude that the potential contribution of public (e) procurement is constrained by being seen as a non-strategic activity and by the frequency of major changes, which can mean there is no opportunity to reap the benefits of reorganizations and special initiatives.

However it is largely recognized that there are common goals and strategies to be achieved in public procurement. Obtaining better value for money is a common objective of reform plans, but not one which seems to be well elaborated or easy to achieve. Reducing transaction costs is also a common theme across the cases.

One of the most interesting application of procurement cooperation is purchasing group, which takes government procurement and contracting professions out of their comfort zones and requires a major effort on behalf of interested parties. Costs and benefits of purchasing group must be carefully balanced against the costs and benefits of more traditional forms of public sector procurement. Nevertheless, they suggest that the traditional concepts of the "market" and of "market management" are now outdated and need to be revised to take into account the potential of collaborative market-based relationships between multiple stakeholders on both the demand and supply side in the public domain.

Equally, there is a need for cultural changes within public sector organizations: front-line professionals should exercise professional judgment in the management of the procurement process and broader relationships with service suppliers. In this context, staff involved in purchasing should be encouraged to adopt the most appropriate procurement mechanism for each particular good or service purchased. However the most efficient purchasing mechanism may not necessarily be open competitive tendering. The best evidence of this comes from private sector organizations which have identified that the purchasing of complex services such as occupational health is best undertaken through the adoption of more relational approaches. By utilising this flexibility, public sector organizations will be better placed to achieve best value for money and fulfill their role in serving the public. In short, there is no single mechanism that fits all service procurement situations, and flexibility as well as adaptability is the key to the successful and effective procurement of complex services by public sector organizations.

REFERENCES

Aberdeen Group. (2005). *Best practices in e-procurement: Reducing costs and increasing value through online buying*. Boston, MA: Author.

Allen, E. (2002). *Managing strategic service delivery partnerships: From governance to delivery*. London, UK: New Local Government Network.

Andersen, K. V. (2004). *E-government and public sector process rebuilding (PPR): Dilettantes, wheelbarrows, and diamonds*. Boston, MA: Kluwer Academic Publishers.

Bache, I. (2001). Different seeds in the same plot? Competing models of capitalism and the incomplete contracts of partnership design. *Public Administration*, *79*(2), 337–359. doi:10.1111/1467-9299.00259

Ball, R., Heafey, M., & King, D. (2001). The private finance initiative: A good deal for the public purse or a drain on future generations? *Policy and Politics*, *29*, 95–108. doi:10.1332/0305573012501224

Bettis, R., Bradley, S., & Hamel, G. (1992). Outsourcing and industrial decline. *The Academy of Management Executive*, *6*(1), 7–22.

Bovaird, T. (2007). *Strategic management in the public sector*. Oxford, UK: Oxford University Press.

Boyne, G. A. (1998). Competitive tendering in local government: A review of theory and evidence. *Public Administration*, *76*(4), 695–712. doi:10.1111/1467-9299.00132

Byatt, I. (2002). *Delivering better services for citizens: A review of local government procurement in England*. London, UK: Department for Transport, Local Government and the Regions/ The Local Government Association.

Calista, D., & Melitski, J. (2007). E-government and e-governance: Converging constructs of public sector information and communications technologies. *Public Administration Quarterly*, *31*(1).

Coulson, A., Darwin, J., Davis, H., et al. (1998). *Client-contractor relationships in ten local authorities*. Occasional Paper 18. Birmingham, UK: School of Public Policy.

Dror, Y., & Hamel, G. (1998). *Alliance advantage*. Cambridge, MA: Harvard Business School Press.

Drucker, P. F. (1992). Sell the mailroom: Unbundling in the 1990s. In *Managing for the future: The 1990s and beyond* (pp. 220–223). Oxford, UK: Butterworth-Heinemann.

DTLR. (2001). *Local authority procurement: A research report*. Department for Transport, Local Government andthe Regions, London.

Erridge, A., & Greer, J. (2002). Partnerships and public procurement: Building social capital through supply relations. *Public Administration*, *80*(3), 503–522. doi:10.1111/1467-9299.00315

Erridge, A., & Nondi, R. (1994). Public procurement, competition and partnership. *European Journal of Purchasing and Supply Management*, *1*(3), 169–179. doi:10.1016/0969-7012(94)90006-X

Essig, M. (2000). Purchasing consortia as symbiotic relationships: Developing the concept of "consortium sourcing". *European Journal of Purchasing & Supply Management*, *6*(1), 13–22. doi:10.1016/S0969-7012(99)00031-3

Filkin, G., Bassam, G., & Corrigan, P. (1999). *Starting to modernize*. London, UK: New Local Government Network.

Fung, P. (1999). Managing purchasing in a supply chain context evolution and resolution. *Logistics Information Management*, *12*(5), 362–367. doi:10.1108/09576059910295788

Gichoya, D. (2005). Factors affecting the successful implementation of ICT projects in government. *The Electronic. Journal of E-Government*, *3*(4), 175–184.

Hagel, J., & Singer, M. (1999). Unbundling the corporation. *Harvard Business Review*, (2): 133.

Hambleton, R. (1998). Competition and contracting in UK local government. In Oatley, N. (Ed.), *Cities, economic competition and urban policy*. London, UK: Paul Chapman.

Harland, C., Gibbs, J., & Sutton, R. (2000). Supply strategy for the public sector: Framing the issues. *Proceedings of the International Purchasing & Supply Research and Education Association* (IPSERA) Annual Conference, London, Western Ontario.

Harland, C., Graves, A., Knight, L., & Lamming, R. (2002). *The future of public sector supply: Developing a research agenda*. UK: Centre for Research in Strategic Purchasing and Supply. University of Bath.

Heeks, R. (2008). Benchmarking e-government: Improving the national and international measurement evaluation and comparison of e-government. In Irani, Z., & Love, P. (Eds.), *Evaluation of information systems*. Butterworth-Heinemann. doi:10.1016/B978-0-7506-8587-0.50017-2

Henriksen, H. Z., Mahnke, V., & Hansen, J. M. (2004). Public e-Procurement adoption: Economic and political rationality. *Proceedings of the 37th Hawaii International Conference on System Sciences* (HICSS-37). IEEE Computer Society.

Heywood, J. B., Barton, M., & Heywood, C. (2001). *E-procurement: A guide to successful e-procurement implementation*. Financial Times Prentice Hall.

Hui, E. Y. Y., & Tsang, A. H. C. (2004). Sourcing strategies of facilities management. *Journal of Quality in Maintenance Engineering*, *10*(2), 85–92. doi:10.1108/13552510410539169

Huxham, C. (Ed.). (1995). *Creating collaborative advantage*. London, UK: Sage.

Johnson, F. P., & Leenders, M. R. (2003). Gaining and losing pieces of the supply chain. *Journal of Supply Chain Management*, *39*(1). doi:10.1111/j.1745-493X.2003.tb00147.x

Kakabadse, A., & Kakabadse, N. (2005). Outsourcing: current and future trends. *Thunderbird International Business Review*, *47*(2), 183–204. doi:10.1002/tie.20048

Kamann, D. J., et al. (2004). Joint purchasing: Theory and practice. *International Purchasing and Supply Education and Research Association Conference*, Catania, (pp. 511-520).

Kanishka, K., & Hepu, D. (2010). *Exploring the public value of e-government.* 23rd Bled eConference, June 20–23, 2010; Bled, Slovenia.

Kanter, R. M. (1994). Collaborative advantage: The art of alliances. *Harvard Business Review*, (July): 96–108.

Kettl, D. F. (1993). *Sharing power: Public governance and private markets*. Washington, DC: The Brookings Institution.

Kirkpatrick, I. (2001). Out of sight - Out of mind: Assessing the impact of markets for children's residential care. *Public Administration, 79*(1), 49–71. doi:10.1111/1467-9299.00245

Kivisto, T. (2003). *Consortia purchasing and logistics in Kuopio area – Lessons learned from a 4 year project*. Budapest, Hungary: IRSPP Proceedings.

Klijn, E., & Teisman, G. R. (2004). Public-private partnerships: The right form at the wrong moment? An analysis of institutional and strategic obstacles. In Ghobadian, A. (Eds.), *Public-private partnerships: Policy and experience*. Basingstoke, UK: Palgrave Macmillan.

Knight, L. (2003). *Academic report from the 1st International Research Study on Public Procurement*. UK: Centre for Research in Strategic Purchasing and Supply, University of Bath.

Liu, J., Derzsi, Z., Raus, M., & Kipp, A. (2008). E-government project evaluation: An integrated framework. In Wimmer, M. A., Scholl, H. J., & Ferro, E. (Eds.), *Electronic government* (*Vol. 5184*, pp. 85–97). Berlin, Germany: Springer-Verlag. doi:10.1007/978-3-540-85204-9_8

Lorange, P., & Roos, J. (1992). *Strategic alliances: Formation, implementation and evolution*. Oxford, UK: Blackwell.

Mahadeo, J. D. (2009). Towards an understanding of the factors influencing the acceptance and diffusion of e-government services. *Electronic. Journal of E-Government*, *7*(4), 391–402.

Maniatopoulos, G. (2004). Enacting e-procurement technologies within UK local authorities. *Proceedings of the IADIS International Conference e-Society*, Vol. 2, (pp. 850–854).

Martin, S. (2002). Best value: New public management or new direction? In Mclaughlin, K., Osborne, S. P., & Ferlie, E. (Eds.), *New public management: Current trends and future prospects*. London, UK: Routledge.

Muse, (2000). *The role of group purchasing organizations in the US health care system*. Washington, DC: HIGPA.

Nollet, J., & Beaulieu, M. (2003). The development of group purchasing: An empirical study in the healthcare sector. *Journal of Purchasing and Supply Management*, *9*, 3–10. doi:10.1016/S0969-7012(02)00034-5

Parker, D., & Vaidya, K. (2000). An economic perspective on innovation networks. In Conway, S., & Jones, O. (Eds.), *Social interaction and organisational change*. London, UK: Imperial College Press.

Patterson, A., & Pinch, P. (1995). Hollowing out the local state: Compulsory competitive tendering and the restructuring of British public sector service. *Environment & Planning A*, *27*, 1437–1461. doi:10.1068/a271437

Pedersen, J. (1996). Product standardization playing to win. *In Vivo (Athens, Greece)*, (June): 15–20.

Perri, D. (2002). *Towards holistic governance: The new reform agenda*. Basingstoke, UK: Palgrave Macmillan.

Piore, M., & Sabel, C. (1984). *The second industrial order: Possibilities for prosperity*. New York, NY: Basic Books.

Postner, H. (1990). The contracting-out problem in service sector analysis: choice of statistical unit. *Review of Income and Wealth, 36*(2), 177–186. doi:10.1111/j.1475-4991.1990.tb00279.x

Quayle, M. (1998). The impact of strategic procurement in the UK government sector. *International Journal of Public Sector Management, 11*(5), 397–413. doi:10.1108/09513559810226860

Quayle, M., et al. (2000). Comparative study of purchasing in UK and Canadian government. In *Proceedings of the 9th International Annual IPSERA Conference*, University of Western Ontario, Canada. 24–27 May.

Rosenau, J. (2004). Strong demand, huge supply: Governance in an emerging epoch. In Bache, I., & Flinders, M. (Eds.), *Multi-level governance*. Oxford, UK: Oxford University Press. doi:10.1093/0199259259.003.0003

Rozemeijer, F. (2000). *Creating corporate advantage in purchasing*. Eindhoven, The Netherlands: Eindhoven University of Technology.

Schoenherr, T., & Tummala, V. (2007). Electronic procurement: A structured literature review and directions for future research. *International Journal of Procurement Management, 1*(1/2). doi:10.1504/IJPM.2007.015353

Schotanus, F., & Telgen, J. (2005). Implications of a classification of forms of cooperative purchasing. *Proceedings of the 21st IMP Conference*, 1-3 September 2005, RSM Erasmus University, The Netherlands.

Schwester, R. W. (2009). Examining the barriers to e-government adoption. *Electronic. Journal of E-Government, 7*(1), 113–122.

Shackleton, P., & Dawson, L. (2007). *Doing it tough: Factors impacting on local e-government maturity*. 20th Bled eConference, June 4–6, Bled, Slovenia.

Skelcher, C. (2005). Jurisdictional integrity, polycentrism and the design of democratic governance. *Governance: An International Journal of Policy, Administration and Institutions, 18*(1), 89–110. doi:10.1111/j.1468-0491.2004.00267.x

Somasundaram, R., & Damsgaard, J. (2005). Policy recommendations for electronic public procurement. *The Electronic. Journal of E-Government, 3*(3), 147–156.

Steane, P. D., & Walker, D. H. T. (2000). Competitive tendering and contracting public sector services in Australia—A facilities management issue. *Facilities, 18*(5), 245–255. doi:10.1108/02632770010328144

Stefan, J. P., & Santiago, R. E. (1989). The benefits of group purchasing. *Journal of Property Management, 54*(5), 50–52.

Tanner, C., et al. (2007). *Current trends and challenges in electronic procurement: An empirical study*. 20th Bled eConference, June 4–6, Bled, Slovenia.

Thomson, J. T. (2009). Remodelled and restyled e-procurement – New power relationships down under. *Electronic. Journal of E-Government, 7*(2), 183–194.

Tonkin, C. (2003). *E-procurement in the public sector: Story, myth and legend*. Dublin, Ireland: The Policy Institute, Trinity College.

Turner, D. N., & Martin, S. (2004). Managerialism meets community development: Contracting for social outcomes. *Policy and Politics, 32*(1), 21–32. doi:10.1332/030557304772860021

Vaidya, K., Sajeev, A. S. M., & Callender, G. (2006). Critical factors that influence eprocurement implementation success in the public sector. *Journal of Public Procurement*, *6*(2), 70–99.

Walker, A. (2001). Value creation in buyer–seller relationships. *Industrial Marketing Management*, *30*, 365–377. doi:10.1016/S0019-8501(01)00156-0

Walker, H., et al. (2003). *The developing role of purchasing confederations in complex supply networks*. Paper presented at British Academy of Management Annual Conference 2003.

Walsh, K. (1995). *Public services and market mechanisms: Competition, contracting and the new public management*. London, UK: Macmillan.

Walsh, K., & Davis, H. (1993). *Competition and service: The impact of the Local Government Act 1988*. London, UK: HMSO.

Williamson, J. E. (2000). Many purchasers want more from GPOS. *Healthcare Purchasing News*, *18*.

Williamson, O. E. (1975). *Markets and hierarchies: Analysis and anti-trust implications*. New York, NY: Free Press.

ADDITIONAL READING

Arbin, K. (2003). E-procurement maturity in industry. *International Journal of Electronic Business*, *1*(4), 396–407. doi:10.1504/IJEB.2003.004112

Bendoly, E., & Schoenherr, T. (2005). ERP system – And implementation – Benefits: Implications for B2B e-procurement. *International Journal of Operations & Production Management*, *25*(4), 304–319. doi:10.1108/01443570510585516

Benslimane, Y., Plaisent, M., & Bernard, P. (2005). Investigating search costs and coordination costs in electronic markets: A transaction costs economics perspective. *Electronic Markets*, *15*(3), 213–224. doi:10.1080/10196780500208756

Beynon-Davies, P., et al. (2007). *Preparing SME suppliers for sustainable local authority e-procurement*. 20th Bled eConference, June 4–6; Bled, Slovenia.

Bonina, C. M., & Cordella, A. (2008). The new public management, e-government and the notion of public value: Lessons from Mexico. *Proceedings of SIG GlobDev's First Annual Workshop*, Paris, France, December 13 2008.

Croom, S. R., & Brandon-Jones, A. (2005). Key issues in e-procurement: Procurement implementation and operation in the public sector. *Journal of Public Procurement*, *5*(3), 367–387.

Deutscher, T. H., & Gruber, D. (2002). *Global healthcare exchange Canada: Trade exchange adoption*. Richard Ivey School of Business Case Collection.

Engelbrecht-Wiggans, R., & Katok, E. (2006). E-sourcing in procurement: Theory and behavior in reverse auctions with noncompetitive contracts. *Management Science*, *52*(4), 581–596. doi:10.1287/mnsc.1050.0474

Enyon, R., & Dutton, W. H. (2007). Barriers to networked governments: Evidence from Europe. *Prometheus*, *25*(3), 225–242. doi:10.1080/08109020701531361

Essig, M., & Arnold, U. (2001). Electronic procurement in supply chain management: An information economics-based analysis of electronic markets. *Journal of Supply Chain Management*, *37*(4), 43–49. doi:10.1111/j.1745-493X.2001.tb00112.x

Hartley, J. L., Lane, M. D., & Duplaga, E. D. (2006). Exploring the barriers to the adoption of e-auctions for sourcing. *International Journal of Operations & Production Management*, *26*(1–2), 202–221. doi:10.1108/01443570610641675

Kumar, N., & Peng, Q. (2006). Strategic alliances in e-government procurement. *International Journal of Electronic Business*, *4*(2), 136–145.

Puschmann, T., & Alt, R. (2005). Successful use of e-procurement in supply chains. *Supply Chain Management*, *10*(2), 122–133. doi:10.1108/13598540510589197

Salleh, N. A. M., Rohde, F., & Green, P. (2006). The effect of enacted capabilities on adoption of a government electronic procurement system by Malaysian SMEs. *Electronic Markets*, *16*(4), 292–311. doi:10.1080/10196780600999676

Schoenherr, T., & Mabert, V. A. (2006). Bundling for B2B procurement: Current state and best practices. *International Journal of Integrated Supply Management*, *2*(3), 189–213. doi:10.1504/IJISM.2006.008593

Yu, C. C. (2008). Building a value centric e-government service framework based on a business model perspective. *Lecture Notes in Computer Science*, *5184*, 160–171. doi:10.1007/978-3-540-85204-9_14

Chapter 6
E-Procurement:
What Really Matters in B2B E-Reverse Auctions

Davide Aloini
University of Pisa, Italy

Riccardo Dulmin
University of Pisa, Italy

Valeria Mininno
University of Pisa, Italy

ABSTRACT

Although the implementation of e-auction events is not all that new, a current interest in understanding main issues involved in its implementation exists, especially in a business to business (B2B) environment. A clear will to classify and systematize the numerous variables directly or indirectly affecting e-auction suitability and final performance determination is evident also from previous conceptual literature contributions. Nevertheless a lack of empirical work in this field is evident. This work provides a contribution to the body of knowledge on critical factors impacting on e-Reverse Auctions (e-RA) performance in a B2B context. Based on an explorative factor analysis addressed to a panel of academic experts and practitioners, it aims at identifying the main factors affecting price and process performance in B2B e-RA.

DOI: 10.4018/978-1-4666-2119-0.ch006

1. INTRODUCTION

E-Government (eGov) is now pervasive in public sector since it has enabled improvements to internal and external processes and activities. One new and emerging area of eGov is the "Dynamic Purchasing System" as defined in article 1.6 of the Procurement Directive 2004/18/EC; it uses the chronology of a tender procedure, introducing modern purchasing techniques, such as electronic auctions.

Dynamic purchasing system is a completely electronic process for making commonly used purchases which opens throughout its validity to any economic operator which satisfies the selection criteria and has submitted an indicative tender that complies with the specification. Such techniques help to increase competition and streamline public purchasing, particularly in terms of the savings in time and money which their use will allow (Özbilgin and Imamolu, 2011).

Among ICT tools able to reduce different transaction and communication costs, such as e-catalogues, dynamic auctions, intelligent agent applications, e-Reverse Auctions (eRAs) are used to obtain more favourable pricing, shorten time and reduce costs for negotiation.

Compared to traditional negotiation mechanisms in purchasing processes, the significant benefits and savings which e-Reverse Auctions have delivered to many companies in recent years, both in terms of transaction cost reductions and impact on business profitability (Klein, 1997; Van Heck, 1998), have persuaded many consulting firms to hype the advantages of e-Reverse Auctions and thus powered their popularity (Brunelli, 2000). Recent surveys by Forrester and Purchasing magazine (Hannon, 2003; Hannon, 2004; Forrester, 2002; Forrester, 2003) showed that 15-25% of respondents had used e-auctions and 10-15% expected to use them; in addition Forrester predicts that as much as 50 US$ billion could be spent through this intention. The rising number of Business Service providers addressing e-Sourcing and eAuctioning services to industrial companies is today an evident proof of firms' expectations and interest in the e-auction phenomena. According to the Institute for Supply Management, 25% of US companies were using this tool in 2004 (www.napm.org); the findings are confirmed in Purchasing's annual benchmark e-sourcing survey, in which adoption of e-RA by US companies was found to evolve from 27% in 2004 to 31% in 2006 (Hannon, 2006).

The growth of e-commerce has, in fact, led to many business to business auctions for goods whose trade was previously negotiated bilaterally. This is true not only for standard goods (commodity) but also for non-standard products especially when the true value or market price is uncertain. This evidence underscores the need to analyze the mechanism of online auctions and to investigate into what really matters in B2B e-RA design (Klemperer, 2002). In fact, even if auction theorists have made important progress on these topics, for example in economic theory, auction theory, finance, law, most of these contributes are of quite low utility for actually designing e-auctions.

The purpose of this work is to identify and examine the main factors which explain price and process performance in B2B e-RA (final price gain vs cost saving and increased productivity of the negotiation process) and to expand the scope of information on this field in order to study e-RA feasibility and support the formulation of management actions during the e-auction design phase. With this aim a set of relevant variables were selected from literature and an exploratory analysis, based on an online survey to academics experts and practitioners from 4 European Business Providers, was performed.

The chapter is structured as follows. Firstly an overview of the theoretical foundations of e-auction performance and potential critical factors is presented. Next, after presenting the methodological approach, the exploratory factor analysis is demonstrated. Finally the results of the empirical study are reported; the chapter concludes with a discussion of the theoretical and managerial implications of performance drivers in B2B e-auction design, the limitations and further research.

2. LITERATURE REVIEW

The implementation of e-procurement initiatives has been an intensively researched field in the last decade, nevertheless a current interest in understanding issues involved in its implementation still exists, especially in a web-enabled environment. (Angeles and Nath, 2007). This is also the case for B2B e-auctions and related design processes.

Auctions have been widely studied in the fields of economics and operation research. Many economic studies have examined auctions from theoretical and empirical perspectives (Kagel 1995; McAfee and McMillan 1987; Milgrom 1989) dealing almost exclusively with forward auctions. These branches of research generally have mainly focused on identifying optimal auction design in various settings (Rothkopf, 1998; Klemperer P, 1999; Kelly and Steinberg, 2000) and on the "winner's course problem" (Kagel and Levin, 1986; Kagel, Levin, Battalio and Meyer, 1989).

As auctions moved to the Internet, researches extended modeling studies in this new changing and dynamic environment to explore online auctions. Although, in fact, some similarities exist between the online reverse auctions and traditional auctions, several significant differences (including product type, winner determination, interdependent bidding practices, and emphasis on bidder behaviour over context) make it difficult to generalize from the economic literature to industrial settings (Jap, 2003).

Looking at the research objective, literature on e-RA consists of three main streams of research:

- One focuses on the e-RA process features and impacts on purchasing process efficiency (Emiliani, 2000; Mabert and Skeels, 2002; Meier et al., 2002; Gattiker, Huang and Schwarz, 2007), including comparisons with traditional negotiation processes and potential integration strategies in the overall purchasing process (Smeltzer, 2000; Hur Hartley, Lane and Duplaga, 2006).
- A second stream analyzes the auction feasibility, i.e conditions and impediments to the adoption and implementation of e-RA (Hur et al., 2006; Mabert and Schoenherr, 2001; Hartley et al. 2004; Hur, Mabert and Hartley, 2007). It deals with influencing factors, prerequisites, critical success factors, and auction design and format related characteristics (Jap, 2002; Beal et al., 2003; Skjøtt-Larsen, Kotzab and Grieger, 2003).
- A third stream of research addresses the impact of e-RA (from a post adoption view) on the market context and in particular on the buyer-supplier relationship and trust (Beall et al., 2003; Smeltzer and Carr, 2003; Bartezzaghi and Ronchi, 2005; Jap, 2007; Amelinckx, Muylle and Lievens, 2008).

Exploring more in depth the "auction feasibility" branch from the research methodology perspective, it can be seen that the majority of research is conceptual, prescriptive and descriptive in nature. Parente, Venkataraman, Fizel and Millet (2004) suggest a broad conceptual model addressing the basis for future research in online auctions; Amelinckx et al. (2008), based on an extensive literature review and multiple case study research, develop a conceptual model on auction outcomes including posits organizational and project antecedents.

Empirical studies in B2B e-auction's ground and in particular on critical success or performance determinant factors, are in fact relatively young (Lucking-Reiley, 1999; Wagner and Schwab, 2004) and mainly based on qualitative interviews and case studies (Wagner and Schwab, 2004):

- A principal research branch focus on bidder/seller behavior dynamics (Bajari and Hortacsu, 2003; Bapna, Goes, Gupta and Jin, 2004);
- A second field of research concerns the impact of auction features on process performances (Carter, Kaufmann, Beall, Carter, Hendrick and Peterson, 2004; Kaufmann and Carter, 2004; Millet, Parente, Fizel and Venkatraman, 2004; Lucking-Reiley, 2007);
- Several case studies (Handfield, 2002; Emiliani, 2004) have examined factors related to e-auction success or failure.

Empirical research concerning the impact of auction features on final price or focusing on auction price prediction were only deployed in business to consumer (B2C) and consumer to consumer (C2C) markets by AI community (Wellman, 2002; Etzion et al., 2003; Wellman, 2004). Moreover to our best knowledge, there are no empirical-quantitative contributions directly investigating which factors affect price and process performance of an online auction in a B2B environment.

3. RESEARCH OBJECTIVE

This work is motivated by the need for solid empirical findings and contributions supporting the conceptual models or background on e-RA performance determinants in a B2B context (Parente at al., 2004; Amelinckx et al., 2008). The study investigates data gathered in an online survey in an attempt to identify the main factors driving e-auction success and tries to understand and systematize the complex relationships and dependences between the variables affecting auction suitability and final performance.

Assessing the suitability on a B2B e-RA and investigating critical success variables in order to provide the conditions for the event to be successful, is an ambitious and recurring task in literature. Nevertheless, e-auctions are complex processes and literature analyzes different features, in terms of auction class and parameters, market condition, characteristics of purchasing; moreover, variables are often described and organized differently (Walley and Fortin, 2005). For an effective execution of an e-auction in a B2B context and its appropriate integration with the main purchasing process, in fact, several conditions must exist (e.g. selecting the right product, assessing the appropriateness of the supply market). Such conditions for successful e-RA are spread throughout the literature and almost all authors provide suggestions based on their experience, interviews or case studies (Wagner and Schwab, 2004).

The "price" dimension is not the only one from which auction success should be considered, as purchasing price reduction is just one of the primary benefits of e-auctions. It is also important to consider process cost savings in assessing e-auction profitability. Emiliani and Stec (2002), argued that some savings would be lost due to various factors associated with the award decision, data integrity and additional business expenses.

In our analysis we address the auction performance problem from the perspective of the two following dimensions. The first dimension is "price efficiency" which directly analyzes savings on final price obtained for goods auctioned, and refers mainly to the reduction on final purchasing price. The second is "process efficiency" which refers to internal process cost savings due to e-auction adoption. Reverse auctions, in fact, force buyers to structure the bid prior to the event, to standardize the procurement process and to develop a strategy for groups of items;

for repeated auctions it means a shorter cycle time and increased productivity (Carter et al., 2004; Carter and Stevens, 2007). The Process Efficiency dimension includes reductions in some components of typical pre/post transactional costs such as negotiation and monitoring costs, due to improvement in operational activities:

- Total negotiation cycle time reduction (Pre-auction cycle time + Auction cycle time).
- Reduction of man-hours spent in non-value added activities such as comparison of different bid frameworks received in different times.
- Reduction of errors from paper based activities and manual data entry.
- Reduction of post transactional activities due to controversies.

However, many of these process improvements are difficult to quantify or estimate as cost reductions; moreover the relationship with the specific adopted negotiation tool is hard to isolate. This makes the "process" performance dimension harder to explore.

To our best knowledge existing research in this field has several limitations:

1. Many conceptual papers try to systematize the numerous variables affecting e-auction success and their complex relationship in a single comprehensive framework; however, there is a lack of empirical evidence supporting these models.
2. Several empirical works focus from different perspectives (both in B2B and most numerous in B2C and C2C field) on the impact of specific variables on auction success but only a few globally investigate these variables and their relationships.
3. Despite a clear distinction between auction "price" and "process" there still exists a lack of empirical contributions which focus on the extent to which different variables impact on these two factors.

This work aims to fill the gap in literature providing an empirical cross-sectorial study which directly investigates critical success factors impacting on "price" and "process" performance in B2B e-RA design. Evaluations on the relevance of variables were collected from the perceptions of a panel of academic experts and practitioners through an online survey. Finally, data were analyzed based on an Explorative Factor Analysis and the main driving factors identified and discussed.

4. RESEARCH METHODOLOGY

Factor Analysis (FA) is a well known statistical technique grounded on the fact that a series of observed variables or measures may be explained by a smaller number of non-observable hypothetical source variables, usually called "factors" (Pasquali, 2000).

This theory is based on the postulate that there exist "internal" attributes (unobservable characteristic of data) which are more fundamental than "surface" attributes (observable). These attributes (commonly referred to as "factors" or "latent variables") are not directly measurable, but they affect measures on surface attributes.

Main FA outcomes are: the common factors and the common factor weights (loadings) which represent the effect of a given factor on the surface attribute; common factor inter-correlations and communalities which provide a measure of relationships among factors and an evaluation of the surface attribute variance accounted for by the common factor.

FA is usually used both in an exploratory direction, to drive and support the conceptualization purpose, and in a confirmatory direction in order to test a previously developed model. Exploratory factor analysis (EFA) seeks to uncover the underlying structure of a relatively large set of variables.

Main phases of our EFA were: variables selection; sample and data collection; data analysis.

4.1. Variables Selection

Variables were selected from literature evidence (Parente et al. 2004; Kaufmann and Carter, 2003) and by semi-structured interviews to practitioners. In Table 1, variables and main literature sources are shown, according to six main conceptual groups, in order to simplify their interpretation.

4.2. Sample and Data Collection

In order to provide a relevant and significant feedback relative to the principal factors affecting price and process performance in e-auction based negotiations, a heterogeneous experts panel – representative of a highly qualified population, directly involved in the analyzed problem – was assembled from the industrial and academic world. This also enabled researchers to verify the consis-

Table 1. Selected variables

Group	Item	Measures	Main literature
Market Context	MC1 MC2 MC3 MC4	The concentration of supply market The volatility of supply market price The presence of a leading firm The number of potential suppliers	*Parente et al. (2004); Wagner and Schwab (2004); Lösch and Lambert (2007)*
Supplier Characteristic	SC1 SC2 SC3 SC4 SC5 SC6	Supplier reputation Total number of firm's employees Total turnover Relative Dimension Company IT culture E-commerce confidence	*Min (1994); Choi (1996); Carter et al. (2004); Walley and Fortin (2005); Lösch and Lambert (2007); Hur et al. (2007)*
Buyer Characteristic	BC1 BC2 BC3 BC4 BC5 BC6	Buyer reputation Total number of firm's employees Total turnover Relative Dimension Company IT culture E-commerce confidence	*Min (1994); Choi (1996); Carter et al. (2004); Walley and Fortin (2005); Hur et al. (2007); Lösch and Lambert (2007)*
Buyer-Supplier Relationship	BS1 BS2 BS3 BS4 BS5	Age of relationship Relative contractual power Dimensional gap IT / E-commerce gap Information gap	*Jaworski and Kohli (1993); Parente (1998); Carter et al. (2004); Parente et al. (2004); Lösch and Lambert (2007)*
Product Characteristic	PC1 PC2 PC3 PC4 PC5 PC6	Product Type Strategic importance of auctioned goods for final product/service Product standardization or customization degree Description complexity of auctioned item Repeatability of auction event Total value/size of auctioned lot	*Klein (1997), Jap (2002), Levi, Klein, Dorfer and Wu (2003), Parente et al. (2004), Wagner and Schwab (2004), Hur et al. (2007), Lösch and Lambert (2007)*
Auction Process	AC1 AC2 AC3 AC4 AC5 AC6 AC7 AC8 AC9 AC10 AC11	Auction type Aggregation mechanism Winner algorithm Minimum bid setting Reverse price level setting Product information disclosure Process information disclosure Timing mechanism (e.g. auto-extension) Opening bid Total number of bidders Bid visibility	*Jap (2002), Bajari and Hortacsu (2003), Beall at al. (2003), Pinker, Seidmann and Vakrat (2003), Carter et al. (2004), Millet et al. (2004), Parente et al. (2004), Wagner and Schwab (2004), Lucking-Reiley et al. (2007)*

tency between business practices from the point of view of practitioners, consultants and academics.

A reasoned sample of academic auction experts was selected using web search facilities, offered by some major publishers (Emerald, Science Direct, IEEE-Xplore), and analyzing references from articles. 335 different authors of works explicitly dealing with online auctions were identified from all over the world. As for the practitioners' sample, 120 senior consultants with direct experience in e-auction event designing from 4 European Business Providers (i.e. market subjects providing facilities and services supporting companies in auction design and setting), whose identities will be here kept secret, were identified.

A introductive e-mail and an official presentation letter with the survey invitation, the website and personal id and password, were sent to all of them asking for their support. The potential effective size of the academic population was reduced to 435, as 20 of them were not reachable or had left their companies. The initial mailing elicited 93 usable responses. A follow-up mailing was sent two weeks after the initial mailing. An additional 65 usable responses were returned. The total number of usable responses was 158. Therefore, the overall response rate for this study was about 36% (32% for academics and 42% for industry's sample).

The respondents were asked to separately indicate the level of importance (on a seven-point Likert scale) of the selected variables affecting online auction performance: the "price" gain and the efficiency of the negotiation "process", as perceived. Then an online survey was specifically designed to investigate the impact of the contextual and technical variables identified in the conceptual framework both on auction "price" and "process performance". With this aim the answering section of each question was divided in two parts.

The design process followed the stages outlined by Churchill (1991). Variables in the questionnaire were selected from and based on previous studies (Parente, 2004; Kaufmann and Carter, 2003), content validity was ensured through a comprehensive review of the literature, interviews with practitioners and discussions with a number of executives and experts in the e-auction field. The interviews resulted in minor modifications to the wording and definition provided in some measurement items, which were finally accepted. The refined measurement items were included in the final survey questionnaire.

The questionnaire consists of three areas: the first part deals with personal data and some company information; in the second part, variables which were thought to impact on e-auction performance are presented; in the third one some open questions are posed.

Variables were grouped in three sections according to the conditions of the market, characteristics of the product and parameters of the auction. The respondents were asked to separately indicate the level of importance of the factors affecting the online auction price performance" and "process performance", as perceived. These factors were scored using a seven-point Likert scale, where 1 corresponds to "very unimportant" and 7 to "very important".

At the end of this first section two open questions are reported in order to investigate the most important factors (maximum 5) that respondents consider as strongly impacting on "price" and "process" auction performance and that they take into consideration during the auction setting process.

4.3. Planned Steps of the Analysis

Data collected were analyzed according to the following steps (supported by SPSS software):

A. Preliminary Analysis.

A preliminary analysis on data was conducted in order to avoid potential bias (non-response bias). Moreover a descriptive overview of information collected by the online survey was reported in order to globally discuss respondent profiles of the final sample, to present the final response rate and to give directions about the respondents "impact perceptions" of each variable on auction performance (by considerations on the means and standard deviations of collected data).

B. Variables Standardization.

This was automatically performed by the software in order to avoid scale and other dimensional problems (data should have average equal to 0 and standard deviation 1).

C. Factor Analysis

The planned steps included in the factor analysis are:

1. Kaiser-Meyer-Olkin (KMO) sample adequacy test and Bartlett significance test on data. We used the KMO and Bartlett test in order to support the choice for a factor analysis on data. The Kaiser-Meyer-Olkin measurement of sampling adequacy is an index for comparing the magnitudes of the observed correlation coefficients to the magnitudes of the partial correlation coefficients (refer to SPSS User's Guide). Large values for the KMO measure indicate that a factor analysis of the variables is suitable. This measure should be greater than 0.5 for a satisfactory factor analysis to proceed. Bartlett's test of sphericity, on the other hand, is used to test the null hypothesis that the variables in the population correlation matrix are uncorrelated. If the observed significance level (P-value) is <.005, it is small enough to reject the hypothesis (at the α level). In this way it is possible to conclude that the strength of the relationship among variables is strong and so proceed with the factor analysis.
2. Factors Extraction. The selected extraction method used was the Principal Component Analysis (PCA). PCA is mostly suggested for data reduction purpose. Both the PCA and (Principal Factor Analysis) PFA method were tested on data set but no relevant differences in data aggregation were identified. The Kaiser criterion, instead, was adopted for dropping the least important factors from the analysis (Kaiser, 1960). The rule suggests dropping all components with eigenvalues under 1.0; nevertheless it may overestimate or underestimate the true number of factors; Lance, Butts and Michels (2006), based on a simulation study, suggest it usually overestimates the true number of factors, sometimes severely. So even if the Kaiser criterion is the default in SPSS and most computer programs, when used as the sole cut-off criterion and an over check, such as the Scree test (Costello and Osborne, 2005), may be opportune.
3. Factors Rotation. A rotation of the factor matrix was performed according to the Varimax rotation method with the aim of improving factors interpretability. It attempts to achieve loadings of ones and zeros in the columns of the component matrix in order to explicit and clarify data patterns (Garson, 2008).

D. Factors Interpretation.

The most recurrent literature threshold for loadings in factor analysis is .7 or higher in order to confirm that independent variables identified a priori are represented by a particular factor (the .7 level corresponds to about half of the variance in the indicator being explained by the factor) (Garson, 2008). However, in real-life, data may well not meet this criterion so, particularly for exploratory purposes, a lower level is usually accepted (such as .4 for the central factor and .25 for other factors) (Raubenheimer, 2004). In any event, extracted factors should be interpreted in the light of theory, not by arbitrary cutoff levels; so they were named, discussed and compared with the most relevant literature evidences.

5. ANALYSIS AND RESULTS

In this section results from the main steps of the data analysis are presented as follows: in sub-section 5.1 the preliminary analysis is reported, in sub-section 5.2 a brief descriptive analysis on data is presented, the in sub-section 5.3 we resume steps form the factor analysis, extraction and rotation. Finally factors interpretation is presented in section 6.

5.1. Preliminary Analysis

An analysis of a non-response bias was conducted to assess the extent of the potential bias in the data collected. We administered the survey twice and set a cut-off date to classify the responses into one of the two mailings. A comparison of the early (those who responded to the first e-mail or letter) and the late (those who responded to the second e-mail reminder) respondents was carried out to test for the non-response bias (Armstrong and Overton, 1977). The 158 respondents were divided into two groups based on their response wave (first and second waves). T-tests were performed on the responses of the two groups. At the 5% significance level, there were no significant differences between the responses of the two groups. Although the results do not rule out the possibility of a non-response bias, they suggest that non-response may not be a problem to the extent that the late respondents represent the opinions of non-respondents.

5.2. Descriptive Analysis

Table 2 and Table 3 show the profiles of the respondents. Note that they are quite equally distributed according to the respondents profile between Academics and Practitioners, all respondents having a long experience in the auction field (more than 7 years) and they are mostly from Europe and North America.

In Table 4, instead, we report mean and standard deviation (S.d.) of each variable on the whole sample. This could give an overall idea of the respondents perception of the variable's impact on auction performance. From a general overview, according to the mean value, it seems that the main relevant variables for price performance mostly belong to the Market Context, Product Characteristics and Auction Process Group; for process performance, on the contrary, Market Context variables seem to be less important.

For an easier understanding of the difference between price and process perceptions, means and s.d. were also drawn in a radar graph (Figure 1). The perception of variables impact on process performance measures seems to be moderate.

A further comparison of the academic and practitioner perceptions was undertaken (Figure 2) in order to catch a different view of the problem. No relevant differences appeared, with the exception of the Market Context group's variables for the Process performance dimension (Figure 2.b – variables 1-5), and some of the auction parameters in the Auction Process group.

Finally, in Figures 3 and 4, a classification of answers to the open questions and respective

Table 2. Response rate

Location	Number of contacts	Respondents	Response rate
North America	186	51	
Europe	189	73	
Others	70	34	
Tot	435	158	36%

Table 3. Respondents profile

Respondent Profiles	Number of responses
Academics	108
Practitioners (From Business Service Provider)	50
Total	158

Table 4. Mean and Standard Deviation of observed variables

Item ID	Measures	Price		Process	
		Mean*	S.d.	Mean	S.d.
	Market Context				
1 -MC1	The concentration of supply market	**5,54**	**1,47**	4,21	1,71
2 -MC2	The volatility of supply market price	4,54	1,58	3,80	1,76
3 -MC3	The presence of a leading firm	**4,79**	1,75	3,94	1,90
4 -MC4	The number of potential suppliers	**5,79**	**1,25**	**4,69**	1,74
	Supplier Characteristic				
5 -SC1	Supplier reputation	3,92	1,64	4,17	1,96
6 -SC2	Total number of firm's employees	2,63	**1,51**	2,93	1,64
7 -SC3	Total turnover	2,96	1,58	2,91	1,60
8 -SC4	Relative Dimension	2,85	**1,55**	2,87	**1,48**
9 -SC5	Company IT culture	3,30	**1,49**	4,45	1,80
10 -SC6	E-commerce confidence	3,61	1,54	**4,70**	1,56
	Buyer Characteristic				
11 -BC1	Buyer reputation	**4,65**	1,64	4,24	1,71
12 -BC2	Total number of firm's employees	2,93	1,64	3,23	1,64
13 -BC3	Total turnover	3,72	1,81	3,33	1,69
14 -BC4	Relative Dimension	3,12	1,67	3,16	**1,55**
15 -BC5	Company IT culture	3,79	1,74	**4,87**	1,67
16 -BC6	E-commerce confidence	3,97	1,66	**5,03**	1,56
	Buyer-Supplier Relationship				
17 -BS1	Age of relationship	3,90	**1,43**	4,16	1,72
18 -BS2	Relative contractual power	**5,18**	1,57	4,13	1,64
19 -BS3	Dimensional gap	3,82	**1,54**	3,33	**1,53**
20 -BS4	IT / E-commerce gap	3,16	1,65	3,72	1,72
21 -BS5	Information gap	**4,73**	1,76	4,26	1,77
	Product Characteristic				
22 -PC1	Product Type	**4,84**	1,75	4,24	1,70
23 -PC2	Strategic importance of auctioned goods for final product/service	**5,29**	1,65	**4,87**	1,64
24 -PC3	Product standardization or customization degree	4,59	1,62	**5,10**	1,62
25 -PC4	Description complexity of auctioned item	4,28	1,67	**5,10**	1,62
26 -PC5	Repeatability of auction event	**5,22**	1,57	3,76	1,64
27 -PC6	Total value/size of auctioned lot	**4,84**	1,67	3,96	1,65
	Auction Process				
28 -AC1	Auction type	**5,13**	**1,53**	**5,03**	1,74
29 -AC2	Aggregation mechanism	**4,84**	**1,47**	**4,85**	1,67
30 -AC3	Winner algorithm	**5,23**	**1,52**	4,33	1,80
31 -AC4	Minimum bid setting	4,19	**1,49**	3,25	1,77
32 -AC5	Reverse price level setting	**5,00**	**1,54**	3,67	1,78
33 -AC6	Product information disclosure	**4,91**	**1,50**	**5,04**	1,65
34 -AC7	Process information disclosure	**4,70**	1,57	**5,29**	**1,51**
35 -AC8	Timing mechanism (e.g. autoextension)	**5,14**	**1,41**	4,14	1,81
36 -AC9	Opening bid	4,13	**1,41**	3,59	1,59
37 -AC10	Total number of bidders	**5,93**	**1,28**	4,45	1,76
38 -AC11	Bid visibility	**5,44**	**1,28**	4,01	1,88

frequency rate are reported both for the price and process dimension. It appears that, as for the price dimension, top rated variables belong mostly to the market and auction technical fields: Market Context (i.e. Competition of Supply Market), Product Characteristics (i.e. Product type, Product Information) and Auction Process (i.e. Pre-auction phase, Auction design, Auction type, Value and Dimension of lot). As for the process dimension on the other hand, top rated variables belong mainly to the negotiation procedure (i.e. IT infrastructure, Clear rules, Clear documentation, Product type and users' Training).

Figure 1. Means and Standard Deviations of perceived variables impact

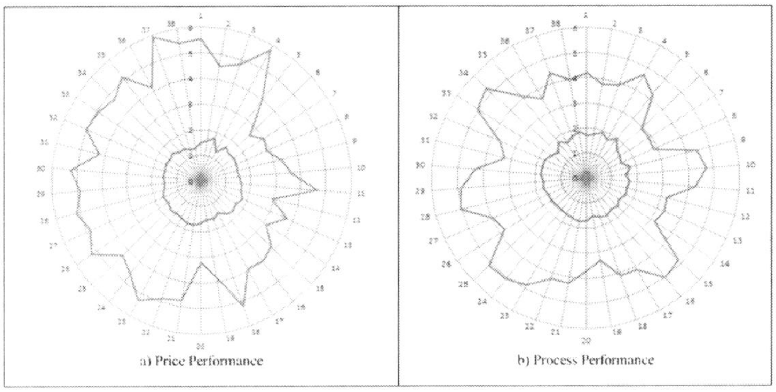

Figure 2. Business Providers and Academic perceived variables impact

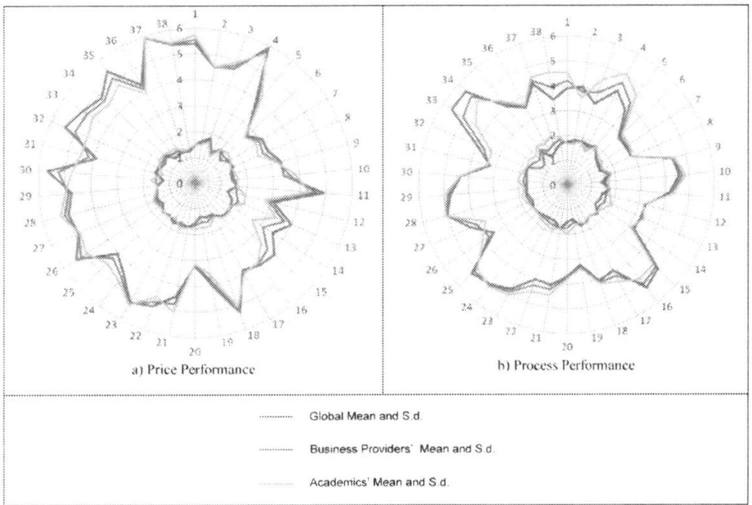

5.3. Factor Analysis

Before going on with the FA analysis and in order to support our choice, the Kaiser-Meyer-Olkin (KMO) sample adequacy test and the Bartlett significance test were separately performed on a price and process data sample. Looking at the table below (Table 5 and 6), related to the price data, the KMO measure is 0.711 (it is a "moderate" but acceptable value for FA), while the Bartlett's test of sphericity is significant (i.e. its associated probability is less than 0.05). This means that the correlation matrix is not an identity matrix and we can induce that the FA is a suitable strategy of analysis. The same conclusion can be carried out for the process data sample since the KMO measure is 0.76 and the Bartlett's test is significant too (Tables 5).

As previously reported, the exploratory analysis was carried out following the PCA extraction methodology and the Kaiser extraction criteria. Lastly, a Varimax rotation was undertaken on the extracted factors. In Tables 7 and 8 rotated matrix for price and process data sample

Figure 3. Classification of answers to the open question on price performance

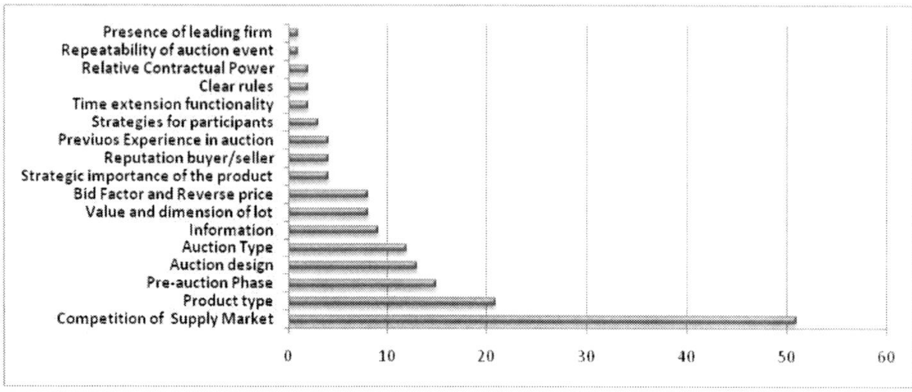

Figure 4. Classification of answers to the open question on process performance

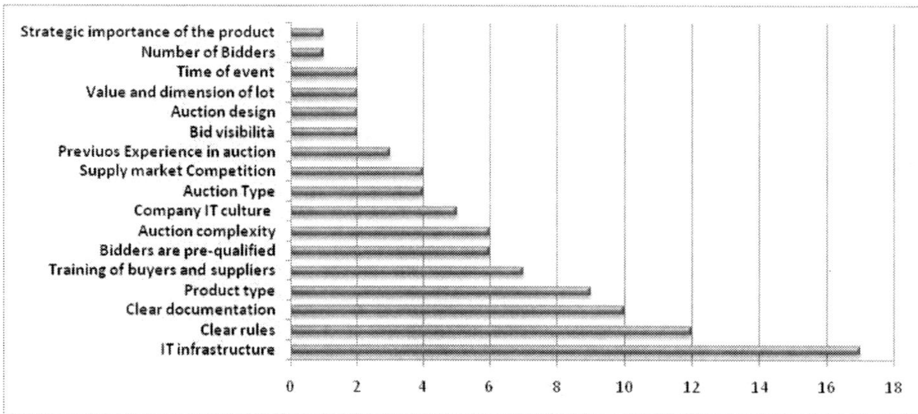

Table 5.KMO and Bartlett significance test on price data

KMO and Bartlett's test		
Kaiser-Meyer-Olkin measure of sampling adequacy		0,711
Bartlett's test of sphericity	Approximate Chi-square	1674,14
	D.f.	703
	Sig.	<0.000*

Table 6. KMO and Bartlett significance test on process data

KMO and Bartlett's test		
Kaiser-Meyer-Olkin measure of sampling adequacy		0,76
Bartlett's test of sphericity	Approximate Chi-square	1937,65
	D.f.	703
	Sig.	<0.000*

Table 7. Rotated matrix for price data

Item: Variables	Factors (Components)								
	I1	I2	I3	I4	I5	I6	I7	I8	I9
6. SC2: Total number of firm's employees (supplier)	0.68								
7. SC3: Total turnover (supplier)	0.85								
8. SC4: Relative Dimension (supplier)	0.88								
12. BC2: Total number of firm's employees (buyer)	0.67								
13. BC3: Total turnover (buyer)	0.76								
14. BC4 Relative Dimension (buyer)	0.76								
9. SC5: Company IT culture (supplier)		0.77							
10. BC6: E-commerce confidence (supplier)		0.81							
15. BC5: Company IT culture (buyer)		0.71							
16. BC6: E-commerce confidence (buyer)		0.82							
20. BS4: IT / E-commerce gap		0.58							
22. PC1: Product Type			0.69						
23. PC2: Strategic importance of auctioned goods for final product			0.62						
24. PC3: Product standardization or customization degree			0.68						
25. PC4: Description complexity of auctioned item			0.59						
26. PC5: Repeatability of auction event			0.71						
27. PC6: Total value/size of auctioned lot			0.55						
30. AC3: Winner algorithm				0.69					
31. AC4: Minimum bid setting				0.62					
32. AC5: Reverse price level setting				0.78					
36. AC9: Opening bid				0.47					
28. AC1: Auction type					0.79				
29. AC2: Aggregation mechanism					0.79				
5. SC1: Supplier reputation						0.72			
11. BC1: Buyer reputation						0.40			
17. BS1: Age of relationship						0.72			
21. BS5: Information gap						0.41			
4. MC4: The number of potential suppliers							0.79		
37. AC10: Total number of bidders							0.79		
1. MC1: The concentration of supply market								0.50	
2. MC2: The volatility of supply market price								0.62	
3. MC3: The presence of a leading firm								0.72	
33. AC6: Product information disclosure									0.42
34. AC7: Process information disclosure									0.54
35. AC8: Timing mechanism (e.g. auto-extension)									0.82
Cumulative Explained Variance (0-1)	0.23	0.34	0.42	0.48	0.54	0.58	0.62	0.66	**0.70**

Table 8. Rotated matrix for process data

Items: Variables	Factors (Components)							
	O1	O2	O3	O4	O5	O6	O7	O8
6. SC2: Total number of firm's employees (supplier)	0.78							
7. SC3: Total turnover (supplier)	0.80							
8. SC4: Relative Dimension (supplier)	0.79							
11. BC1: Buyer reputation	0.42							
12. BC2: Total number of firm's employees (buyer)	0.81							
13. BC3: Total turnover (buyer)	0.73							
14. BC4 Relative Dimension (buyer)	0.80							
20. BS4: IT / E-commerce gap	0.48							
26. PC5: Repeatability of auction event		0.46						
30. AC3: Winner algorithm		0.59						
31. AC4: Minimum bid setting		0.84						
32. AC5: Reverse price level setting		0.77						
35. AC8: Timing mechanism (e.g. auto-extension)		0.71						
36. AC9: Opening bid		0.75						
37. AC10: Total number of bidders		0.60						
38. AC11: Bid visibility		0.64						
17. BS1: Age of relationship			0.62					
18. BS2: Relative contractual power			0.83					
19. BS3: Dimensional gap			0.77					
27. PC6: Total value/size of auctioned lot			0.42					
15. BC5: Company IT culture (buyer)				0.58				
16. BC6: E-commerce confidence (buyer)				0.68				
33. AC6: Product information disclosure				0.66				
34. AC7: Process information disclosure				0.75				
28. AC1: Auction type					0.79			
29. AC2: Aggregation mechanism					0.79			
9. SC5: Company IT culture (supplier)						0.81		
10. BC6: E-commerce confidence (supplier)						0.87		
28. PC1: Product Type							0.52	
29. PC2: Strategic importance of auctioned good for final product							0.77	
30. PC3: Product standardization or customization degree							0.59	
31. PC4: Description complexity of auctioned item							0.61	
1. MC1: The concentration of supply market								0.76
3. MC3: The presence of a leading firm								0.50
4. MC4: The number of potential suppliers								0.71
5. SC1: Supplier reputation								0.55
Cumulative Explained Variance	0.25	0.37	0.47	0.53	0.58	0.62	0.66	**0.70**

are presented. Eleven factors (eigenvalues>1) were retained for the price issue and ten for the process, one representing 75 percent of the explained variance; the threshold for factor retention was 0.4.

In this way, by using factor analysis, common factors were generated grouping variables explaining basic characteristics of a specific area. Eleven factors were identified (Table 7) in the price data sample, however just nine were considered relevant for our proposal since the last two components were "unstable" and characterized by few and conceptually heterogeneous variables. The nine main factors are: General Firms' Features (I1), IT Culture (I2), Product Characteristics (I3), Auction Settings (I4), Auction Class (I5), Trust (I6), Number of Participants (I7), Market Context (I8) and Information Process (I9). For the same reasons, also in process dimension, just eight of ten identified factors were considered relevant. These are: General Firms' Features (O1), Auction Settings (O2), Buyer-Supplier Relationships (O3), Buyer's IT Culture and Information Process (O4), Auction Class (O5), Supplier's IT Culture (O6), Product Characteristics (O7), Market Context (O8).

6. DISCUSSION

As indicated earlier, in this exploratory study a high number of observed values (p=38), and a relatively small number of responses (n=158) were eventually used. The responses to the variables ratio (n/p) is almost 4:1. Hence caution in interpreting the results is needed. The importance of sample size and data quality is essential in FA. Usually n/p ratio is adopted as a predictor of stability in factor structures. Based on a simulative study Costello and Osborne (2005) demonstrated that even samples with the smallest N:p ratios produced correct solutions. In any case when strong data are available (i.e. with uniformly high communalities, low cross-loadings and variables loadings strongly on each factor) significant directions can still be obtained from the analysis.

Data from the online survey are, however, significant given that respondents are representative of a highly qualified population; in addition the more unstable factors were dropped from the analysis and discussion.

A careful examination of outcomes revealed a number of "common" factors recurring both in the Price and Process dimension, others factors, instead, are more "specific" and present some singularity (Figure 5).

In the following sub-sections, we firstly report common factors, clarifying which variables they explain and comparing them with literature evidences. Then, we discuss specific factors, discriminating between price and process dimension.

6.1. Common Factors

Common factors mostly confirm findings reported in previous conceptual frameworks as suggested by Parente et al. (2004) or Amelinckx et al. (2008). Main outcomes are:

General Firms' Features (I1 - O1)

The first common factor (I1 and O1) covers the traditional firm's characteristics (i.e. Buyer or supplier firm's employees (SC2 - BC2), Total turnover (SC3 – BC3), Relative dimension (SC4

Figure 5. Common and specific factors

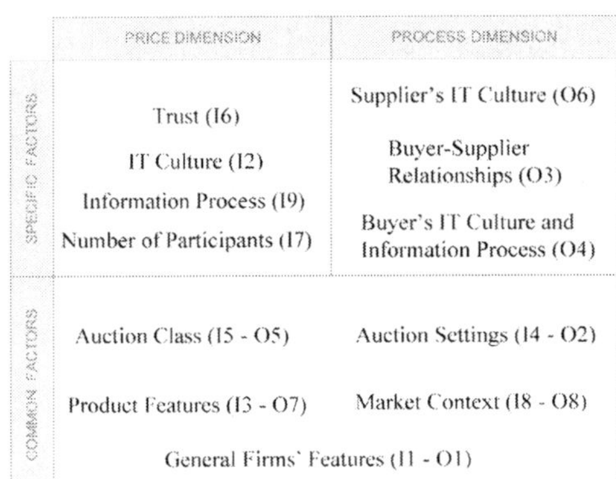

– BC4); factor O1 also includes Buyer reputation (BC1) and IT / E-commerce gap (BS4)) and was called "General Firm's Features". As reported by Parente et al. (2004) and other previous research (Ellram, 1990), such features strongly influence the market and process context in which procurement exchange occurs.

From a managerial point of view, critical buying mass and other benefits such as volume discount, process cost saving, contractual power and other variables which are indirectly influenced by a firm's profile, could have a significant weight on auction players motivation to competition and finally on price reduction. Recommendations for these elements to be included in the pre-auction phase for an earlier screening of potential suppliers are recurrent in literature since they could influence the winner determination algorithm and post negotiation phase, especially for multi-attribute competitions.

Product Features (I3 - O7)

Factors I3 and O7 were called "Product Features", they include Product Type (PC1), The strategic importance of auctioned goods for final product/service (PC2), Product standardization or customization degree (PC3), Description complexity of auctioned item (PC4). Repeatability of auction events (PC5) and Total value/size of auctioned lot (PC6) appears only in factor I3. In accordance with Parente et al. (2004), product attributes, could modify auction costs, dynamics and players motivation. Klein (1997) suggested that a specific auction format may be better for certain types of products; as an aside, Jap (2007) also finds that e-RA can yield price savings but that these savings are product category-specific. In scientific literature a number of researchers investigating on the impact of product characteristics on e-auction suitability, assert that the following set of variables can affect the online negotiation process:

A. Product class, buying situation (New Buy, Rebuy, Straight Rebuy) (Faris, Robinson and Wind, 1967) and Strategic Importance (Kraljic, 1983);
B. Product standardization or customization degree (Parente et al., 2004);
C. Description complexity (Parente et al., 2004; Amelinckx et al., 2008);
D. Repeatability of auction event (Carter et al., 2004).

Purchasing organization should consider that the variables here presented are correlated with relative value as perceived by buyers and sellers, process managerial complexity and business risk perception. These aspects impact negotiation complexity and negotiation costs of the auction and information process, auction cost amortization as well as supplier motivation to e-auction tool adoption, supplier adaptation and opportunistic/collusive behaviors. So effectiveness, efficiency and the dynamics of the auction process, motivation to competition, price acceptance thresholds and finally auction results could be affected.

Auction Settings (I4 - O2) and Auction Class (I5 - O5)

Factors I4 - O2 and I5 - O5 were called respectively "Auction settings" and Auction classes and we will discuss them together since they are both related with the auction process rules and dynamic. In agreement with Pinker et al (2003) the global set of rules for online auctions are here divided in two sub-sets, referred one to the mechanism design and the second to bid constraints.

The factor "Auction Settings" groups: Winner algorithm (AC3), Minimum bid setting (AC4), Reverse price level setting (AC5), Opening bid (AC9) for Price dimension, while in the process one it includes also: Repeatability of auction event (PC5), Timing mechanism (AC8), Total number of bidders (AC10), Bid visibility (AC11). The

"Auction Class" includes both in I5 and O5: Auction type (AC1), Aggregation mechanism (AC2).

These factors refer directly to the auction process variables that may impact on final performances, in particular auction mechanism and related characteristics. In literature a variety of auction formats is available and each format allows personalization through numerous parameter settings, and so thousands of different combinations are effectively configurable. Many authors have studied how auction type and other parameters can impact on final auction price, adopting different analysis approaches especially in the B2C and C2C context (Bajari and Hortacsu, 2003; Pinker et al., 2003; Lucking-Reiley et al., 2006). Millet et al. (2004) based on data from 14,188 auctions concluded that different auction formats result in different levels of supplier participation and price savings. Carter et al. (2004), for example suggest that auctions that utilize multiple lots are more likely to be successful and that the size of the auction in terms of monetary volume is in general significantly greater for "successful" auctions. So, these outcomes highlight that attention should be paid as to how design parameters could influence the participative behavior of consumers over time.

Market Context (I8 - O8)

Factor I8 covers: The concentration of supply market (MC1), The volatility of supply market price (MC2), The presence of a leading firm (MC3). Factor O8 includes: The concentration of supply market (MC1), The presence of a leading firm (MC3), The number of potential suppliers (MC4), Supplier reputation (SC1).

In both groups observed variables refers to supply market competition: more successful e-RA are characterized by higher levels of competition among suppliers (Beall et al. 2003; Carter et al. 2004; Amelinckx et al., 2008). Market conditions and information are relevant in good price definition; the bidding behavior, as also the buyer reserve price, depends on the buyers and sellers perception and confidence of market uncertainty. Market concentration gives important information on potential motivation to auction competition. In particular matching supply and demand concentration would make it possible to better understand the market attitude to auction sourcing and draw supplier motivation to compete in e-auctions. Also regularity of demand, market capacity, elasticity (Smeltzer and Carr, 2003) and price volatility may meaningfully emphasize this phenomena since this could induce suppliers to a more aggressive/protective behavior during negotiations.

6.2. Specific Factors

The other identified factors are more specific and present singularity according to the problem dimension. We have called them "Specific factors" and divided them into the following groups: a) "Price specific" factors and b) "Process specific" ones.

A. For Price dimension, we identified the following.

IT Culture (I2)

It groups: Company IT culture (SC5 - BC5), E-commerce confidence (SC6 - BC6) both supplier and buyer side and IT / E-commerce gap (BS4).

Information technology (IT) confidence and e-commerce attitude have an impact influence on adoption and learning rate of new tools and practices, influencing participation level in e-auctions. Carter et al. (2004) affirm that there is no initial relationship between the level of buyer experience and auction success, but suppliers tend to be unsuccessful in the initial events in which they participate. Parente et al. (2004) suggest the firm's own resources, experience and involvement in e-commerce-related activities can play an important role in online auction success and more experienced firms are likely to be high performers. Amelinckx et al. (2008) identified supplier "e-readiness" and supplier "e-sourcing expertise" as two important antecedents in e-auction outcomes.

Trust (I6)

The "Trust" factor includes: Supplier and Buyer reputation (SC1 - BC1), Age of relationship (BS1), Information gap (BS5). This factor has to do with several attributes such as quality and delivery reliability, economic performance, financial stability and others criteria traditionally used for supplier selection (Ellram, 1990; Min, 1994; Choi, 1996), which contribute to define a market supplier profile.

Trust should be considered in the preliminary stages of auction event settings, even if, as Walley and Fortin (2005) affirm, reputation is a subjective concept that resides in the mind of the buyer; so the inability to observe and quantify reputation makes it difficult to estimate its effect on price, wherever it exists. Also Losch and Lambert (2007) identify trust as an intrinsic feature of the buyer-supplier relationship.

The next two factors deal with the number of competitors and the process of information disclosure. The literature suggests that market potentiality and auction performance are strongly affected by the number of potential bidders, and that the process through which product or auction information is diffused to bidders is a critical aspect for success.

Number of Participants (I7)

The factor covers: The number of potential suppliers (MC4) and Total number of bidders (AC10).

Additional quasi-experimental research by Jap (2007), using 25 e-RA conducted by four buyers across different industries, shows that the larger the number of bidders, the larger the economic stakes, and the less visible the price, the more positive the impact on performance and interorganizational relationships.

Information Process (I9)

The factor aggregates: Product information disclosure (AC6), Process information disclosure (AC7), Timing mechanism (AC8). As reported by Beall et al. (2003) and Carter et al. (2004) the use of rank visibility instead of price visibility in the e-RA impact on auction performance.

B. As for Process dimension instead, we isolated the following.

Buyer-Supplier Relationships (O3)

Factor O3 includes: Age of relationship (BS1); Relative contractual power (BS2); Dimensional gap (BS3); Total value/size of auctioned lot (PC6).

As Parente et al. (2004) suggest "among the other characteristics that are important for auction success, interaction between buyer and seller is the most critical". Factors influencing companies relationships are numerous, many were identified in marketing research (Jaworski and Kohli, 1993; Parente, 1998; Finch, 2007). Many researches investigated this feature both to analyze causal relationship between existent buyer-supplier relationship and auction suitability and to understand the back impact of e-RA on them (Emiliani and Stec, 2005; Amelinckx et al., 2008).

It seems that long relationship between buyer and seller could prejudice auction applicability and motivation to competition. Carter et al. (2004) say that reverse auction are viewed more favorably by buyers than by suppliers; this condition, in same cases, may cause decrease in the level of trust, collusive behavior and less motivation to competition. Moreover, also other variables like contractual power, dimension and lot value are significant for contractual power equilibrium of a trading transaction. It depends on credibility and effectiveness by which a player may represent a treat for the other one and differences in contractual power can influence bidding behavior.

The last two groups (O4 and O6) give evidence of the importance of IT culture and e-commerce experience both buyer and supplier side. Pearcy and Giunipero (2006) suggest that possible explanation for the positive relationship between the frequency of use and price reduction for these two types of products is that "the experience gained through the frequent use of e-RA provides the buying firms with the knowledge required to maximize the purchase price reductions".

Buyer's IT Culture and Information Process (O4)

Factor O4 collects buyer-side: Company IT culture (BC5), E-commerce confidence (BC6), Product information disclosure (AC6), Process information disclosure (AC7).

Supplier's IT Culture (O6)

It brings together from supplier-side: Company IT culture (SC5) and E-commerce confidence (BC6).

As mentioned above factors I10, I11, O9 and O10 were excluded from discussion and further analysis as low significant and un-stable (low number of items on a factor, and low loadings). They should probably be included in some other factors or be dropped.

7. CONCLUSION, LIMITATIONS, AND FUTURE RESEARCH

This chapter presents an application of Factor Analysis in order to understand the complex relationships and dependences between variables affecting e-RA success. The study has reduced the total of 38 variables into a small set of common factors comparing price and process dimension of auction performance.

Nine main factors, belonging to the organizational, technical and market dimension were isolated and discussed starting from the known literature for the price performance and eight main factors for the process performance. Moreover comparing the two different perspectives, some commonalities and recurrent factors were highlighted: General Firms' Features (I1 - O1), Product Features (I3 - O7), Auction Settings (I4 - O2), Auction Class (I5 - O5) and Market Context (I8 - O8). Other specific factors were finally isolated and discussed separately according to the two dimensions.

Limitations for this study concern mainly the sample size, with an n/p ratio of 4:1 generalization problems occur. So even if data for the study are strong and significant, caution should be observed against drawing substantive conclusions and generalizations based on exploratory analysis. In this light, definitively our conclusions are not intended as normative but only suggest some directions and issues for further research. Confirmatory factor analysis as well as other modelling techniques are suggested since they can allow researchers to test hypothesis via inferential techniques.

It should be noted that the factor analysis does not give information on how deeply each factor impacts on final auction performance, about which there are common factors, constructs and dynamics explaining hidden relations in multivariate observed data.

The results achieved from the analysis contribute to the body of knowledge on critical factors impacting on e-Reverse Auction performance in a B2B context and aim to be a support to the formulation of managerial decisions in designing the auction event or process and a support to the definition of the most appropriate negotiation strategies. Such outcomes could also lead to a variables selection for the development of a quantitative model performing a sensitivity analysis on final auction performance.

REFERENCES

Amelinckx, I., Muylle, S., & Lievens, A. (2008). Extending electronic sourcing theory: An exploratory study of electronic reverse auction outcomes. *Electronic Commerce Research and Applications*, *7*(1), 119–133. doi:10.1016/j.elerap.2007.11.003

Angeles, R., & Nath, R. (2007). Business-to-business e-procurement: success factors and challenges to implementation. *Supply Chain Management: An International Journal*, *12*(2), 104–115. doi:10.1108/13598540710737299

Bajari, P., & Hortacsu, A. (2003). Winner's curse, reserve prices, and endogenous entry: Empirical insights from Ebay auctions. *The Rand Journal of Economics*, *3*(2), 329–355. doi:10.2307/1593721

Bapna, R., Goes, P., Gupta, A., & Jin, Y. (2004). User heterogeneity and its impact on electronic auction market design: An empirical explanation. *Management Information Systems Quarterly*, *28*(1), 21–43.

Bartezzaghi, E., & Ronchi, S. (2005). E-Sourcing in a buyer–operator–seller perspective: Benefits and criticalities. *Production Planning and Control*, *16*(4), 405–412. doi:10.1080/09537280500063459

Beall, S., Carter, C., Carter, P. L., Germer, T., Hendrick, T., & Jap, S. L. … Petersen, K. (2003). *The role of reverse auctions in strategic sourcing.* Retrieved from www.capsresearch.org

Brunelli, M. (2000). E-auctions online save millions for Quaker Oats and SmithKlineBeecham. *Purchasing*, *128*(4), S22.

Carter, C. R., Kaufmann, L., Beall, S., Carter, P. L., Hendrick, T. E., & Peterson, K. J. (2004). Reverse auctions-grounded theory from the buyer and supplier perspective. *Transportation Research Part E, Logistics and Transportation Review*, *40*, 229–254. doi:10.1016/j.tre.2003.08.004

Carter, C. R., & Stevens, C. K. (2007). Electronic reverse auction configuration and its impact on buyer price and supplier perceptions of opportunism: A laboratory experiment. *Journal of Operations Management*, *25*(5), 1035–1054. doi:10.1016/j.jom.2006.10.005

Choi, T. Y. (1996). An exploration of supplier selection practices across the supply chain. *Journal of Operations Management*, *14*(4), 333–343. doi:10.1016/S0272-6963(96)00091-5

Costello, A. B., & Osborne, J. W. (2005). Best practices in exploratory factor analysis: Four recommendations for getting the most from your analysis. *Practical Assessment, Research & Evaluation*, *10*(7).

Ellram, L. M. (1990). The supplier selection decision in strategic partnerships. *Journal of Purchasing & Materials Management*, *26*(4), 8–14.

Emiliani, M. L. (2000). Business-to-business online auctions: Key issues for purchasing process improvement. *Supply Chain Management: An International Journal*, *5*(4), 176–186. doi:10.1108/13598540010347299

Emiliani, M. L. (2004). Sourcing in the global aerospace supply chain using online reverse auctions. *Industrial Marketing Management*, *33*(1), 65–73. doi:10.1016/j.indmarman.2003.08.012

Emiliani, M. L., & Stec, D. J. (2002). Realizing savings from online reverse auctions. *Supply Chain Management: An International Journal*, *7*(1), 12–23. doi:10.1108/13598540210414355

Emiliani, M. L., & Stec, D. J. (2005). Wood pallet suppliers' reaction to online reverse auctions. *Supply Chain Management: An International Journal*, *10*(4), 278–287. doi:10.1108/13598540510612758

Etzion, H., Pinker, E., & Seidmann, A. (2003). *Analyzing the simultaneous use of auctions and posted prices for online selling*. Working paper CIS-03-01. University of Rochester.

Faris, C. W., Robinson, P. J., & Wind, Y. (1967). *Industrial buying and creative marketing*. Boston, MA: Allyn & Bacon.

Finch, B. J. (2007). Customer expectations in online auction environments: An exploratory study of customer feedback and risk. *Journal of Operations Management*, *25*(5), 985–997. doi:10.1016/j.jom.2006.10.007

Forrester. (2002). ISM/*Forrester research report on ebusiness*. Institute for Supply Management, April.

Forrester. (2003). *ISM/Forrester research report on ebusiness*. Institute for supply management, April.

Garson, G. D. (2008). *Topics in multivariate analysis*. Retrieved from http://www2.chass.ncsu.edu

Gattiker, T., Huang, X., & Schwarz, J. (2007). Negotiation, email, and internet reverse auctions: how sourcing mechanisms deployed by buyers affect suppliers' trust. *Journal of Operations Management*, *25*(1), 184–202. doi:10.1016/j.jom.2006.02.007

Handfield, R.B., Straight, S. L., & Stirling, W. A. (2002). Reverse auctions: how do supply managers really feel about them. *Inside Supply Management*, *13*(11), 56–61.

Hannon, D. (2003, August 14). Purchasing survey shows e-sourcing adoption stalls. *Purchasing*.

Hannon, D. (2006). E-Sourcing finds its place. *Purchasing*, *135*(16), 51–52.

Hannon, D., Hartley, J., & Lane, M. D. (2004, June 3). GSK closes the loop using e-sourcing tools. Purchasing.

Hartley, J., Lane, M. D., & Hong, Y. (2004). An exploration of the adoption of e-auctions in supply management. *IEEE Transactions on Engineering Management*, *51*(2), 153–161. doi:10.1109/TEM.2004.826010

Hur, D., Hartley, J., Lane, M. D., & Duplaga, E. (2006). Exploring the barriers to the adoption of e-auctions for sourcing. *International Journal of Operations & Production Management*, *26*(2), 202–221. doi:10.1108/01443570610641675

Hur, D., & Mabert, V. (2006). Implementing reverse e-auctions: A learning process. *Business Horizons*, *49*(1), 21–29. doi:10.1016/j.bushor.2005.05.001

Hur, D., Mabert, V., & Hartley, J. (2007). Getting the most out of reverse e-auction investment. *Omega*, *35*(4), 403–416. doi:10.1016/j.omega.2005.08.003

Jap, S. (2002). Online reverse auctions: Issues, themes and prospects for the future. *Journal of the Academy of Marketing Science*, *30*(4), 506–525. doi:10.1177/009207002236925

Jap, S. (2003). An exploratory study of the introduction of online reverse auctions. *Journal of Marketing*, *67*, 96–107. doi:10.1509/jmkg.67.3.96.18651

Jap, S. (2007). The impact of online reverse auction design on buyer–supplier relationships. *Journal of Marketing*, *71*(1), 146–159. doi:10.1509/jmkg.71.1.146

Jaworski, B. J., & Kohli, A. K. (1993). Market orientation: antecedents and consequences. *Journal of Marketing*, *57*, 53–70. doi:10.2307/1251854

Kagel, J. H., & Levin, D. (1986). The winner's curse and public information in common value auctions. *The American Economic Review*, *76*(5), 894–920.

Kagel, J. H., Levin, D., Battalio, R., & Meyer, D. J. (1989). First-price common value auctions: Bidder behavior and the winner's curse. *Economic Inquiry*, *27*(2), 241–258. doi:10.1111/j.1465-7295.1989.tb00780.x

Kagel, J. H., & Roth, A. E. (1995). *Auctions: A survey of experimental research. The handbook of experimental economics*. New York, NY: Princeton University Press.

Kaufmann, L., & Carter, C. R. (2003). Deciding on the mode of negotiation: To auction or not auction electronically. *Proceedings of the 14th ANARSPSCM*, (pp. 191-226).

Kelly, F., & Steinberg, R. (2000). A combinatorial auction with multiple winners for universal service. *Management Science*, *46*(4), 586–596. doi:10.1287/mnsc.46.4.586.12054

Klein, S. (1997). Introduction to electronic auctions. *Electronic Markets*, *7*, 3–6. doi:10.1080/10196789700000041

Klemperer, P. (1999). Auction theory: A guide to the literature. *Journal of Economic Surveys*, *13*(3), 227–286. doi:10.1111/1467-6419.00083

Kraljic, P. (1983). Purchasing must become supply management. *Harvard Business Review*, *61*, 109–117.

Lance, C. E., Butts, M., & Michels, L. (2006). The sources of four commonly reported cutoff criteria: What did they really say? *Organizational Research Methods*, *9*, 202–220. doi:10.1177/1094428105284919

Levi, M., Kleindorfer, P., & Wu, D. (2003). Codifiability, relationship-specific IT investment, and optimal contracting. *Journal of Management Information Systems*, *20*(2), 77–98.

Lösch, A., & Lambert, J. S. (2007). E-reverse auctions revisited: An analysis of context, buyer-supplier relations and information behavior. *The Journal of Supply Chain Management*, *43*(4), 47–63. doi:10.1111/j.1745-493X.2007.00040.x

Lucking-Reiley, D. (1999). Using field experiments to test equivalence between auction formats: Magic on the Internet. *The American Economic Review*, *89*(5), 1063–1080. doi:10.1257/aer.89.5.1063

Lucking-Reiley, D., Bryan, D., Prasad, N., & Reeves, D. (2007). Pennies from eBay: The determinants of price in online auctions. *The Journal of Industrial Economics*, *55*(2). doi:10.1111/j.1467-6451.2007.00309.x

Mabert, V., & Schoenherr, T. (2001). Evolution of online auctions in B2B procurement. *PRACTIX*, *5*(1), 15–19.

Mabert, V., & Skeels, J. (2002). Internet reverse auctions: Valuable tool in experienced hands. *Business Horizons*, *45*(4), 70–76. doi:10.1016/S0007-6813(02)00229-X

McAfee, P. R., & McMillan, J. (1987). Auctions and bidding. *Journal of Economic Literature*, *25*(2), 699–738.

Meier, R., Williams, M., & Singley, R. (2002). The strategic role of reverse auctions in the quotation and selection process. *PRACTIX*, *5*(3), 13–17.

Milgrom, P. (1989). Auctions and bidding: A primer. *The Journal of Economic Perspectives*, *3*(3), 3–22.

Millet, I., Parente, D., Fizel, J., & Venkatraman, R. (2004). Metrics for managing online procurement auctions. *Interfaces*, *34*(3), 171–179. doi:10.1287/inte.1040.0073

Min, H. (1994). International supplier selection: a multi-attribute utility approach. *International Journal of Physical Distribution & Logistics Management*, *24*(5), 24–33. doi:10.1108/09600039410064008

Özbilgin, I. G., & Imamalu, M. Y. (2011). The impact of dynamic purchasing systems in the electronic public procurement processes. *Procedia Computer Sciences, 3*, 1571–1575. doi:10.1016/j.procs.2011.01.051

Parente, D. H. (1998). Across the manufacturing-marketing interface: classification of significant research. *International Journal of Operations & Production Management, 18*(12), 1205–1222. doi:10.1108/01443579810236638

Parente, D. H., Venkataraman, R., Fizel, J., & Millet, I. (2004). A conceptual research framework for analyzing online auctions in a B2B environment. *Supply Chain Management: An International Journal, 9*(4), 287–294. doi:10.1108/13598540410550037

Pearcy, D. H., & Giunipero, L. C. (2006). The impact of electronic reverse auctions on purchase price reduction and governance structure: An empirical investigation. *International Journal of Services Technology and Management, 7*(3), 215–236.

Pinker, J., Seidmann, A., & Vakrat, Y. (2003). Managing online auctions: Current business and research issues. *Management Science, 49*(11), 1457–1484. doi:10.1287/mnsc.49.11.1457.20584

Raubenheimer, J. E. (2004). An item selection procedure to maximize scale reliability and validity. *South African Journal of Industrial Psychology, 30*(4), 59–64.

Rothkopf, M. H., Pekec, A., & Harstad, R. M. (1998). Computationally manageable combinational auctions. *Management Science, 44*, 1131–1147. doi:10.1287/mnsc.44.8.1131

Skjøtt-Larsen, T., Kotzab, H., & Grieger, M. (2003). Electronic marketplaces and supply chain relationships. *Industrial Marketing Management, 32*(3), 199–210. doi:10.1016/S0019-8501(02)00263-8

Smeltzer, L., & Carr, A. (2003). Electronic reverse auctions: promises, risks and conditions for success. *Industrial Marketing Management, 32*(6), 481–488. doi:10.1016/S0019-8501(02)00257-2

Smeltzer, L., & Ruzicka, M. (2000). *Ana'lise fatorial para pesquisadores. LabPAM.* Brası'lia.

Smeltzer, L., & Ruzicka, M. (2000). Electronic reverse auctions: integrating the tool with the strategic sourcing process. *PRACTIX, 3*(4), 1–6.

Van Heck, E. (1998). How should CIOs deal with Web-based auctions? *Communications of the ACM, 41*, 99–100. doi:10.1145/278476.278495

Wagner, S. M., & Schwab, A. P. (2004). Setting the stage for successful electronic reverse auctions. *Journal of Purchasing and Supply Management, 10*(1), 11–26. doi:10.1016/j.pursup.2003.11.001

Walley, M. J. C., & Fortin, D. R. (2005). Behavioral outcomes from online auctions: Reserve price, reserve disclosure, and initial bidding influences in the decision process. *Journal of Business Research, 58*, 1409–1418. doi:10.1016/j.jbusres.2003.10.014

Wellman, M. P., Reeves, D. M., Lochner, K. M., & Vorobeychik, Y. (2002). *Price prediction in a trading agent competition. Technical report.* University of Michigan.

Wellman, M. P., Reeves, D. M., Lochner, K. M., & Vorobeychik, Y. (2004). Price prediction in a trading agent competition. *Journal of Artificial Intelligence Research, 21*, 19–36.

APPENDIX A

SECTION 1

Questionnaire Form

Personal Data Name: Surname: City/Country: Nationality: Telephone: E-mail:
Firm Data Firm Name: Job Position Firm Turnover: Firm Country: Number of firm's employees:
IT DATA How long have you been using Information Technology for process support? (years): How long have you been using IT in the purchasing process? (years): How long have you been using online auctions? (years):

SECTION 2

Weight	Description	
1	Extremely Low Impact	
2	Very Low Impact	
3	Low Impact	
4	Normal Impact	
5	High Impact	
6	Very High Impact	
7	Extremely High Impact	
**Likert's Scale for Section 2		
SECTION 2		
Question - To what extent do you agree with saying that the following variables are important for e-auction performance?		
A - MARKET CONDITION		
2.1 Market Context	**Weight**	
MC1 - The concentration of supply market This variable refers to the number of firms and their respective market shares in the supply market.		

continued on following page

Table Continued

Weight	Description	
MC2 - The volatility of supply market price This variable refers to medium variation of the auctioned item price in supply market during a specified timeline.		
MC3 - The presence of a leading firm This variable refers to the presence of a big player which has a dominant position in the market.		
MC4- The number of potential suppliers This variable refers to the total number of potential suppliers in a particular supply market.		
2.2 Supplier Characteristics		
SC1 - Supplier reputation This variable includes several attributes such as image, quality and delivery reliability, financial stability and other criteria usually used for suppliers selection.		
SC2 - Total number of firm's employees This variables is linked to a firm's dimension and managerial complexity.		
SC3 - Total turnover This is an economic index of a firm's dimension.		
SC4 - Relative Dimension (total turnover/total number of employees) This is a relative indicator of a firm's dimension and complexity.		
SC5 - Company IT culture This variable refers to the general IT culture of firms in terms of awareness of potential improvements of business performance and management of IT introduction processes.		
SC6 - E-commerce confidence This variable refers to the experience using e-commerce tools: how long since the company introduced it and the number of reiterations of the specific auction event.		
2.3 Buyer Characteristics		
BC1 - Buyer reputation This variable includes several attributes such as image, quality and delivery reliability, financial stability and other criteria traditionally used.		
BC2 - Total number of firm's employees This variables is linked to a firm's dimension and managerial complexity.		
BC3 - Total turnover This is an economic index of a firm's dimension.		
BC4 - Relative Dimension (total turnover/total number of employees) This is a relative indicator of a firm's dimension and complexity.		
BC5 - Company IT culture This variable refers to general IT culture of a firm in terms of awareness of potential improvements of business performance and management of IT introduction processes.		
BC6 - E-commerce confidence This variable refers to the experience using e-commerce tools: how long since the company introduced it and the number of reiterations of the specific auction event.		
2.4 Buyer/Supplier Relationship		
BS1 - Age of relationship This variable refers to the length of relationship between seller and buyer (the number of years they have been doing business).		

continued on following page

Table Continued

<table>
<tr><th>Weight</th><th>Description</th><th></th></tr>
<tr><td colspan="2">BS2 - Relative contractual power
The contractual power of a firm is a function of the dependency degree that the opposing party has toward it. It is linked to dimension, concentration both demand-side and offer-side, or other technical dependencies.</td><td></td></tr>
<tr><td colspan="2">BS3 - Dimensional gap
The dimensional gap includes differences related to total turnover of company “A” compared to company “B”.</td><td></td></tr>
<tr><td colspan="2">BS4 - IT / E-commerce gap
This variable is related to the experience and confidence gap using IT support and in particular E-commerce tools.</td><td></td></tr>
<tr><td colspan="2">BS5 - Information gap
This variable resumes the information asymmetry between suppliers and buyers in terms of quality and quantity of technical and market information.</td><td></td></tr>
<tr><td colspan="2">2.5 Product Characteristics</td><td></td></tr>
<tr><td colspan="2">PC1 - Product Type
This variable refers to the class which the auctioned item belong to. That is for example: Manufacturing (Speciality or Commodity) vs MRO goods (Maintenance, Repair or Operation).</td><td></td></tr>
<tr><td colspan="2">PC2 - Strategic importance of auctioned goods for final product/service
This variable is related to the perceptual incidence of the total value of auctioned items on total procurement value and/or the contribution to the innovation, image, quality level and value of final product/service.</td><td></td></tr>
<tr><td colspan="2">PC3 - Product standardization or customization degree
This variable refers to the specificity and uniqueness of auctioned product/service.</td><td></td></tr>
<tr><td colspan="2">PC4 - Description complexity of auctioned item
This variable estimates the complexity of the auction product and costs associated with the communication process of product capitulate</td><td></td></tr>
<tr><td colspan="2">PC5 - Repeatability of auction event
This variable refers to the repeatability of an auction event so that general auction settings and capitulate specifications can be reused more than once.</td><td></td></tr>
<tr><td colspan="2">PC6 - Total value/size of auctioned lot
This variable refers to the dimension and value of the auctioned lot.</td><td></td></tr>
<tr><td colspan="2">2.6 Auction Process Parameters</td><td></td></tr>
<tr><td colspan="2">AP1 - Auction type
This variable indicates if the auction is a single attribute or multi attribute auction</td><td></td></tr>
<tr><td colspan="2">AP2 - Aggregation mechanism
This variable describes the auction use: simple aggregation, multi-lot aggregation (yankee e-RA), combinatorial aggregation</td><td></td></tr>
<tr><td colspan="2">AP3 - Winner algorithm
This variables refers to award modality (automatic or with award reservoir) and the typology of the award price (first price or second price)</td><td></td></tr>
<tr><td colspan="2">AP4 - Minimum bid setting
This parameter indicates the existence of the minimal offer.</td><td></td></tr>
<tr><td colspan="2">AP5 - Reverse price level setting
This variable indicates the existence of a minimum price for the auction to be successful.</td><td></td></tr>
<tr><td colspan="2">AP6 - Product information disclosure
This variable indicates the adoption of a structured process for product information communication (RFx, etc).</td><td></td></tr>
</table>

continued on following page

Table Continued

Weight	Description	
AP7 - Process information disclosure This variable indicates the adoption of a structured process for auction process information communication (Supplier qualification, invitation, training).		
AP8 - Timing mechanism and presence of auto-extension This parameter indicates the auction timing and the auto-extensions due to a bid at the last minute (if the auction is hard close or soft close).		
AP9 - Opening bid This variable refers to the minimum bid for entry into the auction process.		
AP10 - Total number of bidders This variables refers to the total number of participants of the auction event.		
AP11 - Bid visibility This parameter indicates if the auction is: an open auction or sealed bid. It is related to visibility of the bidding process.		

SECTION 3

Question 1: Please indicate, from your point of view, the most important factors (max 5) that you consider strongly impacting on price auction performance and which you take into consideration in the auction setting process.

Question 2: Please indicate, from your point of view, the most important factors (max 5) that you consider strongly impacting on e-auction process efficiency and which you take into consideration in the auction setting process.

Chapter 7
Euroalert.net:
Aggregating Public Procurement Data to Deliver Commercial Services to SMEs

José Luis Marín
Gateway Strategic Consultancy Services, Spain

Mai Rodríguez
Gateway Strategic Consultancy Services, Spain

Ángel Marín
Gateway Strategic Consultancy Services, Spain

Ramón Calmeau
EXIS-TI, Spain

Jose María Alvarez
WESO RG, University of Oviedo, Spain

José Emilio Labra
WESO RG, University of Oviedo, Spain

ABSTRACT

This chapter aims to describe a use case of information re-use in the field of public procurement in the European Union (EU). It describes how the lack of a pan-European information platform providing one single access point to EU public procurement notices, hampers the access for companies to this market, especially for SMEs. To bring one possible solution to this significant issue, Euroalert.net– a company powered by open data –, is currently developing commercial services fuelled by the re-use of public sector information (PSI) related to public procurement. The chapter also describes 10ders information Services (10ders IS), a Euroalert.net R&D project aimed at building a pan-European platform to aggregate public procurement information data generated by hundreds of thousands of contracting authorities in the EU.

DOI: 10.4018/978-1-4666-2119-0.ch007

INTRODUCTION

Euroalert.net (Euroalert.net, 2012) (ISSN 1988-3382) is a brand owned by Gateway Strategic Consultancy Services, S.L. (Gateway, 2012), which is focused in delivering innovative and cost-effective information services. These innovative services are designed to add value to public sector information generated within the framework of public contracts published by government bodies in EU Member States, as well as within the activities and policies developed under an EU general framework. Euroalert.net monitors, processes, and stores information in four main areas: (1) News about EU Institutions activity, (2) EU Legislation, (3) EU Funding opportunities and (4) Public Contracts issued in EU Member States.

The use case described in this chapter is specifically focused on public procurement information which, by itself, is a big challenge to be solved in order to provide new customized services to organizations and companies across Europe. Once processed, all data about public procurement is indexed, enriched, mashed-up and repackaged to deliver products under the brand *10ders*, mainly focusing in SMEs market.

Although they might seem apparently unrelated, there are two main driving forces in this context which are crucial in order to understand why Euroalert.net decided to meet the challenge and build such a platform to contribute to a more competitive EU single market. These two elements are, on the one hand, the EU political determination to modernise and simplify public procurement rules as a way to support growth and employment (European Commission, 2011) and, on the other, the development of the European Commission Open Data Strategy (European Commission, 2011b).

BACKGROUND

Modernising European Public Procurement Market: Situation and New Developments

Government bodies and public administrations as a whole are the most important buyers in the European Union, since all their purchases are estimated to represent around 19% of EU Gross Domestic Product (GDP). However, the lack of a pan-European information service which would provide one single access point to this huge market of business opportunities estimated by the European Commission at more than €2,406.98 billion in 2010 (European Commission, 2010)., is seen as a key obstacle for companies willing to get access to them, especially in the case of SMEs.

Since 2008, the European Commission has made significant efforts in order to improve European public procurement market, making it more transparent and efficient. The "Small Business Act for Europe" adopted in June 2008 (Commission of the European Communities, 2008, p. 394), already highlighted the need to make the public procurement environment more SMEs friendly and to facilitate access for these type of companies to this huge market. This target, which was one of the ten principles identified by the Commission to bring added value, create a level playing field and improve SMEs business environment; was then developed by the "European Code of Best Practices Facilitating Access by SMEs to Public Procurement Contracts" (European Commission, 2008, p. 2593).

As an important part of the European Single Market, public procurement in the European Union has been in the agenda as a way to create growth and improve competitiveness. In his Report to the President of the European Commission on a new strategy for the Single Market, ex commissioner Mario Monti (Monti, 2010), highlighted some of the problems for governments and businesses to fully enjoy the benefits of a strong public procurement single market as well as the gains that could be obtained by lowering barriers to procurement, especially by improving access to cross-border procurement. Furthermore, the role of procurement as a driver for trade has not only been advocated within the EU single market, but also at a global level. This has been the case, e.g., for the deal on the Plurilateral Government Procurement Agreement (GPA) reached within the World Trade Organization in December 2011 (World Trade Organization, 2011) and to which the EU is also signatory.

However, one particular concern within the European Union is the fact that, despite the level of transparency achieved by EU Directives on public procurement, cross-border procurement figures are still low. According to a study commissioned by DG Internal Market and Services (European Commission, 2011c), cross-border public procurement represented only 1.4% of all above EU-thresholds contracts awarded in the European Union in 2009, or 3.6% in terms of their value. The study also showed that, despite some differences depending on the type of purchase – goods, services or works; about half of above EU-thresholds contracts are awarded within 100 kilometres. Administrative burdens, language in publication of tender notices and bidding processes, submission costs, etc., are some of the barriers most commonly identified by businesses. Furthermore, fragmentation in the publication of business opportunities for below EU thresholds procurement is also hindering the access to public procurement within the Single Market.

In its view to modernise European public procurement to support growth and employment, the European Commission presented in December 2011 a reform on the legislation on public procurement (European Commission, 2011d). According the schedule put forward in the Single Market Act, these proposals are expected to be adopted by the end of 2012, once they had undergone the legislative process with the Parliament and the Council.

In the proposals' preparatory works, the European Commission's impact assessment for the revision of EU Public Procurement directives (SEC (2011) 1585 final), identified both regulatory and natural barriers in the access to public procurement in the European Union, especially for SMEs. According to this assessment, a level playing-field has not yet been achieved in the European Single Market in terms of public procurement, and an asymmetric market access still remains. This situation which causes losses in terms of insufficient cost-efficacy in public spending as well as missed opportunities for society, also leads to a situation where 27 national procurement markets co-exist rather than an EU-wide public market. The IA also indicates that fragmented national procurement markets are considered to be economically inefficient.

This particular inefficiency due to fragmentation was in fact already pointed out in the "European Code of Best Practices Facilitating Access by SMEs to Public Procurement Contracts" in 2008, which identified eight groups of difficulties in this field. Two groups of these difficulties referred to the barriers faced by SMEs in accessing relevant information about tenders. The document states that "the (big) number of such web portals being used by the government and by regional and local authorities makes it difficult for tenderers to maintain an overview".

By aggregating data on public procurement in all Member States and at all administrative levels, 10ders IS project developed by Euroalert.net aims to contribute solutions to some of these issues affecting public procurement, improving a situation which affects more than 20 million non-financial companies established in the EU.

European Open Data Strategy

The availability of government data enables (Bennett & Harvey, 2009) greater transparency; delivers more efficient public services; and encourages stronger public and commercial use and re-use of government information. Following this approach, over the past two years an increasing amount of governments in Europe and all over the world, have launched data catalogues for Open Government Data (OGD) to ease the access and re-use of public sector information (Fundación CTIC, 2012).

Although the signature in 2009 of the Memorandum on Transparency and Open Government by Barack Obama (2009) is often cited as the moment when OGD policies became relevant at a higher level, the fact is that the European Commission adopted the Directive 2003/98/EC (European Parliament, 2003, p. 345/90) on the re-use of public sector information in 2003. This Directive, which has been transposed to national law in all EU Member States, introduced a first set of measures to make it easier for businesses to get access and permission to re-use government-held information. The results of the implementation of the Directive were evaluated in 2009 and the legal text is currently under revision with the contributions gathered in a public consultation closed in November 2010.

Along with this process, the Digital Agenda for Europe (European Commission & DG Information Society, 2010), Europe's strategy for a flourishing digital economy by 2020, is explicitly supporting Open Data strategies. In fact, one of the Digital Agenda's Big Ideas for the 1st Digital Agenda Assembly entitled "Beyond raw data: public sector information, done well" (European Commission & DG Information Society, 2010b), was especially focused on this topic.

The Open Data Strategy for Europe, led by vice-president Neelie Kroes and presented in December 2011 outlines three types of measures that will help to unleash potential of data held by governments in Europe. The strategy is strongly focused on the commercial value of the re-use of public sector information, by which the Commission expects to deliver a €40 billion boost to the EU's economy each year. A new version of the 2003 PSI Directive is also expected by 2012 as the European Commission is determined to act as a global leader along with United States, Canada or Australia.

It is also worth mentioning that UK Government, advised by sir Tim Berners-Lee and Professor Nigel Shadbolt among others members of the Public Sector Transparency Board (Government of United Kingdom & Transparency Board, 2010), has been supporting Open Data actions beyond EU policies and regulations. Prime Ministers Gordon Brown and David Cameron have even included the re-use of OGD in several occasions in their speeches, as a key element for economic recovery.

Global Initiatives such as Linking Open Data (LOD) (W3C SWEO, 2012) and EU funded projects like LOD2 (2012) or LAPSI (2012) thematic network, provide additional background to exploit this new context of publishing government data, which full potential has not been unleashed yet.

Euroalert.net is aware of this context and interacts with the open data community as well as with governments (at local, regional, national and EU level) who are, in the end, the holders of public procurement data used by 10ders IS (2012) in order to promote the release of new datasets in machine-readable formats. Euroalert was featured as a relevant Open Data company (Marín, 2011) in the 1st Digital Assembly in June 2011 where contributed with its experience building successful products on top on data released by governments along with main barriers found.

OPEN DATA AND PUBLIC PROCUREMENT: NEW OPPORTUNITIES IN COMMERCIAL INTELLIGENCE

In a highly competitive environment such as public procurement market, information is crucial and has to be searched and treated in the most comprehensive way. Within this framework, Euroalert.net has adopted an innovative approach combining the need to tackle asymmetric market access and information within European public procurement market, with the potential gains in delivering reliable data by applying PSI re-use principles to public procurement. This new approach intends, not only to aggregate as many data as possible in order to create a pan-European platform on public procurement, but also to improve the exploitation of these data in order to deliver reliable and cost-effective commercial intelligence services specially designed for SMEs.

Indeed, public procurement notices include valuable information which can be an important asset not only for potential bidders, but also for exporters and for any company in general to feed their market intelligence systems. However, the huge amount of information and its fragmentation makes it virtually impossible to extract these data manually. Besides, commercial intelligence services currently in the market do not provide a comprehensive set of information and are also unaffordable for most companies, especially for SMEs.

Following this path, this approach aims at improving services which are already in the market by aggregating more data and applying the best search technology, and to lower their prices so that all type of businesses can benefit from them. This is the case, e.g., of services such as public procurement alerts. In addition, new innovative products and services can be created to be used by any company as business and competitive intelligence.

Getting lists of potential partners who can distribute, install or sell one' products; identifying competitors already operating in one particular market; contacting potential partners to build up a consortium to bid for cross-border tenders; accessing some particular data about technical specifications required by authorities in that market; knowing more about one market's price level; among others, are some of the elements which can help businesses to build up their strategy and get better results. Re-using and exploiting public procurement data can help to bring this information to companies.

Furthermore, other prospective benefits coming from data analysis such as matching different product and services codifications - e.g., TARIC, NACE codes, etc.; are also expected to be delivered by 10ders IS. Although not being part of the main targets set out in the project, this particular issue would represent a significant step in bringing public procurement information closer to companies which are not familiar with procurement jargon such as common procurement vocabulary, CPV, but usually employ other coding systems such as the code for their products in the Combined Nomenclature.

10ders Information Services, the Platform

The development of Tenders Electronic Daily, TED (European Commission, 2012), can be considered as the biggest EU-wide effort so far, made to ease interoperability within Europe's e-Procurement framework. TED is the online version of the S Series of the *Official Journal of the European Union*, OJEU, which is a supplement to the Journal particularly focused on European public procurement. TED publishes over 1,500 new over EU-threshold value procurement notices (European Commission, 2012b) every day and, according to Eurostat estimates, it covered 3.70% of EU27 GDP (Eurostat, 2011) in 2010. This means that below EU threshold tenders represented over 16% EU27 GDP, a huge amount of opportunities which are out of the scope of TED.

The objective of building a pan-European platform aggregating data from the huge amount of tender notices posted by contracting authorities in all Member States which are not published by TED, involves a set of overwhelming challenges that Euroalert.net is currently addressing within its big investment in R&D. These challenges can be summed up in the five following points: (1) finding and retrieving the data; (2) defining a unified data structure from heterogeneous sources; (3) efficiently storing big amount of data extracted from millions of documents; (4) understanding the richness of languages used in public procurement in the European Union; and (5) exploiting the aggregated data in products and services of different nature. Ultimately, the platform intends to define an efficient architecture on top of which Euroalert.net can then build more viable commercial services powered by public sector information, affordable for SMEs.

In order to accomplish this important challenges, *10ders IS* platform is developing innovative approaches to tackle the above five challenges. These approaches, that will also set the grounds for the architecture of the platform, are:

1. **Finding and Retrieving Data**: Tender notices are published in a wide range of public sources at European, national, regional and local levels. Furthermore, lower-value tenders following restricted publication procedures are often posted only on the websites of each institution, agency or public authority. *10ders IS* is working on an efficient architecture to track and monitor thousands (estimate) sources of data. Low value procurement can be modelled as a long tail of commercial opportunities scattered throughout thousands of heterogeneous sources of information which publish new information with unpredictable frequency. While some small agencies might be publishing one single tender once a year, national gazettes publish hundreds of new procurement announcements every day. The system, currently in a prototype stage, will be able to identify new opportunities posted every day in all those dispersed sources and will also be able to add new sources as they are identified. In addition to the huge technological challenge involved in this first step, there are also important related issues regarding the negotiation process with the main data holders. However, these administrative challenges are not fully described, as they fall out of the scope of this chapter.
2. **Defining a Unified Data Structure from Heterogeneous Sources**: Despite the data included in tender announcements are public by itself, though not always re-usable, there is not a single format for these notices, not even a limited number of possibilities to express the information. Downloading and processing documents from each source in order to aggregate them, involves a number of complex issues in order to understand the structured or unstructured information included in the notices. Moreover, the available data and their format can vary over time given that most public sources do not provide a guarantee of stability and future compatibility of the formats used to publish tender notices. As an additional difficulty, and depending on the applicable legislation, one same tender notice can be published simultaneously in more than one source, even with different formats, and without a unique identifier or reference code that would help merging data from different sources. There is a big interest in solving this issue in order to determine if data coming from different sources actually refer to the same tender notices, and to use the best quality data in each case. This would not only avoid the duplication of information, it would

also provide the best possible quality for data by merging the best elements of each publication.

3. **Efficiently Storing Big Amount of Data Extracted from Millions of Documents**: The amount of information to be processed by the platform is so huge, that another issue to be solved relates to make it necessary to solve the issue about how to store and efficiently exploit it. In this regard, it is worth pointing out that only the OJEU itself adds more than 20,000 documents every day. The storage strategy has the additional challenge to be scalable in order to include new sources of information at a large scale. A unified data storage for public procurement announcements offers many opportunities to exploit such data by means of different products, some of which will arise as an answer to eventual needs that will be identified long after closing the system design. As an example of this kind of challenge, the platform must be designed in such a way that its architecture can manage multiple subsets of information optimized for different operational requirements, from data-mining to online publishing of information.
4. **Understanding the Richness of Languages Used in Public Procurement in the European Union:** As an additional challenge, the platform deals with the fact that tender documents may be published in one or more of the 23 official languages of the European Union. In addition, each country sometimes uses other co-official languages in its territory. Every algorithm and subsystem is designed to process, aggregate and understand information which is written in a large number of languages and also deals with cultural differences such as currency, tax system or the way postal addresses are encoded. Additionally, when the same tender notice is published in more than one language it is not a good approach to focus only in one of the languages. The platform analyses each of the different versions of documents in different languages in order to use the parts with higher quality data obtained between the different versions of the same tender notice.
5. **Exploit the Aggregated Data in Products and Services of Different Nature**: A unified information system with structured data from public procurement announcements offers multiple possibilities of exploitation in different products, with a wide range of operational requirements. Some of these services will even be designed in the future, so original documents might have to be re-processed without penalizing the performance of existing products and services.

Further to finding new approaches to tackle all these challenges, it is also worth describing some of the publicly available contributions that Euroalert.net will make to the community in the process of building the *10ders IS* platform:

- The transformation of vocabularies developed by governments such as Common Procurement Vocabulary CPV (European Union, 2010), Eurovoc (2011) (now available in SKOS), etc. to RDF, RDF(S), SKOS or OWL. Euroalert.net will publish through its infrastructure the information via an SPARQL endpoint providing a linked data node based on standards. This work is currently available in beta version at MOLDEAS website (WESO, 2012), and it is expected to be released during the first quarter of 2012.
- A new model to express the information available in public procurement notices as web information resources, enriched with controlled vocabularies, geographical information and other datasets now available in the linked data cloud. Euroalert.net expects to release its own model (code name

opXML) for representing tender information, so it can be adopted by any interested stakeholder in the public procurement ecosystem. It could also be potentially standardised by any interested body.

10ders Information Services, Main Services, and Products

All the technology and processes put in place within the *10ders IS* project are ultimately aimed to exploit the information contained in public procurement notices using new and innovative business models. Euroalert is especially focused in the provision of value-added and cost-effective services which can be more easily accessed by SMEs. Following this approach and based on the results which have been obtained so far, Euroalert.net is already offering to its clients both free and subscription services (Euroalert.net, 2012b) packaged in many different innovative products. Some of these products, especially intended to be cost-effective for SMEs, are:

10ders Alerts: Tenders Alerting Systems (Euroalert.net, 2012c)

Euroalert.net helps companies to keep track of the business opportunities available with EU public sector which are relevant for their products or services. The system allows each subscriber to set a customised profile and define priorities in a very easy to use dashboard (Figure 1). This dashboard allows to manage the settings and change them as many times as necessary, so the results can be adapted to evolving needs. Among other criteria, subscribers can set the countries they are targeting, the CPV codes which better define the product or sector they want to track, any keyword that can help to define the profile; the type of announcement they want to track depending on their needs, etc.

Once the profile is set, subscribers can choose the delivery options to receive the information which includes the e-mail or e-mails where they want to receive the alert, the language and the maximum number of announcement to be included at each delivery (Figure 2). It also includes

Figure 1. 10ders Information Services high level architecture

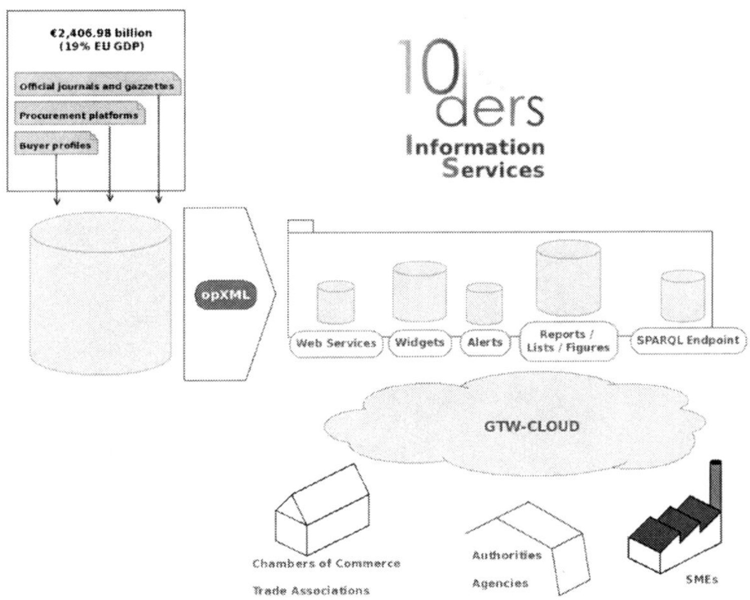

the possibility to choose the periodicity of the alerts and the data to be included in the e-mail.

Apart from these traditional options, Euroalert.net has introduced a new feature which allows to choose the format in which the subscriber wants to receive the data. This new feature enable 10ders Alerts subscribers to receive information in a re-usable format, so they can store and analyse it more easily with their own information systems. Subscribers can choose between inline HTML, an attached Excel document or an attached Open-Document.

Building an accurate profile is crucial to get the right results. For that reason, 10ders Alerts allows to send previous results every time a subscriber makes changes in the profile (Figure 3). With this feature, results can be tested on the go and it is not necessary to wait for upcoming alerts to know whether the profile needs to be reshaped or not.

10ders Reports - Customised Product Reports on Public Procurement (Euroalert.net, 2012d)

Euroalert.net also helps its clients to access new markets. Customised product reports on public procurement offer a simple and clear report listing with the most relevant public buyers and the most successful bidders for the products and services they select, in the country or countries of their choice (Figure 4). It also contains the main figures of that particular market, such as the number of contracts awarded or its estimated economic volume.

Clients only have to fill in the details of the 10ders Report they want to receive in a simple interface and then proceed to on-line payment. The Report is delivered within two days to the e-mail address indicated in the order.

Figure 2. Personal 10ders alerts product profile dashboard

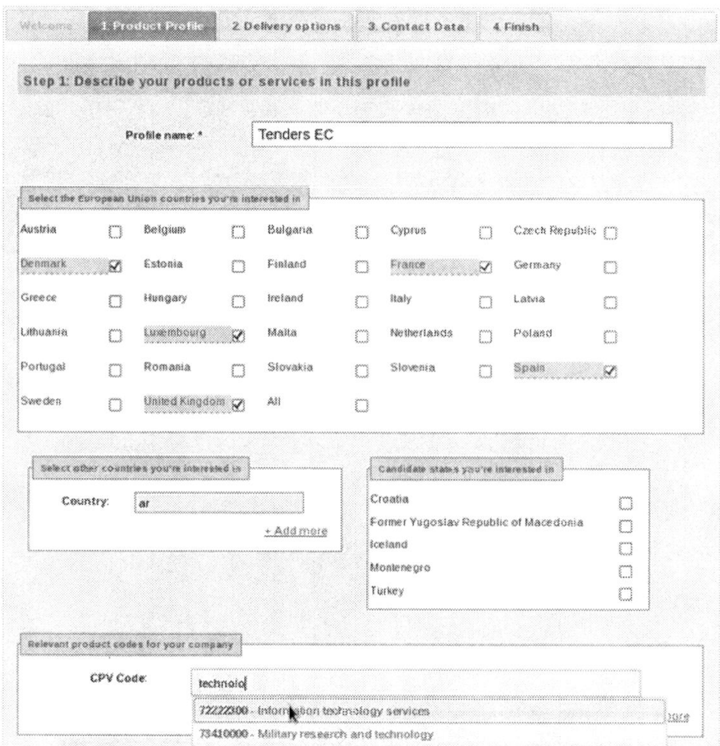

Figure 3. 10ders alerts delivery options

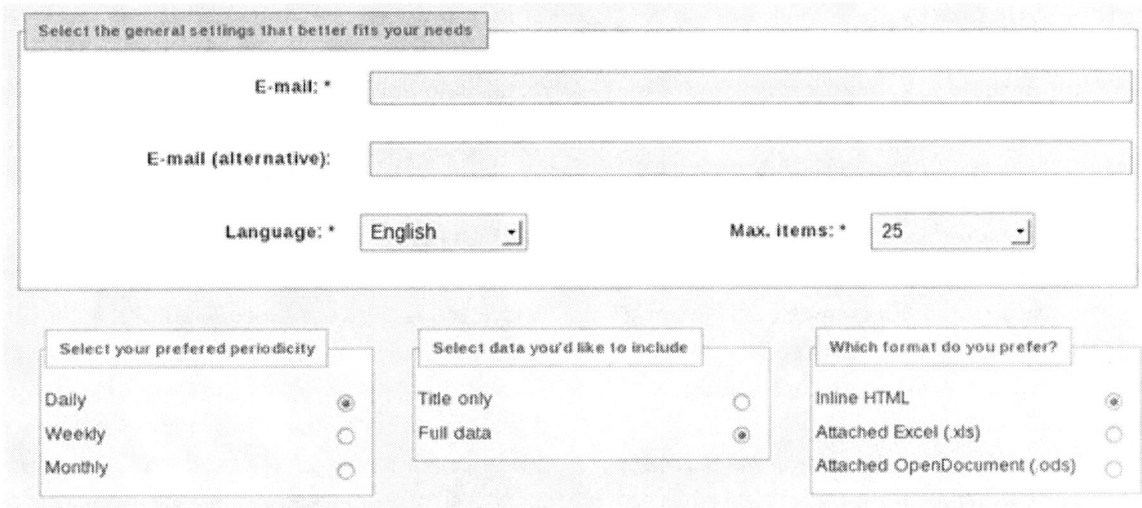

Figure 4. 10ders Alerts prior tenders delivery option

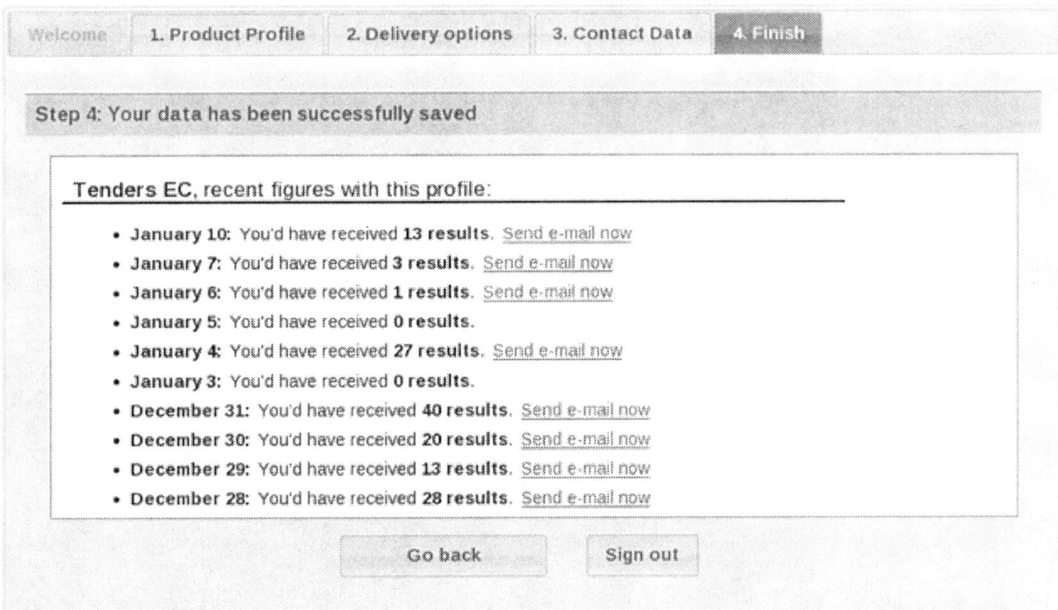

10ders Lists: Lists of Companies Winning Contracts

As one step further, Euroalert.net also provides with more concise lists including the companies winning contracts in any country or sector the client is interested in (Figure 5). These successful bidders can be extracted to a 10ders List using customised criteria, i.e. companies winning in one particular country, companies established in a certain country, or those companies winning contracts related to a certain group of products or services (Euroalert.net, 2012e).

These lists provide information such as the name of the contract winner and its contact details, when available; the title of the tender procedure in which the awarded contract is included as well as its references and value, when available; the details of the contracting authority; and the links to the announcement, where any further detail can be accessed.

Outsourcing of Alerting Systems and Customized Newsletters

Euroalert.net also provides solutions for institutions and organizations willing to disseminate contents among their members. It offers the possibility to outsource information systems on public procurement as well as on the other contents managed in its databases, in order to be distributed under a *private-branded* model.

Figure 5. 10ders customised product reports samplesFigure 1. 10ders Information Services high level architecture

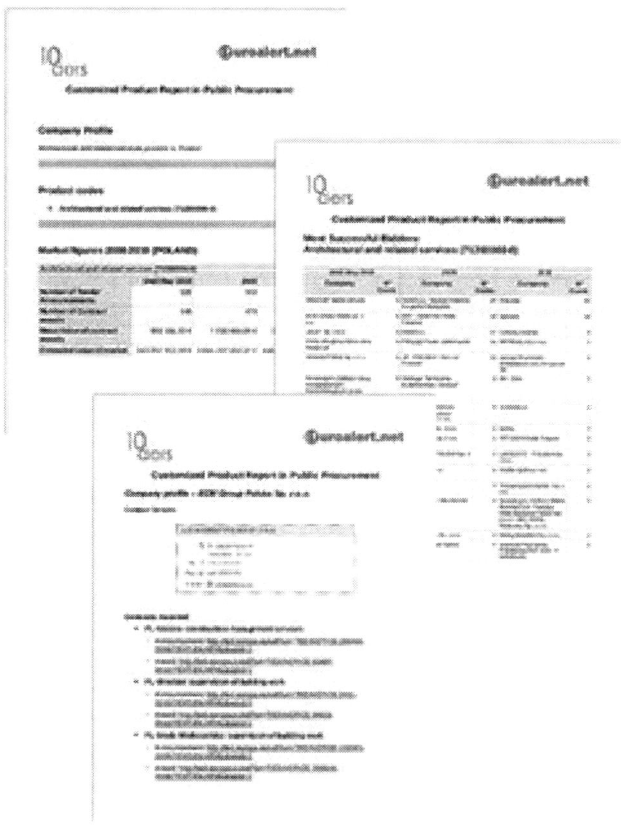

Following the model put in place by Euroalert.net in all the products and services which are traded for organizations worldwide, flexibility and simplicity are two of the main features in outsourcing solutions. They allow to significantly enhance the services provided by any organization without making big investments or compromising future decisions. All these solutions are easy to install and easy to remove, should it be necessary.

Euroalert.net systems to outsource tender alerting systems only involve the installation of a client-side, four-step management system in the client's website (Enterprise Europe Network Flanders, 2009) where final users can register and set their profile. This management system adopts a friendly design in order to be fully integrated within the corporate layout of the site (Figure 6). It is an embedded implementation in order to keep development and integration cost as low as possible.

Flexibility is also ensured by allowing organizations to gradually increase the number of final users that will be receiving information, always enjoying the same benefits in terms of volume for the packages (Figure 7).

These kind of private-branded model is a way for organizations to deliver cost-effective high value services with no investment and benefiting from Euroalert's economies of scale. Low implementation costs, flexibility to add new features gradually and a licensing model which allows to renews or termination of the service with no big economic impacts; are the most valued characteristics of these services within Euroalert.net clients, especially in the present economic situation.

Free Widgets or One Web Full Content Widgets (Euroalert.net, 2012f)

Euroalert.net also provides customized widgets which allow its subscribers to automatically publish in their own website any content distributed by Euroalert.net. In this case, automatic web publication of tender announcements, allows to filter them according to the client's criteria and to fully adapt them to the layout of the website. This kind of automatic publication allows to disseminate opportunities in a completely up-to-date

Figure 6. 10ders lists sampleFigure 1. 10ders Information Services high level architecture

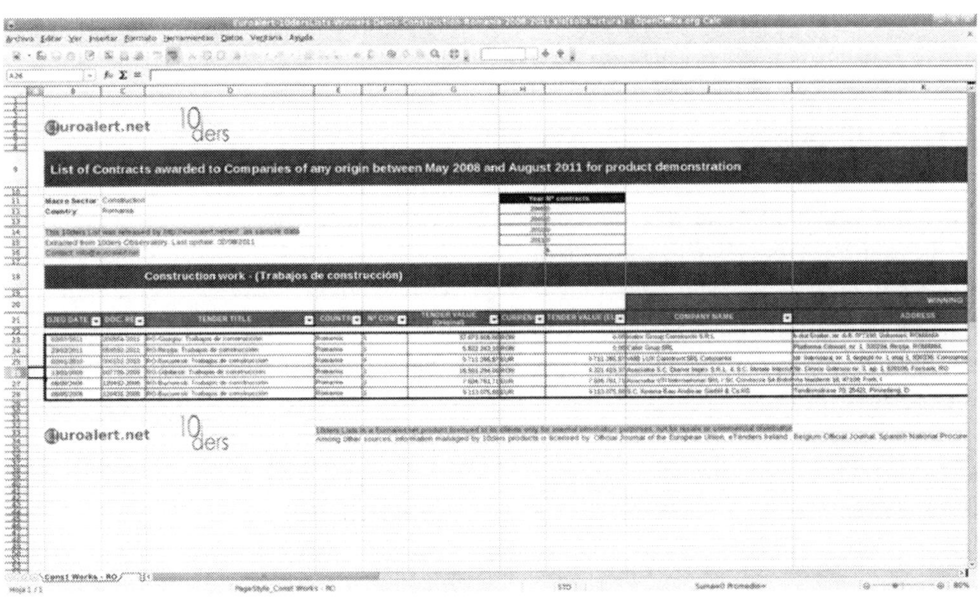

Figure 7. Image of the customisation made for Enterprise Flanders which shows the integration with the layout of the subscriber's

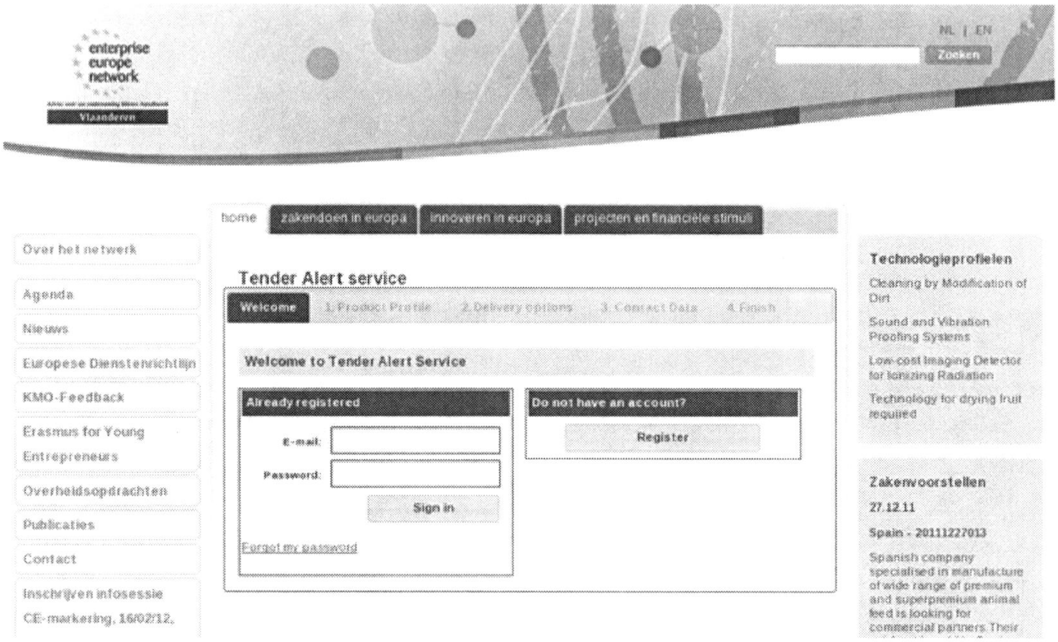

website with no maintenance nor dedication of additional resources on the client's side.

This service has also proven to be quite useful for organizations to upgrade other services they were already delivering. Used as a marketing tool for services such as counselling and expertise, widgets have also turned out to be a way for new sources of revenue.

Customized Data Mining for Market Intelligence

Exploiting the full potential of all the data aggregated in the platform previously described, Euroalert.net provides raw statistics on public procurement, tailored to the interests of each client. Working hand in hand with its clients, Euroalert.net team of experts helps them to extract knowledge from the hundreds of thousands of tender announcements which are published every day in all the sources of information managed within 10ders IS.

These data are provided in a re-usable format, so they can be treated and analysed within a commercial intelligence strategies. Long-term data allow to exploit them, drawing conclusions and identifying trends.

Once again, flexibility, scalability and affordability are the main features in this service. Data packages can be gradually added respecting the economic conditions offered in terms of bigger volumes, and periodic updates are available at low costs.

Web Services

All Euroalert.net contents, including tender announcements, are also provided so they can be automatically stored in clients' databases. This type of service allows them to combine the information provided by Euroalert.net with other sources of information and to enrich the chain of information re-use.

Contents are made available for clients through a private SOAP web service, with a data structure previously agreed with the subscriber over the customization process in order to facilitate as much as possible the integration process. Data are regularly retrieved in order to be stored in the client's infrastructure, and to be later integrated in any product development envisaged by the client - web integration, alerts, newsletters, etc.

Its main feature is the flexibility to develop further services and integrate them in those already put in place by the client, combining Euroalert.net contents with other contents coming from different sources as well as with other in-house contents developed by the client. However, although these kind of services provide a high potential for their exploitation, they also involve higher implementation, storage and development costs which fall outside the licence and must also be foreseen by subscribers.

Some of Euroalert.net products have already been in the market for a few years and are benefiting from the increasing amount of sources of information aggregated by *10ders IS*, making them even more valuable for its clients. This continuous improvement has allowed Euroalert.net to achieve a growing clients portfolio (Euroalert.net, 2012g) across Europe, ranging from regional governments to chambers of commerce, business and trade associations, as well as public agencies supporting international trade and investment promotion, apart from private held companies.

Some outstanding examples of the organizations that are currently trusting Euroalert.net services in this field are the London Chamber of Commerce (UK), the Birmingham Chamber of Commerce (UK), Enterprise Ireland (IE), Poland Trade and Investment (PL), Promo Madrid (ES), Yorkshire Regional Development Agency (UK) or Junta de Castilla y León (ES).

CONCLUSION AND FUTURE WORK

Euroalert.net started providing business information services for public authorities and companies long before the publication of the 2003 Directive on the re-use of public sector information. Despite the global economic downturn, the increasing amount of government information available in re-usable formats represents a new opportunity for innovation as well as for growth and job creation, an approach which is fully in line with the objectives set by the Europe 2020 Strategy launched by the Commission in March 2010 (European Commission, 2012c). It is clear for Euroalert.net that this is a great opportunity for growth and that it opens new possibilities to develop more advanced services.

At this point, Euroalert.net is investing large resources in order to reach the full potential of the 10ders IS platform by reducing the current degree of dispersion of information, standardizing data models and formats, enriching public procurement notices, and implicitly addressing multilingual and multicultural issues.

The amount of information which is currently processed has grown significantly, and now comes from many different public authorities in most European countries. This increases the possibility to add value to information by combining data coming from multiple sources. Also, it should be underlined that the quality of the data processed has been considerably improved and contains fewer errors.

However, and despite the important steps made over the past two years, a scenario where all governments work together with re-users to get the maximum value of the information they are holding, is still a distant future. Being aware of it, and trying to contribute to create the appropriate environment for the commercial re-use of public sector information, Euroalert.net has been active in disseminating open data culture. In so doing, the company has participated in a number of conferences and events (Euroalert.net, 2012h), and is also releasing the knowledge acquired in the process of opening up new sources of public procurement data.

Euroalert.net hopes that all these actions made in its field of interest as well as the joint efforts contributed to the Open Data community, will help to raise awareness among public authorities so that the opening of data sources and the procedures to request raw datasets will soon be put in place and clarified.

ACKNOWLEDGMENT

This chapter is a revised and expanded version of a paper entitled "Euroalert.net: Building a pan-European platform to aggregate public procurement data and deliver commercial services for SMEs powered by open data", a peer-reviewed position paper presented at the 1st Digital Agenda Assembly, Brussels - Belgium, 15-16 June 2011.

This work is also part of "10ders Information Services" project partially funded by the Spanish Ministry of Industry, Commerce and Tourism with code TSI-020100-2010-919 and the European Regional Development Fund (EFDR). The project is leaded by Gateway Strategic Consultancy Services" and developed in cooperation with "EXIS TI" (2012) and WESO Research Group (2012).

REFERENCES

W3C SWEO. (2012). *Community project. Linking open data*. Retrieved http://www.w3.org/wiki/SweoIG/TaskForces/CommunityProjects/LinkingOpenData

Barak Obama. (2009). *Transparency and Open Government. Memorandum for the Heads of Executive Departments and Agencies*. Government of the United States. The White House. Retrieved from http://www.whitehouse.gov/the_press_office/TransparencyandOpenGovernment

Bennett, D., & Harvey, A. (2009). *Publishing open government data*. W3C Working Draft 8 September 2009. Retrieved http://www.w3.org/TR/gov-data/

Commission of the European Communities. (2008). *Communication from the Commission to the Council, the European Parliament, the European Economic and Social Committee and the Committee of the Regions: "Think Small First". A "small business act"*. COM. 394.

10*ders Information Services Project*. (2012). Reviewed http://rd.10ders.net/

Enterprise Europe Network Flanders. (2009). *Tender alerting service*. Reviewed http://www.enterpriseeuropevlaanderen.be/nl/home/overheidsopdrachten/tender-alert-service.html

Euroalert.net. (2012). Retrieved from http://euroalert.net/

Euroalert.net. (2012b). *On-line store web site*. Reviewed http://euroalert.net/en/buy.aspx

Euroalert.net. (2012c). *On-line store, 10ders alerts page*. Reviewed http://euroalert.net/en/tenders-alerts

Euroalert.net. (2012d). *On-line store, 10ders reports page*. Reviewed http://euroalert.net/en/Tenders-Reports

Euroalert.net. (2012e). *On-line store, 10ders lists sample*. Reviewed http://euroalert.net/dl/docs/10dersLists/Euroalert-10dersLists-Winners-Demo-Construction-Romania-2008-2011.xls

Euroalert.net. (2012f). *On-line store: Widgets services page*. Reviewed http://euroalert.net/en/widgets_service_options.aspx

Euroalert.net. (2012g). *Client portfolio*. Reviewed http://euroalert.net/en/clients-portfolio.aspx.

Euroalert.net. (2012h). *Euroalert presents its experience at the Open Software World Conference 2012 and the W3C Day in Spain*. Retrieved from http://en.blog.euroalert.net/search/label/Open%20data

European Commission. (2008). *European code of best practices facilitating access by SMEs to public procurement contracts*. SEC. 2193

European Commission. (2010). *Public procurement indicators 2009*. Retrieved from http://ec.europa.eu/internal_market/publicprocurement/docs/indicators2010_en.pdf

European Commission. (2011). *Modernising European public procurement to support growth and employment*. Press release. Retrieved http://europa.eu/rapid/pressReleasesAction.do?reference=IP/11/1580

European Commission. (2011b). *Digital agenda: Turning government data into gold*. Press release. Retrieved from http://europa.eu/rapid/pressReleasesAction.do?reference=IP/11/1524

European Commission. (2011c). *Final report. Cross-border procurement above EU-thresholds*. Rambøll Management. Retrieved http://ec.europa.eu/internal_market/publicprocurement/docs/modernising_rules/cross-border-procurement_en.pdf

European Commission. (2011d). *Public procurement. Modernising the rules: News legislative proposals*. Retrieved from http://ec.europa.eu/internal_market/publicprocurement/modernising_rules/reform_proposals_en.htm

European Commission. (2012). *TED: Tenders electronic daily*. Reviewed http://ted.europa.eu/

European Commission. (2012b). *Simap: Information about European public procurement*. Reviewed http://simap.europa.eu/supplier/opportunities-in-europe/index_en.htm

European Commission. (2012c)... *Europe, 2020*, (n.d). Retrieved from http://ec.europa.eu/europe2020/index_en.htm

European Commission & DG Information Society. (2010). *A digital agenda for Europe*. Retrieved http://ec.europa.eu/information_society/digital-agenda/index_en.htm

European Commission & DG Information Society. (2010b). *Beyond raw data: public sector information, done well*. Retrieved http://ec.europa.eu/information_society/events/cf/dae1009/item-display.cfm?id=5257

European Parliament. (2003). *Directive 2003/98/EC of the European Parliament and of the Council on the re-use of public sector information*, 345/90. Retrieved from http://eur-lex.europa.eu/LexUriServ/LexUriServ.do?uri=OJ:L:2003:345:0090:0096:EN:PDF

European Union. (2011). *Summaries of EU legislation: Common procurement vocabulary*. Retrieved from http://europa.eu/legislation_summaries/internal_market/businesses/public_procurement/l22008_en.htm

Eurostat. (2011). *Value of public procurement which is openly advertised, as a percentage of GDP*. Retrieved from http://epp.eurostat.ec.europa.eu/tgm/table.do?tab=table&init=1&plugin=1&language=en&pcode=tsier090

Eurovoc. (2010). *Multilingual thesaurus of the European Union*. Reviewed http://eurovoc.europa.eu/.

EXIS-TI. (2011). Retrieved from http://www.exis-ti.com/

Fundación, C. T. I. C. (2012). *Public dataset catalogs faceted browser*. Retrieved ttp://datos.fundacionctic.org/sandbox/catalog/faceted/

Gateway Strategic Consultancy Services. S.L. (2012). *Company web site*. Retrieved from http://gateway-scs.es/en/

Government of United Kingdom & Transparency Board. (2010). *New public sector transparency board and public data transparency principles*. Retrieved http://data.gov.uk/blog/new-public-sector-transparency-board-and-public-data-transparency-principles

LAPSI Project. (2012). *The European thematic network on legal aspects of public sector information*. Reviewed http://www.lapsi-project.eu/

LOD2 Project. (2012). *Creating knowledge out of interlinked data*. Retrieved from http://lod2.eu/

Marín, J. L. (2011). *Euroalert.net: Building a pan-European platform to aggregate public procurement data and deliver commercial services for SMEs powered by open data*. Presented at the Digital Agenda Assembly.

Monti, M. (2010). *A new strategy for the single market – At the service of Europe's economy and society*. Retrieved from http://ec.europa.eu/bepa/pdf/monti_report_final_10_05_2010_en.pdf

WESO (Oviedo Semantic Web). (2012). *MOLDEAS-Methods on linked data for e-procurement applying semantics*. Reviewed http://purl.org/weso/moldeas/

WESO (Oviedo Semantic Web). (2012b). Retrieved from http://www.weso.es/

World Trade Organization. (2011). *Historic deal reached on government procurement*. Government Procurement Agreement. Retrieved from http://www.wto.org/english/news_e/news11_e/gpro_15dec11_e.htm

Chapter 8
The Benefits and Barriers of Electronic Public Procurement System:
A Case Study on Public Hospitals in Turkey

Tolga Demirbaş
Uludağ University, Turkey

Erdal Eroğlu
Uludağ University, Turkey

Özhan Çetinkaya
Uludağ University, Turkey

ABSTRACT

In almost every country, public procurements are the primary issue which citizens are the most sensitive to in terms of how public money is spent. Electronic procurement systems in the public sector have been adopted as a solution in order to respond to the sensitivity of citizens because of the benefits promised. In the early 2000s, Turkey both made the public procurement legislation approximate to the European Union standards and began to develop an e-procurement system within the scope of e-transformation Turkey project. As a result of the works carried out under the leadership of the Public Procurement Authority, which is an independent administrative authority, the e-procurement system started to be used in some stages of the procurement process. Four public hospitals were determined as pilot administrations in order to improve the implementation and it was aimed to make the implementation common in all sectors according to the experiences gained in this field. The objective of this chapter is to reveal benefits gained and barriers faced during the development process of the e-procurement by focusing on the above mentioned pilot implementation field. In order to attain this objective, the method of case study was adopted in this research, and guiding experiences were tried to be gained for the e-procurement implementations in the future.

DOI: 10.4018/978-1-4666-2119-0.ch008

INTRODUCTION

Gaining candidate status for the European Union (EU) membership in 1999, Turkey was shaken by two big financial crises in November, 2000 and February, 2001. The efforts to overcome these crises highly accelerated the efforts to restructure Turkish public administration. Within this scope, various reforms have been introduced in a number of areas such as increasing transparency in public finance, focusing on decentralization and guaranteeing freedom of information. Developing projects for using e-government technologies in public administration became an indispensable part of these reforms. Making a great effort for the EU membership, Turkey adopted the e-Europe+ Action Plan which all candidate countries are expected to adopt and launched e-Turkey Initiative in 2001 (Office of the Prime Minister, 2002). Then, Turkey also launched a new project called e-Transformation Turkey which combined the studies carried out by different institutions (Office of the Prime Minister, 2003). The main objective of this project was laid down as follows: "to become a government that adopts having participatory, transparent, efficient and simple work processes as a principle in order to provide its citizens with rapid public services of high quality." (Office of the Prime Minister, 2003, p. 1)

Electronic public procurement system is one of the milestones of e-Transformation Turkey which is defined as "a social transformation project towards becoming an information society" (State Planning Organization, 2004, p. i). When the system which is among 11 e-government projects prioritized by the Prime Ministry is completely implemented, it is expected to make great contributions to primarily public sector institutions, businesses and citizens (E-Government Advisory Group, 2008). E-procurement is estimated to provide an annual saving of 5 billion Turkish liras in Turkey where about 25000 public institutions make tenders of 70 billion Turkish liras annually and 100 thousand tenderers participate in these tenders (Gül, 2011). The task of developing the e-procurement project launched in order to gain such benefits as above stated or similar ones was assigned to the Public Procurement Authority (PPA) which is an independent administrative authority (State Planning Organization, 2005).

Many countries in the world including Turkey have adopted developing an e-procurement system as a national policy. Moreover, the EU Ministers set such an ambitious goal as 100 percent e-procurement availability until 2010 in the Manchester Declaration of 2005 (Manchester Declaration, 2005). However, developing and adopting an e-procurement system connecting thousands of public institutions and businesses is a task which is complex and takes long time. E-procurement is not a simple, technical application which is based on the use of information and communication technologies (ICTs) instead of paper based systems (European Commission, 2010). Successful implementation of an e-procurement system requires a fundamental transformation ranging from modernizing public procurement legislation to user-friendly, organizational reconstruction in public sector. The fact that every country has different organizational structures, procurement processes, habits, technological infrastructures makes the process more and more difficult. As a matter of fact, it is said that the reason why EU was very far away from realizing the objective set in 2005 was the technical, logistical and administrative complexity of the change (European Commission, 2010). In summary, there is not a standard e-procurement template fitting every country. That is why e-procurement system should be implemented gradually and finding out the problems faced during the implementation process is crucial.

E-procurement system in Turkey is being gradually developed under the responsibility of the PPA. Having taken important steps for digitizing the procurement processes since 2003, PPA is working in cooperation with the relevant parties. Great progress in improving the application of e-procurement system has been made and four public hospitals have been chosen for pilot e-procurement applications in the sector of medical devices and consumables. According to the applications at these hospitals, the e-procurement system is aimed to be made common in other sectors (PPA, 2008; PPA, 2009). Therefore, it can be stated that the e-procurement processes in Turkey are at a crossroads and the current situation at pilot hospitals is crucial for successfully turning the crossroads.

This chapter aims at evaluating the efforts made to develop the e-procurement system in Turkey by focusing on pilot public hospitals. By conducting semi-structured interviews with medium and high ranking officials of 4 hospitals chosen as pilot institutions as well as with authorized staff from the PPA, a case study was carried out. The sub-objectives of this study are (a) finding the organizational benefits of the works carried out, (b) understanding what the current barriers are and (c) finding out the institutions' perceptions of the future of the e-procurement system.

Within this scope, the paper consists of five sections. The first section focuses on the potential benefits and barriers by reviewing the literature on e-procurement in public sector. The second section gives information about at which stage Turkey is currently in terms of developing public e-procurement. The research methodology is described in the third section and the findings are discussed in the following section. The paper concludes with some lessons learned from the case study on pilot public hospitals in Turkey.

ELECTRONIC PROCUREMENT IN PUBLIC SECTOR: POTENTIAL BENEFITS AND BARRIERS

A highly big amount of tax revenues is utilized for public administrations' purchase of goods and services in almost every country. That is why public procurement is one of the issues citizens devote the closest attention to in terms of how public money is expended. It is difficult to state that a bureaucratic state in which the procurement process is carried out in a paper-based way has a positive image in the minds of its citizens. Procurement processes having a complex legal framework, progressing slowly and generally lacking transparency are often criticized by citizens and regarded as one of the most important resource of corruption (Thai, 2004). Nonetheless, it is seen that electronic procurement is increasingly adopted as an e-government solution (Ronchi, Brun, Golini & Fan, 2010) in public sector for the above stated criticism.

In broad terms, e-procurement means using ICT based communication systems instead of paper based procedures during the whole or partial procurement process. According to this definition, various processes such as need identification, publishing tender notices, acquiring tender documents, making offers, evaluation, award, ordering, invoicing and payment can be within the scope of e-procurement (European Commission, 2010).

The most important reason why e-procurement initiatives are becoming common in public sector may be the fact that it has so many potential benefits. These benefits have an important place in e-procurement literature.

When the literature on e-procurement is analyzed, it is seen that "a decrease in administrative costs and an increase in efficiency" is the foremost benefit to be gained from e-procurement. Transition to electronic based procurement process leads to a decrease in paper usage and accelerates the procurement process by simplifying the administrative procedures. Moreover, it prevents repetitive works such as registration and certification of contractors. In other words, it can decrease the administrative costs by saving labor and time up (Singer, Konstantinidis, Roubik, & Beffermann, 2009; PLS-Ramboll, 2000; Croom & Brandon-Jones, 2007; Boff & Previtali, 2007; Somasundaram, 2008; Joia & Zomat, 2002).

E-procurement can also contribute to the effectiveness of public administration. One of the most important conditions for presenting effective service in public sector is to purchase goods and services of good quality at a fair price. By increasing the number of the firms making tender offers to the administration, enhancing competition and simplifying the use of advanced tools such as e-auctions, e-procurement can decrease the price of goods and services without decreasing their quality (Gardenal, 2010; Engström, Wallström & Salehi-Sangari, 2009; Joia & Zomat, 2002).

Another potential benefit of e-procurement is its ability to increase accessibility and transparency (European Commission, 2010; Singer et al., 2009; Somasundaram, 2008). Transparency can be shortly defined as generating reliable, sufficient, timely, comprehensive and accessible information (Kopits & Craig, 1998). E-procurement enhances transparency for not only the public administration itself but also the businesses. For instance, tender notices, the number of applications or tender results can be seen via e-procurement systems immediately. As a matter of fact, e-procurement systems can also be designed to alert suppliers to particular opportunities and provide immediate access to tender documentation (European Commission, 2010; Ronchi et al., 2010).

E-procurement system can also ensure the control. According to this, the system automatically organizes the documents produced for both public administrations and suppliers during the procurement process. It also enables staff and auditors to carry out safety control more easily by removing such risks as loosing or mismatching documents (Gardenal, 2010; Bof & Previtali, 2007). Moreover, the integration of tender and purchasing processes with budget process provides public administrations with fast and reliable control of the spending. Controlling procurement process closely can also prevent maverick buying (Ronchi et al., 2010; Hawking, Stein, Wyld & Foster, 2004).

E-procurement technologies can not automatically provide the above stated benefits. In order to gain these benefits, some pre-conditions such as education and expertise, process effectiveness, technical infrastructure and political support need to be fulfilled. When the complex structure of public sector is taken into consideration, there are a number of potential barriers which decrease the number of benefits expected to be gained from e-procurement and which need to be overcome (Boff & Previtali, 2007; Ronchi et al., 2010; Moon, 2005).

One of the barriers is related to human resources. E-government technologies require knowledgeable and efficient human resources. It is seen in some examples that lack of technical specialists causes a barrier to e-procurement solution (Somasundaram, 2008; Hawking et al., 2004; Boff & Previtali, 2007; Gunasekaran & Ngai, 2008).

Another barrier is lack of legal framework. Supporting e-procurement technologies via legal infrastructure is an unavoidable necessity to be met. Lack of legal basis for especially digital signature and encryption techniques causes an important barrier (PLS-Ramboll, 2000; Hawking et al., 2004).

Lack of motivation observed in both public administrations and suppliers can cause a barrier to the application of e-procurement. Such factors as high cost of reorganizing internal systems (European Commission, 2010) and unawareness of the benefits to be gained from e-procurement (Gunasekaran & Ngai, 2008) have an important impact on this situation.

Literature on e-procurement also point out the problems specific to suppliers. Lack of know-how among suppliers and low user acceptance; SMEs' not having internet access (PLS-Ramboll, 2000) and small companies' not being able to get into the market because of the formal defects they cause in tender offers (Meyer, 2011) are some of these barriers.

Resistance to change is another barrier, which is generally related to the intra-organizational factors such as repudiation of new working methods by users, inefficient knowledge and safety systems (PLS-Ramboll, 2000).

One of the barriers adversely affecting the success of e-procurement systems is related to technical standardization. Usage of different browsers, interfaces, program languages and software packages in public administrations prevents the data from being standard. Such technological problems are connected with the fast development of the Internet and lack of standards, especially within security systems (PLS-Ramboll, 2000).

In addition to the above stated ones, lack of support and commitment by senior management, lack of financial support (Gunasekaran & Ngai, 2008), costly technologies, low level of interaction between buyers and suppliers due to lack of trust (Croom & Brandon-Jones, 2007; Hawking et al., 2004), ethical issues, price pressures (Yu, Yu, Itoga, & Lin, 2008) can be stated as other barriers.

ELECTRONIC PUBLIC PROCUREMENT SYSTEM IN TURKEY: FROM PAST TO PRESENT

An effective electronic procurement system in public sector requires a transparent, competitive and modern procurement legislation which primarily regulates the conventional public procurement process. As a result of both its efforts for EU membership and the commitments made to the International Monetary Fund (IMF) and the World Bank, Turkey introduced a new law (Public Procurement Law No. 4734) complying with the United Nations Standards in 2002, which was a crucial step. With this law, an independent, central administrative authority, namely Public Procurement Authority (PPA), was established in order to regulate and audit the public procurement system. By this way, the principles of competition, transparency, reliability, confidentiality, equal treatment and public supervision in public procurement were guaranteed (PPA, 2003).

The PPA that started to actively carry out its activities in 2003 began to use ICTs rapidly. The Authority put a web-based module for preparing tender notices into service for public administrations within the scope of the Public Procurement Law (PPL) in 2004. Thanks to this module, the administrations started to prepare their tender notices with minimum mistakes and send them to the PPA for approval. In addition, tender notices approved by the PPA started to be announced in Public Procurement Bulletin which has been on the website of the PPA since 2004 (PPA, 2004; PPA, 2005a). All public procurements in Turkey started to be registered in one center and various statistics started to be kept thanks to these practices.

The PPA understood the importance of electronic procurement quite early. O. Sener Akkaynak, the president of the PPA in 2003, declared their ultimate goals in the introduction of 2003 activity report as follows:

Our ultimate goal is to ensure that public procurements, in all procurement methods, are completely carried out on electronic media. By this way, all proceedings will be carried out according to the rules on computer by putting a computer between buyers and suppliers (Akkaynak, 2004, p. 5)

This strong institutional motivation was strengthened by the 2005 action plan of e-transformation Turkey project launched by the government in 2003. The article No 22 of the action plan set forth the establishment of an electronic platform in order to set up the infrastructure of electronic procurement system and this task was assigned to the PPA. It was stated that the platform would set database about the public administrations making tenders by using public resources and the firms making sales to them and would provide reliable exchange of documents between buyers and suppliers. In addition, it was also emphasized that legal regulations necessary for these issues would be made (State Planning Organization, 2005).

The fact that e-procurement has become a national policy has accelerated the works. A road map was prepared by the "electronic procurement working group" that was set up within the PPA in order to prepare an e-procurement model applicable in Turkey by examining the developments and projects in the world and in the EU countries (See Figure 1). The road map envisaged that all stages from the preparation of tender documents to the evaluation of tender offers would be carried to the electronic media and a legislation compliance package would be prepared. Moreover, electronic procurement system was also planned to operate in parallel with the current conventional procurement process for a certain period of time (PPA, 2008; PPA, 2005b). The said road map was announced to the public and private sector via an e-procurement forum held in June, 2005 (PPA, 2005c). After a short period of time, the web-based electronic public purchase platform prepared and managed by the PPA as a part of the road map was put into use by an e-procurement summit organized (PPA, 2005d). This platform which constitutes of three main components, namely administrations, tenderers and citizens, has enabled some activities mostly related to the information dissemination to be carried out, which is the first stage of e-government. Some of these activities are tender registration, advertisement preparation, sending, monitoring, notice search, access to updated list of prohibited tenders and tender results. Some initiatives in order to decrease the use of paper were also launched the same year. Accordingly, tender notices are no longer sent by

Figure 1. E-procurement road map

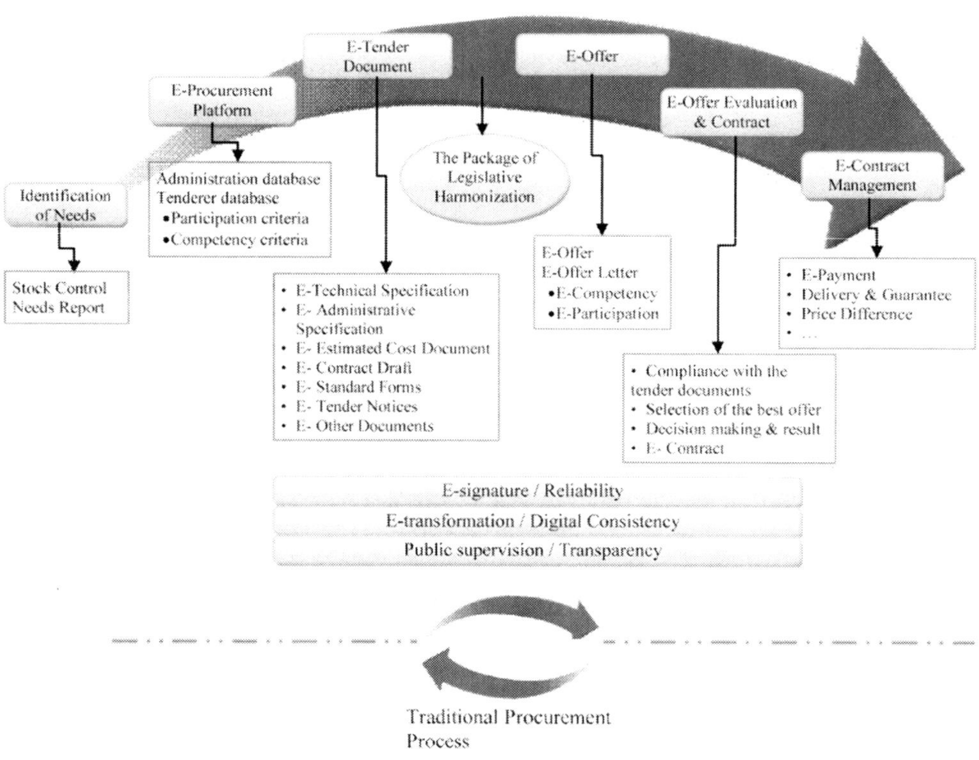

Source: PPA, 2005d.

post separately but sent only on electronic media to the PPA once they are prepared by the public administration after a protocol has been signed with the former in advance (PPA, 2008).

Transition from conventional to electronic procurement process in public sector requires an intensive cooperation among the parties of the process. For instance, tenderers are required to submit the public administration 20-25 official documents obtained from various administrations for a tender made by a public administration in Turkey, which normally makes the participation in tenders more difficult and leads the price offers of the tenderers to increase. That is why the PPA has been making cooperation protocols with various public administrations and non-governmental organizations in order to obtain the above stated documents online since 2005. The Social Security Institution, the Ministry of Health, the Presidency of Development and Support of Small and Medium Sized Enterprises Administration, the Union of Chambers and Commodity Exchanges of Turkey are some of these institutions and organizations (PPA, 2006; PPA, 2007). In spite of the efforts for cooperation and the enactment of E-Signature Law in 2004, the course of the process has not been brisk due to the fact that there is not a framework law regulating the electronic public procurement (Solak, 2011).

The legal basis for electronic public procurement in Turkey was set up with the amendments to the Public Procurement Law (PPL) in November, 2008. With an article added to the PPL No 4734, the PPA has become the fully competent authority for developing and managing the electronic procurement.

In procurements conducted within the scope of this Law, every stage of a procurement process such as... tender notice, preparation and submission of tender documents, submission of the documents regarding participation and qualification, preparation, submission and evaluation of tender offers, finalization and approval of the procurement, notification of contract award decisions and signing contracts and all kinds of notifications can be partially or wholly performed on Electronic Public Procurement Platform established by the Authority.

The principles and procedures regarding the establishment and operation of the Electronic Public Procurement Platform and the use of electronic means during the procurement process shall be determined by the Public Procurement Authority (PPA).

Systems for evaluating the qualification of candidates or tenderers can be set up on the Electronic Public Procurement Platform. The Public Procurement Authority is authorized for establishing these systems, having these systems established, supervising them, canceling the authority of authorized institutions or making precautionary decisions (The PPL, 2002, Additional Article 1).

It is important to state that e-procurement was chosen as one of the 11 e-government projects of high priority a couple of months before the said law amendment (E-Government Advisory Group, 2008). Following the law amendment, the PPA set up a new web-based platform (EKAP - Electronic Public Procurement Platform) stated in the law so as to transfer all procurement process into electronic media by making use of its previous experiences. The platform was aimed to become completely operational at four stages (PPA, 2011a).

Accordingly, 1.0 version of the EKAP was put into use on September 1, 2010. This version made the proceedings prior to sending e-offers (tender document preparation, sending, and downloading without e-signature) digital for all sectors. At the second stage, the 1.1. version of the EKAP was put into use on December 1, 2010. This version enabled natural and legal persons registered for the platform to download the tender documents via e-signature. Moreover, public administrations are able to search such information about the tenderers as their identities, social security premium dept, balance sheets and income statements by using the EKAP thanks to the cooperation of the PPA with other institutions. When the 1.2. version of the EKAP was put into use on March 1, 2011, the third stage started. This version was designed in a way to enable e-procurement application to be tested while purchasing medical devices and consumables to be carried out by following the open tender procedure in four public hospitals in the health sector determined as pilot sector. The first paperless electronic procurement initiative was performed by Hacettepe University Hospital on March 4, 2011. The 2.0 version of the EKAP is planned to be put into use in near future. This version aims to make e-procurement system used in pilot sectors to be also used in other sectors and to integrate such applications as electronic catalogue with the EKAP (PPA, 2011a; Akyer, 2011).

To sum up, tendering administration database, tenderer database and procurement legislation more than 1000 pages have been transferred into digital media thanks to the practices up to now. Purchasing items have only been digitized in health sector that is the pilot sector (Solak, 2011). The efforts for improving the EKAP, promotional activities and training are currently continuing. An EKAP call center (444 0 545) which can be dialed without area code from all over Turkey provides services to its users. Although it is new, EKAP seems to have positive statistics (See Table 1). It is possible to consider these statistics as indicators suggesting that the EKAP, one of Turkey's key e-government projects, will yield fruitful results when completely operational in all sectors.

Table 1. EKAP statistics (June 20, 2011)

Explanation	Number
Registered Administration	22 473
Registered Tenderer	17 129
Registered User	249 519
Published Notice	201 483
Documents downloaded by E-signature / M-signature	34 611
Daily average web visitor	60 000

Source: PPA (2011b), EKAP Statistics

A CASE STUDY ON PILOT PUBLIC HOSPITALS IN TURKEY

Study Backround

As it is known, health sector is one of the critical areas in which public procurements are intensive. The idea of testing the e-procurement in this sector in Turkey dates back to 2005. While the e-procurement development process was progressing, the PPA signed a protocol with the Ministry of Health on November 11, 2005. In the above mentioned protocol, it was stated that the e-procurement was aimed to save time and cost, ensure unity and standard while purchasing medicines, prevent the legislation from being misinterpreted or differently interpreted by buyers and suppliers (PPA & Ministry of Health, 2005). The underlying reason why the health sector was determined as the pilot sector was that there was a national health sector database (Gül, 2010). The name of this database conducted in cooperation with the Ministry of Health and the Social Security Institution was Turkish National Drug and Medical Device Data Bank (TİTUBB). This is a data bank which registers the medical devices and consumables sold in Turkey as well as the firms selling these devices and consumables according to the international denomination and classification standards. The data bank has a Branch Tree and a product codes system separately prepared for every branch in order to use these registrations within national land. The integration of this database with e-procurement processes has enabled online usage of these data by public administrations and tenderers in the health sector (PPA, 2009; Solak, 2010; Social Security Institution, 2011).

Four public hospitals were determined as pilot implementation units in order to test the e-procurement tools in the sector of medical devices and consumables. These hospitals are Hacettepe University Medical Faculty Hospital, Ankara Training and Research Hospital, Dış Kapı Yıldırım Beyazıt Training and Research Hospital and Atatürk Training and Research Hospital, which are all in Ankara just like the Public Procurement Authority. For test-works, the PPA trained the tenderers operating in the sector of medical devices as well as the pilot hospitals. As a result of the works carried out, the 1.2. version of the EKAP has become appropriate for the tenders in the sector of medical devices and consumables made by open tender procedure and the first paperless procurement was performed by the Hacettepe University Hospital on March 4, 2011 (PPA, 2009; PPA, 2010; Gül, 2011, Solak, 2011)

Methodology

It can be stated that an important progress has been made in terms of carrying out public procurements on wholly electronic media in Turkey. The public administrations within the scope of the PPL prepare tender documents and tender notices over the EKAP and the tenderers can get the tender documents by using e-signature. At these four pilot public hospitals, the tender offers can be received, evaluated, concluded and notified over the EKAP. According to the results gained in this sector, it is planned to proceed to the following stages of the e-procurement application in all other sectors. Therefore, it can be stated that the experiences gained from pilot applications are vital.

The objective of this case study is to focus on the experiences the pilot hospitals gained during the e-procurement process and to find out the benefits gained and barriers faced during this process. The findings of this study are aimed to contribute to the implementers and policy makers during the following stages of e-procurement development process. Authors believe that the experiences Turkey has gained during the development process of the e-procurement system can contribute to the international literature on public procurement.

The reason for adopting case study as a methodology is that it is an appropriate research strategy for understanding the dynamics lying behind the current situation (Eisenhardt, 1989). Case studies tell the history behind the result by understanding what happened to cause it and provides a good opportunity to emphasize a projects success or to point out a particular challenge or difficulty in a project. Within this scope, the most important advantage of a case study is that it provides more detailed information than that obtained by using other methods (Neale, Thapa, & Boyce, 2006).

Interviews are used as a data collection method in most qualitative researches. This method is highly useful for researchers to learn experiences and truths that cannot be observed (Hatch, 2002). That is why the method of semi-structured interview was adopted in this study. The data were collected from the face-to-face interviews conducted in June 2011with mid-level managers who are EKAP users in four pilot public hospitals as well as with senior managers from the PPA leading the EKAP. Within this scope, 11 authorized people were interviewed and each interviews lasted approximately 1 hour. The interviews focused on three main issues: the benefits gained from the e-procurement processes, the barriers faced during the process and the expectations for the future of the e-procurement system. Some of the interviews were recorded and deciphered later on. During some of the interviews, what the interviewees said were not recorded but noted down by at least two researchers due to the fact that they did not give permission. After the interviews finished, the notes of the researchers were compared in order to minimize the possible mistakes

FINDINGS AND DISCUSSION

The main findings of this study focusing on the benefits gained and barriers faced during the development process of the public e-procurement system which is one of the 11 e-government projects of high priority in Turkey as well as the expectations of the interviewees for the future of the system are as follows:

The interviews have showed that the foremost benefit gained from the e-procurement system is the progress made in the control of the regulatory compliance. All the interviewees stated that the EKAP guided the procurement process gradually, thereby ensuring the automatic control of the information and documents that the administration uploaded by the system. They also stated that the transaction errors that the administrations made were minimized thanks to these controls and the risks of losing or mismatching documents were removed since all the documents were on the electronic media. For instance, two of the interviewees stated these benefits as follows:

The EKAP guides us to the fields we need to fill in while we are preparing specifications. For example, it tells us to make adjustments according to the relevant article of the regulation. In other words, it directs us to the regulation. By this way, we read the regulation and make necessary adjustments accordingly. Thus, it shows us the mistake we make on the program. We cannot proceed to a next stage without correcting the mistake...

...the EKAP provides choices step by step while preparing tender notices. Therefore, the possibility of making mistakes or forgetting something decreases. It also enables us to save time since it prepares the tender notice itself.

Another benefit of the system that the interviewees stated is decrease in paperwork and administrative costs. During the conventional procurement process, a firm has to go to the administration in order to see and buy the tender document and also to make tender offers. However, the e-procurement system enables all the tender documents to be seen and obtained over the EKAP. During the interviews, it was observed that their workload decreased, they didn't need to make so much effort while preparing and approving the documents during the procurement process and the costs of paperwork such as paper, photocopy decreased thanks to the e-procurement system. These benefits dramatically decrease the costs the administration has to bear. For example, an interviewee highlights paper and time saving the system provides by his statement below:

In the past, as an administration, we had to go to several departments in order to have documents approved. However, transactions now progress gradually over the EKAP. The most important advantage of this system is that we don't have to prepare files of countless pages.

In addition, some of the interviewees said that the paperwork of tenderers significantly decreased. It seems that the costs of tenderers have decreased since they are no longer obliged to go to the administration in order to get or submit a document; they have got rid of travel and accommodation expenses as well as the preparation of some documents. For example, two of the interviewees reflected on these benefits:

Firms have benefitted from this process the most. Firstly, there are no longer obliged to come to the administrations while preparing required documents during the public procurement process. They communicate with us only when they have a problem. This naturally decreases costs.

...In the past, a firm used to come to the administration in order to get the necessary documents during the procurement process. The firm had to both bear travel expenses and spend time just for getting the documents. However, the firm now not only saves time but also gets rid of the costs of paperwork...

When the interviewees were asked whether cost savings the firms made led the prices to decrease, a positive answer was not received. The interviewees stated that they did not see a noticeable decrease in the prices of products. It is thought that this results from the fact that the e-procurement system is still in development process.

Another benefit the interviewees emphasized is that the e-procurement has increased accessibility and transparency. Undoubtedly, this result from the fact that firms registered for the EKAP which is a web-based program can access to tender information without going to the administration. In addition, it is important to state that the EKAP has become a central database regarding public procurement in Turkey, thereby providing not only the PPA but also citizens with important statistics. The interviewees reflected on the increase in accessibility and transparency:

In the conventional system, for a tender of an administration in Ankara, only the firms in Ankara could participate in that tender. However, tenderers from all over Turkey can participate in the procurement process thanks to the e-procurement system. This has increased the accessibility of the procurement process.

...thanks to the e-procurement, firms in every region of Turkey can now examine tender documents...

When the interviewees were asked whether the increase in accessibility and transparency led to an increase in participation in tenders and competition, a positive answer was not received. We think that this also results from the fact that the e-procurement system is still in development process.

Apart from the benefits, the development process of e-procurement system in public sector has also brought about some barriers. After analyzing the interviews, it was found out that the most important barrier faced in the e-procurement process was related to the standardization of the data on medical devices and consumables. Most of the interviewees said that Turkish National Drug and Medical Device Data Bank (TİTUBB) did not completely meet the needs. In spite of some progress made from past to present, it has been understood that the problem has not been solved due to the fact that there are so many products and branch codes. The interviewees said that they had difficulty preparing lists of requirements and they could not find the materials they searched on the database. For example, one of the interviewees reflected on this issue in summary:

There are many branch codes. The number of these branch codes needs to be decreased and standardized.

Products of about 1,8 million with both catalogue and legislation information are registered on the above mentioned database. These products are classified under the branch code of 18 at the first level, and 3287 at the second and lower levels respectively (Solak, 2010). It can be stated that the integration of this huge database with the e-procurement system plays a key role in the applications of the pilot hospitals.

Another finding is that some authorized people have not been able to break some of their past habits during the e-procurement system. Some of the interviewees said that they continued some of their habits they had in the conventional procurement system such as preparing paper-based files. For example, one of the interviewees said that:

...in case something wrong happens, I still prepare some documents in a paper-based way. Then, I transfer them to the electronic media.

Another barrier stated by the interviewees is related to the lack of human resources and technological equipment. Some of the interviewees said that they need workforce both competent in legislation and full of technical knowledge. For example, two of the interviewees pointed to this issue:

...institutions should have permanent staff to only deal with e-procurement process.

...In short, I now have to work more...

Another barrier stated during the interviews is related to the tenderers' adaptation to technology. Some interviewees said that some tenderers felt obliged to go to the administrations although they could download all of the tender documents on the electronic media. As an example for this issue, one interviewee said that:

...some tenderers come to the administration in order to check whether they have really purchased the tender document, although they, in fact, have purchased the tender document over the EKAP since they think that technology cannot be trusted. Since the system is not completely operational, tenderers have problem with trusting the technology....

Another finding shows that some barriers are faced while transferring the conventional procurement process into electronic media. The problems resulting from the fact that the technologists and tender experts do not understand each other at some points are generally noticed by the users. Some of the interviewees said that from time to time they were faced with such problems. For example, two of the interviewees said that:

...the list of materials we prepare on excel may include 300-400 items. We had to choose each item one by one on the EKAP and it took us a lot of time. However, we, in any case, prepared the list of materials on excel. Therefore, we asked the file on excel to be directly transferred to the EKAP...

...there was some information that needed to be on the EKAP but didn't exist...For example, there was not a button for adding items...There was not a search engine...

Most of the interviewees said that such barriers were removed in a short period of time thanks to the close interaction with the PPA.

Researchers think that benefits gained from a new technology and barriers faced while using this technology determine the expectations of actors for the future. That is why the interviewees were also asked what their expectations were for the future of the e-procurement system. When their answers were analyzed, it was found that all the interviewees had positive ideas about the future of the system. Most of the interviewees said that the e-procurement system would work better when the current problems were overcome and the implementers became completely integrated with the process. For example, one of the interviewees supported the system by saying:

...the e-procurement system has provided us with numerous benefits. As an implementer, I personally think that e-procurement system is a crucial step. I am really hopeful about the future.

Moreover, the interviewees stated that the system would provide some other benefits which had not been gained such as an increase in participation and competition and a decrease in the prices of products when the e-procurement system was used all over the health sector.

CONCLUSION

In this research, the main focus was to figure out the barriers and benefits that pilot public hospitals chosen in order to improve the e-procurement system in Turkey had during the implementation process of the system. After analyzing the findings of the case study, it can be said that five main results have been reached.

Firstly, although the e-procurement system is on the onset in four public hospitals, the system has provided most of the benefits it promised. Getting this result from the health sector, which is a complex sector by nature, makes the result more valuable.

Secondly, an independent authority regulating procurement processes has played a key role in the development of the e-procurement tools in pilot sector. When the works of the PPA since 2003 are taken into consideration, it can be said that the Authority has made a great effort. The cooperative approach the PPA adopted for the solution of the problems experienced in pilot hospitals supports this result.

Thirdly, that product range is wide and procurement volume is high in public health sector has a high possibility of causing a barrier to the e-procurement. As seen in the case, standard classification of product information on electronic media can be difficult. In order to avoid such barriers, while digitizing product database, all relevant actors and a healthy planning process are thought to be useful.

The fourth result is that the fact that the health sector which is complex is the pilot implementation field may have some advantageous aspects for the e-procurement practices in public sector. In other words, making e-procurement system common starting from health sector to other sectors may have some advantages. As a matter of fact,, most of the interviewees in this case said that they were aware of the difficulties of the health sector but choosing the health sector as the pilot implementation field was a right decision. For example, one interviewee reflected on this issue:

...Hospitals have very complex structures. Perhaps, they are the most complex for pilot implementation. However, doing what we do here via e-procurement system in other sectors will be quite easier...

Finally, the case shows that the pilot implementation in the health sector provides a positive environment for the future of the e-procurement system in Turkey. The ideas of the interviewees about the future of the system in spite of the difficulties they faced support this result.

Undoubtedly, this study is mainly based on the findings gained from the interviews carried out in four pilot public hospitals. Therefore, it cannot be claimed that it reflects the whole public sector. When the fact that there are only a few empirical studies in the field of e-procurement in Turkey is taken into consideration, it can be said that this subject has the possibility of being studied in many aspects in the future.

REFERENCES

Akkaynak, O. S. (2004). *In PPA, 2003 Yılı Faaliyet Raporu* [2003 Activity Report]. (pp. 3–5). Ankara: Sunuş.

Akyer, M. (2011). *E-İhale ve EKAP Uygulamaları*. Retrieved July 14, 2011, from http://www.diskapieah.gov.tr/dokumanlar/ekap.ppt

Bof, F., & Previtali, P. (2007). Organisational pre-conditions for e-procurement in governments: The Italian experience in the public health care sector. *The Electronic Journal of E-Government*, *5*(1), 1–10. Retrieved July 12, 2011

Cromm, S., & Brandon-Jones, A. (2007). Impact of e-procurement: Experiences from ımplementation in the UK public sector. *Journal of Purchasing and Supply Management*, *13*(4), 294–303. doi:10.1016/j.pursup.2007.09.015

E-Government Advisory Group. (2008). *Öncelikli 11 E-Devlet Projesi*. 12 Haziran, Ankara.

Eisenhardt, K. M. (1989). Building theories from case study. *Academy of Management Review*, *14*(4), 532–550.

Engström, A., Wallström, A., & Salehi-Sangari, E. (2009). Implementation of public e-procurement in Swedish government entities. In *Proceedings of the International Multiconference on Computer Science and Information Technology* (pp. 315-319). Retrieved July 14, 2011, from http://www.e-procurement.nu/eprocurement/download/publicatiesoverig/implementatie-e-procurement-in-zweedse-overheid.pdf

European Commission. (2010). *Green Paper on expanding the use of e-Procurement in the EU.* Retrieved July 14, 2011, from http://ec.europa.eu/internal_market/consultations/docs/2010/e-procurement/green-paper_en.pdf

Gardenal, F. (2010, August 26-28). *Public e-procurement define, measure and optimize organizational benefits*. Paper presented at the 4th International Public Procurement Conference, Seoul, South Korea. Retrieved July 14, 2011, from http://www.ippa.org/IPPC4/Proceedings/05e-Procurement/Paper5-1.pdf

Gül, H. (2010). Kamu İhale Kurumu Başkanı Hasan Gül'ün Bilişim Ajandası Dergisine verdiği bilgi, *Bilişim Dergisi, 127*. Retrieved July 14, 2011, from http://www.bilisimdergisi.org/s127

Gül, H. (2011, April 4). *Kamu İhale Kurumu Başkanı Hasan Gül'ün Telekom Dünyasına verdiği bilgi.* Retrieved July 14, 2011, from http://www.telekomdunyasi.com/?action=haber_detay&id=78

Gunasekaran, A., & Ngai, E. W. T. (2008). Adoption of e-procurement in Hong Kong: An empirical research. *International Journal of Production Economics, 113*, 159–175. doi:10.1016/j.ijpe.2007.04.012

Hatch, J. A. (2002). *Doing qualitative research in education settings*. Albany, NY: State University of New York Press.

Hawking, P., Stein, A., Wyld, D. C., & Foster, S. (2004). E-procurement: Is the ugly duckling actually a swan down under? *Asia Pacific Journal of Marketing and Logistics, 16*(1), 3–26. doi:10.1108/13555850410765140

Joia, L. A., & Zamot, F. (2002, June 17-19). *Eprocurement by the Brazilian government some findings from a case study.* Paper presented at the 15th Bled Electronic Commerce Conference eReality: Constructing the eEconomy, Bled, Slovenia. Retrieved July 14, 2011, from http://ecom.fov.uni-mb.si/proceedings.nsf/Proceedings/6C6F126D51DD7065C1256E9F00354995/$File/joia.pdf

Kamu İhale Kurumu ile Sağlık Bakanlığı Arasında İmzalanan İşbirliği Protokolü. (2005, November 11). Retrieved July 14, 2011, from http://www.ihale.gov.tr/e_zirve/3_program.pps

Kopits, G., & Craig, J. (1998). *Transparency in government operations.* Occasional Paper. Washington, DC: IMF.

Manchester Declaration. (2005, November 24). Retrieved July 14, 2011, from http://ec.europa.eu/information_society/activities/egovernment/docs/pdf/manchester_declaration.pdf

Meyer, T. (2011, February). *E-procurement: Public procurement worth two trillion euros needs smarter spending.* Deutsche Bank Research, Germany. Retrieved July 14, 2011, from http://www.dbresearch.de/PROD/DBR_INTERNET_DE-PROD/PROD0000000000269867.PDF

Moon, M. J. (2005). E-procurement management in state governments: Diffusion of e-procurement practices and its determinants. *Journal of Public Procurement, 5*(1), 54–72.

Neale, P., Thapa, S., & Boyce, C. (2006). *Preparing a case study: A guide for designing and conducting a case study for evaluation input.* Pathfinder International. Retrieved July 15, 2011, from http://www.pathfind.org/site/DocServer/m_e_tool_series_case_study.pdf

Office of the Prime Minister. (2002). *e-Türkiye Girişimi I. Ara Rapor*, Mayıs.

Office of the Prime Minister. (2003). *e-Dönüşüm Türkiye Projesi.* 27 Şubat 2003 tarihli genelge.

PLS-Ramboll. (2000). *Analysis of electronic public procurement pilot projects in the European Union.* Retrieved July 10, 2011, from http://www.eproc.org/site/guides/analysisofeprocurement.pdf

PPA. (2003). *2002 Yılı Mali Raporu* [2002 Financial Report]. Ankara.

PPA. (2004). *2003 Yılı Faaliyet Raporu* [2003 Activity Report]. Ankara.

PPA. (2005a). *2004 Yılı Faaliyet Raporu* [2004 Activity Report]. Ankara.

PPA. (2005b). *Elektronik Kamu Satınalma Sistemi Bilgi Notu, Ankara*. Retrieved July 14, 2011, from http://www.ihale.gov.tr/eihalecs/EKSAS_bilgi_notu.pdf

PPA. (2005c, June 13). *E-İhale Forumu, Ankara*. Retrieved July 14, 2011, from http://www.ihale.gov.tr/Elektronik_Ihale/Elektronik_Ihale.htm

PPA. (2005d, November 16). *E-İhale Zirvesi, İstanbul*. Retrieved July 14, 2011, from http://www.ihale.gov.tr/Elektronik_Ihale/Elektronik_Ihale.htm

PPA. (2006). *2005 Yılı Faaliyet Raporu* [2005 Activity Report]. Ankara.

PPA. (2007). *2006 Yılı Faaliyet Raporu* [2006 Activity Report]. Ankara.

PPA. (2008). *2007 Yılı Faaliyet Raporu* [2007 Activity Report]. Ankara.

PPA. (2009). *E-İhale: EKAP-Elektronik Kamu Alımları Platformu.* 14 Aralık 2009 Sunum.

PPA. (2010). *2009 Yılı Faaliyet Raporu* [2009 Activity Report]. Ankara.

PPA. (2011a). *EKAP Nedir? Eğitim Sunusu*. Retrieved July 14, 2011, from http://www.dmo.gov.tr/Duyurular/egitim/KİKEĞİTİMi2011SUNUMLARI/EkapNedir.pptx

PPA. (2011b). *EKAP statistics*. Retrieved July, 20, from https://ekap.kik.gov.tr/EKAP/Default.aspx

Public Procurement Law. *Laws of Turkish Republic*, No 4734 of 2002. Retrieved July 14, 2011, from http://www.mevzuat.gov.tr

Ronchi, S., Brun, A., Golini, R., & Fan, X. (2010). What is the value of an IT e-procurement system? *Journal of Purchasing and Supply Management*, *16*, 131–140. doi:10.1016/j.pursup.2010.03.013

Singer, M., Konstantinidis, G., Roubik, E., & Beffermann, E. (2009). Does e-procurement save the state money? *Journal of Public Procurement*, *9*(1), 58–78.

Social Security Institution. (2011). *2010 Yılı Faaliyet Raporu* [2010 Activity Report]. Ankara.

Solak, F. (2010). *Elektronik İhale Projesi*. 7. Ulusal Tıp Bilişimi Kongresi Sunusu. Retrieved July 14, 2011, from http://www.turkmia.org/files/konusma2010/solak.pptx

Solak, F. (2011). E-İhale ve Ayrıntıları. *Röportaj*, 44-46.

Somasundaram, R. (2008). Challenges in ımplementation of e-procurement in the Indian government. In Anttiroiko, A.-V. (Ed.), *Electronic government: Concepts, methodologies, tools, and applications* (pp. 2106–2121). New York, NY: Information Science Reference. doi:10.4018/978-1-59904-947-2.ch159

State Planning Organization. (2004). *e-Dönüşüm Türkiye Projesi Kısa Dönem Eylem Planı (2003-2004)*. Ankara.

State Planning Organization. (2005). *e-Dönüşüm Türkiye Projesi 2003-2004 Kısa Dönem Eylem Planı Uygulama Sonuçları ve 2005 Eylem Planı.* Ankara.

Thai, K. V. (2004). Challenges in public procurement. In K. V. Thai, et al., (Eds.), *Challenges in public procurement: An ınternational perspective* (Vol. 3). Boca Raton, FL: Academics Press. Retrieved July 14, 2011, from http://www.ippa.ws/ippc1_book.html

Yu, Y., Yu, H., Itoga, H., & Lin, T. (2008). Decision-making factors for effective industrial e-procurement. *Technology in Society*, *30*, 163–169. doi:10.1016/j.techsoc.2007.12.004

ADDITIONAL READING

Dooley, K., & Purchase, S. (2006). Factors influencing e- procurement usage. *Journal of Public Procurement*, *6*(1), 28–45.

Garrido-Samaniego, M. J., Gutiérrez-Arranz, A. M., & José-Cabezudo, R. S. (2010). Assessing the impact of e-procurement on the structure of the buying centre. *International Journal of Information Management*, *30*, 135–143. doi:10.1016/j.ijinfomgt.2009.08.004

Gilbert, M. (2008). Public procurement in developing countries. *3rd International Public Procurement Conference Proceedings,* August, 28-30, (pp. 1055-1064).

Hardy, C. A., & Williams, S. P. (2008). E-government policy and practice: A theoretical and empirical exploration of public e-procurement. *Government Information Quarterly*, *25*, 155–180. doi:10.1016/j.giq.2007.02.003

Henriksen, H. Z., & Mahnke, V. (2005). E-procurement adoption in the Danish public sector: The influence of economic and political rationality. *Scandinavian Journal of Information Systems*, *17*(2), 85–106.

Prier, E., & McCue, C. P. (2009). The implications of a muddled definition of public procurement. *Journal of Public Procurement*, *9*(3-4), 326–370.

Qiao, Y., Thai, K. V., & Cummings, G. (2009). State and local procurement preferences: A survey. *Journal of Public Procurement*, *9*(3-4), 371–410.

Reddick, C. G., & Frank, H. A. (2007). The perceived impacts of e-government on U.S. cities: A survey of Florida and Texas city managers. *Government Information Quarterly*, *24*(3), 576–594. doi:10.1016/j.giq.2006.09.004

Snider, K. F., & Rendon, R. G. (2008). Public procurement policy: Implications for theory and practice. *Journal of Public Procurement*, *8*(3), 310–333.

Vaidya, K., Sajeev, A. S. M., & Callender, G. (2006). Critical factors that influence e-procurement implementation success in the public sector. *Journal of Public Procurement*, *6*(1), 70–99.

KEY TERMS AND DEFINITIONS

Electronic Public Procurement Platform (EKAP): An electronic environment accessible from PPA website, in which the contracting entities and other stakeholders can conduct the proceedings related with the procurement process via internet (PPL, Article 4).

Needs Report: A report showing the characteristic, type and amount of purchase of goods and services as well as those of the construction work of administrations.

Open Procedure: A procedure whereby any tenderer may submit a tender (PPL, Article 4).

Public Procurement Authority (PPA): An independent administrative authority regulating public procurement field in Turkey.

Public Procurement Bulletin: A free electronic bulletin including tender notices and published by PPA (PPA, 2006, p. 142).

Public Procurement Law (PPL): A law establishing the principles and procedures related to all procurement process of public administrations in Turkey.

Tender Document: Administrative specifications including the instructions to tenderers, technical specifications including the project, draft contract and other required documents and information related to goods, services or works to be procured (PPL, Article 4).

Chapter 9
Electronic Tax Filing: Preliminary Evidence from a Developing Country

Viveka Ramoo
Universiti Sains Malaysia, Malaysia

T. Ramayah
Universiti Sains Malaysia, Malaysia

May-Chiun Lo
Universiti Malaysia Sarawak, Malaysia

Teoh Ai Ping
Universiti Sains Malaysia, Malaysia

ABSTRACT

Governments are seeking to benefit from information technology by incorporating various government services online for the benefits of the citizen. The Malaysian government as part of its Multimedia Super Corridor (MSC) project introduced e-filing in 2006, which is the process of filing taxes using the Internet as one of the e-government services. This is an exploratory study to model the determinants of intention to use an Internet tax filing system. The authors used 4 variables as predictors or intention to use which were perceived usefulness, perceived ease of use, perceived risk, and facilitating condition. Data was collected from 100 respondents using non probability purposive sampling via a structured questionnaire. As hypothesized, perceived ease of use, perceived usefulness, and facilitating condition were positively related to intention to use. The findings show that perceived usefulness has the strongest influence on intention to use ($\beta = 0.341$), followed by perceived ease of use ($\beta = 0.278$) and facilitating condition ($\beta = 0.234$). As hypothesized, perceived risk was negatively related ($\beta = -0.223$) to intention to use indicating that users are concerned by the risk involved in filing taxes online. The regression results show that the four variables can explain 52.2% of the variation in intention to use which indicates good explanatory power. Understanding these factors can extend the knowledge, which can lead to better planning and implementation of e-Filing in Malaysia.

DOI: 10.4018/978-1-4666-2119-0.ch009

INTRODUCTION

Over recent years, government use of the Internet as a platform to provide services to citizens has grown significantly. One of the major priorities already identified by many officials in charge of introducing electronic government is tax. Governments around the world have quickly realized that electronic filing of tax, if properly used; provide a way to greatly simplify the revenue collection process.

Considerable savings can be derived from propagating Internet tax filing system or e-Filing as it is known in Malaysia. Forrester Research (2001), has identified that savings fall in the following three categories.

- Automated data entry yields great savings. Government clerks need not reenter tax information once entered by taxpayer and sent electronically to the relevant government database. As a result, the productivity of data entry and checking doubles to 10 tax files a day-reducing labor expenses for data handling personnel by 80 percent.
- Fewer errors lighten verification and correction burden. Intelligent data entry and the elimination of data re-entry, combine to bring the error rate to 5 percent in countries like Ireland.
- Electronic data exchange reduces printing and mailing costs. Tax departments may spend considerable amount of money to subcontract printing and mailing of tax forms.

In the Asia-Pacific region, Malaysia and Japan were the 2 countries with the lowest number of users making transactions using online government with just 12% and 13% respectively. Singapore leads the region with 53% although Australia has seen the most significant increase in online government service usage from 31% to 46%. (The Star, Nov 12, 2002)

Starting in 2006, Malaysian citizens are able to choose from two methods tax-filing: manual and Internet based or e-Filing. This is the first year the Inland Revenue Board (IRB) Malaysia introduced the use of online tax return filing.

According to The Star May 1 2006, 120,000 taxpayers have filed their returns electronically. IRB chief executive officer Tan Sri Zainal Abidin Abdul Rashid said the IRB wants to play a proactive role by encouraging taxpayers to adopt e-Filing, which is easier and faster. This is inline with the Government's Information Technology policy. He added that the IRB would begin a nation-wide campaign at the end of this year to encourage people to file their tax return electronically. The 120,000 tax returns represent about 1.2% of the population of the tax payers. The number of taxpayers is expected to steadily rise. The predicted number of the population that is expected to be within the age group of 25-55 years of age in 2010 is expected to rise to 12 million. Unofficial sources have put the cost saving of processing each tax return form at RM10.00. This point to a potential cost saving of millions of dollars.

The objective of this paper is to study what factors influence intention to use e-Filing among taxpayers in Penang, Malaysia.

RESEARCH MODEL AND HYPOTHESES

The basic theory that forms the basis of this research is the Technology acceptance model developed by Davis (1989). Technology Acceptance Model (TAM) is tailored for IS contexts, and was designed to predict information technology acceptance and usage on the job (Venkatesh, Morris, Davis & Davis, 2003). TAM introduced by Davis (1986) specifies two particular beliefs- perceived usefulness and perceived ease of us. Perceived usefulness (PU) is defined by (Davis, 1989) as the degree to which a person believes that using a particular technology will enhance his performance. Perceived Ease of Use (PEU) is defined by (Davis, 1989) as the degree to which a person believes that using a particular system would be free of effort. Behavioral intention (BI) is defined as the extent to which an individual intends to perform a specific behavior (Davis et al., 1989).

Further to that we added two other variables which are facilitating condition and also perceived risk as these two variables are deemed as important predictors of intention to use E-filing. The research framework is presented in Figure 1.

Perceived Ease of Use

Perceived ease of use is defined by (Davis, 1989) as the degree to which a person believes that using a particular system would be free of effort. Past research provides evidence of the significant effect of perceived ease of use on usage intention either directly or indirectly through its effect on perceived usefulness (Agarwal & Prasad, 1999, Davis et al.,1989, Venkatesh, 2000; Ramayah & Aafaqi 2004, Ramayah 2006a, 2006b).

Information systems that users perceive easier to use and less complex will increase the likelihood of its adoption and usage (Teo et al., 1999). Perceived ease of use has been shown to influence behavior (i.e., IT adoption) through two causal ways: (1) a direct effect on behavior intention and (2) indirect effect on behavior intention via perceived usefulness.

Perceived ease of use positively influences behavioral intention. Past research by Hong et al., (2001), Gefen et al., (2003), Venkatesh et al., (2003) and Heijden et al., (2003) also found perceived ease of use to influence behavioral intention. In order to encourage tax payers in Malaysia to use e-Filing, it is paramount to understand the factors that influence the intention to use e-Filing. Thus, the suggestion for the hypothesis is:

H1: Perceived ease of use is positively related to intention to use

Perceived Usefulness

Perceived usefulness is defined as a degree which a person believes that using a particular system would enhance his or her job performance (Davis, 1989). When an individual believes that a technology can bring achievement in their job, when the particular system is used then this also signifies perceived usefulness (Davis, 1989; Davis et al 1989). Igbaria (1990) found that perceived usefulness has a positive relationship with system usefulness. Perceived usefulness is the main key to encourage the positive attitude of using (Davis et al. 1989; Ramayah et al., 2003; Ndubisi et al., 2005; Fu et al., 2006). The asynchronous adoption of different types of services relates to perceived usefulness, enjoyment and new possibilities (Carlsson et al., 2005). For example, some services

Figure 1. The research model

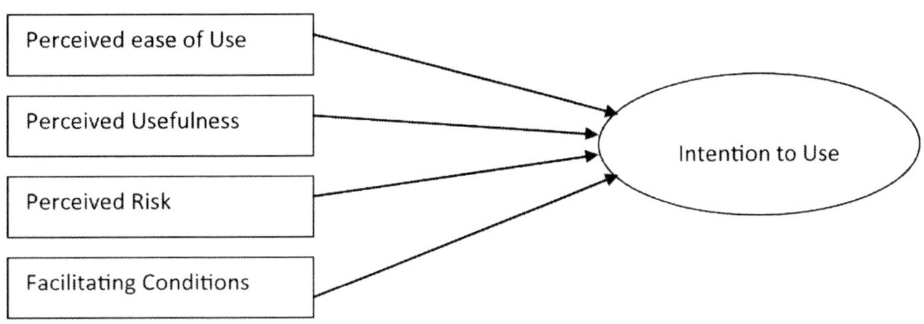

have not been as successful as others because of their business ideas or business models have not been understood or considered attractive by users. According to our line of thinking, if users find the technology to be useful or enjoyable, they will use them. On the other hand, people will be likely to use e-Filing services if they think it will be useful and can help them in their job or performance of a particular task. Thus the next hypothesis was formulated as:

H2: Perceived usefulness is positively related to intention to use

Perceived Risk

A common and widely recognized obstacle to electronic commerce adoption has been the lack of security and privacy over the Internet (Bhimani, 1996; Cockburn & Wilson, 1996; Quein & Klein, 1996). According to Chan and Lu (2004), this has led many people to view e-commerce and Internet application as risky undertakings. Therefore in the context of this study, individuals who regard e-Filing as low risk would have a tendency to accept and use e-Filing.

Studies have shown significant negative relationship between perceived risk and attitude (Jarvenpaa & Todd, 1997; Bobbitt & Dabholkar, 2001; Heijden et al., 2003; Liu & Wei, 2003). Studies showing negative relationship between perceived risk and perceived usefulness includes (Lee et al., 2001; Lee & Ho, 2002; Featherman, 2001; Chan & Lu, 2004; Ramayah et al., 2005).

Frambach (1993, 1995) contends that the speed of adoption is negatively related to the level of perceived risk. The perceived risk surrounding an innovation might cause a potential adopter to postpone the decision to adopt or reject the innovation. Users of e-Filing are influenced by risks they perceive, whether or not such risk actually exists is another matter. Their perception of e-Filing will affect their speed of adopting the system. Therefore, perceived risk was included as one of the determinants of use in the present study. Thus the hypothesis is as follows:

H3: Perceived risk is negatively related to intention to use

Facilitating Conditions

An environment with proper facilitating conditions will promote the exhibition of the appropriate behavior (Triandis, 1977). Taylor and Todd (1995) suggested that facilitating conditions be made up of 2 aspects, namely resource facilitating conditions and technological facilitating conditions.

Fu, Fan and Chao (2006) elaborated that the absence of facilitating resources results in barrier to usage which may inhibit usage. Thus, a taxpayer might be unwilling to accept e-Filing if little or no computer equipment is available and if technical support is low. Facilitating conditions was tested in a number technology acceptance study. The finding from Thompson et al. (1994), Venkatesh and Davis (1996), Taylor and Todd (1995), and, Jiang (2000) empirically supported the impact of facilitating conditions on use. Facilitating conditions was found to have a direct relationship on infusion and adoption of a number of new information system innovations (Cheung & Chang, 2000; Jones, Sundaraman & Chin, 2002).

For this study facilitating conditions encompasses government support and resource support such as computers, connectivity to Internet and training. This includes government provisions of computer support. Training could lead to increased self-efficacy which ultimately facilitates the diffusion and utilization of technology (Agarwal, Sambamurthy & Stair, 2000). Therefore, the proposed hypothesis is:

H4: Facilitating conditions is positively related to intention to use

METHODOLOGY

The population of this study is individuals who are tax payers' in Malaysia. As it would be impossible to get a list of all tax payers and it would be very difficult and time consuming to conduct the survey nationwide we decided to only sample taxpayers in Penang. As this is a preliminary study we used a non-probability convenient sampling method. A self administered structured questionnaire was used to gather the data. A total of 100 responses were used for the purpose of the analysis. The measures were adopted from various literature identified in the literature review section.

Goodness of Measures

To assess goodness of measures we used the factor analysis and reliability analysis. A principal component factor analysis with an orthogonal rotation (Varimax) was executed and the results show a 4 factor solution presented in Table 1. The Kaiser-Meyer-Olkin (KMO) measure of sampling adequacy value was 0.776 indicating sufficient correlation for a factor analysis and the Bartlett's test was significant (χ^2 = 1186.83, p< 0.01). The total variance explained was 79.493%. We used the criteria used by Igbaria et al., (1995) to identify and interpret factors as: each item should load 0.50 or greater on one factor and 0.35 or lower on the other factor. The reliability values were also high ranging from 0.86 to 0.93 indicating excellent reliability. For intention to use the reliability was also a high 0.94. Thus we can conclude that the measures used for this study is both valid and reliable.

Table 1. Results of the factor analysis

	Component			
	1	2	3	4
PU1	-.171	**.810**	.161	-.051
PU2	-.207	**.747**	.285	.006
PU3	-.272	**.865**	.225	-.057
PU4	-.288	**.864**	.248	-.035
PEU1	.084	.343	**.531**	-.333
PEU2	-.070	.142	**.880**	-.003
PEU3	.063	.293	**.841**	-.017
PEU4	-.100	.200	**.894**	-.038
FC1	.006	-.017	-.102	**.899**
FC2	.110	.022	-.001	**.890**
FC3	.146	-.102	-.040	**.902**
PRISK1	**.857**	-.273	-.010	.084
PRISK2	**.853**	-.251	-.126	.055
PRISK3	**.944**	-.123	-.007	.083
PRISK4	**.863**	-.171	.050	.075
Eigenvalue	3.387	3.166	2.814	2.557
Variance (79.493)	22.581	21.105	18.761	17.046
Reliability	0.93	0.91	0.86	0.89

RESULTS OF THE STUDY

Table 2 shows the profile of the respondents. There was a good mix of male and females with a majority from the 30-55 age-group, married, Indians, with a degree or above qualification working in the private sector earning RM 3000 a month and above. Most are heavy users of the Internet having a dial up or broadband connection.

To test the hypotheses developed, we used a multiple regression analysis. All the basic assumptions of the regression analysis (Hair et al., 2010) were checked before interpreting the results. The results are presented in Table 3.

The results indicate that 52.2% of the variance in intention to use can be explained by all the four variables. Perceived ease of use (β= 0.278, p< 0.01), perceived usefulness (β= 0.341, p< 0.01) and facilitating conditions (β= 0.234, p< 0.01) were positively related to intention to use whereas perceived risk (β= -0.223, p< 0.01) was negatively related to intention to use. These results support H1, H2, H3 and H4 of this study. In terms of the impact, as predicted perceived usefulness was the most influential followed by perceived ease of use, facilitating conditions and perceived risk.

Table 2. Profile of respondents

	Frequency	Percentage
Gender	52	52
• Male	48	48
• Female		
Age		
• 18-29 years	26	26
• 30-55 years	73	73
• Above 55 years	1	1
Marital Status		
• Single	28	28
• Married	72	72
Race		
• Malay	20	20
• Chinese	35	35
• Indian	44	44
• Others	1	1
Education Level		
• Secondary and below	8	8
• Diploma	16	16
• Professional	8	8
• Bachelors	51	51
• Masters and above	17	17
Work Sector		
• Government	22	22
• Private	76	76
Income		
• RM 1000-RM 2000	16	16
• RM 2001-RM 3000	24	24
• RM 3001-RM 4000	21	21
• Above RM 4000	39	39
Internet Use		
• Never	5	5
• Less than once a month	9	9
• Once a month	1	1
• Once a week	5	5
• Few times a week	80	80
Computer and Network facilities at home		
• Have no computer	4	4
• Have computer but no Internet connection	19	19

continued on following page

Table 2. Continued

	Frequency	Percentage
• Dial up	36	36
• Broadband	41	41
Computer and Network facilities at work		
• Have no computer	1	1
• Have computer but no Internet connection	11	11
• Dial up	13	13
• LAN	36	36
• Broadband	33	33

DISCUSSION

As hypothesized perceived usefulness was the most influential variable identified in this study. This can be due to the fact that when an individual believes that a technology can bring achievement in their job when the particular system is used then this will lead to more usage. (Davis et al. 1989; Igbaria, 1990; Ramayah et al., 2003; Ndubisi et al., 2005; Carlsson et al., 2005; Fu et al., 2006). For example, some services have not been as successful as others because of their business ideas or business models have not been understood or considered attractive by users.

Consistent with past research, perceived ease of use was found to be a significant predictor of intention to use. This finding supports previous researchers evidence of the significant effect of perceived ease of use on usage intention (Agarwal & Prasad, 1999; Davis et al.,1989; Venkatesh 2000; Ramayah & Aafaqi 2004; Ramayah 2006a, 2006b). Information systems that users perceive easier to use and less complex will increase the likelihood of its adoption and usage (Teo et al., 1999). This, points to the need for developing user interfaces that are easy to use to entice reluctant users to get into the e-Filing mode.

Facilitating conditions also has strong positive relationship with perceived ease of use. Although 88% of the respondents had computer and Internet connection at work and 77% of the respondents had computer and Internet connection at home, the respondents think that more facilitating resources like computer and network connections will be a key factor in influencing ease of using e-Filing. This is in sync with past literature that found facilitating condition having a direct relationship on infusion and adoption of a number of new information system innovation (Cheung & Chang, 2000; Jones, Sundaraman & Chin, 2002; Yu, Lu & Liu, 2005). Government could provide provisional support to aid tax payers' to own computers. The provisional support could be in the form of tax exemptions or quick EPF withdrawal for the purpose of purchasing computers.

Perceived risk was an important factor to influence tax payers. Lack of security and privacy

Table 3. Result of multiple regression

Variable	Standardized beta
Perceived ease of use	0.278**
Perceived usefulness	0.341**
Perceived risk	-0.223**
Facilitating conditions	0.234**
F	25.153
R^2	0.522
Adjusted R^2	0.502

Note: **p < 0.01

over the Internet (Bhimani, 1996; Cockburn & Wilson, 1996; Ramayah et al., 2003a) has been identified as a common and widely recognized obstacle to electronic commerce adoption. This has led many people to view e-commerce and Internet application as risky undertakings. As such the government should provide assurance to the users that their data and privacy will be maintained to mitigate this factor.

CONCLUSION

The findings of this study has indicated perceived ease of use, perceived usefulness as significant factors influencing intention to use e-Filing. Focal training at work place, road shows on how to use e-Filing and a step by step procedure to use e-Filing could be sent to all tax payers in the country. This in many ways will encourage users to get into the e-transaction mode. Government could also provide provisional support to aid tax payers' to own computers. The provisional support could be in the form of tax exemptions or quick EPF withdrawal for the purpose of purchasing computers. Another important factor would be to provide reasonable rates for broadband network connections for home users. This would allow more tax payers to adopt e-Filing.

The new system, e-Filing will eventually save the government millions of dollars that can be used for the development of the country but it will be of no benefit if the users, tax payers themselves are reluctant to get into the electronic mode. The government should step up efforts to promote the new system so as to reap the full benefit of the system.

REFERENCES

Agarwal, R., Lewis, W., & Sambamurthy, V. (2003). Sources of influence on beliefs about information technology use: An empirical study of knowledge workers. *Management Information Systems Quarterly*, *27*(4), 657–678.

Agarwal, R., & Prasad, J. (1998). The antecedents and consequences of user perceptions in information technology adoption. *Decision Support Systems*, *22*(1), 15–29. doi:10.1016/S0167-9236(97)00006-7

Agarwal, R., Sambamurthy, V., & Stair, R. M. (2000). Research report: The evolving relationship between general and specific computer self-efficacy – An empirical assessment. *Information Systems Research*, *11*(4), 418–430. doi:10.1287/isre.11.4.418.11876

Bhimani, A. (1996). Securing the commercial internet. *Communications of the ACM*, *39*(6), 29–35. doi:10.1145/228503.228509

Bobbitt, M. L., & Dabholkar, P. A. (2001). Integrating attitudinal theories to understand and predict use of technology-based self-service. *International Journal of Science Industry Management*, *12*(5), 423–450.

Carlsson, C., Hyvonen, K., Repo, P., & Walden, P. (2005). *Adoption of mobile services across different technologies.* Retrieved October 13, 2006, from http://www.bledconference.org/

Chan, S. C., & Lu, M. T. (2004). Understanding Internet banking adoption and user behavior: A Hong Kong perspective. *Journal of Global Information Management*, *12*(3), 21–43. doi:10.4018/jgim.2004070102

Cheung, W., & Chang, M. K. (2000). Prediction of Internet and World Wide Web usage at work: A test of an extended Triandis model. *Decision Support Systems, 30*(1), 83–100. doi:10.1016/S0167-9236(00)00125-1

Cockburn, C., & Wilson, T. D. (1996). Business use of the World-Wide Web. *International Journal of Information Management, 16*(2), 83–102. doi:10.1016/0268-4012(95)00071-2

Davis, D. F., Bagozzi., P, R., & Warsaw, R. P. (1989). User acceptance of computer technology: A comparison of two theoretical models. *Management Science, 35*(8), 982–1003. doi:10.1287/mnsc.35.8.982

Davis, F. D. (1986). *A technology acceptance model empirical testing new end-user information systems: Theory and results*. Doctoral dissertation, Sloan School of Management, Massachusetts Institute of Technology.

Davis, F. D. (1989). Perceived usefulness, perceived ease of use and user acceptance of Information Technology. *Management Information Systems Quarterly, 13*(3), 319–340. doi:10.2307/249008

Featherman, M. S. (2001). Extending the technology acceptance model by inclusion of perceived risk. *Proceedings of the Seventh Americans Conference on Information Systems,* (pp. 758-760).

Forrester Research Inc. (2001, April). *eFiling kick-starts government.*

Frambach, R. T. (1993). An integrated model of organizational adoption and diffusion of innovations. *European Journal of Marketing, 27*(5), 22–41. doi:10.1108/03090569310039705

Frambach, R. T. (1995). Diffusion of innovations in business –to-business markets. In M. Bruce & W. G. Biemans (Eds.), *Product development: Meeting the challenge of the design-marketing interface*, (pp. 249-245). John Wiley and Sons Ltd.

Fu, J. R., Fan, C. K., & Chao, W. P. (2006). Acceptance of electronic tax filing: A study of tax payers intentions. *Journal of International Management, 43*(1), 109–126.

Gefen, D., Straub, D. W., & Karahana, E. (2003). Trust and TAM in online shopping: An integrated model. *Management Information Systems Quarterly, 27*(1), 51–90.

Hair, J. F., Black, W. C., Babin, B. J., & Anderson, R. E. (2010). *Multivariate data analysis*. Upper Saddle River, NJ: Prentice-Hall.

Heijden, H., Verhage, T., & Creemers, M. (2003). Understanding online purchase intentions. Contributions from technology and trust perspective. *European Journal of Information Systems, 12*(1), 41–48. doi:10.1057/palgrave.ejis.3000445

Hong, W., Thong, J., Wong, W., & Tam, K. Y. (2001). Determinants of user acceptance of digital libraries: An empirical examination of individual differences and system characteristics. *Journal of Management Information Systems, 18*(3), 97–124.

Igbaria, M., Parasuraman, S., & Baroudi, J. J. (1996). A motivational model of computer usage. *Journal of Management Information Systems, 13*(1), 127–143.

Jarvenpaa, S. L., & Todd, P. A. (1997). Consumer reactions to electronic shopping in the World Wide Web. *International Journal of Electronic Commerce, 1*(2), 59–88.

Jones, E., Sundaram, S., & Chin, W. (2002). Factors leading to sales force automation use: A longitudinal analysis. *Journal of Personal Selling & Sales Management, 22*(3), 145–157.

Lee, D., Park, J., & Ahn, J. (2001). On the explanation of factors affecting e-commerce adoption. *Twenty-Second International Conference on Information Systems,* (pp. 109-120).

Lee, J. E., & Ho, P. S. (2002). A retail investor's perspective on the acceptance if Internet stock trading. *Proceedings of the 36th HICSS,* (pp. 1-11).

Ndubisi, N. O., Gupta, O. K., & Ndubisi, G. C. (2005). The moguls' model of computing: Integrating the moderating impact of users' persona into the technology acceptance model. *Journal of Global Information Technology Management*, *8*(1), 27–47.

Ramayah, T. (2006a). Doing e-research with e-library. *The International Journal of Technology Knowledge & Society*, *1*(4), 71–82.

Ramayah, T. (2006b). Interface characteristics, perceived ease of use and intention to use an online library in Malaysia. *Information Development*, *22*(2), 123–133. doi:10.1177/0266666906065575

Ramayah, T., & Aafaqi, B. (2004). Role of self-efficacy in e-library usage among students of a public university in Malaysia. *Malaysian Journal of Library & Information Science*, *9*(1), 39–57.

Ramayah, T., Dahlan, N., Teck, T. K., & Aafaqi, B. (2003a). Perceived web security and web-based online transaction intent. *Multimedia Cyberspace Journal (MMCJ), 1.*

Ramayah, T., Ignatius, J., & Aafaqi, B. (2005). PC usage among students in a private institution of higher learning: The moderating role of prior experience. *Educators and Education Journal*, *20*, 131–152.

Ramayah, T., Zainudin, Y., & Youn, F. C. (2003b). The effect of self-efficacy on internet usage in the organization. *Jurnal ANALISIS*, *10*(2), 187–220.

Taylor, S., & Todd, P. (1995). Understanding the information technology usage: A test of competing models. *Information Systems Research*, *6*(2), 144–176. doi:10.1287/isre.6.2.144

The Star. (2002a, 12 November). Malaysia sees growth in e-government usage. *The Star, Business*, p.11

The Star. (2006a, May 1). IRB won't send out the tax forms from next year. *The Star*. *Nation (New York, N.Y.)*, (n.d.), 1.

The Sun. (2006a, 19 April). eFiling digital certificate. *The Star*, p.5

Triandis, H. C. (1977). *Interpersonal behavior*. Monetary, CA: Brooks/Cole.

Venkatesh, V. (2000). Determinants of perceived ease of use: Integrating control, intrinsic motivation, and emotion into the technology acceptance model. *Information Systems Research, 11*(4), 342–365. doi:10.1287/isre.11.4.342.11872

Venkatesh, V., & Davis, F. D. (1996). A model of the antecedents of perceived ease of use: Development and test. *Decision Sciences*, *27*(3), 451–481. doi:10.1111/j.1540-5915.1996.tb01822.x

Venkatesh, V., & Davis, F. D. (2000). A theoretical expansion of the technology acceptance model: four longitudinal field studies. *Management Science*, *46*(2), 186–204. doi:10.1287/mnsc.46.2.186.11926

Venkatesh, V., Morris, G. M., Davis, B. G., & Davis, D. F. (2003). User acceptance of information technology: Toward a unified view. *Management Information Systems Quarterly*, *27*(3), 425–478.

Chapter 10
Implementing Authentication in an E-Procurement System

Miloš Milovanović
University of Belgrade, Serbia

Miroslav Minović
University of Belgrade, Serbia

Dejan Simić
University of Belgrade, Serbia

Dušan Starčević
University of Belgrade, Serbia

ABSTRACT

E-government can provide citizen with better and/or more convenient services as oppose to traditional government services. Using electronic approach in completing a procurement process opens up a lot of issues regarding security. Transparent nature of the process at hand is requiring a sophisticated security system. Unauthorized access or different intrusion types are presenting a legitimate threat. On the other hand, developing such system in a developing country as Serbia bears many difficulties. Some of them are legal obstacles, technical weaknesses, as well as human resistance towards change. The focus of this chapter lies on methods used to overcome those difficulties as well as provide a strong security system that will guarantee the protection of sensitive data.

E-GOVERNMENT AND E-PROCUREMENT

The communication technologies, Internet especially, caused a big change, maybe even a revolution in people's everyday lives, work activities and conducting of business in companies. Today, large amount of transaction can be done online. Some of them are paying taxes, changing your address of residence or automatic registration. For these transactions to be conducted it is necessary to connect the government with citizen, businesses or some other social entities by use of Internet. E-government, electronic govern-

DOI: 10.4018/978-1-4666-2119-0.ch010

ment or online government presents a concept whose purpose is to allow access to governmental institutions through Internet. There are different definitions of E-government. It can be defined as use of technologies in order to improve access to and delivery of government services for citizen, business and employees wellbeing. It presents the use of Internet technologies as a platform for exchange of information, providing of services as well as transactions for citizen, businesses and other users. According to Institute for Software Technology at UN University E-government is the use of informational-communication technologies by public government in providing the information and services to citizen, businesses and other social entities. E-government is focused on citizen, business community, government employees and other governments.

Another definition states that the term E-government, in a wider sense, is aimed at simplifying the informational, communication process as well as performing transaction between government institution, citizen and businesses.

Informational process is defined as one-way gathering of information. Communication, on the other side, represents a two-way information exchange. Transaction is a transfer of objects or right among two entities in communication process.

E-government consists of E-Administration, E-Democracy and E-Justice. “E” stands for electronic. E-Administration is actually E-government in a nutshell since is mainly focused on simplifying the administration process. E-Democracy could for example be electronic electoral voting by SMS or Internet service with no need to visit the voting post. E-Justice represents a conduct of juditional process via electronic communication. Instead of writing a complaint and sending it in paper form, you can send it by e-mail or submit it by use of court’s web portal. Court’s web portal represents an interface for communication with public. Communication in that process is mostly done electronically.

Some advantages for E-government use are:

- Simplifying a process of service providing to citizen
- Eliminating management levels in government
- Downsizing of costs
- Broadening the number of services that government can provide
- Makes information and services easily accessible to citizen, businesses and government agencies.

Basic interaction models within e-Government are:

- Government-to-Citizen or Government-to-Customer (G2C),
- Government-to-Business (G2B),
- Government-to-Government (G2G), and
- Government-to-Employees (G2E).

Inside each of these models four activities are executed:

- Sending information via Internet,
- Two-way communication between agency and citizens, companies or other government agencies,
- Transactions processing, and
- Management system.

Government-to-Business (G2B) model includes different forms of non-commercial interactions between government and business sector. As defined by UN University – International Institute for software technologies, services enabled with this model are: new company registration, payment for social insurance of employers, taxes, VAT, custom declarations, eco permissions, public procurement and other services. Public procurement is one of the eight most important G2B services. E-procurement is a B2B buying or selling goods and services over the Internet. E-procurement utilizes electronic tools and methods in every phase of the procurement process. Public E-procurement covers all phases from initial announcement to final settlement and payment.

E-procurement should enable functionalities listed below:

- E-Announcement
- E-Tender
- E-Conclusion
- E-Auction
- E-Catalog and E-Ordering
- E-Invoice and E-Payment

In the document *The Role of eGovernment for Europe's future* (2003), by European parliament, public procurement are entitled as area where application of Information and Communication technologies will be very productive. It also states that old-fashion procurement methods are complex, time consuming and resource intense. Information and communication technologies will provide improvement of efficiency, quality and total value in public procurement. One of the major barriers to introduce electronic public procurement is poor law regulation of this area. Without law regulation it is not possible to create efficient electronic public procurement system.

Strong accent in public procurement systems is set on security. By nature, public procurement process is and it should be transparent. By following this rule we avoid possible corruption or misuse of the process. Unfortunately, transparency poses a problem concerning security. Information's posted on procurement portal must be available to all interested parties for review as well as commenting. Since the process is very sensitive identity of those accessing the portal must be authenticated. That is why authentication process must be the corner stone of each e-Procurement system. Proving the identity of each user is necessary in order to provide liability and transparency. The main goal in every security system is to implement triad, confidentiality, integrity and availability, so called C - I – A. The only way for a good implementation of this is to set a strong authentication.

STAKEHOLDERS OF E-PROCUREMENT PORTAL

Stakeholders identified in public procurement process (Larman, 2001), according to our country procurement law are:

A. Ordering Party (The Purchaser)

It is a user that publishes announcement about public procurements to web portal (system user). All purchasers have same permissions. Role of the purchasers in system could be exploited only after successful login to the system. While performing login, system check out which role user belong to and set adequate user privileges on the portal. Purchaser can perform predefined set of tasks, such as: public procurement setup, procurement documents upload.

B. Portal Visitor

He uses portal in order to be informed on active public procurements. Role of the visitor represent basic role on the portal. Every portal user has this role.

C. Offering Party (The Bidder)

Domestic or foreign company or person, or syndicate of more companies or persons, which offer delivery of goods or services. Role of the offering party becomes active only after successful login to the system. While performing login, system check out which role user belong to and set adequate user privileges on the portal. Bidder can perform predefined set of tasks, such as: setup offer, and add offer documents.

D. Administrator

A person who determines the validity of temporarily placed open competition offers and registered users. The role of the administrator in the system starts only after the successful logging to the system. The system checks which role belongs to entered user name and the password, and based on this, it opens privileges for access to certain parts of the portal. The administrator has the right to perform the verification of users, as well as verification of purchase itself. Also, it could have access to parties for survey of open competitions, but in that case, its role is being observed as a role of portal visitor.

PROBLEM STATEMENT

Unauthorized access to public electronic systems presents an outstanding problem for its developers. Those systems are by default open for wide use of all interested parties. Open systems are vulnerable to intrusion and misuse. There are many motives that drive the attackers to break in to such systems. Open systems usually have to types of data contained within. First there are those data that are opened for public review and commenting, and other data represents data that is crucial for establishing system functionality as well as identity confirmation that are usually hidden from the public eye.

Acquiring hidden data can provide attackers with useful information that they can use to gain financial and other types of benefit. By realizing that we should acknowledge that one of the main objectives of such systems is providing security for sensitive data.

There are the potential attacks on a remote authentication method. Here, we are threatened with three types of attack: phishing, malicious software, and man in the middle. All three are attacks against the client, whose protection mechanisms are arguably less sophisticated than those typically found at a server. Figure 1 offers a general perspective of the three attack types.

Figure 1. Typical credentials attack types

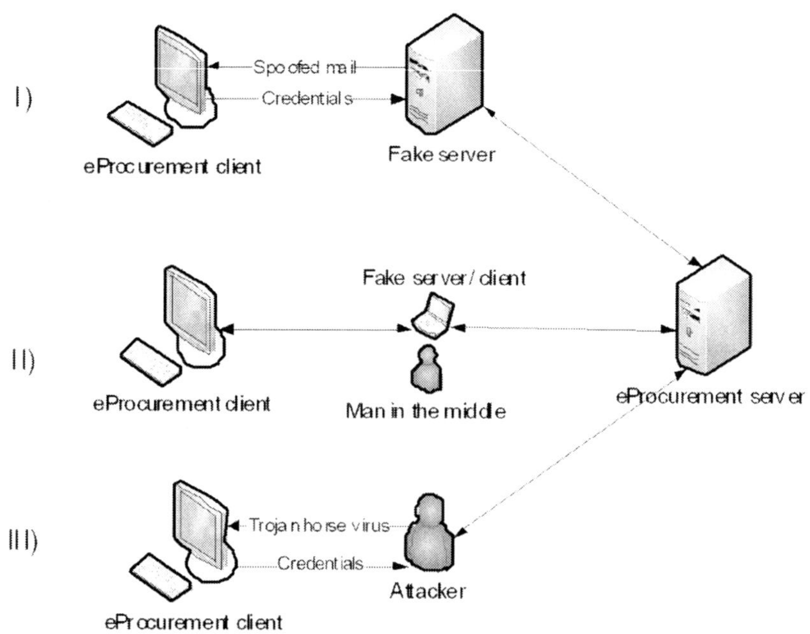

A. Phishing

In the field of computer security, phishing is the criminally fraudulent process of attempting to acquire sensitive information such as usernames, passwords and credit card details, by masquerading as a trustworthy entity in an electronic communication.

B. Man in the middle

The man-in-the-middle attack or bucket-brigade attack (often abbreviated MITM), sometimes Janus attack, is a form of active eavesdropping in which the attacker makes independent connections with the victims and relays messages between them, making them believe that they are talking directly to each other over a private connection when in fact the entire conversation is controlled by the attacker. The attacker must be able to intercept all messages going between the two victims and inject new ones, which is straightforward in many circumstances (for example, the owner of a public wireless access point can in principle conduct MITM attacks on the users).

C. Malicious software

Software designed to infiltrate or damage a computer system without the owner's informed consent. The expression is a general term used by computer professionals to mean a variety of forms of hostile, intrusive, or annoying software or program code. For example, once established, a Trojan horse could read and forward a private key stored on the PC's hard drive while monitoring keyboard activity to access the pass phrase used to decrypt the private key.

The danger of invading a public system such as eProcurement is evident. We have chosen these three attack types because they usually target identity information. Access to public services is actually quite vulnerable process. Stealing someone's credentials and accessing a system without authorization poses a large issue with these types of systems. By use of *Phishing* attacker can acquire username and password from the user and then use them for false impersonation. *Man in the middle* is a particularly good way to misuse systems such as this. Attacker can intercept the communication during authentication process and act as a genuine server while stealing the user's credentials. *Malware* can attempt to steal all the information that is accessible to it. Then it can send them to attacker to use for false impersonation. All these threats pose a problem of confirming someone's true identity.

Establishing a person's identity is usually a simple process. It consists out of comparing information provided, with information from an officially issued document and also by comparing some physical characteristics of a person with the one that can be seen usually on a photograph. As you can notice this type of authentication requires a "face to face" interaction. During the process of the transactions which make use of a 'non-face-to-face', 'non-connection oriented' skills, the identity of the authenticity and non-repudiation of transactions are particularly important, in addition to the safety of the transaction itself (Xian-ge et al, 2008). The problem is that for electronic authentication you cannot establish a "face to face" communication.

In order to confirm identity of a person accessing the system you need to create some form of remote authenticating. By confirming someone's identity you cannot ensure the proper use of your system, but you can ensure liability of person that misuses the system.

USE CASES

In Figure 2, we can see the system boarders with cases of the highest level usage, as well as participants in the process of e-Procurement (Tatnall,

Figure 2. Model of use cases

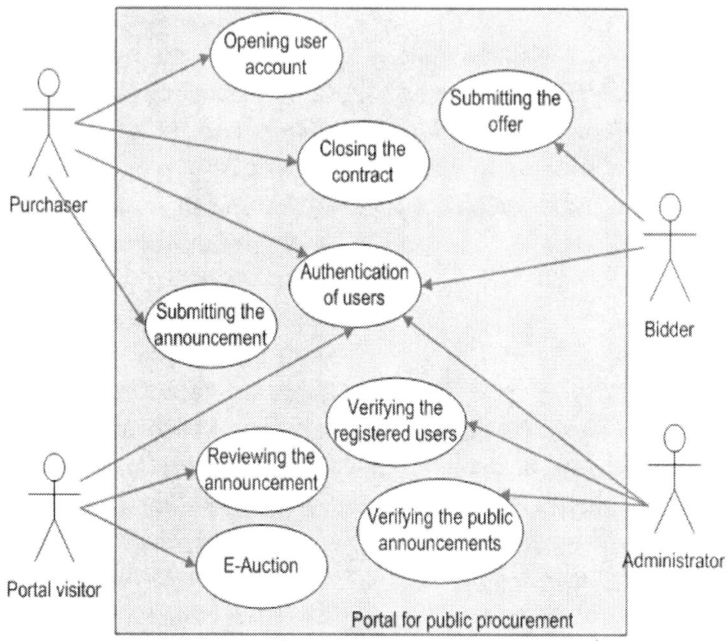

2005; Starcevic et al, 2008). The case of using E-auction is suggested as a system option if this is the way to carry out one part of giving offers to ads concerning such open competitions.

Use cases (Booch et al, 2005) on the highest level are as follows: opening user accounts, change of user accounts, authentication of users, submitting the Announcement, updating the Announcement, closing the contract on public e-procurement, reviewing the Announcement, verification of registered users, verification of submitted Announcements, submitting the offer and attaching the document.

As for opening the user account as an initial action, the owner opens the page for creating new user accounts, and then enters all the relevant user data, chooses user name and sends a request to the system to open new account.

If it is necessary to change some data, the purchaser opens the page for user account update, carries out the change of user data, and then sends the request to the system to update the user account. While logging to the system, the authentication of all entities is necessary. User name and the password are entered, and the request is being sent to the system to carry out the authentication of the account.

The key concept of such web portal is submitting of the Announcement. The purchaser opens the page for submitting the Announcement, and enters all relevant data for wanted Announcement. He sends a request to the system to put into storage this open competition. Of course, sometimes there might be a need to update the Announcement, and then he chooses the Announcement he wants to update. The purchaser enters relevant data for wanted Announcement, and sends a request to the system to put into storage a new version of Announcement. All present Announcements could be reviewed in such way that the visitor chooses search criteria, and then the system lists the search results.

Of course, once the Announcement is entered to the web portal, the bidder can place his own offer for selected purchase. The bidder chooses whether he will enter the offer for the whole purchase, or only for certain items. The system, depending of the type of public e-procurement procedure, enters adequate offer status. He informs the purchaser of this offer via e-mail system. The system informs the bidder of successfully entered offer.

The option for attaching the adequate document for selected Announcement is also predicted. After the selection of Announcement, the user enters the name of the document and the following description, after which he chooses the document he wishes to place. He sends a request to the system to put the document into storage, and in return, the system informs the user of successful document storing.

Under the functionality of this portal, there comes the verification of registered users and verification of placed Announcement. The administrator surveys data and decides on validation not only of users, but of open competitions as well.

The final goal is closing the contract for public e-procurement, where the purchaser chooses his previously selected Announcement or certain items of this Announcement (depending on whether the contract is being closed in accordance with items of Announcement or the whole of Announcement). After that, he chooses the offer which is given for items or the whole Announcement, and enters the text of this contract (or he enters the scanned copy of the contract). Then, the request is sent to the system to put the contract into storage, and close the items, or the whole Announcement.

We proposed using of digital signature (Paine et al, 2002) on all portal documents. Step further is implementation of PKI system – Public key infrastructure (Adams & Lioyd, 2002). This automatically implies using PKI authority. PKI a kind of key management system or security platform following standard, it can transparently provides public key and certificate management needed by public key encryption and digital signatures, and other key services for all network applications (Hua-ging & Sheng-hui, 2008). This authority is responsible for digital certificates publishing. These certificates will be responsible for document integrity preservation and users authentication.

THE PROPOSAL OF AUTHENTICATION

Public procurement process in Serbia is unique from a legal point of view. The Law recognizes two different procurement types. First type are procurements of low financial value, a certain financial amount is set as a prerequisite for this type. Second type is procurements of high financial value, those that overpass the value intended for the first type. Realizing that classification, a unique model of security measures can be applied. Since the Law already recognizes two different groups, security measures can also be divided.

Why is there a need to authenticate a user? People are authenticated to authorize their requests or to capture information that holds them accountable for something (Beardsley, 1972). In order for a client to publish a public procurement, natural condition of proving ones identity is established. In order to make system as efficient as possible, it is important to recognize its primary purpose – publishing a public procurement.

It is a good practice to implement a reliable authentication process by using a separated layer in charge of security and authentication (see Figure 3). This particular layer makes sure there is no unauthorized access to specific business process. Each request for a sensitive operation must go through security layer which is aware of business process limitations according to authorization.

Even though the public procurement is a sensitive process regarding the security, burdening the publishing process with a complicated authentication can consume large time portion and in that way security action prevails over the primary purpose. In our system we differentiated three groups of users, and consequently three authentication types.

Figure 3. Security/authentication layer architecture

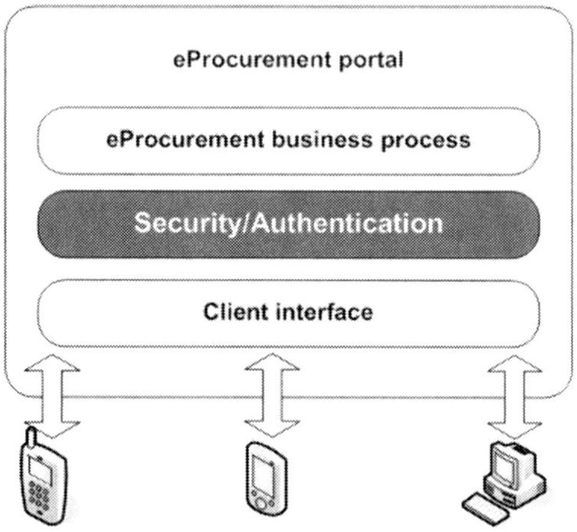

First group are users that are only visitors to procurement portal and are looking for information. They can only post comments or send messages. The authentication process for them is established by use of username and password. This automatically implies the lowest security level, but on the other side rather efficient way of conducting desired action.

Second group are users that use e-Procurement portal to publish only low value public procurements. Since this action is more sensitive than just posting a comment or sending message, authentication level must be on a higher end. In addition to first process we introduce a one-time code authenticating to e-Procurement system. Remote authentication with one-time codes is based on the idea that both client and server share a secret (Lynette & Stephen, 2003). In our implementation it is a mobile based solution. Upon request for authentication from client, web server requests from an application server to generate a one-time code (further referred to as token) and send it to the client via SMS-gateway. Client receives a token through his mobile phone device, whose number he registered with our administrator when opening an account. Then he sends a token back to web server. Finally web server and application server communicate on authenticity of the posted request as shown in Figure 4. Token has a time slot for its validity. This protects misuse of phone device in case of theft. During one working day there can be over 400 low value procurements opened. By applying this process we raise the security to a slightly higher level, but on the same time ensure efficient way of executing the publishing process.

Figure 4. Authentication process for low value procurement

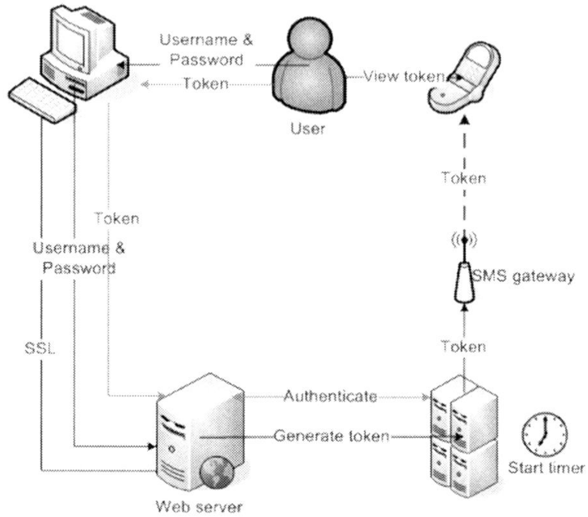

Third group represents the users that usually publish high value procurements, but still retain the right to publish low value procurements as well. Examples of this type of entities would be large companies, state and local government entities, health institutions etc. Number of these entities does not surpass few hundred. Number of high value procurement published during one working day is not a large number. On the other hand a process of publishing high value procurements is rather sensitive since a large amount of financials are involved. This requires raising a security level to the highest possible state. Knowing that, we proposed to implement a three generic authentication which involves using a smart card and biometric abilities. We can describe the three generic means of authentication loosely as "something you know," "something you have," or "something you are." (Beardsley, 1972) This model for authentication that combine biometrics, smartcard and public key infrastructure (PKI) to authenticate the user was already applied in several systems (Yoshiaki et al, 2001; Yoichi, 2002; Bing et al, 2002).

A PKI is a framework for the management of public keys and certificates that is responsible for issuing, maintaining and revoking of the public key certificates over unsecure networks, in particular the Internet. PKI is the combination of software, encryption technologies and services. A PKI permits users of such networks to exchange data through the use of a public and private key pair that is obtained and shared through a trusted authority. The public key is widely distributed, whereas the private key is held secretly by an individual. Messages are protected from malicious people by scrambling them with the public key of the recipient. Only the recipient can decrypt the message by using his / her private key, thus retaining the privacy of the message. The public key is distributed with a digital certificate that contains information that uniquely identifies an individual. Digital certificates identify individuals or organizations. Also, by using digital certificates we can digitally sign messages to protect the integrity of the information itself and achieve non-repudiation. A PKI is built upon the concept of trust, that is, how much confidence users may give to the digital certificates provided by the PKI. A trust domain is a set of PKI systems linked by a uniform management or subjected to a common set of security policies. A certification authority, CA, is a trusted third party that issues digital certificates.

There are the different types of CA architectures that are generally considered when implementing a PKI. PKI may be constructed as a:

- Single architecture
- Hierarchical architecture
- Mesh architecture
- Bridge CA
- Hybrid. (Satizábal et al, 2006)

Single CA model is the simplest to deploy, because all PKI users trust the only CA of the architecture, but is not suitable for very large or diverse communities of users. *Hierarchical* model is the most common model. In this configuration, all the users trust the same root CA (RCA). Thus, a user of a hierarchical PKI begins its certification paths with the RCA public key. In a hierarchical PKI, trust relationships are unidirectional, that is, subordinate CAs does not issue certificates to their superior CAs. *Mesh* model is also known as cross-certificate architecture, here the trust anchor of a user is its local CA and all CAs are autonomous, so a CA does not rely on a superior CA. In this model the number of trust relationship is directly proportional to the number of CAs, what brings a lot of scalability problems. *Bridge* CA model must use certificate information to establish trust relationships among different enterprise PKIs. In this model, certification path discovery is easier than in a mesh PKI, but it is more complex than in a hierarchical PKI. *Hybrid* model allows mixing the previous certification architectures and depends of relationships among user communities.

Since PKI is used only for third group of users, and eProcurement process is limited to a certain number of such users, choosing the right PKI architecture is crucial. Since we have to use our own CA authority and also consider the costs single model stands out as a valid solution. As you can see (Figure 5) this architecture uses only one CA authority that represents all users in the system. Deployment of such architecture is a low cost option. On the other side it provides a sufficient amount of protection. Even though the replacement of CA implies reissuing of certificates for all users, limited number of them allows it to be done easily enough.

In biometrics, the server matches one or more client biometric—such as a fingerprint, facial feature, iris pattern, or hand geometry—with the

Figure 5. Single CA model

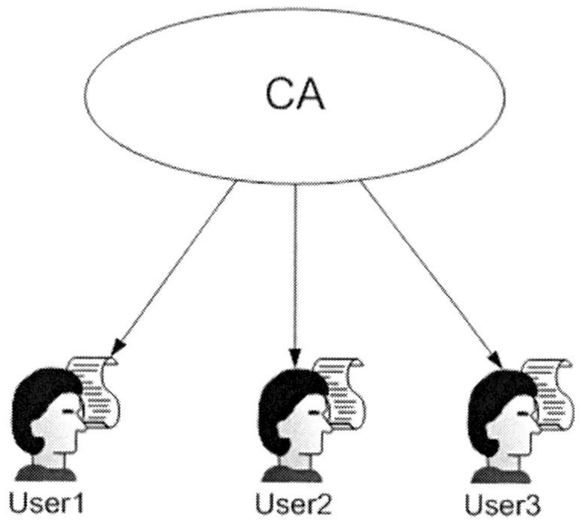

same information previously stored at the server during enrollment (Weigold et al, 2008). Biometrics authentication system has been widely used in physical access control. However, it has been little translated into network security (Zhenhua, 2008). On the other hand, biometric technology used in the authentication of e-commerce, can overcome the threat of forgotten, embezzlement, sharing, losing of the password, cards, certificates used in the traditional authentication (Xiaoming, 2008). In spite of all the upsides of biometric use in authenticating process there are significant downsides. Each biometric feature has limitations, for example, the feature of some fingerprints are difficult to extract, the identification rate of face recognition is impacted because of makeup, facial expressions, posture, light changed, the voice will be changed when the health status is changed, the effort and direction of handwriting signature will be changed by specialized training (Xiaoming, 2008). Generally, biometrics systems make two type of error: one is false accept which occurs when recognizing two different persons as the same person; the other is false reject which occurs when recognizing the same person as two different persons. False accept is also call false match, and false reject is also call false not match. There is a tradeoff between false accept rate (FAR) and false reject rate (FRR) in every biometrics system (Zhenhua, 2008). Finding the right balance is crucial. On the other hand economic side of the process is also relevant. Since this authentication will be done by public entities that represent a descent number the overall cost of system implementation must be considered. Distributing expensive equipment to each public entity of interest represents an unacceptable solution. That is why we need to choose a solution that lowers the overall cost for installing biometric scanning system. This led us to choose the fingerprint scanning as the optimal solution to this problem. Equipment for scanning is significantly cheaper and also the installation costs are on the low side. On that perspective we decided to use smart cards that can store biometric data. This way biometric comparison can be done directly on card as shown in Figure 6. On the picture smart card and biometric reader are separated but this is only done to represent logical difference and accentuate the steps of authentication process. Physically it can be done via one device. Client inserts his smart card, enters the PIN and provides his finger for fingerprint scanning. Client PC signs the response

Figure 6. Authentication process for high value procurement and bidding

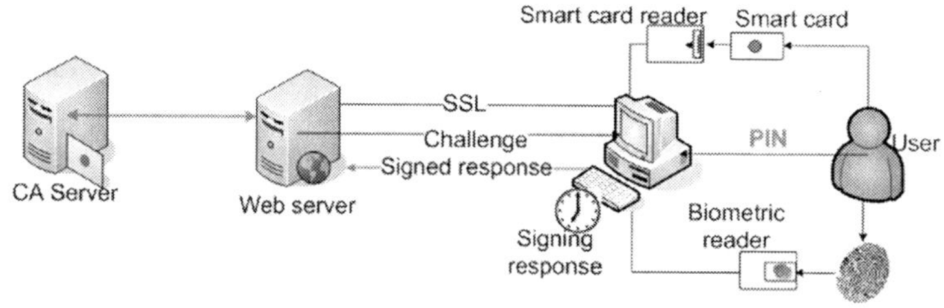

to the challenge provided by server and sends it back. Finally web server and CA server communicate to complete authentication.

It is important not to leave out an important group of users from authentication process. This group represents Offering parties (The Bidders). Due to sensitivity of this role same three generic authentication processes should be applied.

CONCLUSION

Rapid development of information technologies caused adequate actions from public administration in the field of e-procurement.

Process of executing electronic procurement is by its nature quite sensitive. Transparency is a requirement that must be honored in order to provide citizen with the insight in to procurement process, and all that in the purpose of preventing corruption and misuse.

However, this application can still be subject to some changes, or even some better applications can be developed in the meantime and new security methods can be applied. This is not a revolutionary leap forward, but it is an important move towards the future; towards the concept of electronic government.

REFERENCES

Adams, C., & Lioyd, S. (2002). *Understanding PKI: Concepts, standards, and deployment considerations* (2nd ed.). The Addison-Wesley Professional.

Beardsley, C. T. (1972). Is your computer insecure? *IEEE Spectrum*, *9*(1), 67–78. doi:10.1109/MSPEC.1972.5218476

Bing, H., Zheng-Ding, Q., & Dong-Mei, S. (2002). Secure authentication system incorporating hand shapes verification and cryptography techniques. *Proceedings of IEEE Region 10 Conference on Computers, Communications, Control and Power Engineering*, Vol. 1, (pp. 156-159).

Booch, G., Rumbaugh, J., & Jacobson, I. (2005). *Unified modeling language user guide* (2nd ed.). New York, NY: The Addison-Wesley.

Huang, X.-G., Shen, L., & Feng, Y.-H. (2008). A user authentication scheme based on fingerprint and USIM card. *International Conference on Intelligent Information Hiding and Multimedia Signal Processing*, (pp. 1261-1264).

Larman, C. (2001). *Applying UML and patterns: An introduction to object-oriented analysis and design and the unified process* (2nd ed.). NJ: Prentice Hall.

Lynette, I. M., & Stephen, H. H. (2003). *Authentication and its privacy effects*. IEEE Computer Society, National Academy of Sciences.

Paine, von S., Atreya, M., & Hammond, B. (2002). *Digital signatures*. McGraw-Hill Professional.

Satizábal, C., Páez, R., & Forné, J. (2006). *PKI trust relationships: From a hybrid architecture to a hierarchical model*. International Conference on Availability, Reliability and Security (ARES'06).

Starcevic, D., et al. (2008). *Inception project for e-procurement web portal*. Belgrade, Serbia: Faculty of Organizational Sciences.

Tatnall, A. (2005). *Web portals: The new gateways to internet information and services*. Hershey, PA: Idea Group Publishing.

Weigold, T., Kramp, T., & Baentsch, M. (2008). Remote client authentication. *IEEE Security & Privacy*, *6*(4), 36–43. doi:10.1109/MSP.2008.93

Xiaoming, M. (2008). *Study on the model of e-commerce identity authentication based on multi-biometric features identification.* International Colloquium on Computing, Communication, Control, and Management ISECS 2008.

Yoichi, S. (2002). Development of personal authentication systems using fingerprint with smart cards and digital signature technologies control. *Proceedings of the Conference ICARCV 2002*, Vol. 2, (pp. 996-1001).

Yoshiaki, I., Yoichi, S., & Masanori, K. (2001). Development of personal authentication system using fingerprint with digital signature technologies. *Proceedings of the Hawaii International Conference HICSS-34*, Island of Maui, Hawaii, (pp. 1-9).

Zhenhua, W. (2008). Biometrics authentication system on open network and security analysis. *Proceedings of ISECS 2008.*

Zhou, H.-G., & Dai, S.-H. (2008). PKI-based e-business security system. *Proceedings of 3rd International Conference on Innovative Computing Information and Control*, June 18 - 20, 2008, Dalian, China.

Chapter 11
Intention to Use E-Government Websites among Universiti Sains Malaysia (USM) Students

Ng Yee Boon
Universiti Sains Malaysia, Malaysia

T. Ramayah
Universiti Sains Malaysia, Malaysia

Teoh Ai Ping
Universiti Sains Malaysia, Malaysia

May-Chiun Lo
Universiti Malaysia Sarawak, Malaysia

ABSTRACT

In almost every country, government agencies are making their services available online. The success of e-Government initiatives is contingent upon citizen's willingness to use these Web-enabled services. This study investigates and examines the intention to use e-Government services among students in Universiti Sains Malaysia (USM), Penang. A research framework based on the PCI (Perceived Characteristics of Innovating) by Moore and Benbasat (1991) to identify factors that would determine and influence the intention to use e-Government websites and services. A survey involving a total of 145 university students was conducted. The results reveal that relative advantage and ease of use are the significant drivers of intention to use e-Government whereas image and compatibility were not important. The implications for research and practice are also explored.

DOI: 10.4018/978-1-4666-2119-0.ch011

INTRODUCTION

Situated in Malaysia, the Multimedia Super Corridor (MSC) is a Government designated zone, designed to leapfrog Malaysia into the information and knowledge age. The MSC Malaysia Flagship Application consists of seven types of applications, whereby electronic government (e-government) is one of the flagships. Electronic government was initiated in Malaysia on 24 February 2004. The Vision of e-Government is to transform administrative process and service delivery through the use of IT and multimedia. Definition:

- An initiative aimed at reinventing how the Government works
- To improve the quality of interactions with citizens and businesses
- Improved Connectivity
- Better Access
- High Quality Services
- Better Processes/ Systems

The primary aim of this initiative is to create a virtually paperless administration, with an eye towards the widespread use of electronic and multimedia networks in the government. The Electronic Government initiatives were launched to lead the country into the Information Age. It seeks to improve both how the government operates internally as well as how it delivers services to the people of Malaysia, and to improve the convenience, accessibility and quality of interactions with citizens and businesses. Electronic and multimedia infrastructure will eventually encompass all levels of government, and in doing so, information flows and processes related to government affairs will be made faster and more efficient. The vision of Electronic Government is a vision for government, businesses and citizenry to work together for the benefit of Malaysia and all of its citizens. The vision focuses on effectively and efficiently delivering services from the government to the people of Malaysia, enabling the government to become more responsive to the needs of its citizens.

The seven pilot projects of the Electronic Government Flagship Application include Project Monitoring System (SPPII), Human Resource Management Information System (HRMIS), Generic Office Environment (GOE), Electronic Procurement (EP), Electronic Services (E-Services), Electronic Labor Exchange (ELX), E-Syariah.

The myGovernment Portal acts as the one-stop source of Malaysian government information and services for the citizens. Government to Citizen (G2C), the goal is to have the availability of citizen-centric services at any time, any place and by any means. Government to Business (G2B), enterprises will be able to deal with government as speedily as with any other business; processes will be clear, fast, reliable and automated. Governments will provide on-the-spot feedback and ongoing information about the status of their request. Areas include business life cycles, employee reporting and control, procurement, sales tax reporting, and environment compliance. Government to Employee (G2E), the solution is about empowering employees to support citizens in the fastest and most appropriate way, speeding up administrative processes, and optimizing governmental solutions. Government as a Trusted Exchange, this includes collaborative work in the areas of e-authentication, e-training and disaster assistance.

To date, 3,300 government forms can be downloaded for free and 395 online services are available on the Portal. While there seems a big growth in the development of e-Government initiatives, however there is question that how much citizens will accept the use of such services. To date, few studies have explored the core factors that influence citizen adoption of e-Government services. In 2006, on September 30, in Kuala Lumpur, Bernama news reported that the government has again underscored its commitment towards the growth of the ICT sector in the 2006 Budget, say ICT companies operating in Malaysia. These include the extension of MSC-status related benefits (50 percent income tax exemption for five years or investment tax allowance of 50 percent) to ICT and multi-media enablers operating outside the Cyber cities of Cyberjaya, Kuala Lumpur City Centre, Technology Park Malaysia, Bayan Lepas in Penang and Kulim HiTech Park in Kedah. In United States, there are predictions of more than $600 billion of government fees and taxes to be processed through the Web by 2006 (James 2000). In the US, federal government spending is predicted to reach $2.33 billion in 2005 (Gartner Group 2000). According to a survey conducted by the international City/Country Management Association (ICMA) administered to chief administrative officers (CAO) at government agencies, 74.2% of CAOs reported that their government agency had a Web site. However, 90.5% of these agencies have not conducted a survey to see what online services citizens and business actually want (ICMA, 2002).

This study uses Moore and Benbasat's (1991) perceived characteristics of innovating (PCI) to identify fundamental elements of e-Government use. These constructs have been used in IT research (Karahanna et al. 1999; Moon & Kim 2001; Pavlou 2003) and e-commerce research (Van Slyke et al. 2004). Thus the questions this research hopes to answer are as follows:

1. Does relative advantage influence the intention of USM students to use e-Government services?
2. Does compatibility influence USM students about to use e-Government services?
3. Does image influence the intention of USM students to use e-Government services?
4. Does ease of use influence the intention of USM students to use e-Government services?

REVIEW OF LITERATURE AND HYPOTHESES DEVELOPMENT

The main constructs of interest in this research are the perceived characteristics of using an innovation. The reason for focusing on the perceived characteristics of innovations is that the findings of many studies which have examined the primary characteristics of innovations have been inconsistent. According to Downs and Mohr (1976, p.702), the focus on the primary attributes of innovations has created this inconsistency. Primary attributes are intrinsic to an innovation independent of their perception by potential users. The behavior of individuals, however, is predicated by how they perceive these primary attributes. Because different adopters might perceive primary characteristics in different ways, their eventual behaviors might differ. This is the root of the problem of using primary characteristics as research variables. Furthermore, studying the interaction among the perceived attributes of innovations helps the establishment of a general theory. In determining what characteristics to examine, we relied primarily on the extensive work of Rogers (1983). He identified five general attributes of innovations that a variety of diffusion studies had shown to consistently influence adoption which are relative advantage, compatibility, complexity, observability and trialability.

Another construct was identified beyond Roger's classifications which weas thought important in the decision to adopt an innovation. The construct image has been used by some researchers, including Rogers, as an aspect of relative advantage. As discussed by Tornatzky and Klein (1982), some researchers have found the effect of image (social approval) to be different enough from relative advantage to be considered a separate factor (e.g. Holloway 1977). The relevance of the above argument to the study of the diffusion of innovations is clear. Innovations diffuse because of the cumulative decisions of individuals to adopt them. Thus, it is not the potential users' perceptions of the innovation itself, but rather their perceptions of using the innovation that are keys to whether the innovation diffuses. Unfortunately, however, within diffusion research, perceptions have traditionally been defined with the innovation itself, as evidenced by Rogers' definitions. Nevertheless, the perceived characteristics of innovations can easily be recast in terms of using the innovation. (Moore 1987). Thus, all characteristics were redefined in terms of the potential adopters' use, trial or observation of the innovation, and labeled the Perceived Characteristics of Innovating (PCI). Moore and Benbasat (1991) perceived characteristics of innovating (PCI) are based on Rogers' (1995) Diffusion of Innovation Theory (DOI), which is used frequently in information systems research to explain user adoption of technological innovations.

An innovation is "an idea, practice or object that is perceived as new by an individual or other unit of adoption Rogers' (1995)." Moore and Benbasat (1991) identify eight PCI factors that influence the diffusion of an innovation: relative advantage, compatibility, ease of use, result demonstrability, image, visibility, trial ability and voluntariness. Based on previous research (Karahanna 1999; Moore and Benbasat 1991; Plouffe et al. 2001; Tornatzky & Klein 1982; Van Slyke et al. 2004) the effects of relative advantage, compatibility, ease of use and image on citizen intention to use e-Government are studied. Tornatzky and Klein (1982) suggest that relative advantage, compatibility and ease of use are the most relevant constructs to adoption research, thus these three variables are included in this study (see Figure 1).

Relative advantage is "the degree to which an innovation is seen as being superior to its predecessor" (Davis 1989). The concept of relative advantage refers to the degree to which an innovation is perceived to be better than the idea it supersedes (Rogers, 1995). For example, the relative advantage of e-Government mirrors the citizens' acknowledgement that this new online service provides certain advantages over alternative services (e.g. traditional method to pay income tax). If a student believes that she/ he will gain a greater benefit by getting information through the e-Government, he or she would prefer this Internet services for their own good. In this spirit, the relative advantage may be parallel to the balance of contradicting forces, articulated as motive and impediments. Relative advantage also refers to the degree to which an innovation providers benefits which supersede those of its precursor and may incorporate factors such as economic benefits, image enhancement, convenience and satisfaction. (Lee & Lin 2005). In prior technology adoption literature (Karahanna et al. 1999; Moon

Figure 1. Research framework

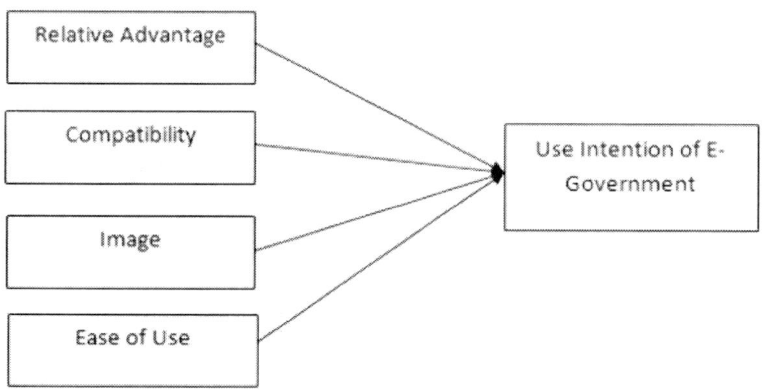

& Kim 2001), variable of relative advantage demonstrate a positive relationship with use intentions. Hence, in this study can expect the nature of this relationship to remain the same in the context of e-Government. Therefore based on prior research in information technology adoption, the following hypothesis is tested:

H1: Relative advantage has a positive direct effect on use intention of e-Government servces

Compatibility refers to "the degree to which an innovation is seen to be compatible with existing values, beliefs, experiences and needs of adopters". (Davis 1989). Rogers also defined compatibility as "the degree to which an innovation is perceived as consistent with the existing values, past experiences and needs of potential adopters" (Rogers, 1995). If e-Government fits with the citizens' life-situation and needs, it would be compatible and, therefore, it would be preferred over alternatives services modes. In this study, compatibility is treated with e-Government as a twofold concern, comprising use of direct services and use of Web browsing activities. Compatibility is also be defined as the degree to which the innovation fits with the potential adopters' existing values, previous experiences and current needs (Rogers, 1995). Verhoef, and Langerak (2001) indicated that citizens who consider e-Government to be compatible with their value, needs and lifestyle and express high willing to use online services. In prior technology adoption literature (Karahanna et al. 1999; Moon & Kim 2001), variable of compatibility demonstrate a positive relationship with use intentions. In this study can expect that the nature of this relationship to remain the same in the context of e-Government. Therefore based on prior research in information technology adoption, the following hypothesis is tested:

H2: Compatibility has a positive direct effect on use intention of e-Government services

Image refers to the "degree to which the use of the innovation is seen as enhancing to an individual's image or social status" (Van Slyke et al. 2004). Moore and Benbasat (1991) define Image as "the degree to which use of an innovation is perceived to enhance one's status in one's social system (Chan & Lu, 2004). The increased power and influence resulting from elevated status provides a general basis for greater productivity. An individual may thus perceive that using such a system will lead to improvements in his/her job performance indirectly due to system use (Chan & Lu, 2004). In prior technology adoption literature (Karahanna et al. 1999; Moon & Kim 2001), variable of image demonstrate a positive relationship with use intentions. So, in this study can expect that the nature of this relationship to remain the same in the context of e-Government. Therefore based on prior research in information technology adoption, the following hypothesis is tested:

H3: Image has a positive direct effect on use intention of e-Government services

Ease of use reflects how simple the e-Government is to use. Ease of use is a construct in the Technology Acceptance Model (Davis, 1989). Ease of use is "the degree to which a person believes that using a particular system would be free of effort (Davis 1989). This finding concurs with the results of many previous studies (Davis, 1989; Mathieson, 1991; Adams et al., 1992; Segars & Grover, 1993, Igbaria et al. 1995; Ndubisi et al., 2001; Ramayah et al., 2002; Ramayah et al., 2003a; Ramayah et al., 2003b; Ramayah & Aafaqi, 2004). Other findings have also indicated that ease of use impacts online trust. For example, ease of searching, transaction interaction, broken links and navigation have all been associated with changes in online trust (Igbaria et al., 1997; Lohse & Spiller, 1998; Nielsen et al., 2000). Ease of use, a plausible reason for this is that when a system is learning to use it becomes much easier, thus the likelihood of potential users to use would increase.

Similar findings by Mathieson (1991) reported that perceived ease of use explains significant amount of the variance in perceived usefulness.

According to Jantan et al. (2001), perceived usefulness and perceived ease of use have direct effect on system usage. Cooper (1997) argued that ease of adoption is one of the important characteristics in technological adoption from the customer's perspectives. The degree to which an innovation is complicated and difficult to understand was one of the reasons for failure of home banking in United States (Dover, 1988). In addition, Daniel (1999) identified ease of use as one main factor for customer acceptance for Internet banking in the United Kingdom and Ireland.

Venkatesh (2000) once proclaimed that for any emerging IT/IS, ease of use is an important determinant of users' intention of acceptance and usage behavior. In prior technology adoption literature (Karahanna et al. 1999; Moon & Kim 2001), variable of ease of use demonstrate a positive relationship with use intentions. So, in this study can expect the nature of this relationship to remain the same in the context of e-Government. Therefore based on prior research in information technology adoption, the following hypothesis is tested:

H4: Ease of use has a positive direct effect on use intention of e-Government services

METHODOLOGY

Data was collected through a questionnaire based on previous researches and was adapted to better reflect the use intention of e-Government. In this study, information was elicited on 4 independent variables which are relative advantage, compatibility, image, and ease of use; and use intention as the dependent variable. This study was conducted in the natural setting where the respondents are around the USM campus. The unit of analysis in this study is individual USM student. This research is a cross-sectional research where the data is collected once from each of the respondents at a particular time. This research is to study the intention of USM students to use e-Government. The number of items and the sources of the instrument are presented in Table 1.

The questionnaire is divided into 2 sections, section A and section B. Section A is all the variables questions and section B is demographic questions. Ease of use, Relative advantage, Compatibility, Image, and Use intention have 4 items in each of these variables. Section B obtain the demographic questions such as age, gender, race, course, year entered university, programmed registered, living arrangement, status of candidacy and medium to get to know about e-Government. Furthermore, the questionnaire has a paragraph of information brief about e-Government so that the respondents can recall and understand better before they do the questionnaire. We used the Likert scale to measure the variables. The respondents are asked to agree or disagree with each statement. Each response is given a numerical score to reflects the degree of attitudinal favorableness, and the scores maybe summed to measure the respondents overall attitudes. In this study, 5-point scale is used: (1=disagree, 2=slightly disagree, 3= neutral, 4= slightly agree and 5=agree). The data was cleaned and anlyzed using SPSS version 19. The following section discusses the results.

Table 1. Description of questionnaire used

Construct	Item	Source
Ease of use	4	Davis (1989)
Relative advantage	4	Van Slyke et al. (2004)
Compatibility	4	Van Slyke et al. (2004)
Image	4	Van Slyke et al. (2004)
Intention	4	Gefen and Straub (2000); Pavlou (2003)

ANALYSIS AND RESULTS

A total of 150 questionnaires were all collected back. There were 5 incomplete questionnaires that were discarded. Therefore, only 145 questionnaires were used for data analysis, thereby giving a response rate of 96.67%.

From Table 2, the respondents comprised of 50 males (34.5%) and 95 females (65.5%). The profile of the respondents is shown in 25.5% of the respondents' age between 20-21 years followed by 40.7% whose age is between 22-23 years old. 24.1% of the respondents' age between 24 till 25 years old followed by 9.7% whose age is more than 25 years old. From the table also shows the 3 main races in Malaysia there are 37 Malays (25.5%), 96 Chinese (66.2%), 12 Indians (8.3%). There are 98 students (67.6%) from Art stream which be the respondents. Mainly their courses are Management, Social Science, Education, Mass Communication and Accounting. 47 students (32.4%) are from Science stream (Biology, Pharmacy, Computer Science, HBP, Chemistry and Statistic). There are 11 respondents (7.6%), who entered USM at year 2003, 5 respondents (3.4%) entered USM at year 2004, 81 respondents (55.9%), who entered USM at year 2005 and 48 respondents (33.1%), who entered USM at year 2006. In this research there are 100% undergraduate be the respondents. There are more students live in campus (60.7%) compared to those who live outside (39.3%). The respondents showed full time students (94.5%) are more than part time students (5.5%).

Table 2. Frequency and percentage of respondent profile

Variable	Frequency	%
Age 20 till 21 years old 22 till 23 years old 24 till 25 years old More than 25 years old	37 59 35 14	25.50 40.70 24.10 9.70
Gender Male Female	50 95	34.50 65.50
Race Malay Chinese Indian	37 96 12	25.50 66.20 8.30
Course registered Art stream Science stream	98 47	67.60 32.40
Year entered university 2003 2004 2005 2006	11 5 81 48	7.60 3.40 55.90 33.10
Living arrangement Inside campus Outside campus	88 57	60.70 39.30
Status of candidacy Part time Full time	8 137	5.50 94.50

From Table 3, medium which is used most by students to get to know about e-Government is newspaper 96 students, followed by Internet 82 students. There are 53 students who got to know e-Government through their friends, 37 students who get to know e-Government by television. The same amount of students (17) gets to know e-Government by radio and family / relatives. 20 students get to know e-Government by their lecturer and 19 students get to know e-Government trough other mediums.

Table 4 shows the reliability coefficients for the major variables. Cronbach alpha values above 0.7 are deemed acceptable. From Table 4 it can be seen that the values are all acceptable without deleting any item. Hence, we can conclude that the reliability of the measuring instruments are acceptable.

The average mean compute by the major variables are between 3 and 4. Relative advantage obtained the highest mean 3.43 while Image obtained the lowest mean 3.10. The highest standard deviation is computed by Image 0.93 while the lowest standard deviation is computed by Compatibility 0.73 (refer to Table 5).

Multiple regression analysis was done to determine the relationships between ease of use,

Table 3. Frequency table of medium used by USM students to get know e-government

Variable	Frequency (use)	Frequency (do not use)
Newspaper	96	49
Radio	17	128
Television	37	108
Internet	82	63
Family / relatives	17	128
Professors	20	125
Friends	53	92
Others	19	126

Table 4. Reliability coefficients for the major variables

Variables	Number of items	Items dropped	Cronbach alpha
Ease of use	4	0	0.815
Relative advantage	4	0	0.807
Compatibility	4	0	0.804
Image	4	0	0.882
Use intention	4	0	0.821

Table 5. Descriptive for the major variables

Variables	Mean	Standard Deviation
Ease of use	3.21	0.76
Relative advantage	3.43	0.78
Compatibility	3.25	0.73
Image	3.10	0.93
Intention	3.28	0.87

(Note: All items used a 5-point Likert scale with (1= Disagree, 2= slightly disagree, 3= Neutral, 4= slightly agree and 5= Agree)

relative advantage, compatibility, and image towards intention of USM students to use e-Government. This regression analysis was conducted to test hypothesis H1, H2, H3, H4.

The coefficient of determination (R^2) is 0.528 indicating that this model is significant whereby 52.8% of the variance on use intention of USM students towards e-Government system is explained by ease of use, relative advantage, compatibility, and image. The Beta value of ease of use (β=0.252, $p<$ 0.01) and relative advantage (β=0.577, $p<$ 0.01) are positive and significant. Therefore, H1 and H4 are supported whereas H2 and H3 are not supported. (see Table 6).

DISCUSSION AND IMPLICATIONS

The objective of this study is to investigate factors that influence USM students' intention to use e-Government in Malaysia. This study has 4 main variables that will affect the intention to use e-Government. They are ease of use, relative advantage, compatibility, and image.

The variable ease of use shows direct positive effect on the use intention of e-Government. In prior technology adoption literature (Karahanna et al. 1999; Moon & Kim 2001), the variable of ease of use demonstrate a positive relationship with use intentions. Hence, the findings support previous study.

Relative advantage in this study has a direct positive effect on the use intention of e-Government in Malaysia. This result supports the earlier research by Karahanna et al. (1999) and, Moon and Kim (2001), where relative advantage demonstrates a positive relationship with use intentions. The relative advantage of e-Government mirrors

Table 6. Multiple regression analysis

	Standardized Beta	t-value	p-value
Relative Advantage	.577	5.919	0.000
Compatibility	.065	.709	0.479
Image	-.108	-1.474	0.143
Ease of Use	.252	3.777	0.000
R^2 Adjusted R^2 F-value	0.528 0.514 39.130**		

**p< 0.01

the students' acknowledgement that this new online service provides certain advantages over alternative services. If a student believes that she/he will gain a greater benefit by get information through e-Government, he or she would prefer this Internet services for he or she own good. In this spirit, the relative advantage may be parallel to the balance of contradicting forces, articulated as motive and impediments. State government agencies should identify and communicate to students about the benefits or advantages to use online services. As a result, good thinking of e-Government will appear in students mind and hence students will use the services of e-Government more frequently. For example, government could encourage students to use online service to renew the license by emphasizing the speed and convenient of using this service instead of going to JPJ to renew the car or motor license. Yet online license renewal is available 24 hours; it is not limited to business hours only.

In addition, in this finding show that compatibility does not have direct positive effect on use intention of e-Government. This findings does not support the previous research by Verhoef and Langerak (2001) who indicated that citizens who consider e-Government to be compatible with their value, needs and lifestyle and express high willing to use online services. In prior technology adoption literature (Karahanna et al. 1999; Moon & Kim 2001), variable of compatibility demonstrate a positive relationship with use intentions. Although this finding showed that it does not have direct effect on use intention, however, there are medium correlations (0.558) between each other. Hence, maybe compatibility will indirectly influence use intention of e-Government.

On the other hand, in this study also shows that image does not have effect on use intention of e-Government. The findings do not support the previous study by (Chan & Lu, 2004) who concludes that an individual may thus perceive that using such a system will lead to improvements in his/her job performance indirectly due to system use). In prior technology adoption literature (Karahanna et al. 1999; Moon & Kim 2001), variable of image demonstrate a positive relationship with use intentions. This finding seems goes against their results. This findings show that since students have not yet started working, hence they will not have too much consideration about the image of using e-Government.

IMPLICATIONS AND CONCLUSION

There are many considerations and potential implications of implementing and designing e-government, including disintermediation of the government and its citizens, impacts on economic, social, and political factors, and disturbances to the status quo in these areas.

In countries such as the United Kingdom, there is interest in using electronic government to re-engage citizens with the political process. In particular, this has taken the form of experiments with electronic voting, aiming to increase voter turnout by making voting easy. The UK Electoral Commission has undertaken several pilots, though concern has been expressed about the potential for fraud with some electronic voting methods. Hence maybe this is a good suggestion for government in Malaysia.

Since there are very few similar researches done, this research can serve as a starting point to provide a guideline for future research to better understand e-Government. Future researches can cover a wider geographical area to do this research so that more precise results can be obtained. On the other hand, researches can be conducted to examine users' satisfaction on using e-Government compared to traditional government services or integrate constructs from the technology acceptance model and the Web trust, Internet security literature to develop a more complete, comprehensive model of e-Government. Therefore, it is definitely worthwhile to conduct and intensified the future research in this area.

This study revealed that the significant elements of students' intention to use e-Government services are relative advantage and ease of use. State government should always encourage students to accept and use e-Government services by focusing on these two factors. Alternatively, state government agencies should capitalize on the unique benefits of online services. They could send letter, through newspaper, television or radio to explain the speed, convenience and accessibility of online government services. When students have explored these information, and as times go by, they will increase their intention to use e-Government.

This study used constructs from Moore and Benbasat's (1991) perceived characteristics of innovating to develop this model of USM students' adoption of e-Government services in Malaysia. Relative advantage is the most important element to influence the intention of USM students to use e-Government. Hence, in this coming technology world, e-Government growth is important, an understanding of the factors that influence students' adoption of e-Government services is needed as students play an important role in the future to contribute to the country.

REFERENCES

Adams, D. A., Nelson, R. R., & Todd, P. A. (1992). Perceived usefulness, ease of use, and usage of information technology: A replication. *Management Information Systems Quarterly*, *16*(2), 227–247. doi:10.2307/249577

BERNAMA. (n.d.). *2006 Budget underscores govt continued commitment for ICT*. Retrieved March 19, 2007, from http://www.e-government research/msc/BUDGET 2006.com/

Chan, S. C., & Lu, M. T. (2004). Understanding Internet banking adoption and use behavior: A Hong Kong perspective. *Journal of Global Information Management*, *12*(3), 21–43. doi:10.4018/jgim.2004070102

Cooper, R. G. (1997). Examining some myths about new product winners. In Katz, R. (Ed.), *The human side of managing technological innovation* (pp. 550–560).

Daniel, E. (1999). Provision of electronic banking in the UK and Republic of Ireland. *International Journal of Bank Marketing*, *17*(2), 72–83. doi:10.1108/02652329910258934

Davis, F. D. (1989). Perceived usefulness, perceived ease of use and user acceptance of information technology. *Management Information Systems Quarterly*, *13*(3), 319–340. doi:10.2307/249008

Dover, P. A. (1998). The effect of technology selection on consumer adoption of in home computerized banking. *International Journal of Marketing*, *2*, 31–37.

Downs, G. W. Jr, & Mohr, L. B. (1976). Conceptual issues in the study of innovation. *Administrative Science Quarterly*, *21*, 700–714. doi:10.2307/2391725

Gartner Group. (2000). *E-government strategy: Cubing the circle*. Research Notes, Strategic Planning Assumption.

Holloway, R. E. (1977). *Perception of an innovation*. Syracuse University Project Advance, Unpublished Doctoral Dissertation, Syracuse University.

ICMA. (October 2002). *Electronic government survey findings*. Retrieved March 20, 2003, from http://egov.e21corp.com/site/html/eNewsletter/oct2002/survey.html

Igbaria, M., Guimaraes, T., & Davis, G. B. (1995). Testing the determinants of microcomputer usage via a structural equation model. *Journal of Management Information Systems, 11*(4), 87–114.

Igbaria, M., Zinatelli, N., Cragg, P., & Cavaye, A. (1997). Personal computing acceptance factors in small firms: A structural equation model. *Management Information Systems Quarterly, 21*(3), 279–302. doi:10.2307/249498

James, G. (2000). Empowering bureaucrats. *MC Technology Marketing Intelligence, 20*(12), 62–68.

Jantan, M., Ramayah, T., & Chin, W. W. (2001). Personal computer acceptance by small and medium sized companies evidence from Malaysia. *Journal Management & Business, 3*(1), 1–14.

Karahanna, E., Straub, D., & Chervany, N. (1999). Information technology adoption across time: A cross-sectional comparison of pre-adoption beliefs. *Management Information Systems Quarterly, 23*(2), 183–213. doi:10.2307/249751

Lee, G. G., & Lin, H. F. (2005). Customer perceptions of e-service quality in online shopping. *International Journal of Retail and Distribution Management, 33*(2), 161–176. doi:10.1108/09590550510581485

Lohse, G. L., & Spiller, P. (1998). Electronic shopping. *Communications of the ACM, 41*(7), 81–87. doi:10.1145/278476.278491

Mathieson, K. (1991). Predicting user intention: Comparing the technology acceptance model with theory of planned behavior. *Information Systems Research, 2*(3), 173–191. doi:10.1287/isre.2.3.173

Moon, J. M., & Kim, Y. G. (2001). Extending the TAM for a World-Wide-Web context. *Information & Management, 38*, 217–230. doi:10.1016/S0378-7206(00)00061-6

Moore, G. C. (1987). End user computing and office automation: A diffusion of innovations perspective. *INFOR, 25*(3), 214–235.

Moore, G. C., & Benbasat, I. (1991). Development of an instrument to measures the perceptions of adopting an information technology innovation. *Information Systems Research, 2*(3), 173–199. doi:10.1287/isre.2.3.192

Multimedia Development Corporation. (n.d.). *The MSC Malaysia flagship applications*. Retrieved from http://www.MSCMalaysia.com

MyGovernment. *The Malaysia Government's official portal*. Retrieved March 19, 2007, from http://www.myGoverment.com/

Ndubisi, N., Jantan, M., & Richardson, S. (2001). Is the technology acceptance model valid for entrepreneurs? Model testing and examining usage determinants. *Asian Academy of Management Journal, 6*(2), 31–54.

Nielsen, J., Molich, R., Snyder, C., & Farrell, S. (2000). *E-commerce user experience: Trust*. Fremont, CA: Nielsen Norman Group. Retrieved March 1, 2001, from http://www.nngroup.com/reports/ecommerce/

Pavlou, P. A. (2003). Consumer acceptance of electronic commerce: Integrating trust and risk with the technology acceptance model. *International Journal of Electronic Commerce, 7*(3), 69–103.

Plouffe, C. R., Hulland, J., & Vandenbosch, M. (2001). Research report: Richness versus parsimony in modeling technology adoption decisions – Understanding merchant adoption of a smart card-based payment system. *Information Systems Research, 12*(2), 208–222. doi:10.1287/isre.12.2.208.9697

Ramayah, T., & Aafaqi, B. (2004). Role of self-efficacy in e-library usage among students of a public university in Malaysia. *Malaysian Journal of Library & Information Science*, *9*(1), 39–57.

Ramayah, T., Jantan, M., & Bushra, A. (2003a). Internet usage among students of institutions of higher learning: The role of motivational variables. *The Proceedings of the 1st International Conference on Asian Academy of Applied Business Conference*, Sabah, Malaysia, 10 – 12th July, 2003.

Ramayah, T., Jantan, M., Mohd Noor, M. N., Razak, R. C., & Koay, P. L. (2003b). Receptiveness of Internet banking by Malaysian consumers: The case of Penang. *Asian Academy of Management Journal*, *8*(2), 1–29.

Ramayah, T., Siron, R., Dahlan, N., & Mohamad, O. (2002). Technology usage among owners/managers of SMe's: The role of demographic and motivational variables. *The Proceedings of the 6th Annual Asian-Pacific Forum for Small Business on "Small and Medium Enterprises Linkages, Networking and Clustering,* Kuala Lumpur, Malaysia.

Rogers, E. M. (1983). *Diffusion of innovation* (3rd ed.). New York, NY: The Free Press.

Rogers, E. M. (1995). *Diffusion of innovations*. New York, NY: The Free Press.

Segars, A. H., & Grover, V. (1993). Re-examining perceived ease of use and usefulness: A confirmatory factor analysis. *Management Information Systems Quarterly*, *17*(4), 517–525. doi:10.2307/249590

Tornatzky, L. G., & Klein, J. K. (1982). Innovation characteristics and innovation adoption-implementation: A meta analysis of findings. *IEEE Transactions on Engineering Management*, *29*(1), 28–45.

Van Slyke, C., Belanger, F., & Communale, C. L. (2004). Factors influencing the adoption of Web-based shopping: The impact of trust. *The Data Base for Advances in Information Systems*, *35*(2), 32–49. doi:10.1145/1007965.1007969

Venkatesh, V., & Davis, F. D. (2000). A theoretical extension of the technology acceptance model: Four longitudinal field studies. *Management Science*, *45*(2), 186–204. doi:10.1287/mnsc.46.2.186.11926

Verhoef, P. C., & Langerak, F. (2001). Possible determinants of consumers' adoption of electronic grocery shopping in the Netherlands. *Journal of Retailing and Consumer Services*, *8*(5), 275–285.

Wikipedia. (n.d.). *Multimedia super corridor*. Retrieved December 23, 2006, from http://www.wikipedia.com/

Chapter 12

Business Process Integration within Lightweight Semantic-Enabled Enterprise Service-Oriented Architecture

Tariq Mahmoud
Carl von Ossietzky University of Oldenburg, Germany

Marc Petersen
Carl von Ossietzky University of Oldenburg, Germany

David Rummel
Carl von Ossietzky University of Oldenburg, Germany

ABSTRACT

In the last decade, the Small and Medium Enterprises (SME) market has been enormously raised, and the major vendors are trying to adapt their software to suit it. One important factor to be taken into consideration in such context is the support of internal and external business process integration. Service-oriented systems are offering reasonable business process integration support. However, they lack semantic definition of their service interfaces. The research presented in this chapter tries to solve this issue by proposing a lightweight semantic-enabled enterprise service-oriented framework where services can be semantically grouped based on the domains to which they belong. The proposed framework is merging both business processes and service orientation concepts to provide an agile and flexible enterprise solution that utilizes reusability, better quality, and faster time-to-market factors. This chapter will illustrate this framework, its goals, and outcomes, together with demonstration of a business case built on top of it.

DOI: 10.4018/978-1-4666-2119-0.ch012

INTRODUCTION

It is very rare nowadays to find any enterprise that is based merely on a single information system. Rather it has a bundle of systems specialized for different organizational sections within the business. As far as e-procurement is concerned, the most three significant systems are Supply Chain Management (SCM), Customer Relationship Management (CRM), and Enterprise Resource Planning (ERP) systems. One of the most problematic issues that these businesses have to overcome is the integration issue. In clearer words, how to handle the data exchange among heterogeneous dissimilar information systems? We will try to answer this question in this chapter by proposing our approach.

The remainder of this chapter is organized as follows: section two will provide background information about service orientation and business process management. A literature review and brief comparison between the proposed approach and existing frameworks and techniques is presented in section three. Section four presents the semantic-enabled SOA concept together with its main components interactions. Section five details a business case built on top of the proposed concept with highlights on its corresponding prototype. The main system's outcomes are then listed in section six. Finally, we conclude the chapter and present a brief outlook and future directions.

BACKGROUND INFORMATION

Service-Oriented Architecture and its Limitations

This section illustrates the main service-orientation concept. The OASIS SOA Reference Model group defines SOA as follows: "SOA is a paradigm for organizing and utilizing distributed capabilities that may be under the control of different ownership domains. It provides a uniform means to offer, discover, interact with and use capabilities to produce desired effects consistent with measurable preconditions and expectations" (MacKenzie et al., 2006, p. 29). Several technologies are used to realize SOA but Web Services are accorded the most common ones. A Web Service as defined by the W3C consortium is "a software system designed to support interoperable machine to machine interaction over a network" (Booth et al., 2004). A Web Service in general can be implemented through the use of technologies and standards like the Simple Object Access Protocol (SOAP) and the Web Services Description Language (WSDL) using the Extensible Markup Language (XML) (Graham, 2006).

SOA concept has in general three main ingredients namely: service provider, service consumer and service registry. The service provider creates a Web Service and possibly publishes its interface and access information to the service registry. This latter (also known as service broker) is responsible for making the access information of both Web Service interface and implementation available to any potential service consumer, and categorizing the results in taxonomies. The Universal Description Discovery and Integration (UDDI) (Clement et al., 2004), defines a way to publish and discover information about Web Services. Finally, the service consumer or Web Service client locates entries in the registry using various find operations and then binds to the service provider in order to invoke one of its Web Services.

Based on SOA (see Figure 1), the vision of software integration has been carried out by realizing systems' functionalities in the form of Web Services. From the perspective of application developers, this means composing new applications can rely on using existing services. There is no need for the developer to have knowledge about the underlying implementation of the used Web Services in order to assemble these services into a productive application.

The 2000s decade came to strengthen the concept of information system integration by be-

Figure 1. Web service-enabled SOA

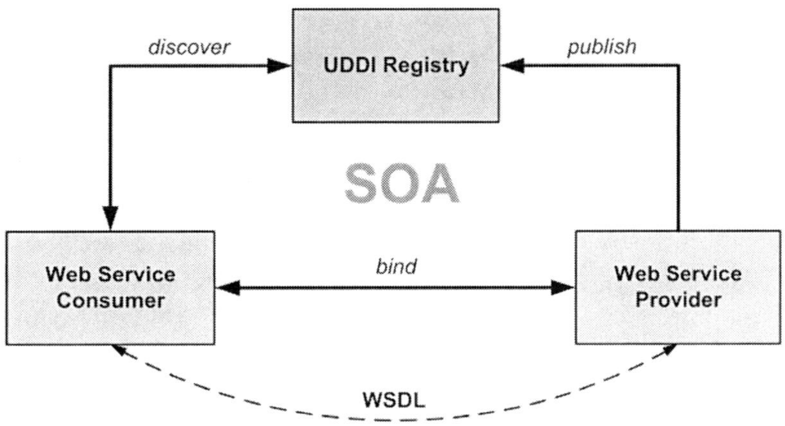

ing relied on the service orientation paradigm. Service-Oriented Architectures are one recent architectural and design discipline in the IT application architecture. One typical and widely used approach for implementing SOA is the use of Web Services. This aligns the business along with the technology by providing a powerful integration of applications and data. Instead of being connected to several disparate applications, Web Service-enabled SOA solutions provide connectivity between these heterogeneous applications by avoiding a central point of integration, which was often a bottleneck in prior architectural designs (Mahmoud, 2009). Such a SOA solution is the opposite of a central point of integration – it provides a loosely coupled integration of services. On the one hand, existing SOA-based solutions are just reducing the number of the point-to-point adapters by designing each interface following the WSDL standard. Nevertheless, what these solutions really lack is the semantic documentation of these interfaces (Hu et al., 2008).

On the other hand, after the evolution of the Semantic Web (Berners-Lee, Hendler, & Lassila, 2001), the semantic documentation of the Web Service interfaces has been defined making it possible for the Web to understand and satisfy the requests of people and machines to use the Web content. However, the emerging semantic approaches are considered as complex solutions that are founded on expressive formalisms to provide semantics first. Moreover, they are accorded inaccurate to somaticize the Web content in a standardized way because of the vague representation of their evolving ontologies.

The reason for applying SOA concepts to enterprise systems is based on the statement that the product a company distributes to its customers is the result of a sequence of actions. Referring to e-procurement enterprises it is obvious that many actions within a sequence are automatically performed by information systems. Effective and efficient support and fulfillment of the necessary sequences requires process-oriented solutions (Weske, 2007). In other words, the activities that constitute the companies' business processes can be realized using Web Services. In this context, business process management plays an important role. This term is explained in details in the following section.

Business Process Management

Current business process integration solutions allow modeling and implementing of actual business processes of an enterprise. Based on (Bartonitz, 2011) and his yearly updated overview for business process modeling standards, the commonly used techniques and languages for modeling business processes are:

- Business Process Modeling Notation (BPMN),
- Event-driven Process Chain (EPC)
- Business Process Execution Language (BPEL) and
- Unified Modeling Language (UML).

It is important to analyze a business process before it is used in the production system. This prevents problems that might appear like unsatisfied customers, damage claims, as well as the need to exceed capacities (van der Aalst, 2008).

Business process analysis is one of the major parts of Business Process Management (BPM). It aims at identifying the current information systems states besides pointing out their problems and bottlenecks. Analyzing a business process can be performed through validation, verification, and performance analysis. While validation's main role is to test the business process whether it behaves as expected or not, verification intends to establish the correctness of a process definition. Last but not least, performance analysis aims to meet requirements regarding service levels, resource usage and flow rates (Celino et al., 2007).

However and like traditional SOA limitations, the modeling and implementation of business processes lack the options to semantically describe the services they contain. This means that the problem that a service consumer in a process-oriented SOA solution can hardly detect new appropriate services at runtime. This leads to a decreased trust level in the reliability of the complete SOA concept since only services that are known at design time can be invoked.

Based on the aforementioned brief state of the art analysis we will propose in this chapter a semantic enterprise SOA solution based on lightweight semantic annotated Web Services. This annotation is mainly done by assigning Resource Description Framework (RDF[1]) statements to services' relations. This will try to overcome the aforementioned weaknesses of current technologies. It enhances SOA with semantic annotation but avoids the introduction of current semantic frameworks complexity. We also assume our framework to impact BPM by describing business process scenarios in a more general, semantic manner, moving away from concrete, specific Web Services assemblies towards dynamic, requirements-driven, on-demand groups of Web Services.

RELATED WORK

In this section we will list some approaches and technologies that are conceptually similar to our proposed work and compare them with it. The main approach behind our work will be compared with semantic conceptual frameworks and lightweight semantic annotation techniques. Moreover, implementing a business case on top of this approach together with related enterprise integration systems will be listed and compared.

Currently different conceptual frameworks for semantic Web Services already exist. These frameworks allow Web Services to be annotated semantically, so a Web Service consumer in can discover and consume them even if the Web Service did not exist at design time. The most notable frameworks in this field are the Web Ontology Language for Web Services (OWL-S[2]) (Martin et al., 2007), the Web Service Modeling Ontology (WSMO) (Domingue, Roman, & Stollberg, 2005), and the Semantic Web Service Framework (SWSF) (Battle et al., 2005). However, these frameworks have in common the following disadvantages:

- They are classified as heavyweight frameworks
- They are based on complex ontology specification and rules
- They introduce new languages based on expressive formalisms.

In contrast, our solution is accorded more lightweight, based on simple RDF statements. Therefore, it does not introduce any new languages.

On the other side, lightweight semantic annotation techniques like Semantic Annotations for WSDL (SAWSDL) (Kopecký et al., 2007), WSMO-LITE (Kopecký, & Vitvar, 2008), and MicroWSMO (Fensel, Kopecký, & Vitvar, 2008) are:

- Supporting augmentation of the existing service specifications with semantic descriptions
- Covering the other grounding approaches: WSDL-based services and RESTful-based services[3]
- Classified as lightweight service ontologies

These frameworks extend existing service descriptions with semantics but they still miss the semantic annotation of relations between services which is handled by our solution.

Business processes are technically implemented as workflows that are executed using different workflow engines. The third version of the Microsoft.NET Framework provides the Windows Workflow Foundation technology that includes the workflow engine concept (Schichtenberg, 2007; Scribner, 2007). This engine can be used to implement workflows within .NET applications. It is integrated in several products like for example in the Microsoft Office SharePoint Server[4] (2007 and newer versions) and Microsoft Dynamics CRM[5] (starting from the 4th version). Second workflow engine example is the Java-based software framework: Yet Another Worfklow Language (YAWL[6]). It is based on its own modeling language and integrates organizational resources and Web Services (van der Aalst et al., 2004). Other existing workflow engines in the market are: the J2EE-based project WfMOpen[7], ActiveVOS (previously known as ActiveBPEL) and WebSphere Process Server (which execute Business Process Execution Language for Web Service[8] modeled business processes). These workflow engines do not natively support the dynamic discovery of Web Services at runtime but require the business process designer to define all participating Web Services at design time. In contrast, our solution enables business process designers to semantically describe Web Services in general and dynamically invoke them.

In the following sections, these points are going to be explicated more in details by giving an in-depth overview of the overall architecture in which its reference architecture and an accompanying business case are demonstrated.

SEMANTIC-ENABLED ENTERPRISE SERVICE-ORIENTED ARCHITECTURE

In this section we will explain the Semantic-enabled Enterprise Service-Oriented Architecture (SESOA), its components and main interactions together with the potential application fields to which it can be applied.

SESOA framework can be defined as an enterprise solution that links businesses to external systems based on business process and service-orientation concepts. It represents a lightweight Web framework that annotates Web Services coming from different service providers with semantics so that the indexing and discovery of these services can be more comprehensive. Examples of service providers can be those who provide product shipment or payment services. These providers publish their services in a common registry called SESOA semantic service repository. Because of that, SESOA can be considered as an enhanced SOA concept in which the service consumer can discover its repository and invoke the provider's services. The Web Services published in this repository are semantically annotated using RDF triples. These triples are merely subject-predicate-object statements that link the services in groups called assemblages. The subject in such statement is for example the assemblage, the predicate is has member, and the object is the Web Service. Doing so, any service can be queried based on the group to which it belongs using any RDF query language like SPARQL Protocol and RDF Query Language (Prud'Hommeaux, & Seaborne, 2008). Last but not least, SESOA framework offers also the traditional discovery provided using former techniques like the Universal Description Discovery and Integration (UDDI) standard.

The research process that has been followed to design SESOA is derived from the design science research methodology proposed by (Peffers et al., 2008). In SESOA, all the business functionalities are realized using Web Services that can be invoked by service consumers. Moreover, the main characteristics of this framework are:

- It is a process-oriented framework where business processes are managed, implemented, and executed using the Web Services;
- SESOA validates Web Services following predefined businesses' criteria, evaluates them and annotates their relations with semantics;
- It is a lightweight semantic-enabled SOA solution;
- It groups Web Services based on the business domains to which they belong;
- It provides semantic annotations to the Web Services relations using RDF statements;
- It supports service reuse because of the adoption of the SOA concept.

Figure 2 illustrates the SESOA reference architecture. Consumer system, provider system and Web Service directory are the typical ingredients of the SOA concept. The main and centric component in this framework is the processing system. It is a workflow-based system from which all the business processes can be initiated in form of workflows with connection to the other SESOA components.

As we mentioned earlier, the Web Services are grouped into assemblages based on the domain to which they belong. These assemblages are placed in the assemblage unit within the semantic Web Service-based system component that is responsible of managing (create, update and delete) the assemblages. Each assemblage is having

Figure 2. Semantic-enabled enterprise SOA reference architecture

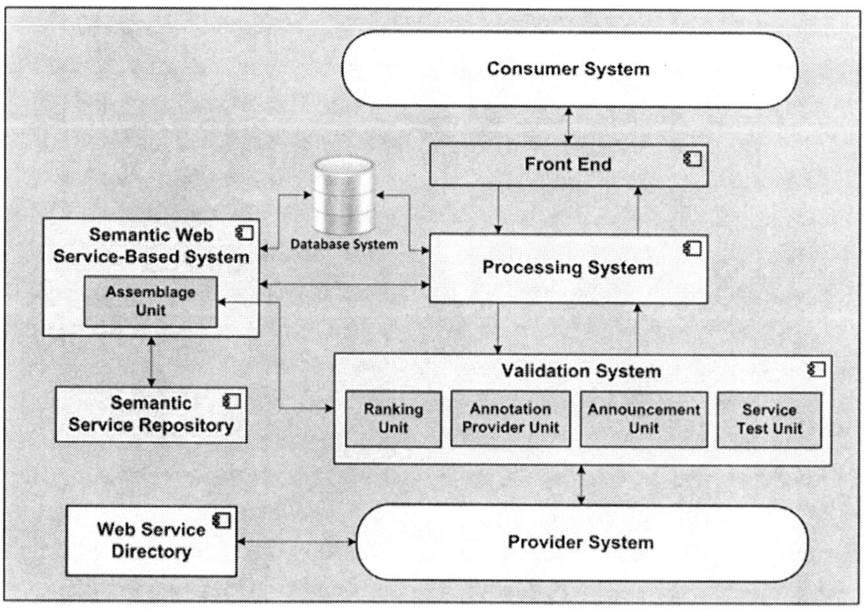

as properties an id, category, domain, and members (the Web Services).

All Web Services are registered in one or more assemblages as members. The relations between the services and the assemblages are semantically annotated using RDF statements. These semantic annotated relations are advertised in the semantic service repository. All the RDF statements, the business and user management data are stored in the SESOA database system.

Listing 1 shows an example of RDF statement between an assemblage and one of its services.

Based on that any system that have access to the semantic service repository can use a SPARQL engine to query the listing based either on the subject, the predicate, or the object to call the service and get the data from the external systems.

The validation system has four subsystems namely: service test unit, ranking unit, annotation provider unit and announcement unit. Service test unit subsystem is providing set of tests exposed as Web Services like primitive data types tests (integer, string, decimal, etc.). The ranking unit subsystem evaluates the services supplied by the provider system in form of machine to machine evaluation (services' response time and availability are the adopted criteria to perform the service evaluation). The annotation provider unit is responsible of semantically annotating the relations between the services and the assemblages using RDF statements besides storing these relations in the SESOA database system. The announcement unit advertises for new service functionalities where the service provider system may implement in the future.

The main interactions between the SESOA components are explained as follows: consumer system starts to run one of the activities within the processing system. The processing system forwards this request to the assemblage unit to check whether there is a corresponding service or not. The semantic Web Service-based system discovers the semantic service repository relations to see in which assemblage the service(s) is located. Upon finding corresponding service(s), it will respond back to the consumer system via the processing system and direct binding between the consumer system and the service(s) will be made. The services that are supplied by the provider system are validated and ranked using the validation system.

As for the SESOA database system, it is responsible of managing:

1. The semantic service-assemblage relations where they are stored as entities and statements between these entities (subject-predicate-object expressions),
2. The assemblages and service properties,
3. The system's user profiles (user management) and
4. The data of the implemented business processes.

The SESOA implementation is done as a Web application that can be used to enable the realization of several business cases on top of it. Table 1 shows an example of an online shop ordering system using the SESOA prototype. It calls the responsible service and returns the order number,

Listing 1. Assemblage - service RDF-annotated relation

```
<?xml version="1.0"?>
<rdf:RDF xmlns:assemblage="http://asbl.wi-ol.de/sesoa" xmlns:rdf="http://www.w3.org/1999/02/22-
 rdf-syntax-ns#" xmlns:sesoa="http://asbl.wi-ol.de/sesoa/">
<rdf:Description rdf:about="http://asbl.wi-ol.de/sesoa/assemblage/Payment">
 <sesoa:hasMember rdf:resource="http://asbl.wi-ol.de/sesoa/services/CreateInvoice" />
</rdf:Description>
</rdf:RDF>
```

Table 1. Online shop ordering system example

Order number	Date	Status	
6	30/03/2012 3:42:56 PM	To be Processed	Select
5	25/03/2011 4:17:14 PM	Processed	Select
4	18/11/2011 4:15:06 PM	Processed	Select
3	12/07/2011 4:09:11 PM	Done	Select

the date, and the status of this order. Status can be either *done, in progress,* or *to be processed.*

More insights on the business case realization are explained in more details below in the following section.

PRACTICAL BUSINESS CASE REALIZATION

This section describes the business case that is built on top of SESOA prototype and depicts some prototypical implementation aspects and technologies that were utilized to realize it.

The business case is described as follows: enterprise systems have normally three business processes clearly connected to create and deliver products and services, these processes are: the buying process (procurement), the producing process (production) and the selling process (completion). The implemented business case is more concerned about representing one business process namely the selling process. This process includes all the activities to sell and deliver the final product to the end customer.

The implementation of the selling business process leads to five main tasks:

1. Receiving the customer purchase order and creating a sales order out of it.
2. Creating the invoice and sending it to the customer
3. Packaging the requested products
4. Shipping the packages to the customers delivery address.
5. Customer notification about the current order state to point out whether his/her order has been processed and finalized or not.

The business case has been divided into six main components namely: Website, Shop, Payment, Logistics, Shipping and Coordination.

The Website component represents the frontend as an interface to enable the customer to perform a purchase order. It could easily be replaced by any other frontend due to the fact that it only needs to communicate with the Shop component realized using Web Services. The Shop component provides the database access to all other components. Logistics is an internal component within the system that accomplishes the packaging of the ordered articles and products by taking the warehouse management into account.

With Payment and Shipping components represent the implementations of external payment and shipping companies. Finally, the Coordination component has been realized to reflect the whole business process management. Its main task is to integrate each activity coming from the other components into one primary workflow.

Figure 3 shows a mapping of the business case model. The Website is representing the Consumer System and it communicates via an interface to the Shop component which represents one database within the SESOA database system. The Coordination is placed in the processing system and can be seen as the heart of the system. Both of the mentioned external components are representing several instances of the SESOA's provider system.

For the realization of the prototype, several technologies have been utilized. All the components have been implemented using the Microsoft .NET Framework 4.0. The frontend is implemented using ASP.NET. As for the workflows, they have been realized using the Microsoft Workflow Foundation. The databases are hosted using Microsoft SQL Server 2008 and are mapped

Figure 3. The selling business process

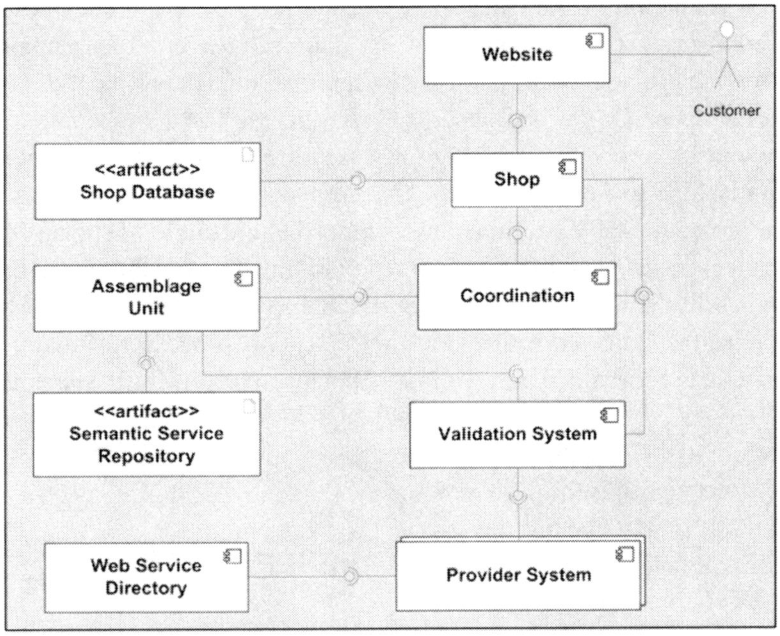

with the object-relational wrapper Language Integrated Query (LINQ).

The implemented prototype represents a Web shop that reflects the mentioned business process. The key feature is the dynamic retrieval of external services through the semantic service repository. This opens the chances for new service providers to offer new payment and shipping options to the customer (differences in forms of price, availability, response time, etc.). Moreover, service providers can easily add new services, semantically annotate them and publish them to the repository using the SESOA prototype.

SYSTEM OUTCOMES

The main outcomes from the SESOA framework can be summarized as follows:

- Open the market for SMEs
- Web Service validation and evaluation
- Lightweight Semantic annotation of Web Service relations

In this work, Web Services are not just supplied by one single company rather they can be provided by a wider set of services providers. This will *open the market for SMEs* that was for long time dominated by huge software vendors, like Microsoft®, IBM®, Oracle®, SAP®, etc. All of the enterprises (regardless of their sizes) can supply their services to the SESOA semantic service repository so that each company can use them if it has access to it. In this way, we extend the traditional service market to include external data that were not accessible before.

One of the gained advantages that can be harvested from SESOA concept is *Web Service validation and evaluation*. On the one hand, service validation is applied as a set of validation data types' tests realized in form of Web Services and applied on services operations and messages where data types, such as integer, decimal, string, etc. can be validated. To make it more clear, the string data type, for example, can be split into alpha, numeric, alphanumeric and non-alphanumeric sub-data types. Based on the usage of Web Service operation, a validation test can be applied on one of these sub-data types or the generic string data type. In this way, the validation of the external data imported to the company's application can be guaranteed and all service providers can be sure that they use the same data types. On the other hand, service evaluation represents secure service rating protocol based on a machine-to-machine evaluation protocol. This protocol enables automatic ranking of Web Services based on two criteria, namely: service availability and response time. Service evaluation helps the managers to decide which external services can be invoked based on their reputation.

As mentioned before in this chapter, SESOA semantic service repository groups the Web Services into assemblages. It is up to the business to decide how many assemblages are sufficient to group their supplied Web Services. All the relations between the services and the assemblages are annotated using RDF statements. Therefore, SESOA supports *the Lightweight Semantic annotation of Web Service relations*. This annotation is done using RDF subject-predicate-object statements in which the subject is an assemblage, the object is the actual Web Service, and the predicate is the relationship (e.g. hasMember, isMemberOf, or any other relation).

Based on the aforementioned outcomes and from an evaluation point of view, SESOA can be applied to a bunch of business domains like ERP, Sales Leads, Business Intelligence, or Environmental Information Management Systems.

CONCLUSION AND OUTLOOK

In this chapter, the main focus was to present the SESOA framework with an accompanying business case built on top of it. SESOA is a SOA-based architecture that deals with semantic-annotated Web Services' relations. Using SESOA assures the high reusability of its components where each component can be seen as a standalone system. SESOA enables the realization of business processes as Web Service-based workflows that takes benefit from the market's best practices.

Moreover, one of the main purposes of this architecture is to group the Web Services into assemblages based on their actual domain to which they are related. We introduced also the current development of the overall framework. As an outlook behind this work, using Task Parallel Library (TPL) along the prototypical implementation will scale up the system to have a better performance on multi-core processors. Finally and from semantic perspective, only RDF statements have been used and the system can be enhanced to support higher level ontologies like OWL.

REFERENCES

Barnaby, T. (2002). *Distributed. NET programming in C*. Berkely, CA: Apress.

Bartonitz, M. (2011). *Vom Status Quo der Standards im Geschäftsprozessmanagement*. SAPERION. Retrieved from http://www.saperionblog.com/lang/de/vom-status-quo-der-standards-im-geschaftsprozessmanagement-und-der-wende-in-deutschland/5428/

Battle, S., Bernstein, A., Boley, H., Grosof, B., Gruninger, M., & Hull, R. ... Tabet, S. (2005). *Semantic Web services framework (SWSF) overview*. Retrieved from http://www.w3.org/Submission/SWSF/

Berners-Lee, T., Hendler, J., & Lassila, O. (2001). The Semantic Web. *Scientific American, 284*(6), 34–35. doi:10.1038/scientificamerican0501-34

Booth, D., Champion, I. M., Ferris, C., Haas, H., McCabe, F., Newcomer, E., & Orchard, D. (2004). *Web services architecture*. Retrieved from http://www.w3.org/TR/ws-arch/

Celino, I., Karla, A., De Medeiros, A., Zeissler, G., Oppitz, M., Facca, F., & Zoeller, S. (2007). Semantic business process analysis. *Business, 251*, 1–4.

Clement, L., Hately, A., von Riegen, C., & Rogers, T. (2004). *UDDI version 3.0.2.* UDDI Spec Technical Committee Draft. Retrieved March 24, 2012, from http://uddi.org/pubs/uddi-v3.0.2-20041019.htm

Domingue, J., Roman, D., & Stollberg, M. (2005). Web service modeling ontology (WSMO): An ontology for Semantic Web services. *Architecture (Washington, D.C.)*, (n.d), 776–784.

Fensel, D., Kopecký, J., & Vitvar, T. (2008). MICROWSMO: Semantic description of restful services. WSMO Deliverable. Retrieved from http://wsmo.org/TR/d38/v0.1/20080219/d38v01_20080219.pdf

Graham, I. (2006). *Business rules management and service oriented architecture*. John Wiley & Sons.

Hu, Y., Yang, Q. P., Sun, X., & Wei, P. (2008). Applying Semantic Web services to enterprise Web. *Engineering, September,* 9–11.

Kopecký, J., & Vitvar, T. (2008). WSMO-Lite: Lowering the Semantic Web services barrier with modular and light-weight annotations. In *Proceedings of the 2008 IEEE International Conference on Semantic Computing,* (pp. 238–244). Washington, DC: IEEE Computer Society.

Kopecký, J., Vitvar, T., Bournez, C., & Farrell, J. (2007). SAWSDL: Semantic annotations for WSDL and XML schema. *IEEE Internet Computing, 11*, 60–67. doi:10.1109/MIC.2007.134

MacKenzie, C. M., Laskey, K., McCabe, F., Brown, P. F., & Metz, R. (2006). *Reference model for service oriented architecture 1.0* (pp. 1–31). OASIS Open.

Mahmoud, T. (2009). Semantic SOA-based model to be applied in business environments. *CENTERIS 2009 Conference on ENTERprise Information Systems Proceedings,* (pp. 473-482). Ofir, Portugal.

Martin, D., Burstein, M., Mcdermott, D., Mcilraith, S., Paolucci, M., & Sycara, K. (2007). Bringing semantics to Web services with OWL-S. *World Wide Web (Bussum), 10*, 243–277. doi:10.1007/s11280-007-0033-x

Peffers, K., Tuunanen, T., Rothenberger, M., & Chatterjee, S. (2008). A design science research methodology for information systems research. *Journal of Management Information Systems, 24*(3), 45–77. doi:10.2753/MIS0742-1222240302

Prud'Hommeaux. E., & Seaborne, A. (2008). SPARQL query language for RDF. W3C Recommendation. Retrieved March 24, 2012, from http://www.w3.org/TR/rdf-sparql-query/

Richardson, L., & Ruby, S. (2007). *RESTful Web services*. O'Reilly Media.

Schichtenberg, H. (2007). *Microsoft. NET 3.0 - Crashkurs*. Microsoft Press.

Scribner, K. (2007). *Microsoft Windows workflow foundation*. Microsoft Press.

Van Der Aalst, W. M. P. (2008). *Challenges in business process analysis* (pp. 27–42). Springer-Verlag.

Van Der Aalst, W. M. P., Aldred, L., Dumas, M., & Ter Hofstede, A. H. M. (2004). Design and implementation of the YAWL system. *Proceedings of the 16th International Conference on Advanced Information Systems Engineering CAiSE04, 3084,* (pp. 281–305).

Weske, M. (2010). *Business process management: Concepts, languages, architectures*. Springer Publishing Company, Incorporated.

ENDNOTES

1 http://www.w3.org/TR/rdf-concepts/ (Retrieved: 24.03.2012)
2 http://www.daml.org/services/owl-s (Retrieved: 24.03.2012)
3 Representational State Transfer or RESTful Web Services (Richardson & Ruby, 2007)
4 http://sharepoint.microsoft.com/ (Retrieved: 24.03.2012)
5 http://crm.dynamics.com/ (Retrieved: 24.03.2012)
6 http://yawlfoundation.org/ (Retrieved: 24.03.2012)
7 http://wfmopen.sourceforge.net/ (Retrieved: 24.03.2012)
8 It is also known as BPEL4WS.

Chapter 13
A Complex Adaptive System Thinking Approach of Government E-Procurement in a Cloud Computing Environment

Marc Rabaey
University of Hasselt, Belgium

ABSTRACT

The main focus on e-Procurement in this chapter will be the public (government) e-Procurement, which is part of a larger whole, namely e-Government. e-Procurement and e-Government are very important tools for the government to act in this fast changing society. But as for must business, the tools may be important, but the vision and the strategy to use these tools are much more important. Therefore the chapter discusses e-Government and e-Procurement in their strategic contexts, in which intelligence (contextual integrated information) is a key factor to survive. The reason is because the government is a Complex Adaptive System (CAS). Without intelligence and the agility of its structure and processes, the government will not survive, or at least it will be less efficient and effective in developing strategies and in executing these strategies. The game theory discussion will show that the flexibility and agility of the e-Procurement system (together with a good strategy) are key factors for a successful system; otherwise e-Procurement is more of weakness in the government's value chain of procurement of goods and services. In the last part of the discussion on Cloud Computing and e-Procurement, the author argues that ERP systems (so called best practices) are not well adapted to other contexts than the simple context of the Cynefin Framework. Service Oriented Architecture solutions can provide better (adapted) solutions for e-Procurement. Cloud Computing in combination with SOA may be the next generation solution.

DOI: 10.4018/978-1-4666-2119-0.ch013

INTRODUCTION

The main focus on e-Procurement in this chapter will be the public (government) e-Procurement, which is part of a larger whole, namely e-Government. Therefore we will first discuss e-Government and its strategic context. Here we will show the importance of intelligence (contextual integrated information) in the decision making processes from the perspective of systems thinking.

In the next point we approach the procurement function from game theory. We will show that depending on the role that a government wants or has to play, the e-Procurement system has to be able to adapt to this role. Therefore the management of e-Procurement must enable and promote the agility of such system.

The need for different types of interactions with the environment will lead us to the discussion on Complex Adaptive System (CAS), more precisely on the dimensions and the characteristics of CAS and the agility to survive in a fast changing and dynamic environment. Also in this context the command and control (C2) and the Cynefin framework will be brought into the spotlight.

The last part of this chapter before the conclusions deals with Cloud Computing, and the technological framework in which we will place the e-Procurement.

For one person Cloud Computing is hype, for another it is a paradigm shift. We will not argue this, but we will investigate the full potential of Cloud Computing for e-Procurement. The actual platform of e-Procurement is formed by Enterprise Resources Planning (ERP) systems. Vendors of ERP systems are pretending that they sell the "Best Practices" solutions. However in this part, we will see that the notion (awareness) of being a CAS is very relevant for defining the structure, the processes and the functions of e-Procurement. In this context we will argue that Service Oriented Architecture (SOA) is providing – at this moment – the better solutions to orchestrate e-Procurement.

E-GOVERNMENT

Government

A government is a collection of institutions that act with authority and create formal obligations. A Government may administer or supervise a state, a set group of people, or a collection of assets (UNU-IIST-SP, 2008). Therefore an information system is needed to manage its functions and responsibilities, but a common characteristic for many governments is that the information systems of all the departments of the governments were in the beginning of Information Technology (IT) isolated and barely integrated.

The picture of an archipelago with a deep sea in-between represents better this situation. They were certainly not (inter)connected governmental departments, and every department had its own procurement service (automated or not). Later with the introduction of automated information systems, every island of the archipelago was automated differently and certainly not with integration of systems in mind. The Information Technology (IT) implemented by these governmental bodies was logically based on their own needs and way of working.

At the level of the (overall) system of government, this approach led often to incompatibilities and vulnerabilities, which result in considerable expenses due to the inability to collaborate or communicate between the different governmental bodies in an efficient and effective way, but worse the citizen is suffering from this: less service, more tax, and thus a less productive government.

Efforts to centralize the IT and/or to develop Enterprise Application Integration (EAI) were very costly projects and thus never fully executed. Luckily we are observing that the IT industry is moving towards an affordable form of technological integration solutions. This is not caused by an altruistic reflex of those companies, but by the Internet as the concept of interconnecting everything, everywhere at any time (Rabaey, 2012).

The newest trend is cloud computing (pay per use IT-services), which uses models such as the public cloud (for everybody), private cloud (only for one organization), hybrid cloud (mixture of public and private) and community cloud. Cloud Computing was first preceded by another (however related) technology: Service Oriented Architecture (SOA). SOA will be the glue to combine legacy systems and Cloud Computing.

Types of E-Government

Mainly three sorts of e-Government exist: Government-to-Government (G2G), Government-to-Citzen (G2C) and Government-to-Organization (G2O).

Government-to-Government can be national (amongst departments), intranational (higher and lower governmental authorities like provinces) or international (like the European Union (EU)). Collaboration on itself can be difficult (contradicting interests), and electronic collaboration is certainly not always trivial. Although SOA is at first glance the more obvious solution, cloud computing in a community model may offer more secure and economical possibilities (see below). However, it is at the political level that the commitment should be made and just like in any other business if the top is not committed to move things forward, then nothing will happen.

Government-to-Client (G2C) is client-oriented (citizens, companies). The time of information portal is over. Cloud computing is the enabler of knowledge portals in combination with services portals (Rabaey, 2012).

In the context of e-Procurement, the Government-to-Organizations, more particularly enterprises plays an important role. e-Procurement is "the use of the internet or a company's intranet to procure goods and services used in the conduct of business. An e-procurement system can streamline all aspects of the purchasing process while applying tighter controls over spending and product preferences." (Business Dictionary, 2012)

Connected Government

The tendency is to look at governments as business enterprises; however they are more complex (different levels of government, political influences, etc.) and therefore integration and even interoperability are more difficult because they don't follow the common (economical) business logic. Pallab Saha writes: "Most governments worldwide are in the midst of substantial public sector transformation activities. A majority of these initiatives are triggered by the need to have better and seamless government services delivered online. The focus on automating government services often is a largely limited to specific ministries and agencies. However such initiatives lack the cross-ministry / agency viewpoint and coordination. This creates challenges in taking a whole-of-government (W-O-G) approach and concomitant benefits, which are much more than benefits derived by taking agency-centric viewpoints." (Saha, 2010, p.7)

He defines three key goals of Enterprise Architecture (EA) in government organizations: make them citizen-centered, results-oriented and market-based. One of the possible ways to achieve this is by introducing the concept of "Connected Government": "Connected government enables governments to connect seamlessly across functions, agencies, and jurisdictions to deliver effective and efficient services to citizens and businesses."(Saha, 2010, p. 8).

The dimensions of Connected Government are:

- Citizen centricity;
- Common infrastructure and interoperability;
- Collaborative services and business operations;
- Public sector governance;
- Networked organizational model;
- Social inclusion;
- Transparent and open government.

Those dimensions can be drawn in a "cause-and-effect diagram" (based on the Balanced ScoreCard philosophy, (Rabaey, 2012)) and show in this way the interdependency of these dimensions of Connected Government (Figure 1). This interdependency will point to possible risks of failure if lower (causing) goals are not attained.

The public sector governance is the base of all and found its justification through the overall policy defined by the government. For economical (effectiveness and efficiency) and technological (efficiency) reasons, the government(s) should have at least an interoperable IT-capabilities (SOA) and/or a common infrastructure (Cloud Computing, see below). To form generic collaborative services and business operations, the organizational structures of the governments must be taken into account. From the perspective of systems thinking, this is necessary but not sufficient because all stakeholders should be included (see below). However we have introduced this dimension "Generic" collaborative services and business operations because it is fundamental in an ever changing environment (caused by the society, the globalized economy and the politics self) to describe the IT-capabilities. These capabilities are then instantiated in "Real" collaborative services and business operations by taking into account the social inclusion, citizen centricity and another additional dimension "Economical & Business Inclusion". Governments cannot ignore the economical reality and they need to collaborate with business to acquire services and resources to attain their objectives.

In the modelling of systems thinking loops will come to the surface. One example would be in the context of e-Procurement: resources and services will be used to acquire a system of e-Procurement, and once established the e-Procurement will be responsible for acquiring additional and/or new services and resources for the e-Procurement.

The collaborative services and business operations are representing the operational strategy of the governments, which is responsible for the realization of the objectives of the Grand strategy of the State. This (adapted) cause and effect diagram (Rabaey, 2010) shows in another way the importance of Enterprise Architecture (EA). If EA is not present or not fully developed then the operational level may suffer from inconsistencies

Figure 1. Cause and effect diagram for connected government (adapted from Rabaey (2012)

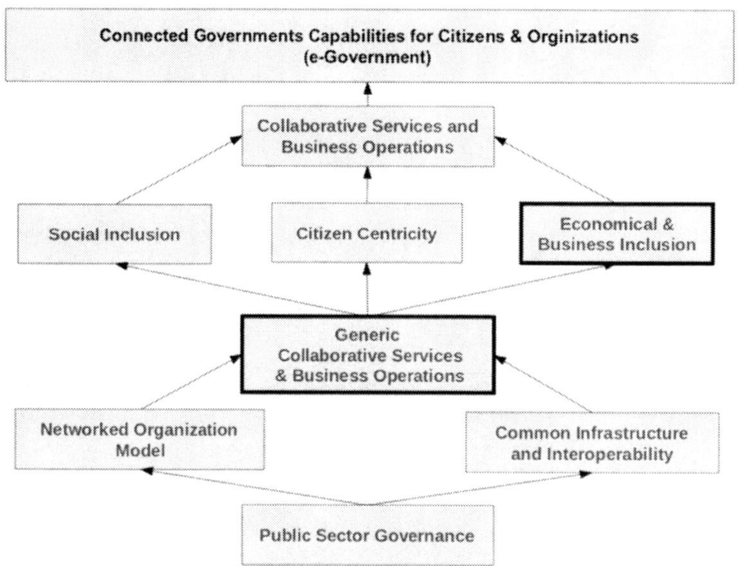

in the allocation of resources or in the definition of operational objectives (Salab, 2010; Rabaey, 2012). So in the case of e-Government, and therefore also of e-Procurement EA is necessary but not sufficient to develop, maintain and extend a good working e-Government.

STRATEGIC CONTEXT OF E-GOVERNMENT

Co-Creating its Environment

A government is not a closed system due to the fact that it interacts with its environment. It will first observe the internal (organization) and external (environment) situation before making decisions to act. These actions will be observed by other actors (agents) in the environment and they will react upon it (ignore, collaborate, compete, agree, disagree, etc.). Of course, the government itself will behave in a similar way upon the actions or reactions of the other actors (Figure 2).

All of these actions and reactions will have effects that cannot be fully assessed on forehand. It is possible that the effects are just the opposite of the goals defined by the governmental strategy. A strategy is the balance between goals and means (Bernard, 1976). If a government engages too many resources than necessary, then it is not efficient. If the resources are insufficient to attain the objectives, then it will not be effective. This of course also applies to the e-government initiatives. Putting up an e-Government infrastructure is most of the time a very budget intensive project.

Uncertainty and Intelligence

As already mentioned the actors do not know beforehand if their actions will have the desired outcomes, because they do not know how the other players will act, therefore deciding is making choices under uncertainty. This uncertainty can be due to wrong information, lack of information, lack of time to analyze information or a wrong collection of information. As a consequence we need a way to reduce the uncertainty and thus to mitigate the risks before making decisions.

Decision making has three dimensions (Gharajedaghi, 2011, pp.33-37): rational, emotional

Figure 2. Mutual influence

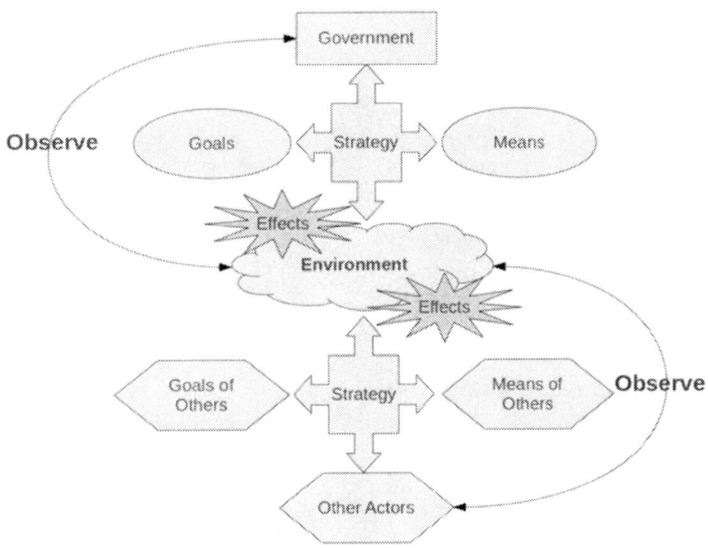

and cultural. A rational choice is the domain of the self-interest of the decision-maker. It reflects the perceived interest of the decision maker at that certain time and is related to extrinsic values (instrumental).

The emotional dimension of decision making is the domain of beauty and excitement and deals with intrinsic values (stylistic). In contrast to rational choice, which is risk aversive, emotional choice is not. As a matter of fact, uncertainty is an important attribute of excitement and challenge. An uncertainty can be positive (opportunity) or it can be negative (threat).

The cultural dimension is about ethical norms of the collectivities to which the decision maker belongs. The ethical values are the constraining elements of the decision process. Culture delivers the default values when the decision maker fails to choose one explicitly.

Moreover literature on behavioral economics (Ariely, 2009; Montier, 2010), intuitive management (Burke et al., 1999), psychology (Libet, 2011; Pucket et al., 2011) and naturalistic decision-making (Brooks, 2007; Berryman, 2007; Shattuck & Miller, 2006) confirms that the decision-making is not always rational. A lot has to do with how people and their brains are coping with uncertainty and the perception of uncertainty.

In an economical context (see also (Rabaey, 2011)), rationality has more to do with the ratio of benefits to costs instead of the philosophical meaning of reasoning. Related to the investments and/or resource allocation issues, is uncertainty management. Uncertainty is more than risk management, which is the identification, assessment, and prioritization of risks (based on uncertainties) followed by coordinated and economical application of resources to minimize, monitor, and control the probability and/or impact of unfortunate events or to maximize the realization of opportunities. Uncertainty is a state in which the outcomes are unknown and perhaps unknowable. The more distant in time (future), the greater the uncertainty is (Funston, 2010, p. xxiii). The decision horizon is farther at the strategic level than at the operational or tactical levels of the organization. For most of the organizations in this ever faster changing environment, the time line at the strategic level is from the present until the long term (at least a year), while the operational level is from now until short term (couple of weeks or months at most).

So, the government as any other organization must always be collecting intelligence (Bernard, 1976). The continuous process of observing, creating and disseminating of intelligence is the only rule for this principle (Rabaey et al., 2012). Intelligence is the product resulting from the collection, evaluation, analysis, integration, and interpretation of all available information, that concerns one or more aspects of the other actors and their actions in the environment, and that is immediately or potentially significant to the planning and operations of an organization (adapted from (Rabaey et al, .2012)).

Intelligence Base

Intelligence Base is a system to manage in essence the unknown and the knowledge. It is composed of (Figure 3):

- Planning and Directing: this cell receives and manages the intelligence needs.
- Collecting cell is responsible for the managing of the network of sensors.
- Network of sensors will collect data on demand or ad hoc
- Knowledge Base is a software system capable of supporting the explicit representation of knowledge in some specific competence domain and of exploiting it through appropriate reasoning mechanisms in order to provide high-level problem-solving performance. The knowledge base, a part of the Intelligence base, stores available knowledge concerning the domain at hand, represented in appropriate explicit form

Figure 3. Government and intelligence base

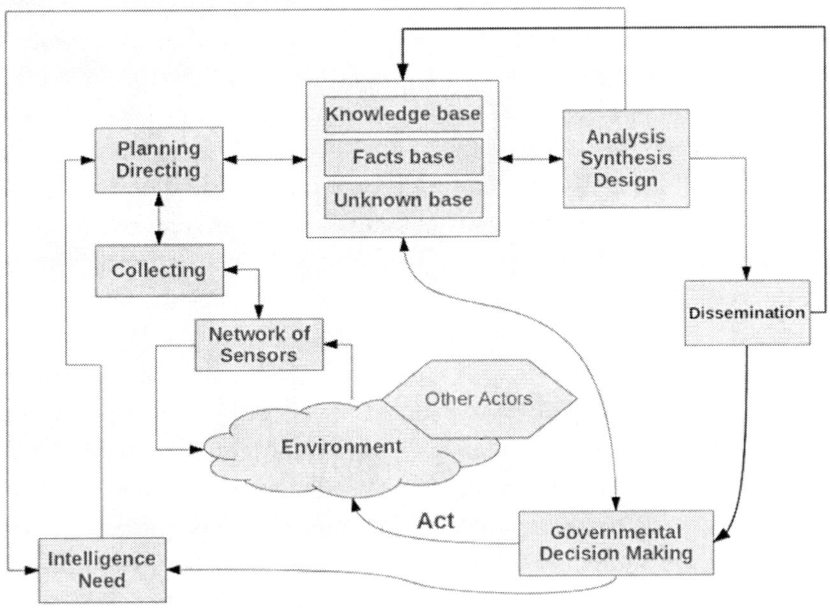

and ready to be used by the reasoning mechanism (Guida & Tasso, 1994)

- Facts Base is the collection of all raw information. This made a later interpretation of facts possible with new inference rules and/or knowledge.
- Unknown Base supports the management of all requests that are still active.
- Analysis, Synthesis and Design: the intellectual interpretation of the collected data in a context relevant to the user and/or organization.

The "Planning and Directing" cell will look in the knowledge base if the intelligence need can be satisfied. If so it will transmit the need to the "Analysis, Synthesis and Design" that will disseminate to the client. If not, the "Planning and Directing" cell will send a request for search to the manager of the sensors "Collecting cell".

Regarding the network of sensors, two events can trigger an interaction between the decision making process and the intelligence process. Firstly, the decision maker expresses an intelligence need. The second trigger is the transmission of newly detected facts by the sensors.

The case of "Information Pull" is when the decision maker does not find the necessary intelligence (in the Intelligence Base or outside of it), he expresses his need to the "Planning & Direction". As mentioned above, the latter will then define the needed intelligence actions. The needed information may not be in the Intelligence Base in which case the network has to be instructed (push). The resulting information (if any) is then interpreted ("Analysis, Synthesis and Design"). Additional information may be required if there is not enough information to be integrated into intelligence. Once the intelligence is acquired, then it will be disseminated to the intelligence client. The information and intelligence are stored respectively in the Facts Base and the Interpreted Information Base, and the Unknown Base is updated.

In the case of "Information Push" the sensors are injecting information in the network (push). The transmitted information is then analyzed. If the information can be integrated, then the resulting intelligence is pushed to the concerned people and/or organizations. The information and intelligence (if any) are stored respectively in the Facts Base and the Knowledge Base.

For a more in depth discussion we refer to the work of Rabaey and Mercken (2012) "Framework of Knowledge and Intelligence Base: From Intelligence to Service" in the book "Knowledge Management and Drivers of Innovation in Services Industries" edited by Patricia Ordoñez de Pablos and Miltiadis D. Lytras.

Systems Thinking and Intelligence

However we would like to add a systems thinking perspective to this matter. An important difference between the work of previous authors and this work is that the former only mentions analysis as "intellectual interpretation" of the data. According to Gharajedaghi (2011) the intellectual interpretation in Systems Thinking (ST) consists of two other elements than analysis: synthesis with systems design.

Analytical thinking has been the essence of classical science, which assumes that the whole is nothing more than the sum of the parts. This implies that understanding of the structure is both necessary and sufficient to understanding the whole and therefore knowing the structure means knowing the system. In ST one of the dimensions is structure.

Synthetic thinking is linked with the functional approach. By defining a system by its outcome, synthesis puts the subject in the context of the environment, which can also be a (larger) system. This corresponds in ST with functions.

Last but not least, Gharajedaghi (2011) added dynamic thinking to the arsenal of intelligence methods. Dynamic thinking is focusing on the processes, so it looks to the how-questions for the necessary answer to define the whole.

Sterman (2010) and Gharajedahi (2011) state that seeing the whole requires understanding structure, function and process at the same time, and moreover they are interdependent.

Structure defines components (capabilities) and their relationships. Functions are defining the outcomes or results to be produced. Processes explicitly define the sequence of activities and the know-how to produce the outcomes. The context defines the unique environment in which the system is situated (Gharajedaghi, 2011) which requires permanent observing and intelligence (Rabaey et al., 2012).

Regarding the capability approach (Rabaey et al., 2007) and ST (Gharajedaghi, 2011) a structure can perform more than one function, or different structures can have the same function. The classical view on structure (one function) fails, because its notion of causality, where cause is both necessary and sufficient for its effect) proves inadequate to explain the other two non-classical cases.

The assessment of function – structure – process – environment is an iterative inquiry (cycle), which has the framework of interdependent thinking models (analytical, synthetic and design) and they have to happen at the same time. Gharajedaghi (2011) refers to the work of Stephen Wolfram when he explains that iteration is the key to understand complexity. An iterative process of applying simple rules is at the core of nature's mysterious ability to produce complex phenomena so effortlessly.

Feedback Loops and Learning

As one can observe in previous points, intelligence is not only needed to support the decision making, but also to increase and update the knowledge of an organization as we have seen above. Knowledge management however is also related to learning and unlearning. Figure 1 "Cause and Effect diagram for Connected Government shows the generic and operational "collaborative services and business operations," which implies processes that have to be optimized. The optimization of the processes of procurement is very crucial for a good functioning government, and thus also for e-Procurement in the e-Government environment. Of course, the content of the different subject matters (knowledge areas) are even more crucial, but in the context of systems thinking we must extend the scope of e-Procurement to the realizations of the bids, so that the feedbacks of these realizations can enrich the e-Procurement processes and knowledge. But first we will discuss feed back loops and mental models.

Action Research has the single and the double loop learning. If the results are in match with the action strategies, the intention and the governing variables (or governing values) then nothing has to be changed. If the results mismatch the intention (of the action strategies) then the first loop learning is activated, meaning that another strategy will be developed, but still with respect to the governing variables. If however there is also a mismatch with the belief system, then the governing variables have to be adapted; this may lead to a scope redefinition of the business (market).

Sterman (2010) added mental models to the double loop. Although he defined a double loopback between (information) Feedback and the mental models, the author esteems that this double loopback can be the cause of an (increasing) gap between the models and the awareness (culture, strategy) of the organization, so that loopback is not drawn (Figure 4).

In the next part we will go more in depth to the strategy.

GAME THEORETICAL APPROACH

Real Options

Certainly project-based procurements are very difficult to decide fully at the beginning of the procurement. It may look contradicting but in an e-Procurement situation it is even more difficult. What follows is based on a paper presented at the 8th Annual Acquisition Research Symposium (Rabaey, 2011)

Game theory on its own analyzes complexities of the equilibriums and the payoffs into detail by determining players' utility functions without any

Figure 4. Action research and mental models

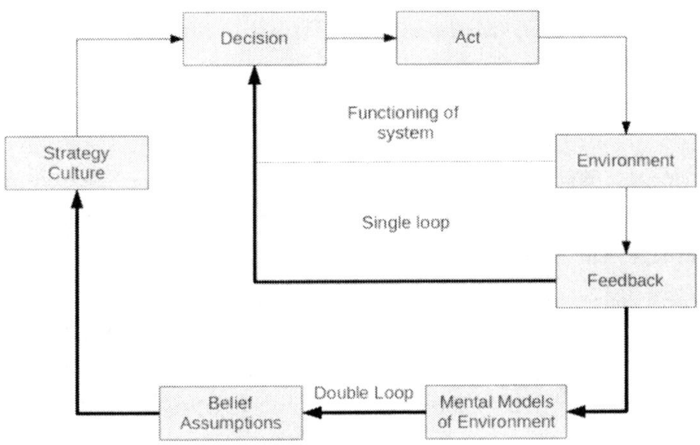

relation to market values. Real options analysis places these payoff values under uncertainty, considering market values and the flexibility of response by the optimal exercise of the options. Real options are the right but not the obligation to buy or sell products (and/or services). However because of the actual actions (and necessary actual decisions), urgent events seem to erode partly the value of waiting. This is the main reproach that we can find in the literature on the option games. The following approach brings both theories together in another way.

Real options are a set of chains of future decisions. In order to make decisions (delay, stop, start up, continue), management is waiting to collect more information, or is waiting for a better environment (market situation, political situation and so on). The situation has to be assessed at that moment in the future, but we will place it in a game theoretic context. Our proposal is not only a chain of possible decisions (as in the non-interactive original version of real options), but also a chain of possible interaction situations represented by games.

Every decision node consists of two phases. The first is to assess the situation in which the decision has to be made, in other words the probable payoff matrix of the game. The second phase is to determine the value of the real option based on this payoff matrix.

If the convention is to always take the same game, then we call this the mono-game chain of options. A more complex version is to consider more than one game, and therefore determine the value of the real option for each game (and its corresponding payoff matrix). As a result, each node with multiple games (in the so called multi-game chain of options) will generate more branches than in the case of a mono-game chain of options.

The multi-game chain has a tendency to become a chaotic (although deterministic) system after a certain point in the time horizon. To select the more relevant games, meaning reducing the number of possible games, it is necessary that the organization collects intelligence about the possibilities on collaborating or competing with one or more actors in the market. Otherwise the system will overload itself.

Moreover Weeds (2006) warns that certain urgent events force the organization to act immediately, indicating that an organization must permanently screen its environment, and therefore implement an intelligence system. It must be stressed that even organizations that are not using ROV must implement a similar system; otherwise it will miss opportunities and be warned too late for eventual threats.

Procurement in Competition (First and Second Mover)

In general there are two kinds of situations: competition and collaboration. A government can be in competition with enterprises, organizations or other governments (agencies) to obtain from the limited number of suppliers, the capabilities to produce goods or to deliver services. In function of the strategic importance, the government can chose between a first mover (leader, innovator), or a second mover (follower).

The first mover advantage (FMA) is when the government invests first, rather than continuing to delay and the competitor continues to delay. The invested cost can be seen as a basis investment for further options, while the government as first mover has as advantage that there will be a strong alignment of the 'new' capabilities on his own strategy. A second advantage is that for a limited time the government has a monopoly and can create market conditions for the suppliers and not to forget also the customers of the suppliers. However it is not without any risk. If it fails then the competitor who has delayed can take advantage of the mistakes of the first mover (this is an example of a Second Mover Benefit (SMB)).

To be a second mover can have many causes. First of all, the government had not enough information to reduce its uncertainty. In this case with the information coming from the actions (failure or not) of the competitor, the government can reevaluate the situation and improve its payoffs.

The government can also consider saving the costs of being the first mover, but it will have to adapt to the solution of the first mover, by sacrificing some of the strategic objectives or part of it, unless the first mover has failed. In the latter case, the second mover can take the lessons learned to determine a better strategy to obtain the necessary capabilities, as already mentioned above.

It can be even a strategy that the follower wants the other one (pushed in the role of leader) to move as first, so that the latter can come with a better strategy or products or gaining better resources (or methodologies) and hope that the follower becomes the leader.

Weeds (2006) states that FMA tend to conflict with real options, because there is a threat of preemption of a rival; however that is more the now-or-never situation (see below). FMA comes from the strategic (competitive) advantage (opportunity) of that moment. By investing (consuming cash flow), the government hopes to create more potential for the future (for attaining the objectives of the political governance) and knows that a possible reaction of the follower can come. In the case of now-or-never, the initiative is not exclusively for the leader.

As for the game-theoretic aspect, the government as first mover must be aware that the competitors will react. These reactions can undermine the FMA, therefore the government should not only consider its own actions, but also the reactions of the competitors and the influence of these reactions on its own payoffs (the case of leader-follower game). Therefore from the point of view of the leader, the government will establish two payoffs matrix, one for the case that the follower reacts quickly, and one for the case that the follower continues delaying any action. By creating intelligence (collecting and interpreting information) the government can better determine the utility functions and the probable reaction of the follower and its impact on the own payoffs.

Procurement in Competition (Now-or-Never)

There is a third type of competition, where the government is obtaining simultaneously the scarce resources. This is the case when it is strategically important to have a specific system (or goods or services) and therefore has to compete with other agencies. In this the competitive pressures to obtain the resources or goods/services is strong and the cost of being preempted is considerable high, then waiting can cause considerable damage by losing the investment opportunities to its competitors.

This is a now-or-never opportunity where the option has no value anymore and classic investment techniques can be used. It is not a failure of the system of real options, only strategic (game) considerations oblige the government to act as soon as possible. Of course, the decision can have significant influence on other projects or investments, of which the option values can change dramatically. Therefore it is not because of the fact that real options have not been used in an urgent case, that the decision nodes along the scenarios tree don't need a ROV anymore.

It must be clear that the government has to develop (strategic) scenarios where not only first and second mover must be taken into consideration but also the now-or-never situations.

E-Procurement in Competition

In this situation, e-Procurement can be rather a weakness than a strength, if the observing capability and early warning system are not automatically linked to the automated processes. So it is not in the interest of a government, as like any other organization, to run the e-Procurement in an automated way, just taking into account only internal alerts. In the discussion about the management of e-Procurement we will propose a system, which interprets data (signals) coming from the environment (competitors, collaborators, citizens, companies, etc.) and disseminates the intelligence (contextual interpreted information) into the whole system. Of course, the information systems need to have the capabilities "to do" (act, react) with the incoming intelligence.

E-Procurement in Collaboration

The second situation for the government procurement is collaboration. The government shares common interests with EU and other member-states of the EU, thus it is in their common interest to collaborate. Collaboration does not necessarily mean that the government is in a less stress situation. "Missing the boat" to collaborate can be as disastrous as in competition.

In the cases of repeated games, the game theory, linked with the real option analysis can be used by the government to steer the decisions in the best possible way to obtain the strategic objectives.

Here e-Procurement must be capable of interfacing with other e-Procurement systems. In this case Service Oriented Architecture (SOA) and Cloud Computing may provide better solutions.

Government as Regulator in the Market for its Own Procurement Environment

The strategic objectives determine the functional requirements of the goals, where the resource strategy is determining the technical requirements based on standards, policy or doctrine of use. The request for procurement or proposal is then published to the suppliers (market) through e-Procurement. As seen above when the government was itself submitted to the market strategic games, the suppliers can be put in two situations: competition or collaboration (coordination).

In this case we don't use the game theory to position the government in the market, but as the organization which creates a particular micro-environment for the suppliers, a market regulator for its own procurement. As a matter of fact, the government is creating the game theory framework in which the suppliers will interact with each other.

In the case of competition only: the government will enforce its own standards or the market standards. The best possible proposal will be chosen.

Competition followed by collaboration: this is the particular situation where the government will let different suppliers compete based on the competences (capability) and it creates a short-list for each capability. Afterwards the government creates an environment in which the chosen suppliers are encouraged to choose one or more partners to collaborate so that the main capability can be formed.

This is a more active steering of the formation of collaborative suppliers than the next situation. Collaborate and competition: if a project is too big for a single company (supplier) then the interested suppliers will look for themselves to find the best partner to collaborate with. So the market itself will be clustering the different players into ad hoc entities. Once these entities are formed the competition can start.

Collaborate: In the situation where there are no clear standards for a specific system, this collaboration of interested suppliers will produce and propose standards. Here the government can play also an active role to determine the future standard(s).

For this part we can conclude that the technical issues are less important than the fact that the market is a Complex Adaptive System (see below). As for any other organization (profit or non-profit), a government must take these dynamic interactions into consideration, and ensure that they are reflected it in the strategy for its procurement of goods and services. If it is not, then any initiative in the domain of e-Procurement will be an expensive failure.

E-PROCUREMENT MANAGEMENT

Extending the Scope

Earlier we quoted the definition of e-Procurement from the Business Dictionary (2012), which states that e-Procurement is "the use of the internet or a company's intranet to procure goods and services used in the conduct of business. An e-procurement system can streamline all aspects of the purchasing process while applying tighter controls over spending and product preferences." So it focuses on the procurement itself, however from the point of view of the government more things are going on. Wikipedia lists up following phases (Wikipedia Public eProcurement (n.d.)):

- **E-Sourcing:** Preparatory activities conducted by the contracting authority/entity to collect and reuse information for the preparation of a call; potential bidders may be contacted, if admitted by the legal rules, by electronic means to provide quotations or manifest interest.
- **E-Noticing:** Advertisement of calls for tenders through the publication of appropriate contract notices in electronic format in the relevant Official Journal (national/EU); electronic access to tender documents and specifications as well as additional related documents are provided in a non-discriminatory way.
- **E-Access:** Electronic access to tender documents and specifications as well support to economic operators for the preparation of an offer, e.g. clarifications, questions and answers.
- **E-Submission:** Submission of offers in electronic format to the contracting authority/entity, which is able to receive, accept and process it in compliance with the legal requirements.
- **E-Tendering:** Is the union of the eAccess and eSubmission phases.
- **E-Awarding:** Opening and evaluation of the electronic tenders received, and award of the contract to the best offer in terms of the lowest price or economically most advantageous bid.
- **E-Contract:** Conclusion, enactment and monitoring of a contract / agreement through electronic means between the contracting authority/entity and the winning tenderer.
- **E-Orders:** Preparation and issuing of an electronic order by the contracting authority/entity and its acceptance by the contractor.
- **E-Invoicing:** Preparation and delivery of an invoice in electronic format.
- **E-Payment:** Electronic payment of the ordered goods, services or works

To simplify the discussion Figure 5 (a) depicts only four phases that the government is going through. The height of the blocks and arrows indicates the level of knowledge related to the subject matter. First the agency expresses its need and a workgroup in charge of the market study for that need will collect information. There are feed forward and feed back loops between them which is why at the end of the market study the knowledge has increased. However the transfer of the requirements to the procurement step (i.e. e-Procurement) cannot fully grasp the knowledge and thus the feedback loop is more related to process technical issues in the procurement phase.

Although e-Procurements can make contracts, the procurement function is not in all agencies capable of managing the life-cycle of a contract (change management, maintenance, problem solving, etc.).

Figure 5(b) shows the possible process paths.

- Agency/Market Study/e-Procurement/e-Contracts: first acquisition
- The same way can be taken for adapting contracts, or

Figure 5. Extending e-procurement

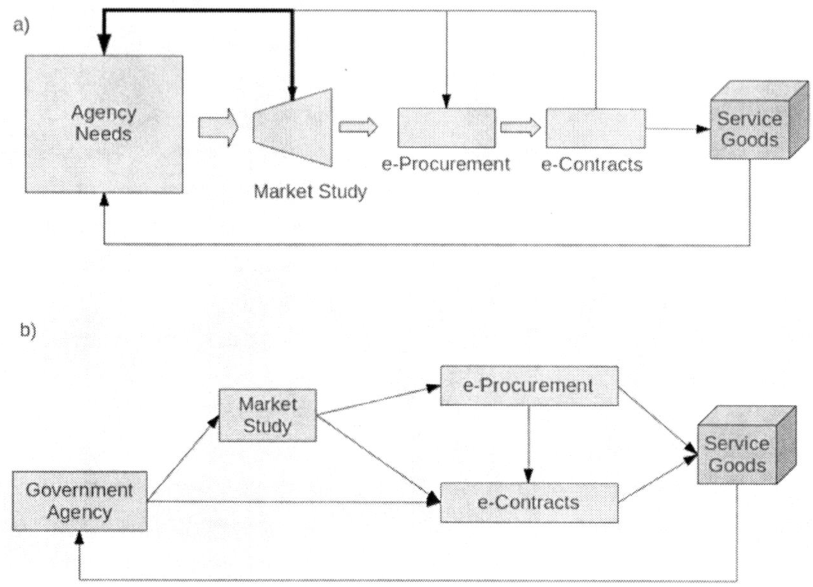

- Agency/Market Study/e-Contracts, or
- Agency/e-Contracts

This cycle can be executed more than once, for instance first for a Request for Information and then for a Request for Proposal and/or Request for Quotation. It can become more complicated if goods and/or services have to be procured for more than one agency. As one can see, simple rules applied in multiple relationships and having multiple iterations are making the procurement complex (see below Complex Adaptive System) and thus they cannot be modeled as a linear system.

Context E-Procurement

Figure 6 shows the procurement interactions not only internally but also externally. As matter of fact, in most cases external actors (from the environment) are in one way or another involved in the different phases of the process. The environment influences the organization, but the organization itself also influences the environment. The agency is the co-creator of its environment (see above).

The information systems (IS) and therefore Information Technology (IT) must be accessible for all parties involved in the procurement of goods and services. Some organizations are using an Enterprise Resource Planning (ERP) system to share data and processes (Business Process Management (BPM)). However this causes problems when actors in the organizational procurement process are outside the borders of the main organization (see discussion below on Cloud Computing).

Communication (Comm.): in a Complex Adaptive System, this is very crucial so the government must foresee a good communication system. Most of the time groupware solutions are put in place in the intranet (document library, forums, e-mail, calendar, help desk, etc.). For a part this can compensate the disadvantage of ERP because the security system can segment and protect different parts of the intranet, so that external actors can have access to the necessary resources (extranet).

Figure 6. E-procurement interactions

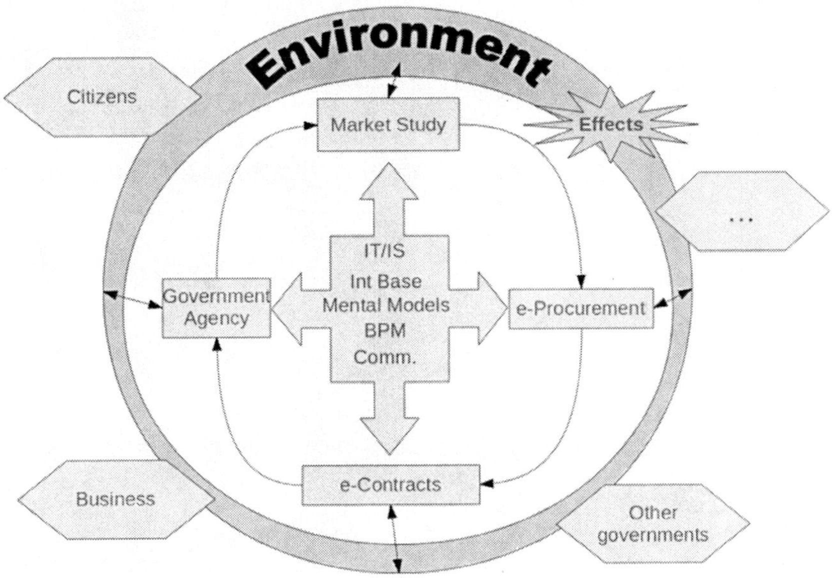

This figure shows the importance of the mental models and intelligence base (Int Base). Every actor can use the intelligence process as shown in "Figure 3: Government and Intelligence Base". In combination with the communication and the intranet, actors can have access to the knowledge (subject matters) of the procurement subject, and as such reduce the knowledge drain when the procurement object goes from one phase to another in the process.

So due to the collaborative system, knowledge workers of different areas can contribute in the analysis, synthesis and design of the procurement matters, and this in every phase of the process (Agency loop (Figure 5: Extending e-Procurement)). In the case of interconnected governments, this feature is even more important because the different governments do not have to duplicate the competences internally, but can share the competences in a networked environment. This will lead to emergent properties which are more beneficial for all concerning governments (Figure 7). The whole is greater than the sum of the parts, as we will see in more depth in the next point.

COMPLEX ADAPTIVE SYSTEM (CAS)

Dimensions of Social System

Earlier we have seen what the perspectives of the decision making to systems thinking were: rational, emotional and cultural. This decision making is happening in the context of following five dimensions of a social system, which a government is: wealth, power, knowledge, beauty and values. The generation and dissemination of these dimensions form a comprehensive set of interdependent variables that collectively describe an organization in its totality. For a good e-Procurement system, all five dimensions must be evaluated at the same time; otherwise not all interactions can be studied, the more because of the fact that is quite feasible for any four to become producers of the fifth

Figure 7. Knowledge workers

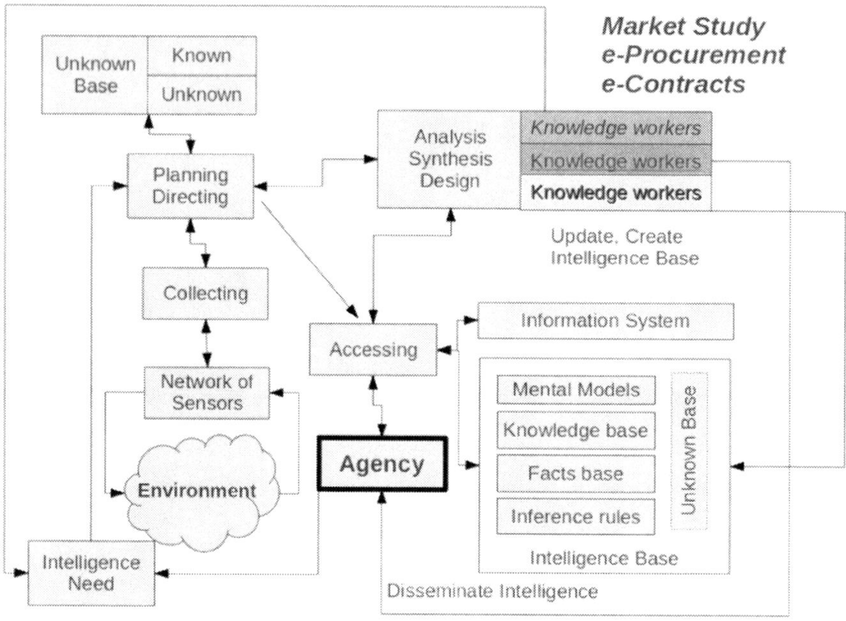

one. Recognition of multidimensionality and the imperative of and-relationships among the five dimensions of a government is one of the most significant characteristics of holistic thinking.

In a Complex Adaptive System (CAS) it is crucial that not only the five dimensions are created, but that they also are circulating and distributed to the whole organization (system of systems). Hovhannisian (2001) and Bowser, Cantle & Allan (2011) state that organizations are CAS. Those organizations are segmented rather than monolithic, in which information flows and interactions between the agents occur. The way this happens is very relevant to understanding the working of the whole and its components because it influences the culture (and subcultures), the hierarchy and the structure and it has an impact on the speed of communication and interpretation of the (internal and external) information.

Hovhannisian (2011) points out that if only the components are analyzed (Taylorian decomposition) and not the whole, analysts are not getting the full picture. They are missing the links, the interconnections between agents, and how the whole interacts with its environment. Bowser et al. (2011) emphasize that the study of CAS is interdisciplinary (and so must be the applicable tools) and that emergence requires a holistic approach before studying the parts.

Characteristics of CAS

A decisive argument for a holistic approach is found in the complexity theory and the theory of CAS. Complexity theory deals with systems that are large collections of interacting agents. Despite their diversity, complex systems share certain fundamental behaviors (Gore, 1996; Lowe & Ng, 2006):

"Emergence": Interactions among agents in complex systems may lead to emerging global (or system-wide) properties that are very different from the behaviors of individual agents. These properties which cannot be predicted from prior knowledge of the agents, in turn affect the environment that each agent perceives influencing its behavior in a synergetic feedback loop.

Thus the "whole" of a complex system is far greater than the sum of its parts and the whole has properties not held by its consisting agents. Therefore the analysis of complex systems requires a holistic approach. An agency may not only be decomposed into business units (business agents). The support of the business processes of these business agents is delivered by resources agents (like human resources, material resources, IT). They also have their culture, goals and processes and therefore must also be considered in the "whole".

"Adaptive Self-Organization": Complex systems tend to adapt to their environments and to be self-organizing. Rather than tending toward disorder or entropy, complex adaptive systems spontaneously crystallize into more highly ordered states but with few leverage points.

"Information Processing": Complex systems exhibit the ability to process information sensed from the environment and react to it based on internalized models, as discussed above. Information processing is closely related to a system's ability to learn and adapt near the edge of chaos. It creates interacting feedback loops which cause highly non-linear behavior (Bowser et al., 2011). If the CAS is an organization then the management will be confronted with counter-intuitive and non-intended consequences.

"Evolution to the Edge of Chaos": All dynamic systems exist in one of three regimes:

- A stable regime. in which disturbances tend to die out;
- A chaotic regime (the province of chaos theory);
- The phase transition between stability and chaos.

Whereas increasing disturbances in the environment cause some systems to move from stability to chaos, complex systems learn from their environments and add new functions to cope with previously unknown situations (cause and symptoms are separated in time and space). Thus they increase their complexity and adapt along the edge of chaos. According to complexity theorists the same type of growth in complexity occurs in nature, man-made systems as well as societies, business and economies (see also Cynefin framework).

Agility

The concept of CAS is important for the leadership of an organization. Lowe et al. (2006) state that good leaders have intuitively understood the nature of complexity and the nonlinearity of leading dynamic organizations. In turn, the science of complexity may reveal the underlying basis of these intuitive truths.

The nonlinearity implies that a given input may produce anything from a disproportionately large effect to no effect at all and this may change over time, meaning there is no Newtonian "cause-and-effect" phenomenon. Moreover the feedback loops may produce effects that propagate and return to impact the original causation in some way (Lowe et al., 2006, p.5). Another characteristic of CAS is that such a system is very sensitive to initial conditions (Hovhannisian, 2001).

Classic "formal" management philosophy does not cope with these issues related to CAS. That's why Lowe et al (2006, p.9) write: "Continuous change means people, structures and processes need to be able to adapt appropriately. Study of CAS indicates that an agile organization can be built on the basis of individuals with a simple but effective set of rules and the ability to communicate and adapt. A study ... showed that the [organization] has functioned effectively in the past through the use of informal networks. ... Organizational rigidity has been seen by those within the system as a restriction that reduces effectiveness to some extent. Rather than attempting to address this by finding the perfect C2 [Command & Control] structure, CAS ideas promote the use of individual initiative through informal networks as part of our C2 culture and not just as a tolerated "work-around".

Weijnen, Herder & Bouwmans (2008) in their work with the accurate title "Designing Complex Systems, A Contradiction in Terms" confirm that a classic C2 is not anymore accepted since no agent is superior to any other, therefore a very good communication system is necessary. Furthermore the authors state that besides the C2, the management by 'expertise of management' based on a content-based is also unlikely to succeed; rather decisions will be based on a negotiated knowledge, which can deteriorate to "negotiated nonsense". (See also Janssen & Kuk, 2006).

E-Procurement is about the acquisition of goods and services which will be allocated/used in business processes and projects, which are designed to achieve the goals (effectiveness) with the most optimal use of resources (efficiency) based on the mental models of the organization and environment.

Nowadays procurement managers have to be very creative to get the most out of these dynamic markets. Rigidly structured procedures (ISO or other norms based systems) are counterproductive. As clearly shown above, classic C2 is not anymore recommended. Holistic or systemic approaches for investing (procuring) are more appropriate to handle these situations. Rabaey (2012, 2012a) describes the Strategic Interdisciplinary Investment Forum (S2IF) in which the decisions can be taken. Related to this context, we have discussed the Intelligence Base framework of intelligence creation and dissemination where experts (knowledge workers) are giving guidance to the investments (see also the part on "Game theoretical approach").

Cynefin Framework

For the IT-architects, it is a quiet a challenge to integrate this agility requirements into the e-Procurement system. However not all systems are CAS and components of CAS are not always complex. In their article in the Harvard Business Review Snowden and Boone (2007) state that wise executives should tailor their approach for decision making to fit the complexity of the

Figure 8. Cynefin framework

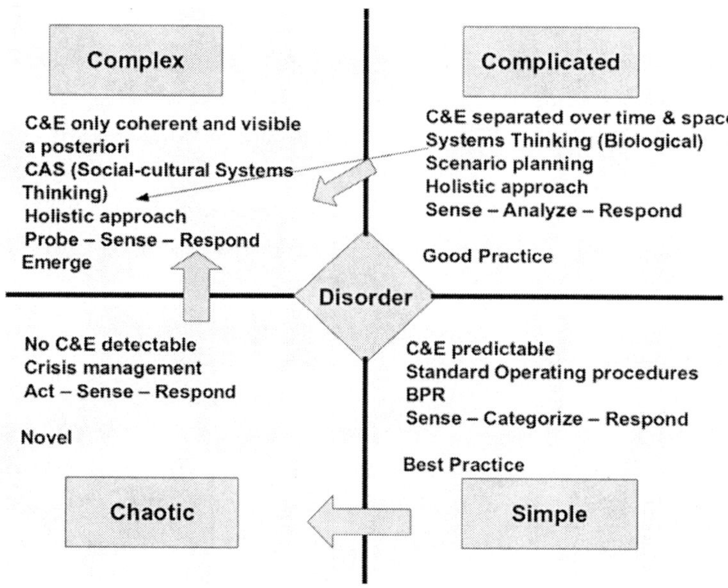

circumstances they face, which are (Figure 8: Cynefin Framework):

"Simple context": Here fits the classical C2 where clear cause-and-effect can be detected. The leader should sense the problems, categorize them and then response with the best practices. It is the domain of the known knowns, however there is a danger to oversimplify the situation. Leaders often become complacent and too often react too late which can be catastrophic. That's why in the Cynefin framework, an arrow is drawn from simple systems to chaotic systems.

"Complicated context": Here also the context is ordered and cause-and-effects exist, only not everybody can see these relationships and therefore experts are needed to detect them. The leaders should sense, analyze and respond. But in this domain of known unknowns, the experts can be overconfident in their own solutions. The so-called "maverick" solutions of non-experts are mostly rejected.

The first two contexts are ordered and based on the philosophy of "cause-and-effect". Mauboussin (2011, p. 90) states that this prevents leaders and managers from dealing effectively with complexity. "The biggest issue, in my mind, is that humans are incredibly good at linking cause and effect—sometimes too good. Ten thousand years ago most cause and effect was pretty clear. And our brains evolved to deal with that. But it means that when you see something occur in a complex adaptive system, your mind is going to create a narrative to explain what happened—even though cause and effect are not comprehensible in that kind of system. Hindsight's a beautiful thing. Also, we have a tendency to think that certain causes will lead to particular effects. .... And we just don't know. I think that's the biggest single bias."

The two following contexts are unordered and don't have this bias. "Complex context" has unknown unknowns (one is not aware of the facts) and it is the domain to which much of contemporary business has shifted. There are no right answers and leaders should probe, sense and respond, meaning that the organization should look at emergent patterns. Snowden et al. (2007, p. 74) warn "If [the managers] try to overcontrol the organization, they will pre-empt the opportunity for informative patterns to emerge. Leaders who try to impose order in a complex context will fail, but those who set the stage, step back a bit, allow patterns to emerge, and determine which ones are desirable will succeed."

"Chaotic context" is the realm of unknowables. A bit counterintuitive, in this case the leader has to act first to create order, so that he can sense where stability is or not to make it possible to transform the situation from chaos to complexity; thus act, sense and respond. So in this case a leader has not much time to think and act quickly. In this context George S. Patton can be quoted "A good plan violently executed now is better than a perfect plan next week'.

Governments and enterprises should look up these contexts because they give the best opportunities. Eisenhardt and Sull write about this phenomenon in their HBR-article "Strategy as Simple Rules" (2001, P. 108): 'The secret of companies like Yahoo! is strategy as simple rules. Managers of such companies know that the greatest opportunities for competitive advantage lie in market confusion, so they jump into chaotic markets, probe for opportunities, build on successful forays, and shift flexibly among opportunities as circumstances dictate. But they recognize the need for a few key strategic processes and a few simple rules to guide them through the chaos." This does certainly not imply that no strategy at all is needed. "Each company follows a disciplined strategy - otherwise, it would be paralyzed by chaos. And, as with all effective strategies, the strategy is unique to the company. But a simple-rules strategy and its underlying logic of pursuing opportunities are harder to see than traditional approaches." (Eisenhardt et al., 2001, p.109)

The fifth context is "disorder" The authors recommend to break down the situation into constituent parts and assign each to one of the other realms. In this way leaders can make decisions and intervene in contextually appropriate ways.

We will now discuss Cloud Computing in general before we will link e-Procurement to CAS and Cloud Computing in particular.

CLOUD COMPUTING

National Institute of Standards and Technology (NIST)

Some terms in the domain of cloud computing need to be defined. We will give an overview of the definitions and characteristics of cloud computing by the National Institute of Standards and Technology (NIST) by Mell & Grance (2011):

In essence, "Cloud computing is a model for enabling ubiquitous, convenient, on-demand network access to a shared pool of configurable computing resources (e.g., networks, servers, storage, applications, and services) that can be rapidly provisioned and released with minimal management effort or service provider interaction. This cloud model is composed of five essential characteristics, three service models, and four deployment models."

The Characteristics of Cloud Computing

Regarding "Broad network access," the network is the computer. On the one hand the governmental bodies need quick and reliable access to the applications and/or data in the Cloud, and on the other hand the citizens should be able to use all communication devices. The network is an issue in cloud computing, and therefore the government should not only look at the internal communication but also approach it from the perspective of the citizen.

A cloud infrastructure is the collection of both hardware and software that enables the five characteristics in Table 1 of Cloud Computing. Therefore a cloud infrastructure contains both a physical layer and an abstraction layer. The physical layer consists of the hardware resources that are necessary to support the cloud services being provided. It typically includes server, storage and network components. The abstraction layer consists of the software deployed across

Table 1. Characteristics of cloud computing

Characteristics	Description
On-demand self-service	"A consumer can unilaterally provision computing capabilities, such as server time and network storage, as needed automatically without requiring human interaction with each service's provider."
Broad network access	"Capabilities are available over the network and accessed through standard mechanisms that promote use by heterogeneous thin or thick client platforms (e.g., mobile phones, tablets, laptops, and workstations)."
Resource pooling	"The provider's computing resources are pooled to serve multiple consumers using a multi-tenant model, with different physical and virtual resources dynamically assigned and reassigned according to consumer demand. There is a sense of location independence in that the customer generally has no control or knowledge over the exact location of the provided resources but may be able to specify location at a higher level of abstraction (e.g., country, state, or datacenter). Examples of resources include storage, processing, memory, and network bandwidth.)."
Rapid elasticity	"Capabilities can be elastically provisioned and released, in some cases automatically, to scale rapidly outward and inward commensurate with demand. To the consumer, the capabilities available for provisioning often appear to be unlimited and can be appropriated in any quantity at any time."
Measured Service	"Cloud systems automatically control and optimize resource use by leveraging a metering capability at some level of abstraction appropriate to the type of service (e.g., storage, processing, bandwidth, and active user accounts). Resource usage can be monitored, controlled, and reported, providing transparency for both the provider and consumer of the utilized service."

the physical layer, which manifests the essential cloud characteristics.

Service Models of Cloud Computing

In Table 2, four different service models of cloud computing are described.

BPaaS in E-Government

BPaaS is pre-assembled business processes which are provided via cloud application platforms to the consumers (Marks et al., 2010). BPaaS can be based on the concept of Business Process Embedded Information System (BPEIS), an additional stage in Enterprise Architecture (EA) (Rabaey et al., 2007; Rabaey, 2012). The principle is that organizations can use a standardized business process (BP) that contains a standardized, automated information system.

A government consists of different departments and agencies. Some of them are the core business of the government; others support the core business, for example Information and Communication Technology (ICT), human resources, budgeting, which are led by resource managers. Every governmental body organizes their core business processes and the support or resources processes (RP). These RP are particular (so therefore different) implementations of higher directives and procedures. So in every governmental unit, we find experts of the different resource domains. If a change of directives has to be implemented, all those experts of every unit need to adapt processes and/or data in the local RP, which may prove problematic, demanding a lot of efforts for each individual unit.

In the context of connected government and Cloud Computing, the concept of BPEIS can be implemented by the respective competent resources-managers through BPaaS. The RP are nothing more than BPaaS and one change of directives are directly implemented in every unit. A governmental unit can have temporary needs of capabilities to launch campaigns, surveys or tasks. An example of task or responsibility in the

Table 2. Service models of cloud computing

Service Model	Description
Cloud Software as a Service (SaaS).	"The capability provided to the consumer is to use the provider's applications running on a cloud infrastructure. The applications are accessible from various client devices through either a thin client interface, such as a web browser (e.g., web-based email), or a program interface. The consumer does not manage or control the underlying cloud infrastructure including network, servers, operating systems, storage, or even individual application capabilities, with the possible exception of limited user-specific application configuration settings."
Cloud Platform as a Service (PaaS)	"The capability provided to the consumer is to deploy onto the cloud infrastructure consumer-created or acquired applications created using programming languages, libraries, services, and tools supported by the provider. The consumer does not manage or control the underlying cloud infrastructure including network, servers, operating systems, or storage, but has control over the deployed applications and possibly configuration settings for the application-hosting environment"
Cloud Infrastructure as a Service (IaaS)	"The capability provided to the consumer is to provision processing, storage, networks, and other fundamental computing resources where the consumer is able to deploy and run arbitrary software, which can include operating systems and applications. The consumer does not manage or control the underlying cloud infrastructure but has control over operating systems, storage, and deployed applications; and possibly limited control of select networking components (e.g., host firewalls).."
Cloud Business Process as a Service (BPaaS)	Business Process as a Service is not a standard Cloud Computing Service (see below).

European Union is the half-yearly presidency of the EU by a member-state. Most of the processes are the same, but need to be, for the duration of the presidency, integrated with the administration of the member state (Rabaey, 2012). However as mentioned above, the management must assess in which context of the Cynefin framework they want to operate with these projects.

The Deployment Models of Cloud Computing

In the situation of e-Procurement we have a combination of "Community Cloud" and therefore in "Hybrid Cloud". It is the government that will decide if it will use only the cloud for the internal communication and processing, or integrate the suppliers in the Cloud (Table 3).

CAS and Cloud Computing

Capital markets are CAS (Mauboussin, 2011). James Urquhart (2010) justly links the "flash crash" as an example of behavior of a CAS and links this to Cloud Computing. On May 6, 2010 several financial indexes experienced a sudden and precipitous drop, losing around 8 percent of their value at the beginning of the day in a matter of minutes. While there has been no definitive cause identified for the day's events, many financial market experts have identified the increasing presence of automated trading and electronic exchanges as a key cause of this "flash crash".

He continues: "High-frequency trading is performed by automated systems that attempt to beat out competition to the best matches of buyers and sellers for particular stocks. These systems are deployed in the same data centers as the exchange systems themselves, and the success of a system is often dependent on shaving milliseconds off of network and computing latencies.

What is critical to note, however, is that the number of high-frequency trading algorithms operating independently against the same market environment creates a sort of complex adaptive system, in which many interdependent agents adhering to known rules create a system which exhibits unpredictable or unexpected behaviors as a whole. In fact, financial markets are often heralded as one of the best examples of complex adaptive behavior. One of the key traits that science has determined about these systems is that sometimes little causes can trigger giant effects."

Table 3. Deployment models of cloud computing

Deployment model	Description
Private cloud	"The cloud infrastructure is provisioned for exclusive use by a single organization comprising multiple consumers (e.g., business units). It may be owned, managed, and operated by the organization, a third party, or some combination of them, and it may exist on or off premises."
Community cloud	"The cloud infrastructure is provisioned for exclusive use by a specific community of consumers from organizations that have shared concerns (e.g., mission, security requirements, policy, and compliance considerations). It may be owned, managed, and operated by one or more of the organizations in the community, a third party, or some combination of them, and it may exist on or off premises." This is the model that Rabaey (2012) is using for connecting governmental units.
Public cloud	"The cloud infrastructure is provisioned for open use by the general public. It may be owned, managed, and operated by a business, academic, or government organization, or some combination of them. It exists on the premises of the cloud provider."
Hybrid cloud	"The cloud infrastructure is a composition of two or more distinct cloud infrastructures (private, community, or public) that remain unique entities, but are bound together by standardized or proprietary technology that enables data and application portability (e.g., cloud bursting for load balancing between clouds)."

Although Urquhart foresees that Cloud Computing could become a CAS, it is already a reality in some cases, particularly in combination with Service Oriented Architecture (SOA) and its web services. Some web services and even whole collections of them in Services (be it through Cloud Computing or other channels) are providing the same and/or customized services to different organizations on the same and different markets. The cascading of web services and SaaS/BPaaS is creating a CAS with interacting organizations (market or business agents) and consumers. But most of all, the necessary feedback loops and thus the iterations make that the whole system becomes a CAS or a network of CAS (forming another CAS) with emergent properties that can not be solely explained by analyzing the different parts (the whole is more than the sum of the parts).

If a government wants to avoid this complexity then it will position e-Procurement as a simple system (see Figure 8: Cynefin Framework). This can cause oversimplification and the government may run the risk to enter into a chaotic context due to the fact that it was not agile enough to respond or to anticipate threats or to catch opportunities (see also Procurement in Competition (Now-or-Never)).

E-Procurement and Cloud Computing

Wikipedia E-Procurement (n.d.) states that e-Procurement is evolving from older technologies (like Electronic Data Interchange (EDI) and Enterprise Resource Planning (ERP)) to new technologies like SaaS (thus Cloud Computing). However it lists up to seven types of e-Procurement, mainly based on ERP:

- **Web-Based ERP:** Creating and approving purchasing requisitions, placing purchase orders and receiving goods and services by using a software system based on Internet technology.
- **E-MRO (Maintenance, Repair and Operations):** The same as web-based ERP except that the goods and services ordered are non-product related MRO supplies.
- **E-Sourcing:** Identifying new suppliers for a specific category of purchasing requirements using Internet technology.
- **E-Tendering:** Sending requests for information and prices to suppliers and receiving the responses of suppliers using Internet technology. May or may not involve e-auctions or eRFx functionality (Request for Information, Request for Proposal, Request for Quotation).
- **E-Reverse Auctioning:** Using Internet technology to buy goods and services from a number of known or unknown suppliers.
- **E-Informing:** Gathering and distributing purchasing information both from and to internal and external parties using Internet technology.
- **E-Market Sites:** Expands on Web-based ERP to open up value chains. Buying communities can access preferred suppliers' products and services, add to shopping carts, create requisition, seek approval, receipt purchase orders and process electronic invoices with integration to suppliers' supply chains and buyers' financial systems.

ERP-based e-Procurement systems are the so-called "best practices" solutions. However referring to the Cynefin framework, these systems correspond to the simple context (Figure 8) and are far from supporting agility (see above).

If a government wants to have a more agile e-Procurement system then it should consider Service Oriented Architecture and/or Cloud Computing. Figure 9: Government Cloud Computing shows the three different possibilities: legacy systems (like ERP), SOA based systems and Cloud Computing solutions.

Figure 9. Government cloud computing

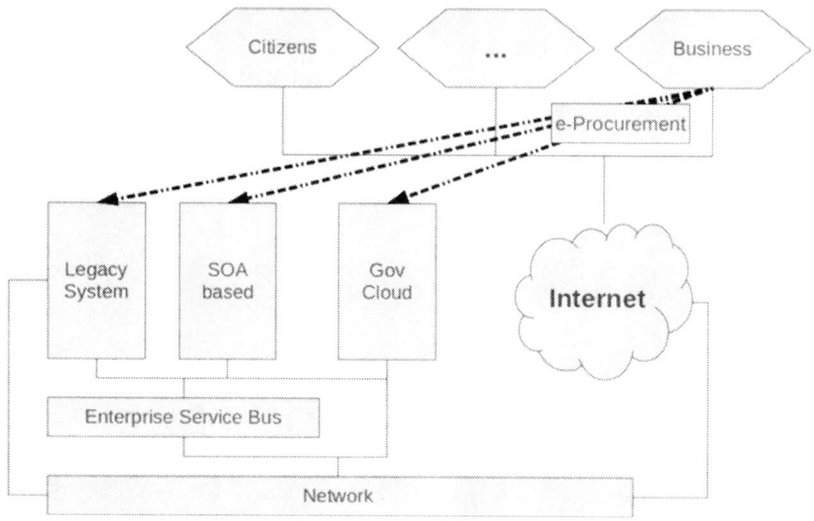

A very important component is the Enterprise Service Bus (ESB), which is a SOA-based technology. Nowadays ERP's have Application Program Interfaces (API) that are web services, thus the communication (by preference) goes through the ESB. Otherwise these API's can be wrapped in web services to enable the ERP to communicate anyway through web services.

These web services have the advantage that a legacy system can be gradually migrated (modules) to SOA- or Cloud Computing based solutions. For a more in depth discussion on this matter we refer to Rabaey (2012): "A Public Economics Approach to Enabling Enterprise Architecture with the Government Cloud in Belgium" in "Enterprise Architecture for Connected E-Government: Practices and Innovations" edited by Pallab Saha.

SaaS does not guarantee more agility. As we have seen in the discussion on CAS, the interrelationships are very important. A SaaS (for instance e-sourcing) should interact with other systems to exchange data or to receive a workflow object and after treating it, send it to another node in the workflow (business process). This is in some cases not possible or it is limited. A higher level system must coordinate (orchestrate) the different processes. It is this higher level system that can make the whole (CAS) agile or not. Due to its flexibility (which implies also complexity) SOA is the best candidate orchestrator.

If the technology of semantic web services were to be at a level that it could be generally used, then Semantic SOA will be even more agile, ad hoc workflows will be formed automatically in function of the strategy of the semantic (web) intelligent agents. At that point, intelligence (context interpreted information) and transaction speed will be very crucial. However, unless programming techniques evolve tremendously fast, large projects (as discussed above) will not be procured and managed completely by semantic web technologies. For more information on semantic SOA we suggest Rabaey, Vandenborre, Vandijck, Timmerman & Tromp (2007a): "Semantic web services and BPEL: semantic service oriented architecture - economical and philosophical issues" in "Semantic Web Technologies and eBusiness: Toward the Integrated Virtual Organization and Business Process Automation" edited by Salam and Stevens.

CONCLUSION

The definition of the architecture of a e-Procurement system is not only determined by the level of ambition of the government, but also by the degree of awareness that e-Procurement is a Complex Adaptive System (CAS), and that is part of bigger whole, another CAS namely e-Government.

A CAS cannot survive if it does not screen its environment. Rabaey et al. (2012) have proposed an intelligence system (called Intelligence Base) that takes into account on the one hand the mental models of the organization and its environment (Sterman, 2010) and on the other hand the dimensions and the perspectives of systems thinking (Gharajedaghi, 2011).

The whole is greater than the sum of the parts, because of the relationships between not only the parts, but also between the parts and the environment. In their interactions, a lot of feedback loops and iterations makes the whole a complex system. The flexibility of the structures and processes and the capability of quickly changing functions can only result in CAS if the whole and its parts dispose of a reliable and quick-responsive intelligence (base) system. This is confirmed by Weeds (2006), who states that urgent events force the organization to act immediately.

The game theory discussion showed that the flexibility and agility of the e-Procurement system (together with a good strategy) are key factors for a successful system; otherwise e-Procurement is more of weakness in the government's value chain of procurement of goods and services.

In the last part of the discussion on Cloud Computing and e-Procurement, we argued that ERP systems (so called best practices) are not well adapted to other contexts than the simple context. Even stand alone Cloud Computing applications (SaaS) are not guaranteeing to perform well in a CAS, unless it can be orchestrated with other software components in a SOA context.

The system requirements of interrelationships, interconnectivity and interoperability force the e-Procurement architects to take the CAS and its environment into account. Otherwise the government will create an inefficient and ineffective e-Procurement system with no added value for the government and its (actual and potential) suppliers.

So as for must business, the tools may be important, but the strategy to use these tools is much more important.

ACKNOWLEDGMENT

Marc J.A. Rabaey was IT-director in the Medical Service and CIO of the Assistant Chief of Staff Evaluation of the Belgian Ministry of Defense. He is currently System Thinking consultant in Business and Information Technology. This research was supported by the Faculty of Applied Economics, University of Hasselt, where Marc Rabaey has an on-going PhD. The subject is investment in Cloud Computing (Information Technology)

REFERENCES

Ariely, D. (2009). *Predictably irrational*. London, UK: Harper Collins Publishers.

Bernard, H. (1976). *Totale Oorlog en Revolutionaire Oorlog* (*Vol. I*). Brussels, Belgium: Royal Military Academy.

Berryman, J. M. (2007). Judgments during information seeking: A naturalistic approach to understanding of enough information. *Journal of Information Science*, *20*(10), 1–11.

Bowser, M., Cantle, N., & Allan, N. (2011). *Unraveling the complexity of risk.* Presented at Open Forum of The Actuarial Profession (January 21, 2011). London.

Brooks, B. (2007). The pulley model: A descriptive model of risky decision-making. *Safety Science Monitor*, *11*(1), 1–14.

Burke, L. A., & Miller, M. K. (1999). Taking the mystery out of intuitive decision making. *The Academy of Management Executive*, *13*(4), 91–99. doi:10.5465/AME.1999.2570557

Business Dictionary. (2012). *Definition of e-procurement.* Retrieved April 22, 2012, from http://www.businessdictionary.com/definition/electronic-procurement-e-procurement.html

Eisenhardt, K.M., & Sull, D. (2001). Strategy as simple rules. *Harvard Business Review*, (1): 106–116.

Funston, F., & Wagner, S. (2010). *Surviving and thriving in uncertainty: Creating the risk intelligent enterprise*. Hoboken, NJ: John Wiley & Sons.

Gharajedaghi, J. (2011). *Systems thinking: Managing chaos and complexity – A platform for designing business architecture*. Amsterdam, The Netherlands: Morgan Kaufmann.

Gore, J. (1996). *Chaos, complexity, and the military*. National Defense University.

Guida, G., & Tasso, C. (1994). *Design and development of knowledge-based systems: From life cycle to development methodology*. Chichester, UK: John Wiley & Sons.

Hovhannisian, K. (2001). *Exploring on the technology landscapes: Real options thinking in the context of the complexity theory.* Paper presented at the DRUID Winter Conference (January 17-19, 2002), Aalborg, Denmark.

Janssen, M., & Kuk, G. (2006). *A complex adaptive system perspective of enterprise architecture in electronic government*. Paper presented at the 39th Hawaii International Conference on System Sciences, Hawaii

Libet, B. (2011). Do we have free will? In Sinnott-Armstrong, W., & Nadel, L. (Eds.), *Conscious will and responsibility* (pp. 1–10). Oxford, UK: Oxford Press.

Lowe, D., & Ng, S. (2006). *The implications of complex adaptive systems thinking for future command and control.* Paper presented at 11th International Command and Control Research and Technology Symposium (September, 2006). Cambridge, UK.

Mauboussin, M. (2011). Embracing complexity. *Harvard Business Review*, (September): 89–92.

Mell, P., & Grance, T. (2011). *The NIST definition of cloud computing*. Gaithersburg, MD: National Institute of Standards and Technology.

Montier, J. (2010). *The little book of behavioral investing*. Hoboken, NJ: John Wiley & Sons.

Pucket, S., & Purdy, S. C. (2011). Are voluntary movements initiated preconsciously? The relationships between readiness potentials, urges, and decisions. In Sinnott-Armstrong, W., & Nadel, L. (Eds.), *Conscious will and responsibility* (pp. 1–10). Oxford, UK: Oxford Press. doi:10.1093/acprof:oso/9780195381641.003.0005

Rabaey, M. (2011, May 10-12). *Game theoretic real option approach of the procurement of department of defense: Competition or collaboration.* Paper presented at the 8th Annual Acquisition Research Symposium. Montery CA, USA.

Rabaey, M. (2012). A public economics approach to enabling enterprise architecture with the government cloud in Belgium. In Saha, P. (Ed.), *Enterprise architecture for connected e-government: Practices and innovations*. Hershey, PA: IGI Global.

Rabaey, M. (2012a). Holistic investment framework for cloud computing: A management-philosophical approach based on complex adaptive systems. In Bento, A., & Aggarwal, A. (Eds.), *Cloud computing service and deployment models: Layers and management*. Hershey, PA: IGI Global.

Rabaey, M., & Mercken, R. (2012). Framework of knowledge and intelligence base: From intelligence to service. In Ordoñez de Pablos, P., & Lytras, M. D. (Eds.), *Knowledge management and drivers of innovation in services industries*. Hershey, PA: IGI Global. doi:10.4018/978-1-4666-0948-8.ch017

Rabaey, M., Tromp, H., & Vandenborre, K. (2007). Holistic approach to align ICT capabilities with business integration. In Cunha, M., Cortes, B., & Putnik, G. (Eds.), *Adaptive technologies and business integration: Social, managerial, and organizational dimensions* (pp. 160–173). Hershey, PA: Idea Group Publishing.

Rabaey, M., Vandenborre, K., Vandijck, E., Timmerman, M., & Tromp, H. (2007a). Semantic web services and BPEL: Semantic service oriented architecture - Economical and philosophical issues. In Salam, A., & Stevens, J. (Eds.), *Semantic Web technologies and ebusiness: Toward the integrated virtual organization and business process automation* (pp. 127–153). Hershey, PA: Idea Group Publishing. doi:10.4018/978-1-59904-192-6.ch005

Saha, P. (2010). *As platform for connected government (Phase 1 Report)*.

Shattuck, L. G., & Miller, N. L. (2006). Naturalistic decision making in complex systems: A dynamic model of situated cognition combining technological and human agents. *Organizational Behavior: Special Issue on Naturalistic Decision Making in Organizations*, *27*(7), 989–1009.

Snowden, D., & Boone, M. (2007). A leader's framework for decision making: Wise executives tailor their approach to fit the complexity of the circumstances they face. *Harvard Business Review*, (November): 68–76.

Sterman, J. D. (2010). *Business dynamics – Systems thinking and modelling for a complex world*. India: Tata McGraw-Hill.

UNU-IIST-SP. (2008). *15th UNeGov.net school on foundations of electronic governance*. Retrieved April 11, 2011, from http://www.egov.iist.unu.edu/

Urquhart, J. (2010). *What cloud computing can learn from 'flash crash'*. Retrieved April 20, 2012, from http://news.cnet.com/8301-19413_3-20004757-240.html

Weeds, H. (2006). *Applying option games: When should real options valuation be used?* Colchester, UK: University of Essex. Retrieved from http://privatewww.essex.ac.uk/~hfweeds/

Weijnen, M. P. C., Herder, P. M., & Bouwmans, I. (2008). Designing complex systems: A contradiction in terms. In M. Eekhout, R. Visser, & T. Tomiyama (Eds.), *Delft science in design: A Congress on interdisciplinary design*, (pp. 235-254). Delft, The Netherlands: IOS Press.

Wikipedia. (n.d.). *E-procurement*. Retrieved April 20, 2012, from http://en.wikipedia.org/wiki/E-procurement

Wikipedia. (n.d.). *Public eProcurement*. Retrieved April 20, 2012, from http://en.wikipedia.org/wiki/Public_eProcurement

Chapter 14
Electronic Procurement (E-Procurement) Implementation in Municipalities:
Lessons Learned

Rugayah Hashim
Research Management Institute, Universiti Teknologi MARA, Malaysia

Mohd Anuar Mazuki
Universiti Teknologi MARA, Malaysia

ABSTRACT

Local authorities or municipalities have different organizational structure and goals and as such implementing a customized information systems project requires a separate evaluation that would fit their needs. In the case of an electronic procurement (e-procurement) system, the implementation of this project at the central government level is not without challenges. Similarly, at the local government level, issues prevailed. Thus, this chapter highlights the issues encountered by twelve local authorities in the state of Selangor, Malaysia. The issues are broken down into four themes, namely, political, economic, social, and technological. It is important to note that local authorities fall within the jurisdiction of the state government; thus, more issues are abound particularly with regards to political interference. Nonetheless, the ultimate goal of having an online public procurement system is a win-win situation for both the local authority concerned and the vendors or suppliers. Hence, identifying the issues and learning from them will limit project failures or extended scheduling. Inherently, the implications of lessons learned from others who have implemented an online public procurement system will provide valuable guidelines for other lagging municipalities, yet at the same time, the late implementers will benefit more as they are able to avoid the pitfalls made by their counterparts that embarked earlier. In fact, the late-comers tend to achieve better success rate and report a significant return of investment.

DOI: 10.4018/978-1-4666-2119-0.ch014

INTRODUCTION

As with most developing countries, Malaysia is witnessing a shift from an industrial-based economy to an information-based economy in which information is intrinsic to organizational functioning. Driven by the need to acquire, manipulate and distribute information, the last decade have seen a massive growth in Information and Communication Technology (ICT) investments by both public and private institutions (Karim, 1999, 2003; Karim & Khalid, 2003). Often described as a characteristic of the information revolution, this increasing rate of investment in technology has also been fueled by both the decreasing costs and increasing capabilities of technological hardware and software (Seneviratne & Garson, 1999). Given all of these events, there is little doubt that the Malaysian society has become increasingly dependent on ICT (Badawi, 2004).

Furthermore, in recent years, the vital development of the Internet offers increasing opportunity for electronic commerce (Mortensen & Arlbjorn, 2012). E-commerce has attracted much attention from businesses, not only to get connection with others and make a profit from their product/service, but also to reduce the costs of internal and external operational procedures including purchasing or procurement (Nelson & Svara, 2012). Procurement is a very critical task because it is a matter not only for making a profit, but also for staying in business in a highly competitive environment (Quesada et al, 2010). In the government sector, procurement is sometimes the source of corruption, scandal and abuse of public resources. Besides inadequately qualified personnel, "transparency" of the procurement environment becomes another source of problems in the procurement procedure (Liao et al, 2003).

The Malaysian scene for e-procurement (EP) is very slow to pick up even though e-procurement is one of the flagships of the Multimedia Super Corridor (MSC) (Hashim, 2006). Since Selangor is the leading state in Malaysia and in view of its economic development, it should play a major role in making Malaysia's Vision 2020 a reality. Also, due to Selangor's economic success, as well as its strategic location in the center of West Malaysia, Selangor has become the regional hub for all things cyber. Of the 14 states in Malaysia, Selangor is the only state that has achieved the status of a developed state as of August 29, 2005 through their Vision 2005.

BACKGROUND: PROCUREMENT AND E-PROCUREMENT

ICT procurement processes exist, formally or informally, in every organization that acquires information and communication technologies. Procurement involves all aspects of ICT acquisition such as competitive bidding, purchasing equipment and services, and evaluation of implemented systems (Mukhopadhyay, 2011; Neef, 2001)

Part of the complication of ICT procurement in particular is that the acquisition of ICTs is not just about the purchase and use of hardware and software, it is also inherently tied to the acquisition of a variety of services, support personnel, intellectual properties, and any items that have either a direct or indirect effect on information and communication technologies (Ren et al, 2012). The ICT procurement process is interdisciplinary and in most circumstances, involves everyone in an organization – IT staff, purchasing, legal, and financial employees, not to mention a number of end users from all departments across the organization and its planning and implementation procedures. This multi-dimensional aspect makes ICT procurement especially complex in relation to an organization's traditional purchasing practices. This complexity, in conjunction with the huge number of available products and services, and the speed with which new products are introduced to the market, makes the area of ICT procurement an extremely intricate and volatile process area.

Literature surrounding this domain is relatively scarce aside from the many prescriptions and guidelines for actually carrying out the procurement process. Much of what is available speaks primarily on major trends like cost-benefit analysis of ICT and specific procurement practices in a particular, individual organization. Essentially, the procurement of information and communication technology (ICT) consists of budgeting for ICTs and the ultimate acquisition of ICTs. The early literature in this area in essence discussed procurement as a set of alternatives for ICT acquisition, the first of which is internal information and communication technology appropriation (Neef, 2001). At its most fundamental level, this means that each individual municipality must take care of all the budgeting, cost-benefit analysis, ICT selection, purchasing and implementation on its own. The second alternative, known as external, is the contracting out of all, or a significant portion of all ICT equipment and services for a given municipality (Neef, 2001).

Most of this early discussion was based on the need for an organization to achieve economies of scale with regard to their ICT processes. To have an internal procurement process meant that the organization could provide ICT services for it and still achieve a great cost-benefit ratio than contracting out would allow. In the 1960s and 1970s in the United States, only the larger local governments could afford the luxury of internal procurement. For smaller municipalities the economies of scale were much smaller and they had to contract out to external agencies that could provide ICT services for them at a substantially lower cost than they could achieve by doing it themselves (Seneviratne & Garson, 1999).

Much of this situation changed in the early 1980s with the arrival of the technology scene in the form of the microcomputer or PC (Personal Computer), which created an environment where most ICT processes could be provided internally by the local government. Even with this technological boost there still remained a contracting out factor. The hardware had become much more cost effective for a locality to own but in many cases some of the operations (like network management) continued to exist beyond the fiscal grasp and expertise level of the organization. Currently, contracting out still occurs for the provision of certain ICT services.

More recent literature with regard to ICT procurement discusses the process of acquiring ICT equipment and services but it refers mostly to the state and federal levels of government. This discussion provides an overview of the bidding and contracting process, which is often defined in statutes and regulations. According to Gansler et al, (2003), this aspect of the procurement process creates special problems for the management of ICTs.

Most of the procurement regulations require the acceptance of minimum bids for equipment and services, which meet proposal guidelines. The procedures are often quite slow and stretch out over a number of planning cycles. In this environment, it is difficult to handle system and software upgrades, which are an integral part of today's information technologies (Gansler et al, 2003). As in the earliest stages of information and communication technology (ICT) procurement, the area of cost-benefit analysis remains a prominent concern. Many of the problems with ICT implementation that local governments face today are drawn from the history of a strict cost-benefit approach to the development of information systems. Over time, the level of concern and frustration that managers have developed with regard to ICT acquisitions have grown substantially. Their main consideration has become a question of how ICT can best be made to work efficiently and economically, and deliver the expected benefits. This view often comes from unrealistic expectations of technology, ignorance of the systems, and excessive expense. Unfortunately, these issues have taken focus away from other important issues, which come into play (Ward, 1995).

Local governments must look on the acquisition of information and communication technologies as an investment decision, which necessarily requires careful evaluation of the risks as well as the benefits. As Gansler et al (2003) pointed out, ICT acquisitions entail future costs, which go far beyond initial procurement decisions. There must necessarily be a substantial commitment to future upgrades, operating expenses, software and personnel. Typical cost-benefit analysis of an ICT investment does not fully realize the implications of the ICT procurement process. ICT investments cannot be calculated the same as other capital investments, that is, by using internal rates of return or net present values to determine whether to invest in specific systems or not. According to Ward (1995), this method only works when the costs and benefits can be accurately predicted over the life cycle of the system and since the actual life cycle is extremely hard to determine, it is very difficult to evaluate ICTs on a financial basis alone.

In order to effectively evaluate (in an appropriate manner) ICT investments, it is necessary to secure a more holistic view of the process – taking into consideration infrastructure investments, personnel investments and, incremental capacities (Ward, 1995). Part of the problem with quantifying the benefits of ICT lies in the inability to convert the many "intangibles" of information (and communication) technologies into financial figures. In effect it is really not possible to quantify all of the benefits of ICT nor does it make sense to try and force these types of quantitative measures on those that are not quantifiable. Dasgupta (2012) mentioned the analysis technique specifically for ICT, which takes into account possible IT applications and then justifies five basic techniques for evaluation. They maintained the traditional cost-benefit analysis and added to it the following techniques:

- Value linking (improvement and performance)
- Value acceleration (improvements in time use)
- Value restructuring (productivity through organizational change)
- Innovation evaluation (the value of new processes and practices).

This approach is one of the more creative of the limited offerings in the literature on this area and provides a better way of interpreting the long-term values of ICT for an organization. Thus, to determine the tangible benefits of ICT, they must be broken down into distinct divisions, which represent the types of technology categories. Dasgupta (2012) suggested three main ways in which ICT systems benefits accrue:

- **Substitutive**: Replacing people power with machine power. This approach is generally driven by economic factors with the ultimate goal of improving efficiency.
- **Complementary**: Improving productivity and personnel effectiveness by providing new ways to perform tasks through ICT.
- **Innovative**: Increasing a competitive edge by creating new applications for ICT. In this particular model, the authors provided a way of looking at ICT acquisitions, that provides for a view which is neither purely based on efficiency, nor solely on innovation. Instead, they provide a framework where integration between cost-benefit analysis and innovative evaluation is possible depending on organization needs and directives.

On the whole, this particular area has proven itself very resistant to change. Guidelines for ICT procurement are still floundering in a traditional approach to budgeting and acquisitions. The publication from the Federal Government of the United States of America actually addressed the procurement process is the 1995 guide to IT investments published by the OMB (1984) for the Office of Information and Regulatory Affairs. This guide lays out a step-by-step acquisition process, which is based on a standardized evaluation of risks, benefits, and costs. Their proposed process begins with a prioritization of all funding requests in an organization in an attempt to maximize the value of scarce public resources. This part of the process requires the balancing of any potential benefits against the costs and risks, while at the same time aligning the organizations' strategic and tactical goals with any proposed ICT investment. A critical factor to this particular guide's approach is the eventual clear evidence of the positive net benefits that the public has garnered for their tax dollars invested (Smart, 2009).

Inherent problems with this process are obvious and intrinsic in ICT procurement efforts (Neef, 2001). As stated by the GAO (1988 and 1997) report, Information Management and Technology Issues, the IT acquisition and management process is reasonable from an ideal view of how the process should function, that is, the delivery of ICT systems that operate as intended, within specific time parameters, and in a measurable and cost-effective manner (Neef, 2001). For overall government efficiency, it is desirable that the procurement process achieves economy through the standardization and sharing of systems across agencies (Erridge & Greer, 2000). Unfortunately, in practice, the process continually fails to meet these ideal objectives – primarily because the realities of ICT systems procurement and implementation are not taken into account (Mortensen and Arlbjorn, 2012). As others have pointed out, the ICT acquisition process is risk-averse and demands a high degree of certainty. Both demands are the exact opposite of the reality of ICT procurement, which is again, uncertain and very risky (Mortensen and Arlbjorn, 2012; Dasgupta, 2012). The typical acquisition process, as illuminated by the United States' federal government's guide to technology investment, calls for the formulation of precise long-term plans and budgets which essentially assume that all systems requirements can be identified and forecasted at the outset (GAO, 1988). Process models like this assume that ICT hardware and software development are predictable and that there is a high degree of accuracy in long-term budgeting for ICTs (Ward, 1995; Gansler et al, 2003). Typical acquisition processes do not work well within the complex and long-term life cycles of ICT systems. The very nature of information technologies makes traditional acquisition processes ineffective and problematic. Information and communication technologies (ICTs) change rapidly and defy predictions as to costs, development time, and ultimate performance measures.

For authors such as Bruch and Bellgran (2012), and Angeles and Nath (2007), one of the most crucial aspects in the ICT procurement and acquisition is the alternative analysis and feasibility. This part of the process takes on the job of deciding whether or not a future ICT acquisition is headed in the right direction and feasible in relation to the organizations' goals and directives. For Bruch and Bellgran (2012), this requires a full review of the financial situation, system possibilities, existing system needs, and specific guidelines for use.

Gansler et al (2003) argued that all information and communication planning and implementation must be subjected to a series of feasibility and trade-offs tests that examine each according to technical, operational and economic factors. A number of important issues arise in an examination of technical feasibility. Is the planned for IT a reliable use of technology? Is it compatible with existing systems? Does it require specialized training or rely on unfamiliar techniques, hardware and software? In the end, IT solutions must be compatible and in line with users' skill levels and expertise. It should also be implementable using existing staff and not overly tax their capabilities and time. Ideally, information and communication technologies are supposed to enhance an organization's effectiveness, not detract from it. The reality of the situation is that if proposed acquisitions cannot meet certain technical requirements, it is more than likely that problems will occur on implementation (Bruch & Bellgran, 2012).

Furthermore, Lanzola and Suarez (2012) emphasized operational feasibility as the most critical and the most often overlooked aspect of the procurement process when dealing with the planning, acquisition, and implementation of ICTs. Operational feasibility speaks of the attempt to determine how well the predetermined technical alternatives will work within the context of the organization's day-to-day operations and environment. In an ideal situation, implemented ICTs will enhance the effectiveness of an organization – at the very least it should not detract from, or disrupt existing operations. In order to be feasible in this way, the technologies must be in line with organizational needs and directives. A main part of the difficulty in this area stems from the fact that in many instances, operational procedures must be changed to accommodate ITs and in a few cases the fundamental culture of the organization may require some modicum of change. Ideally, these sorts of changes should be addressed early on in the planning stages in order to lessen some of the more detrimental impacts (perceived or otherwise) of implementation. In essence, the operational feasibility of any specific information and communication technology affects both the social and work processes of an organization and as such must be treated as a fundamental factor in ICT implementation.

Finally, Angeles and Nath (2007) discussed economic feasibility and specifically places this aspect last to deal with a management predilection toward the pure cost-benefit analysis of ICT. In fact economic feasibility should be considered last or else the probability is high that technological direction could be determined for the wrong reason, that is, low cost (Davila et al, 2002).

Bruch and Bellgran (2012) recognized that funding decisions for ICT are usually dependent on the justification of increased revenue, reduced costs, or better services. In addition, it was cautioned that pure evaluation of costs to benefits does not necessarily provide a full picture of the economic feasibility of any given ICT (Bruch & Bellgran, 2012; Angeles & Nath, 2007). He proposes that they must be evaluated in terms of the whole work process and only on those ICT alternatives deemed technically and operationally feasible. He argues that this is the only way to make sure that the analysis is a true evaluation of all favorable alternatives. Potential benefits should not be masked by unanticipated costs associated with trying to make an unfeasible system work. For any ICT implementation to be successful, it must be funded and justified by enough benefits across the board to allow for full development and implementation. To achieve this, benefits must be projected for the full "useful" life cycle of the system. As discussed previously, this is quite difficult to do and requires the analysis of all three types of feasibility (Bruch and Bellgran, 2012).

One of the earliest recognized problems for ICT implementation in local government has been poor ICT acquisition and development procedures. Many local governments, and particularly those adopting integrated ICTs for the first time are unsure how to go about procuring systems that will meet their needs (Berman, 2012).

As has always been the case, there is a great deal of difference with regard to capability among the range of ICTs available for any given solution. Procuring a system which is too limited for the tasks a local government wants to utilize generally leads to immediate upgrade needs. This in turn creates a disruption of the whole process of implementation – particularly if a system must be upgraded prior to full systems implementation. The opposite situation can also have detrimental effects. If too much systems capacity is acquired there may be desire to "fill-in" the slack capacity so as not to appear underutilized in evaluation.

This may result in the establishment of processes that are not needed by the municipality, but that may eventually become entrenched. In the end it is very important that ICT procurement be tied to the development of specific but integrated systems over a particular period of time. This holds true for the federal government of the United States (GAO, 1997) which stated that difficulties doing business through FACNET (Federal Acquisition Computer Network) have overshadowed the benefits of using it, for example, lost, late and duplicate transactions and network interruptions have frustrated government and industry users and delayed procurements. The report went to state that the United State's federal government lacks a coherent strategy and implementation approach for efficiently and effectively carrying out the agencies' requirements for the acquisition function using various appropriate electronic commerce technologies and purchasing methods (GAO, 1997).

This implementation issue is further backed by their 1995 report, "Evaluating IT Investments: A Practical Guide" of the Office of Information and Regulatory Affairs – Information Policy and Technology Branch (United States) proposed a process model for IT investments which outlined the major aspects of the IT procurement process. Figure 1 shows a model of Information Technology Process used by the Office of Information and Regulatory Affairs of the United States federal government.

In this particular model, three specific processes exist:

- Select refers to the screening of all possible projects requiring IT/ICTs. It also requires an analysis of risks and cost-benefit ratios resulting in the prioritization of projects based on rate of return to risk. The ultimate objective is the determination of the right mix of projects for the organization.
- The second step in this IT/ICT procurement process refers to control of the selected projects. As IT/ICTs are acquired for any given project they must be evaluated against projected costs, implementation schedules and predefined performance

Figure 1. IT process model (Source: OIRA, 2004)

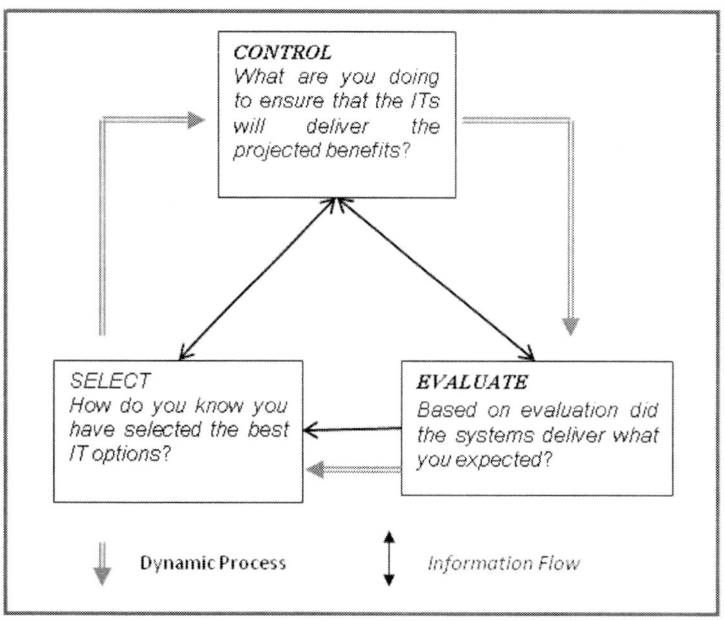

measures. As acquisition and implementation take place, action may be taken to correct any deficiencies with regard to the IT/ICTs and their relationship to the given project.

- Finally, the ICTs must be evaluated to determine whether or not they have met expectations and/or cost-benefit ratios. This step allows for adjustments to the systems and/or their usage in existing or future projects.

While this acquisition process model appears to be fairly standard, it does speak directly to the implementation of information technologies and it does allow for course correction within the process. Unfortunately, as with a multitude of other available models, it places most of its focus on cost-benefit analysis.

SIGNIFICANCE OF STUDY

In order to realize an electronically driven government, an in-depth understanding of the specific issues related to ICT implementation leading to e-procurement implementation, is essential for the establishment of appropriate principals and effective approaches with regard to the management of information and communication systems in an organization. In fact, in the implementation of e-government initiative subsequently leading to e-procurement initiative, many issues and challenges to both initiatives are inter-related such as those pertaining to information security, establishment of a comprehensive, widespread and affordable telecommunications infrastructure as well as adequate education and training which encompass not only government employees but the masses as well (Karim, 1999 & 2003; Karim & Khalid, 2003). Each individual issue is important in its own context as well as producing multiple impacts which affect the organization and implementation of ICTs within it. Subsequently, effective management of ICT and later, e-procurement across the board can only take place when a more comprehensive understanding of the myriad of issues is achieved (Ward, 1995).

In the area of information and communication technology, a good portion of the research conducted prior to this study tended to focus primarily on private sector systems and was based on what Ward (1995) termed "supply-side" issues, or those issues related to how ICT based systems can be made to work effectively, economically, and in the end deliver the expected benefits. In this case the issues were those which surround the cost to benefit ratios of specific ICTs and were usually earmarked for singular applications or projects. While these issues are certainly very important, they are not the be-all and end-all of ICT implementation leading towards e-procurement systems. This study will identify and address the issues that the local government or local councils' ICT officers or managers face when attempting to implement and later adopt e-procurement in their organizations.

The focus of this study is on the ICT planning and e-procurement implementation processes as a whole and not on one specific part, since it is only through a complete review of the spectrum of issues that greater success can be achieved in this relatively new and volatile environment, especially for the Selangor local government.

RESEARCH OBJECTIVES

The objectives of this research were to identify and examine the issues or problems which are specific to the Selangor local government with regard to e-procurement (EP) implementation in their municipality as well as to distinguish a comprehensive view of the overriding barriers and/or facilitators associated with the information and communication technology (ICT) planning, ICT implementation and e-procurement development, deployment and implementation processes in the

Table 1. The Selangor local authorities and district offices

	LOCAL COUNCILS (12)		LAND & DISTRICT OFFICES (9)
1.	Shah Alam City Council	1.	Petaling Land/District Office
2.	Petaling Jaya City Council	2.	Klang Land/District Office
3.	Subang Jaya Municipal Council	3.	Gombak Land/District Office
4.	Ampang Jaya Municipal Council	4.	Hulu Langat Land/District Office
5.	Klang Municipal Council	5.	Kuala Langat Land/District Office
6.	Kajang Municipal Council	6.	Kuala Selangor Land/District Office
7.	Selayang Municipal Council	7.	Sabak Bernam Land/District Office
8.	Sepang Municipal Council	8.	Sepang Land/District Office
9.	Kuala Langat District Council	9.	Hulu Selangor Land/District Office
10.	Hulu Selangor District Council		
11.	Kuala Selangor District Council		
12.	Sabak Bernam District Council		

Selangor local government. For this study, the concept of local government will actually consists of the twelve municipalities or local agencies and nine land/district offices (LDO) within the state of Selangor, Malaysia as shown in Table 1.

LITERATURE REVIEW

Information and communication technology (ICT) has been the catalyst for the new source of economic wealth during the current economic period called the Information or Digital Age. ICT has become the generally accepted umbrella term for a rapidly expanding range of equipment, applications, services and basic technologies that process information (Angeles & Nath, 2007). These elements of ICT fall into three principal categories: computers, telecommunications and multimedia data. Many industries and specific organizations have successfully implemented numerous ICTs and as a result, enjoy great competitive advantages, while others have not.

All electronic, web and internet applications require the use of information and communication technologies (ICTs). Therefore, when talking about e-government, one can not run away from ICT, hence, areas reviewed on ICT and e-government would prevail before focusing on e-procurement. Electronic procurement is one area where governments can reduce inefficiencies in their service provision. Every level of government is involved in purchasing or procuring. Most governments, especially in Malaysia, still use the traditional purchase order method which is a slow and antiquated process requiring multiple levels of bureaucracy for almost any purchasing decisions. These methods satisfy the goal of increased public accountability, but increase the cost of procurement. Definitely, this system has worked and will continue working for all levels of government but in a dragging manner. Thus, by incorporating technology, purchasing will be made easier, cheaper and more accountable through streamlined electronic procurement, that is, a digital or electronic paper trail is recorded at every level of the transaction (Liao et al, 2003; Davila et al, 2002; Berman, 2012). However, for government agencies, particularly the municipalities, have been slow to implement technology to improve the procurement process. At the rate that technology moves, if the Selangor local government does not jump on the bandwagon and adopt e-procurement fast, the chance that they will be left behind other local governments in Malaysia would be inevitable (Badawi, 2004).

Thus, this research will identify and examine the issues or problems which are specific to the Selangor local government with regard to e-procurement (EP) implementation in their municipality as well as to distinguish a comprehensive view of the overriding barriers and/or facilitators associated with the information and communication technology (ICT) planning and development, and e-procurement implementation processes in the Selangor local government. In relation to this, the findings will determine the readiness of e-procurement adoption at the local government level of Selangor.

INFORMATION AND COMMUNICATION TECHNOLOGY IN GOVERNMENT

The growth of computer networks and computer usage during the 1990s has been dramatic. A major factor in this expansion has the simultaneous globalization of markets and communication (Murray, 2008). Globalization has become the "in" concept used to describe trends and forces that are shaping the world which has led the transition from national economies to the global economy. The ICT changes of the 90s differ from the information technology (IT) developments of the 80s (Ward, 1995). In terms of computer sales and markets, spending moved from large mainframe systems to personal computers (PC) with office suite software and networking capabilities. A shift in organizational computer usage occurred from mainframe systems as data-processing tools to networked systems (using e-mail, shared databases and Intranets) as information providers.

The difference between information and communication technology (ICT) and information technology (IT) hinges on the quality and the extent of communication (Mukhopadhyay, 2011). IT involve automation of existing structures to process data and to monitor the systems involved in data-process production; whereas ICTs enhance and enable the exchange of information through electronic networks and information systems. Communication outlets and patterns are increased because the act of communicating is no longer constrained by a physical dependency on time or space. The compass or cost of long distance communication no longer hinders interaction within and between organizations. This virtual freedom, according to Davila et al (2002) has promoted greater access to information through greater access to information through enhanced information exchange.

ICT integration has reshaped organizational structures by increasing communication exchanges. The increase in access and exchange of information has a two-fold impact, effecting external relationships between organizations and internal relations between individuals and organizations. Externally, greater interaction between organizations has promoted integration, thus diminishing organizational boundaries. Internally, structures and working patterns have either been merged or eradicated through organizational integration and improved efficiency gains. The overall effect has been the cascading of middle management functions through the rationalization of resources (Davila et al, 2002).

The private sector was quick to recognize the potential of ICTs and was willing to bear the emotional cost of reducing employment numbers. Government is beginning to follow suit. Current policy initiatives advocate the use of ICTs to modernize government and to provide better services (Aman & Kasimin, 2011). Besides that, globalization and the world economy have changed the social and economic priorities of most of nation's central or federal government. Developing nations like Malaysia must contend with the almost silent but overwhelming forces of globalization. The increased need for competitiveness in a restrictive economic environment is forcing management and administrative modifications. Government must now be cost effective and efficient (Badawi, 2004; Aman & Kasimin, 2011). Besides enhancing Malaysia's competitiveness, the public delivery system must be improved simply because the citizens demand it. It is important to remember that the public sector delivery system has the entire nation and the population as its clientele and therefore, the civil servants at all levels (national, state and local levels) must be able to understand their respective individual, and team roles, in delivering every facet of service to the people, whether those in business, in the schools or those who need services at the counter level (Karim, 1999). Furthermore, to ensure the efficiency of the system, appropriate strategies are required for the necessary political, economic and social governance of the country. And in the Digital Era with convergence, ICT will be the strategic tool and its use must be pervasive in all aspects of human life. Nevertheless, information and communication technologies (ICT) are changing the pattern of people's lives -- very few will disagree with this thought. It also seems unavoidable that relations between citizens and their government are deeply affected by this phenomenon. ICT are powerful tools for change according to some, while for others they will only be the cause of an even greater divide between the haves and the have-nots (Bruch & Bellgran, 2012).

However, ICT is more often determined not just simply as a matter of choice, but rather as a crucial component to ensuring effective human development. It has become very apparent that those communities who do not adopt ICTs will become increasingly isolated. The potential of ICTs to modernize public administration was also recognized at an academic level. The concept of "informatization" sought to use ICTs to complement the New Public Management reforms and assist the modernization of public administration (Karim, 1999; Badawi, 2004, Gansler et al, 2003). Informatization recognized the effects ICTs has on organization and aspired to emphasize the importance of information flows within public administration. Information flow analysis could highlight the "...political dynamics of change in Government" and therefore, aid the process of reform implementation (Gansler et al, 2003). New initiatives would have a greater chance of succeeding if organizational change problems could be identified and incorporated in to a management strategy. The analysis of information flow would become a core element in the modernizing and reinventing of government as it would potentially provide an insight into political interaction with governmental organizations.

Furthermore, ensuring appropriate levels of connectivity with ICT has become a major challenge. Local governments need not only to meet the demand from a new type of citizen who is IT literate, or to improve the quality of services, but they also have to shape their own public administration and develop new forms of social and citizen participation (Karim, 2003; Badawi, 2004). No other sphere of government is making more efforts than the local one in trying to introduce new technologies in the daily life of their citizens, but also in its own operations. Local administrators around the world would benefit by embracing this new paradigm and leverage on ICT to enhance the delivery system, and this is possible through proper implement of an electronic government (EG) initiative.

Electronic Government (e-Government)

It is impossible to discuss e-procurement without venturing into the parent area of electronic government. E-government (EG) generally refers to more use of ICT, but more importantly attempts to achieve more strategic use of ICT in the public sector (Lanzola & Suarez, 2012; Nelson & Svara, 2012). The term "government" covers several aspects of managing a country, ranging from the very form of government, over strategic management to daily operations. The definitions of EG generally covers these areas, but typically contains not only goals of more efficient operations but also of better quality of services and increased and better quality citizen participation in democratic processes (Karim, 2003).

According to Karim and Khalid (2003), a number of definitions for EG have been offered in existing literature but these definitions have come to imply EG as the government's use of technology, particularly the web-based Internet applications to enhance access and delivery of government services to citizens, business partners, employees and other government entities. Despite the citizen-centric focus, the definition of EG is not limited to a service-based view of offering electronic public services to citizens. It has been observed that EG in this Information Age has become an inter-organizational phenomenon and that technological improvements have implied more cooperative initiatives between government departments and organizations in complex, diverse and often divided political systems. Even though there are different views on the concept of EG, the adoption of ICTs by the public sector will definitely affect public service delivery, organizational settings and the social/political system (Karim & Khalid, 2003). Furthermore, Karim (2003) commented that history shows emerging uses rather than strategy-based ones and by now ICT use is so comprehensive and so diverse that ICT strategies have to be revamped in order to get some kind of return on the investment. Typically, so far electronic services have been set up at additional costs, leaving operations much as they were rather than achieving savings or better services by improved logistics.

EG is about changes in two related but distinct fields. First, it is about changes in the internal government operations that come about as ICT is used for automation, cooperation, integration among government agencies and as tools assisting in decision processes. While such ICT use has been going on for a couple of decades, the current spark of interest in the field is most of all due to the fact that now external operations are transformed, as information and services increasingly become available on the Internet. This has meant that government agencies must try to organize their operations based on the premise that citizens and companies will to a large extent manage their interactions with the public sector on a self-service basis (Karim, 2003).

In the last 20 years, Malaysia has experienced a remarkable growth in the economy. The GNP per capita has risen from US$1,710 in 1981 to US$4,284 in 1997 (Badawi, 2004). One consequence of this rapid growth of the Malaysian economy is that, the rise in the level of affluence of the local population has created increasing demands for public goods and services. People not only want to consume what is being provided to them but they also care for the quality of the public goods and services. At the local level, the local government, as one of the levels of government, plays a crucial role in providing public goods and services that are specific to the localities. However, the performance of local governments has been subjected to various criticisms based on the increasing number of complaints and dissatisfaction from the public regarding provision of public goods and the poor services rendered to the locals, suggesting the inefficiency of our local governments. This calls for the local government to be more responsive in meeting local needs and being able to deliver their functions effectively (Gansler et al, 2003). As the public at large is concerned about quality services and the greater role expected from local governments, the need to evaluate the performance of local governments is essential, thus, the implementation of e-procurement by the local government is an important issue to be addressed by the respective state governments in Malaysia.

The local governments in Malaysia are classified into three groups: city council for city centers, municipality for large towns and land/district offices for small sub-urban areas. As of 1999, there are a total of 99 local governments in Peninsular Malaysia comprising of four city councils, 19 municipal councils and 76 land/district offices. They are formed and regulated by the respective state legislation and subordinate to the respective state governments. The local government act of 1976 provides local authorities in Malaysia with a very comprehensive set of functions and responsibilities. The major function of the local governments is to provide public goods and services that are specific to the localities. Local public services that are undertaken by them on behalf of the respective state governments include both mandatory and discretionary functions. The mandatory functions include all critical functions such as refuse collection, maintenance of minor drainage, sewerage treatment, road maintenance, street lighting and activities pertaining to public health. Discretionary functions include all development function such as providing amenities, recreational parks, housing and commercial activities, markets, sports facilities and community centers. The sources of revenue for local governments mainly come from state specific grants that include road maintenance grant, economic development grant, and property tax (ILBS, 2003).

It is important to note that this study was the first attempt to undertake the systematic study of e-procurement implementation in selected local governments of Malaysia. Having a narrow and controlled scope, just for the state of Selangor, have allowed for an in-depth and rigorous study. Though some parts of the findings may be sensitive and painful to acknowledge, the final outcome of sharing the problems or issues encountered with e-procurement project implementation with other local governments of Malaysia, would override the deficiencies as the return on investment on such an expensive project can be seen and charted.

METHODOLOGY

All the 21 or 100% of the local governments in Selangor were studied comprising of the city councils, municipalities and the land/district offices (see Table 1.0), thus, no sampling technique is employed. The study utilized both the primary and secondary data, that is, the research used a combination of qualitative and quantitative methods. As very little is known about the implementation of e-procurement in the local governments of Selangor, the initial data gathering needed to be more qualitative in order to gain a breadth of view on the subject (Miles and Huberman, 1994). Stangor (2004) and Neuman (2003) pointed out the value of using qualitative techniques where research issues are not clear-cut and where respondents' replies are likely to be complex, discursive, and grounded in the culture of the organization. Furthermore, since the population of the Selangor local governments is not large, this study employs the local governments as the unit of analysis.

Data collection for this study was extremely rigorous and was divided into two phases:

Phase 1: Face-to-face interviews were conducted using structured survey questions. The local governments were chosen on the basis of easy access and their geographical closeness to Shah Alam and Klang. The seven local governments were: Petaling Land/District Office, Petaling Jaya Municipal Council (MPPJ), Subang Jaya Municipal Council (MPSJ), Shah Alam City Council (MBSA), Ampang Jaya Municipal Council (MPAJ), Klang Municipal Council (MPK) and the Kuala Selangor Land/District Office. These seven municipalities comprised 33.3% of the overall population. Only the department head of the respective ICT Department of each municipality was interviewed.

Phase 2: A questionnaire was then developed based on the responses received. These questions were structured on a Likert scale of 1 (Extremely Ineffective) to 7 (Extremely Effective). At the request of the respondents during the interview sessions, the questionnaire was translated to Bahasa Melayu as the respondents are more comfortable with this language. The questionnaires were sent to all 21 (100%) local governments of Selangor by snail mail followed by e-mail upon request.

From the 21 questionnaires sent out to the 21 local governments, only seven or 33.3% were returned after repeated phone calls and e-mail. From these seven responses, only one was from the land/district office while the remaining six are from the local councils or municipalities. Following the procedures described in the data gathering processes, the interview sessions were audio-taped and notes taken by the researcher. The interviews were later transcribed and content analysis was performed on the notes to identify the main themes relative to the research questions. Consequently, a questionnaire was drawn up to quantify the responses with questions structured on a (Likert) scale of 1 (Extremely Ineffective) to 7 (Extremely Effective). The software used to analyze the descriptive statistics was the Statistical Package for Social Science or SPSS Version 12.0.1 for Windows.

FINDINGS

In a nutshell, the findings of this study on e-procurement implementation issues in the Selangor local government resonate with the literature on like issues. The findings from this study indicate a paradox in the midst of policies imposed by the State and Federal Governments plus those hyped up by the mass media. The responses made by the various local governments stem more from the perspective of the respective individuals surveyed which are actually reality-checks than from upper management.

Table 2. Comparison of means for the ICT planning issues of the Selangor local governments

	Minimum	Maximum	Mean	Std. Deviation
Municipalities	1.00	13.00	5.7143	4.38613
Inter-departmental coordination	5.00	7.00	5.8571	.69007
Strategic planning	4.00	7.00	5.4286	.97590
Organizational directives	5.00	7.00	5.4286	.78680
Organizational ICT expertise	5.00	7.00	5.5714	.78680
Individual ICT expertise	5.00	6.00	5.7143	.48795
Written procedures	4.00	6.00	5.2857	.75593
Fiscal/budgeting issues	4.00	7.00	5.5714	1.13389
Planning model	5.00	6.00	5.5714	.53452
Drawing up contracts	3.00	6.00	4.4286	.97590
Timeframes and Scheduling	4.00	5.00	4.7143	.48795
Politics, internal/external	4.00	5.00	4.5714	.53452
Individual support	4.00	7.00	5.1429	1.06904
Existing system/legacy sys	5.00	6.00	5.4286	.53452
Organizational culture	4.00	6.00	4.8571	.69007
Standardization issues	4.00	6.00	4.8571	.89974
Rapidly changing technology	5.00	6.00	5.2857	.48795
Human Res. Issues	2.00	6.00	4.5714	1.61835
Organizational support	4.00	7.00	5.4286	1.27242

The findings revealed that the most problematic issues faced by the Selangor local government executives with regard to ICT planning process are the Human Resource issue and the drawing up of contracts issue (Table 2). From the interview transcriptions, almost all of the ICT officers are employed on a contractual basis. This is a de-motivating factor as most of them have been working for their respective local authority for more than three years. Furthermore, the organizational structure of their local authority shows that they are the department heads for the ICT department or unit. Even though most of them are diploma or degree holders, the fact remains that as department heads they should be employed as a permanent staff as their subordinates are full-time employees. Grievances on this matter have been brought up to the top management at every opportunity but bureaucracy hinders the process of recruitment, compensation and benefits at the local government organizations. Therefore, in order to have an effective ICT planning process, the local governments must deal with these issues immediately.

Bearing in mind that the e-procurement project is ICT-based, therefore, the most problematic issues facing the Selangor local government executives with regard to ICT implementation are again the human resource issue, drawing up of contracts and adequate staffing (Table 3). Yet again, the Klang land/district office which represents the rest of the eight land/district offices in Selangor pointed out that Human Resource management is ineffective because of the ripple effect on the contract employment of these ICT executives. Inadequate staffing for ICT-skilled employ-

Table 3. Comparison of means for the ICT implementation in the Selangor local governments

	Minimum	*Maximum*	*Mean*	*Std. Deviation*
Municipalities	*1.00*	*13.00*	*5.7143*	*4.38613*
Inter-departmental coordination	*5.00*	*7.00*	*6.0000*	*.57735*
Strategic planning	*5.00*	*6.00*	*5.2857*	*.48795*
Organizational directives	*5.00*	*7.00*	*5.8571*	*.69007*
Organizational ICT expertise	*5.00*	*6.00*	*5.4286*	*.53452*
Individual ICT expertise	*5.00*	*6.00*	*5.1429*	*.37796*
Written procedures	*4.00*	*7.00*	*5.5714*	*.97590*
Fiscal/budgeting issues	*3.00*	*7.00*	*5.1429*	*1.57359*
Planning model	*5.00*	*7.00*	*5.5714*	*.78680*
Drawing up contracts	*3.00*	*6.00*	*4.2857*	*.95119*
Timeframes and Scheduling	*4.00*	*5.00*	*4.7143*	*.48795*
Politics, internal/external	*3.00*	*6.00*	*5.0000*	*1.15470*
Individual support	*4.00*	*6.00*	*5.4286*	*.78680*
Existing system/legacy sys	*5.00*	*7.00*	*5.7143*	*.75593*
Organizational culture	*4.00*	*6.00*	*5.4286*	*.78680*
Standardization issues	*4.00*	*6.00*	*4.8571*	*.89974*
Organizational support	*5.00*	*7.00*	*5.5714*	*.78680*
Human Res. Issues	*2.00*	*6.00*	*4.4286*	*1.51186*
Internal Leadership	*5.00*	*6.00*	*5.2857*	*.48795*
Adequate Staffing	*1.00*	*6.00*	*4.2857*	*1.79947*

ees is another issue that the state government of Selangor should look into as only one ICT officer heads the ICT department at their municipality, thus these ICT officers are considered a "Jack or Jill of all trades". In particular, the ICT officers at the land/district officers are in charge of everything ICT such as handling the tasks of network administrators, systems analyst, programmer, webmaster, ICT trainer, etc. Therefore, in order to have a successful implementation of ICT at the local government organizations, these issues must also be tackled as soon as possible.

The issues that emerged led to the clustering of barriers to e-procurement implementation. Subsequently, the barriers of e-procurement implementation at the Selangor local governments are simply categorized into political, social, economic, technological and public service issues. Difficulty in adjusting to change, lack of funding, complex and expensive initiatives, and rigid government bureaucracy are some examples of the barriers facing the smooth implementation of e-procurement at the Selangor local governments. On the other hand, the facilitators of e-procurement implementation are again, to a lesser degree, the independent variables such as political, social, economic, technological and public service.

Consequently, from the above findings, it can be deduced that the local governments of Selangor (Municipalities and, Land and District Offices) are **not** ready for e-procurement adoption based on the findings as shown in Table 4. All of the issues such as political, economic, social, technological and public services must be taken care of immediately as they are the barriers to e-procurement adoption in these organizations, in particular, the human resource and the drawing up of contracts issues (Social variable), plus the bureaucratic red-tape on recruitment (Public Service variable). Once these issues are resolved, the adoption of e-procurement

Figure 2. Framework for EP implementation issues in municipalities

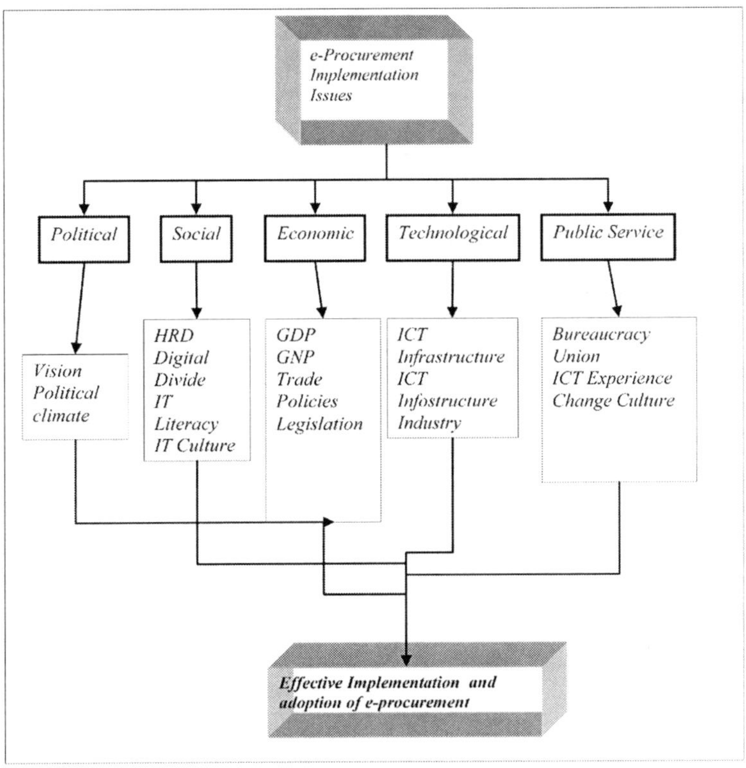

at the local government level of Selangor would be a smooth process (see also Figure 2).

ASSUMPTION AND LIMITATION

Every research project is limited in some way or another and this research too has its limitations and assumptions which are firstly, the small sample size is to aid manageability. The choice of Selangor from the rest of the 13 states in Malaysia is due to her being the only developed state as well as her strategic location of being sandwiched between Putrajaya and Cyberjaya. Other criteria for choosing Selangor are: extensive infrastructure, high population, successful economy, etc.

Secondly, the minimum response rate of 33.3% or 7 out of 21 is the borderline acceptance for reliability in research. It has been anticipated that using the local government as the unit of analysis would cause some problems in getting back a complete response but the need to use them as the scope is important in today's Information Era.

LESSONS LEARNED AND RECOMMENDATION

To reiterate, the e-procurement implementation issues of local governments in the state of Selangor, Malaysia were analyzed relative to ICT planning and ICT implementation. There are several conclusions that can be derived from this study. Firstly, the findings suggest that most of the local governments in Selangor are not ready for e-procurement implementation or to provide procurement/tendering services online. The underlying objective of this research is to enable on-line Federal Government procurement. When fully implemented it will transform the current procurement procedures by making it a faster and cheaper process which will then be handed down to state governments and the local governments throughout Malaysia. Electronic procurement enables the Government to become a smart buyer procuring quality goods and services at reasonable prices (Davila et al, 2002). Suppliers in turn will reap benefits through more expeditious and error-free payments.

From literature, the initial phase of the project is limited to the procurement of Central Contract goods and services involving the automation of the procurement process and establishing connectivity between buyers and suppliers (Neef, 2001). The project will then be extended to other procurement processes, namely direct purchases, quotations and tenders. Two agencies have been identified to implement this project. They are the Administration Division and the Government Procurement Division of the Ministry of Finance and the Management Services Division of MAMPU (Malaysian Administrative Modernization and Management Planning Unit). Pilot implementation will begin in early 1998 before full rollout to all Government agencies in subsequent phases.

Secondly, the variables that influence the local government's implementation issue the most are the type of local government, level of technology usage, political issues and social issues. Lastly, the results indicate that the city and municipal councils would have better preparations to introduce e-procurement compared to the other local councils particularly the land/district offices. This might be due to the bigger-sized, scale of operations and autonomy of the city and municipal councils.

REFERENCES

Abdullah, A. B. (2004). *Keynote address – Managing the national economy in challenging times: Enhancing the delivery systems and mechanism.* Kuala Lumpur, Malaysia: National Institute of Public Administration (INTAN).

Aman, A., & Kasimin, H. (2011). E-procurement implementation: A case of Malaysia government. *Transforming Government: People. Process and Policy*, *5*(4), 330–344.

Angeles, R., & Nath, R. (2007). Business-to-business e-procurement: Success factors and challenges to implementation. *Supply Chain Management: An International Journal*, *12*(2), 104–115. doi:10.1108/13598540710737299

Beaumaster, S. (1999). *IT implementation issues in local government: An analysis*. Unpublished doctoral dissertation, Blacksburg, Virginia, USA.

Berman, S. J. (2012). Digital transformation: Opportunities to create new business models. *Strategy and Leadership*, *40*(2), 16–24. doi:10.1108/10878571211209314

Bruch, J., & Bellgran, M. (2012). Design information for efficient equipment supplier/buyer integration.

Dasgupta, M. (2012). Conceptual paper: Organizational learning and its practices. *Sage Open*, 1-11. DOI: 10.1177/2158244011432198

Davila, A., Gupta, M., & Palmer, R. J. (2002). *Moving procurement systems to the Internet: The adoption and use of e-procurement technology models*. Stanford GSB Research Paper No. 1742. Retrieved, March 22, 2003, at http://ssrn.com/abstract=323923

Erridge, A., & Greer, J. (2000). Policy network analysis of UK Central Government civil procurement. *Public Policy and Administration*, *15*(4), 25–49. doi:10.1177/095207670001500403

Gansler, J. S., Lucyshyn, W., & Ross, K. M. (2003). *Digitally integrating the government supply chain: E-procurement, e-finance, and e-logistics. E-University of Maryland*. USA: Government Series.

Hashim, R. (2006). Electronic procurement (e-procurement) implementation issues in the Selangor local government. *Proceedings of the 6th European Conference on e-Government*, Pilipps-Universitat, Marburg, Germany.

ILBS – International Law Book Series. Laws of Malaysia. (2003). *Local Government Act 1976 (Act 171) & Subsidiary Legislation: As at 25th July 2003*. Kuala Lumpur, Malaysia: Direct Art Company.

Karim, M. R. A. (1999). *Reengineering the public service: Leadership and change in an electronic age*. Kuala Lumpur, Malaysia: Pelanduk Publications.

Karim, M. R. A. (2003). Technology and improved service delivery: Learning points from the malaysian experience. *International Review of Administrative Sciences: Creating Self-Confident Government*, *69*, 191–201. doi:10.1177/0020852303069002005

Karim, M. R. A., & Khalid, N. M. (2003). *E-government in Malaysia: Improving responsiveness and capacity to serve*. Selangor, Malaysia: MAMPU and Pelanduk Publications.

Lanzola, G., & Suarez, F. F. (2012). Closing the technology adoption-use divide: The role of contiguous user bandwagon. *Journal of Management*, *38*(3), 836–859. doi:10.1177/0149206310369938

Liao, S. H., Cheng, C. H., Liao, W. B., & Chen, I. L. (2003). A Web-based architecture for implementing electronic procurement in military organizations. *Technovation*, *23*(6), 521–533. doi:10.1016/S0166-4972(02)00006-8

Miles, M. B., & Huberman, A. M. (1994). *Qualitative data analysis: An expanded source book* (2nd ed.). Thousand Oaks, CA: Sage.

Mortensen, M., & Arlbjorn, J. (2012). Inter-organizational supplier development: The case of customer attractiveness and strategic fit. *Supply Chain Management: An International Journal*, *17*(2), 152–171. doi:10.1108/13598541211212898

Mukhopadhyay, B. (2011). Evaluating public procurement. *Review of Market Integration*, *3*(1), 21–68. doi:10.1177/097492921100300103

Murray, J. G., Rentell, P. G., & Geere, D. (2008). Procurement as a shared service in English local government. *International Journal of Public Sector Management*, *21*(5), 540–555. doi:10.1108/09513550810885822

Neef, D. (2001). *E-procurement: From strategy to implementation*. Upper Saddle River, NJ: Prentice Hall.

Nelson, K. L., & Svara, J. H. (2012). Form of government still matters: Fostering innovation in U.S. municipal governments. *American Review of Public Administration*, *42*(3), 257–281. doi:10.1177/0275074011399898

Neuman, W. L. (2003). *Social research methods: Qualitative and quantitative approaches* (5th ed.). Boston, MA: Allyn and Bacon.

Quesada, G., Gonzalez, M. E., Mueller, J., & Mueller, R. (2010). Impact of e-procurement on procurement practices and performance. *Benchmarking: An International Journal*, *17*(4), 516–538. doi:10.1108/14635771011060576

Ren, Z., Kwaw, P., & Yang, F. (2012). Ghana's public procurement reform and the continuous use of the traditional procurement system: The way forward. *Built Environment Project and Asset Management*, *2*(1), 4–4. doi:10.1108/20441241211235053

Seneviratne, S. J., & Garson, G. D. (Eds.). (1999). *Information technology and organizational change in the public sector*. Hershey, PA: Idea Group Publishing.

Smart, A. (2009). Exploring the business for e-procurement. *International Journal of Physical Distribution & Logistics Management*, *40*(3), 181–201. doi:10.1108/09600031011035083

Stangor, C. (2004). *Research methods for the behavioral sciences* (2nd ed.). New York, NY: Houghton Mifflin.

Ward, J. (1995). *Principles of information systems management*. New York, NY: Routledge.

Chapter 15
E-Procurement Systems as Tools for the Development of Supply Chains

Cuauhtémoc Sánchez-Ramírez
Instituto Tecnólogico de Orizaba, México

Giner Alor-Hernandez
Instituto Tecnólogico de Orizaba, México

Guillermo Cortes-Robles
Instituto Tecnólogico de Orizaba, México

Jorge Luis García-Alcaráz
Instituto de Ingeniería y Tecnología Universidad Autónoma de Ciudad Juárez, México

Alejandro Rodríguez-González
Centre for Plant Biotechnology and Genomics UPM-INIA, Polytechnic University of Madrid, Spain

ABSTRACT

The Supply Chain Management is a strategy that has allowed the organizations that have established in their business models a competitive advantage. The supply chain is a network of elements, where different key process such as: procurement, manufacturing, distribution, inventory, customer services, and information should be managed and controlled to meet customer requirements. To achieve this goal, different tools have been developed to help to the key processes of the supply chain; one of these tools is the e-procurement system, which helps an organization to control the interactions with the most crucial suppliers.

DOI: 10.4018/978-1-4666-2119-0.ch015

INTRODUCTION

Christopher (1998) considered to Supply Chain Management as new strategy in the business models. A supply chain is a network that enables the distribution options for procurement of both raw and finished materials, which can be transformed into finished goods and distributed to the end customer through various distribution channels. Commonly, the main goal of a supply chain is satisfy the customer's requests as soon as they appear. To achieve the above goal it is necessary that the processes and key activities are carried out in a supply chain quickly and effectively. One of these processes is the procurement on line that with advances of technology has had a great develop in recent years. This process is well-known as e-procurement. E-procurement increases efficiency by reducing the cost of human resources in purchasing activities, but e-procurement is more than just a system for making purchases online, because a properly implemented system can connect companies and their business processes directly with suppliers while managing all interactions between them. It provides those who use it with a set of built-in monitoring tools to help control costs and assure maximum supplier performance. It provides an organized way to keep an open line of communication with potential suppliers during a business process. E-Procurement helps with the decision-making process by keeping relevant information neatly organized and time-stamped. Well-managed e-procurement helps reduce inventory levels. Knowing product numbers, bid prices and contact points can help businesses close a deal while other suppliers are struggling to gather their relevant data. E-Procurement systems that allow multiple access levels and permissions help managers organize administrative users by roles, groups, or tasks.

E-PROCUREMENT AS SUPPORT IN THE DEVELOPMENT OF SUPPLY CHAIN

The Supply Chain Management as Competitive Advantage

The companies that competing in a global market must identify and develop their strategies to meet the challenges that market requires, such as: products with high quality, low price and the time required. One of these strategies is the Supply Chain Management, which has proven success factor in world-class industries (Gunasekaran & Ngai, 2004).

Today many manufacturing companies have as their main strategy, improving their production systems using methodologies or tools such as: Just in Time (JIT), Total Quality Management (TQM), Lean Manufacturing, Kaizen among other. The application of these techniques and methodologies have very good results in business processes, however, the Supply Chain Management to Thomas and Griffin (1996), is the most advanced state for the purchase, acquisition, production and distribution companies, because it includes suppliers and end users.

The main elements in a supply chain are (Figure 1): suppliers, logistics and customers (Rushton et al, 2010). To Council of Supply Chain Management Professionals (CSCMP, 2006) *Logistics* "is the planning, implementation and control of the effective forward and reverse flow and storage of goods, services and related information between the point of origin and the point of consumption in order to meet customer requirements".

The actual representation of the supply chain is through the inter-relation of elements above mentioned and others activities at different levels (Figure 2).

Figure 1. Main elements of supply chain

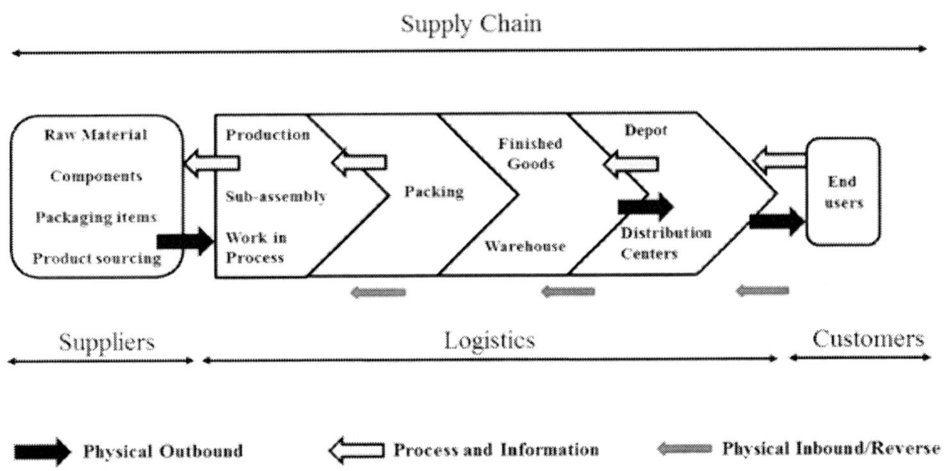

Figure 2. Structure of supply chain

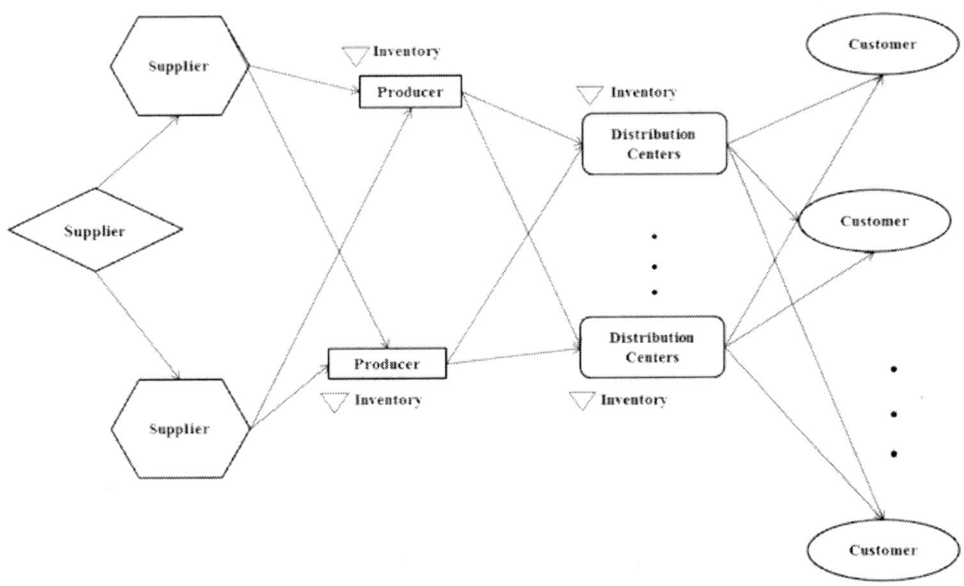

Jay W. Forrester (1961), professor of MIT is considered the pioneer of the formal study of supply chain. Using a basic structure of a supply chain and through the System Dynamics methodology found that delay and feedback information between the elements of supply chain originated the Amplification Effect or Whiplash that occurs when a small change in demand causes a mismatch (increase) in inventories of the elements of a supply chain. At present, this effect is known as the Bullwhip Effect and is still studied by different researchers (Lee et al, 1997).

The Importance of Supply Chain Management as a competitive advantage is that in every company there are movements of raw materials, finished goods, money and information that must be managed and controlled from suppliers to end customers (Waters, 2003).

Moreno-Luzon & Peris (1998) addressed level of decision-making centralization and level of formalization-standardization as the basic organizational design variables of the contingency model relating to quality management. Formalization can be defined as the degree to which roles and tasks performed in the organization are governed by formal rules, and standard policies and procedures. If higher level of flexibility is required by the organization, then level of formalization should be low whereas if the organization requires a rigid structure then higher level of formalization will be suitable.

Degree of formalization can be explained by the existence of independent department responsible for supply chain management and the strategic positioning of the department and the degree of centralization which reflects the scope of responsibilities and the power of supply chain department within the organization (Kim, 2007). The concept of formalization refers to "the extent that the rules governing behavior are precisely and explicitly formulated and the extent that roles and role relations are prescribed independently of the personal attributes of individuals occupying positions in the structure". In other words, formalization describes the degree to which work and tasks performed in the organization are standardized (Dewsnap & Jobber, 2000; Mollenkopf et al., 2000; Manolis et al., 2004).

Bowersox & Daugherty (1995) suggest that the concept of formalization in supply chain management perspective can be consistent with it in organizational perspective. They define formalization as the degree to which decisions and working relationships for supply chain activities are governed by formal rules and standard policies and procedures.

Centralization can be defined as the pattern of authority distribution for various departments within the organization. The management decides the authority distribution pattern on the basis of objectives to be achieved and type of strategy to be followed by the organization. For example, defender's strategy is cost oriented, so centralization should be high whereas prospector's strategy is product innovation oriented, so lower level of centralization will be suitable. Centralization is defined as the extent to which the power to make supply chain management decisions is concentrated in an organization (Mollenkopf et al., 2000; Manolis et al., 2004). Higher degrees of centralization correspond with concentration of decision making authority at more senior levels (Dewsnap & Jobber, 2000).

The degree of centralization is determined partly by hierarchical relationship between supply chain management department and other functional areas over the control and responsibilities for supply chain management activities (Leenders et al., 2002). According to Bowersox & Daugherty (1995) and Tsai (2002), three structural components-formalization, centralization and specialization have considerable influence on organization performance. Factors favouring centralization include standardization of products and business processes, cost reductions created through opportunities to allocate resources efficiently and economies of scale and improved levels of knowledge and expertise through the dedication of staff and resources (Droge & Germain, 1989).

Decentralization offers business units autonomy and control over key functional activities, supporting the principle that business units must carry responsibility for major decisions if they are to be held accountable for performance (Johnson & Leenders, 2006). Potential advantages of centralization include greater buying specialization, coordination of policies and systems and consolidation of requirements. Meanwhile, decentralization improves service and lowers costs by pushing decision-making responsibility closer to the end user, promotes closer working relationships between suppliers and end users and provides increased opportunities for end users to manage total cost of ownership factors (Leenders & Johnson, 2000). There can be other objectives like cost, flexibility, quality and innovation on the basis of which organization structure can be decided. The competitive dimensions can include cost, quality, flexibility, and delivery performance among others (Corbett & Van Wessenhove, 1993; Minor et al., 1994; Vickery, 1991).

Supply chain structure can be defined on the bases of organization's strategy. As defenders, prospectors and analysers have different strategies, there should be a strategic fit between their supply chain and competitive strategies. To achieve strategic fit, supply chain activities of an organization must support their objectives. Supply chain structure has been defined and classified in a number of ways in the literature. A very simple way of describing supply chain structure differentiates between organizations on the dimension of centralization or decentralization (Ghoshal, 1994). One of the major problem of decentralized organization is that the goals of the agents are not aligned with the overall goal of organization (Dirickx & Jennergren1979, Milgrom & Roberts, 1992). Different business subunits have their own objectives.To pursue their private interests; these units may choose to send false, or biased, information to headquarters and other departments (Jennergren & Muller, 1973). Companies must adjust their organizational structure and management processes to adapt to changes in the external competitive environment or its strategy in order to maximize performance (Galunic & Eisenhardt, 1994). The two extremes (prospector and defender) are consistent with findings put forward by the other authors, e.g. Burns and Stalker (1961) and Porter (1980). They labelled these extremes the mechanistic and organic management system, respectively. Burns and Stalker (1961) explicitly mention that mechanistic firms have a functional organization structure with high level of formalization i.e. extent to which rules and roles are precisely and explicitly formulated. Organic firms, on the other hand, have low level of formalization.

Mechanistic firms have a hierarchical structure and the way of coordination between the members of the organization is limited to vertical, that is, between superior and subordinate. Mechanistic systems are appropriate in stable conditions and have a functional organization structure, a high degree of formalization, and many rules and procedures. Organic systems are most appropriate in changing conditions and are characterized by loose structures and few rules. Miles & Snow's (1978) prospector corresponds with Burns and Stalker's organic system and Porter's differentiation strategy, while the defender strategy corresponds with Burns and Stalker's mechanistic system and Porter's cost leadership strategy. Analysers combine cost-leadership and a mechanistic system orthogonally with differentiation and an organic system. That is, they either spatially or temporally separate innovation and operation, but do not do both in the same part of the company or at the same time (Volberda, 1998).

According to Chopra & Meindl (2001), a product-focused organization performs many different functions in producing a single product whereas a functional-focused organization performs few functions on many types of products. A product focus tends to result in more expertise about a particular type of product at the expense of functional expertise that comes from a functional manufacturing methodology. Hybrid organizational structure approach is defined as the structure having features of both centralized and decentralized structures (Leenders & Johnson, 2000). While previous research has found that the hybrid organizational model is the most commonly used within large supply organizations (Johnson et al., 2006), there is still considerable variation with respect to how the hybrid model is implemented.

In 1960s, matrix structures became a popular organizational framework for managing new product and service development. Matrix organization approach manages coordination of activities across unit lines within the organization. The matrix combines the benefits of project and functional organizations by integrating the work of various specialists. The matrix structure operates through a two-dimensional system of control: a project/

product-line chain of command and a functional chain of command (Lawrence et. al., 1982). Project managers retain responsibility for developing products, while functional managers concentrate on the organization's capability to make use of up-to-date technical knowledge (Katz & Allen, 1985). On the basis of above arguments we have main organization structure types of supply chain departments as mechanistic, organic and matrix structure.

According to Min & Zhou (2002), "when structuring a supply chain network, it is necessary to identify who the partners of the supply chain are". Meanwhile, Cooper and Lambert (1997), suggest a guideline to structure a supply chain network, these structures are: (1) the type of a supply chain partnership; (2) the structural dimensions of a supply chain network and (3) the characteristics of process link among supply chain partners.

Importance of Procurement Process in Supply Chain Management

Actually the purchasing also known as procurement is a main process in the organizations because is the link between suppliers and this. If this process is correct, the organization ensures that there are sufficient suppliers of raw material at low prices, in the required quality, in the right place that is crucial to any manufacturing plant. Procurement is not only about raw material but also aspects as utilities, fuel, capital assets, corporate travel and hotels, outsourced services and information technologies (IT) equipment (Rushton et al., 2010).

The procurement process is linked to other key processes, such as the inventory management and transportation. In the case of inventory is about raw materials and the finished goods, because if the organization has a wrong procurement process designed and managed this will generate that the organization accumulate large quantity of raw materials and finished products to fulfill the customer requirements. In the case of transportation the relation is about the type of transport that the organization will use, because if the raw materials will be transported by road, sea, rail or air because the delivery time is different in each and this affect the quantity of orders that the organization will done to suppliers.

The organization, without process of procurement would not have a flow of raw materials into a manufacturing process and this will cause a serious problem in production scheduling. If the plant stops production line, will generate huge costs because the labor capital and machinery would be standing and the orders of customers will not available for delivery at the appropriate time.

To address the above problems, the organization can design a model for management to procurement process and define several policies, such as:

- Calculate the correct safety stocks to help the organization to cover such eventualities;
- Analyze the possibility that supplier move his facilities next to or close to the organization; and
- With products commodities, analyze the option to buy certain quantities may be negotiated in advance.

Other point to consider is the products need to be classified about their criticality to the organization and the value of annual purchases. According to Rushton et al. (2010), there are four categories:

- Routine purchases;
- Commodities;
- Critical items; and
- Strategic items.

Once that the products have been categorized, in the process of procurement may be considering the following options:

- Online catalogues;
- Tendering;

- A system of approved suppliers; and
- Strategic partnerships.

Figure 3 show the two aspects above mentioned both the criticality to the organization and procurement options.

The information technology has helped to consolidate the procurement process as a key tool in the development of supply chains, it is since allows streamline the purchasing process and improve the links between customers and suppliers.

The procurement process through an electronic platform is known as e-procurement. According to Rayport and Jaworski (2002) e-procurement is defined "as the usage of Web-based functions and services that allow employees of a buying organization to purchase goods and services, and allow suppliers to manage and communicate the fulfillment of those purchase orders which have been submitted".

E-procurement provides several options such as: catalog management of suppliers; requisition, control and approval of purchases; payment processing and others activities that are important in logistics systems and Supply Chain Management.

Figure 3. Issues to consider in the classification and acquisition of products

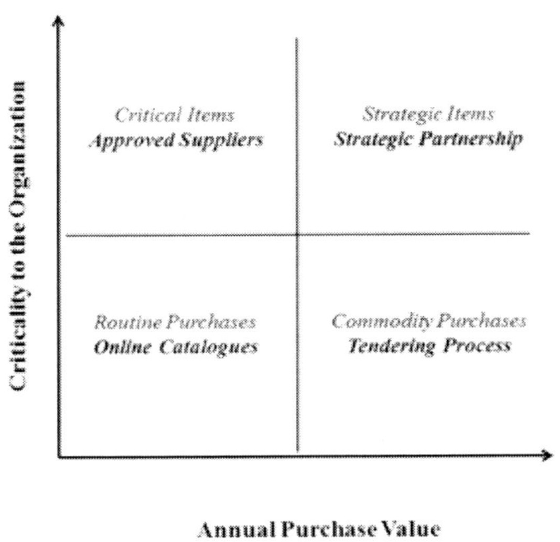

E-Procurement in Supply Chain Management

As the world's economy becomes increasingly competitive, sustaining competitiveness and the resulting profitability depends less on the ability to raise prices. Instead, firms need to compete on the basis of product innovation, higher quality, and faster response times, all of which must be delivered, in most cases simultaneously and always at the lowest costs attainable. Those competitive dimensions cannot be delivered without an effectively managed supply chain. Firms with the most competitive supply chains are and will continue to be the big winners in contemporary business.

The supply chain encompasses all activities associated with the flow and transformation of goods from the raw materials stage through to the end user, as well as associated information flows. Supply Chain Management is the integration of these activities through improved supply chain relationships to achieve sustainable competitive advantage (Handfield & Nichols Jr, 1999).

The definition suggests that all of the links in the supply chain must be strong and well integrated. However, it is argued here that the key link, the one that sets the foundation for the others, is supply management1 on the input end of the chain (Dobler & Burt, 1996). It is the link in the supply chain that serves as the boundary-spanning activity on the input end of the business where the supplier base is built based on the suppliers' ability to help the firm deliver on the competitive dimensions. It is where industrial marketers come face to face with the demands of the buying firm's supply chain.

The increasing emphasis on supply chain management has sharpened top management's focus on the valued-added potential of supply management. A recent survey suggests that 76% of CEOs expect supply management to contribute to shareholder value as firms continue to move toward more outsourcing (Nelson et al., 2002). The potential impact on competitiveness and profitability is enormous because the average manufacturing firm spends about 50% of its sales revenue on the purchases of goods and services needed to produce its final product. It is at the supply end of the supply chain where most of the expenditures on supply chain activities exist. This increasing emphasis on supply management, rather than on the more traditional "purchasing," requires that the professional supply manager move beyond the typical transaction focus of purchasing where price and availability were the key factors to be considered in the purchase decision.

The new basics of supply management require that supply managers take a more strategic view of what they do. Those new basics include a comprehensive understanding of target costing, value engineering, supplier development, and electronic procurement (Nelson et al., 2002). The first three are not really new, having existed as an implicit part of supply management for some time. It is more accurate to say they are being rediscovered. It is electronic procurement, the productive use of the Internet to improve the effectiveness and efficiency of the supply end of the supply chain that is new.

Strategic supply management has the potential for significant value creation for the firm. Business professionals who have long been involved in supply management understand its power to create value. The emergence of e-procurement in the last few years is creating a higher profile for supply management, boosting its visibility to top management. The challenge to those operating on the supply end of the supply chain is to make a convincing business case for what they do. Although CEOs expect supply management to contribute to shareholder value, effective supply managers need to get comfortable with the language of top management to communicate how that value is created. The move to e-procurement provides a unique opportunity for supply managers for two reasons. First, the application of technology to boost competitiveness and profitability is on the agenda of any forward-thinking CEO. Second, the application of technology to supply management, where firms spend most operating dollars, is focusing more top-management attention on that issue. A recent study by Deloitte Consulting of 200 global firms indicates that 30% have begun implementing at least a basic e-procurement solution whereas 61% are either planning or are considering an implementation (Whyte, 2000).

E-procurement is the linking and integration of inter-organizational business process and systems with the automation of the requisitioning, the approval purchase order management and accounting processes through and Internet-based protocol (Podlogar, 2007). In Figure 4, the main

Figure 4. Main concepts in e-procurement

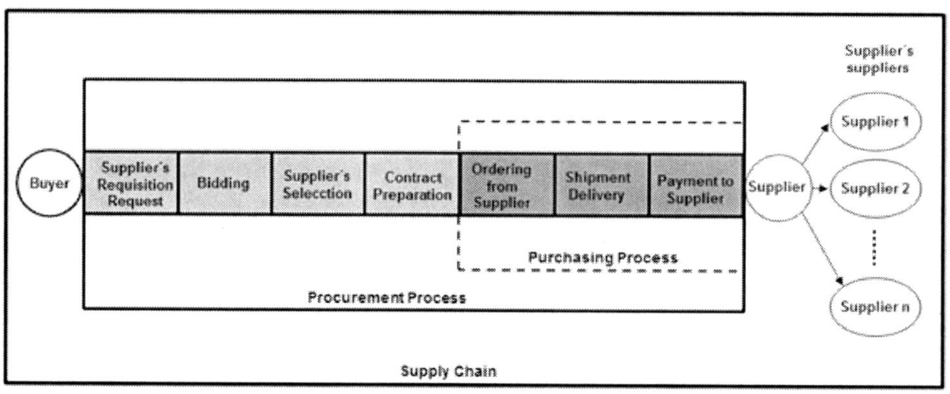

terms in the e-procurement are shown. According to Kalakota and Robison (1999), the purchasing process is within the procurement process and refers to the actual buying of materials and those activities associated with the buying process.

In the supply chain, the procurement process is important, because includes business partners as: suppliers, manufacturers, distributors and customers that use transactions to purchase, manufacture, assemble, or distribute products and services to the customers.

Elements of E-Procurement in the Supply Chain Management

E-procurement (electronic procurement, sometimes also known as supplier exchange) is the business-to-business or business-to-consumer or Business-to-government purchase and sale of supplies, work and services through the Internet as well as other informations and networking systems, such as Electronic Data Interchange and Enterprise Resource Planning (Baily, 2008). Typically, e-procurement Web sites allow qualified and registered users to look for buyers or sellers of goods and services. Depending on the approach, buyers or sellers may specify costs or invite bids. Transactions can be initiated and completed. Ongoing purchases may qualify customers for volume discounts or special offers. E-procurement software may make it possible to automate some buying and selling. Companies participating expect to be able to control parts inventories more effectively, reduce purchasing agent overhead, and improve manufacturing cycles. E-procurement is expected to be integrated into the wider Purchase-to-pay (P2P) value chain with the trend toward computerized supply chain management. E-procurement is done with a software application that includes features for supplier management and complex auctions. The new generation of E-Procurement is now on-demand or a software-as-a-service.

There are seven main types of e-procurement:

- **Web-Based ERP (Enterprise Resource Planning):** Creating and approving purchasing requisitions, placing purchase orders and receiving goods and services by using a software system based on Internet technology.
- **E-MRO (Maintenance, Repair and Overhaul)**: The same as web-based ERP except that the goods and services ordered are non-product related MRO supplies.
- **E-Sourcing:** Identifying new suppliers for a specific category of purchasing requirements using Internet technology.
- **E-Tendering:** Sending requests for information and prices to suppliers and receiving the responses of suppliers using Internet technology.
- **E-Reverse Auctioning:** Using Internet technology to buy goods and services from a number of known or unknown suppliers.
- **E-Informing:** Gathering and distributing purchasing information both from and to internal and external parties using Internet technology.
- **E-Marketsites:** Expands on Web-based ERP to open up value chains. Buying communities can access preferred suppliers' products and services, add to shopping carts, create requisition, seek approval, receipt purchase orders and process electronic invoices with integration to suppliers' supply chains and buyers' financial systems.

The e-procurement value chain consists of Indent Management, e-Tendering, e-Auctioning, Vendor Management, Catalogue Management, and Contract Management. Indent Management is the workflow involved in the preparation of tenders. This part of the value chain is optional, with individual procuring departments defining their indenting process. In works procurement, administrative approval and technical sanction are obtained in electronic format. In goods procurement, indent generation activity is done online. The end result of the stage is taken as inputs for issuing the NIT.

Elements of e-procurement include Request For Information, Request For Proposal, Request for Quotation, RFx (the previous three together), and eRFx (software for managing RFx projects). According to Podlogar (2007), the main elements in the e-procurement are buyers, suppliers and Internet access system. Through this system, the buyer can input their needs using the e-catalog included in the e-procurement program, these needs are the request for procurement. The entire process is totally automated through the electronic interchange. The approval is accomplished online, helping cutting the cycle time.

Due to importance of the e-procurement in the supply chain, we describe some experiences and success stories of adapting e-procurement systems.

Success Cases of Application of E-Procurement in Supply Chain

E-procurement is gaining in popularity in business practice and its benefits encourage its adoption in huge domain diversity. Its positive impact on several key performance indicators in different kind of business it is not questioned. As an example (Ronchi et al., 2010) shown the importance of e-procurement for an information technology chain. (Kothari et al., 2005) explain how the adoption and implementation of e-procurement technology within a hotel chain can generate important benefits. Presutti (2003) analyzed the integration of supply management and e-procurement to create value in the supply chain and generate competitive advantages in organizations. Yu et al. (2008) identified the factors that has been consider to realize an effective e-procurement in the industry. Panayiotou et al. (2004) presents a case study concerning the analysis of the Greek governmental purchasing process, revealing the importance of new services design in this process. Maybe one of the most dynamics domains in e-procurement and typical procurement is the automotive industry; (Perrone et al., 2010) for example, explain how multi-attribute auctions can improve the procurement process in the context of new product development while (Kim, 2006) explain that the supply chain can generate more value if e-procurement is synchronized and involves corporate executives. Thus e-procurement enable: (1) On-line procurement and access to the global supply chain, (2) Effective auction process (quality, quantity and adequate price) and (3) Effective cost reduction.

Some historical developments in supply chain management are described below.

Historical Developments in Supply Chain Management

In today market most of firms have realize the importance of designing, planning and controlling an efficient supply chain. The effect over competitiveness and profit has been analyzed form different perspective: economical (Atkins et al., 2010), social (Griffith, 2006), technological (Min et al., 2002) and recently from an environmental perspective (Türkay et al., 2004), (Laínez et al., 2008). All those research point out that a modern enterprise does not contend in the market as independent unit, but inside a common network or high level supply chain. Supply chain is a synergy among several business processes with common goals: the acquisition of raw material and its transformation into consumer goods, the creation of value and common wealth, distribution and promotion to retailer or costumers and information/knowledge exchange among diverse business entities. The capital objective in the supply chain is to improve the operational efficiency, to increase profitability and competitiveness of all stakeholders involved in the supply chain (Chopra & Meindl, 2001). The evolution in the supply chain is a complex process that could be analyzed from different point of view:

1. The quantity and relationship among business entities and components. Concerning their components, a supply chain is integrated for many components -element, system or any other function- required to fulfill a customer request. The term function comprises design, operation, distribution, pricing, marketing and customer service among other functions. This definition involves evidently, the manufacturer and its suppliers, but also transporters, warehouses, retailers, and even customers themselves.
2. Due to the variety of functions and components, the evolution of the supply chain is a very complex process (Min et al., 2002).
3. As well, the supply chain possesses a forward flow of finished goods and materials and, a second one of information in opposite direction. These are business processes evolving at their own rhythm and thus, considerably increasing the complexity in the evolution of the supply chain.

Evolution tendencies could be extracted from these perspectives. In first place, there is a clear problem of interoperability because many organizations must cooperate in network through the supply chain. The quantity, frequency and intensity of this cooperation are increasing continually. To solve this problem and to minimize heterogeneity, there is an evident tendency in the search of synchronization and standardization in the core business processes (Cellarius, 1998), (Blanc et al., 2006). The number of connections and functions in the supply chain affects its performance, thus a considerable effort was allowed to manage this complexity (Perona, 2004). Then, the inherent complexity of the supply chain is one of the subjacent reasons for the creation of managerial approaches that aims to ameliorate the operation and integration of the supply chain. Concerning the information flow, this is maybe the most dynamic research field.

Companies are continually searching for means and strategies to improve their flexibility, responsiveness and in consequence its competitiveness by changing their methods and technologies, which include the implementation of supply chain management paradigm and information technology (IT) (Gunasekaran et al., 2004), (Bailey et al., 2008), (Verissimo, 2009), (Huang et al., 2010). Information Technology (IT) is responsible for an important change in the evolution of the supply chain: that knowledge could be a decisive success factor (Hult et al., 2006), (Craighead et al., 2009).

The supply chain environment is very flexible due to changing demand and pressure from competitors. Determine the software architecture is needed to allow information systems to be realigned with the changing supply chain without effort or delay. In next section, an historical overview of Web technologies for e-procurement is presented.

WEB TECHNOLOGIES FOR E-PROCUREMENT

The features and requirements of the supply chain of the future matches the advantages and features of a software component architecture. Information technology support for the next generation supply chain systems is critical. This information technology needs to be: (1) Reusable, and (2) Rapidly changeable. Furthermore, it can be seen that the underlying software architecture of a supply chain solution also needs to be: (1) Agile, (2) Flexible, (3) Deployable over a multi-enterprise scope, (4) Multi-function support when used as a suite, (5) Handle complexity, (6) Enable collaboration, and (7) Enable coordination. We identify the main information technologies for developing Web-based systems for e-procurement:

- **EDI (Electronic Data Interchange):** EDI is the computer-to-computer exchange of formatted electronic messages called transaction sets. The most widely used formats are specified in a U.S. standard, ANSI (American National Standards Institute) X.12, and in an international standard called EDIFACT. An EDI message contains a string of data elements, each of which represents a piece of information, such as a price, or model number, separated by delimiters. The entire string is called a data segment (Zilbert, 2000). A transaction set usually corresponds to an equivalent paper document or form, e.g. Set 850 Purchase Order. For security, messages can be encrypted. With forms-based software, including Web pages, users can create or display an EDI transaction in a familiar way, without needing to know the transaction number or any details of the underlying formats. With the growing use of Internet, the transmission costs of EDI-based documents have been reduced. However, the development of EDI translators is still expensive because the codification of EDI documents is complicated due to their emphasis in the data consistency. An alternative to this proposal that eliminates several problems of business process integration was CORBA/IIOP.
- **CORBA/IIOP:** CORBA/IIOP stands for Common Object Request Broker Architecture/Internet Inter-ORB Protocol. CORBA is an industry standard from the Object Management Group -- largely the UNIX/Linux/not Microsoft community. Client programs send requests to a common interface called the Object Request Broker. The ORB sends each request to the appropriate object (application code and data) and returns the results. The standard allows this to be accomplished in a distributed computing environment, across languages, operating systems, hosts and networks. CORBA is essentially a messaging protocol and has helped promote the use of messaging (store & forward/publish & subscribe) as a technical approach to systems integration (Boldt, 1995). IIOP makes CORBA usable on a TCP/IP network (the Internet). CORBA objects can be embedded in a Web page and executed via Java applet. This allows a Web page to be interoperable with remote applications accessible via the Internet. However, CORBA does not offer interoperability for the business processes in a supply chain management. This is mainly to that each commercial partner (represented as a node in CORBA) must execute its own ORB which is highly dependent of the CORBA implementations. This originates a great problem of interoperability in the development of commercial activities among the participants of the supply chain. In order to solve the interoperability among the CORBA implementations, Microsoft proposed an alternative approach well-known as DCOM.
- **COM/DCOM and ActiveX:** Component Object Model/Distributed Component Object Model and ActiveX are Microsoft's Windows-oriented methods for developing and supporting interoperable program component objects. Together, these tools provide ways for Windows-based applications to interact and exchange data (Horstmann & Kritland, 1997). DCOM supports the TCP/IP protocol necessary for Internet- and web-based data interoperability. However, DCOM presents certain lacks of interoperability in the supply chain management. All the business processes of the participants in a supply chain should be executed under the Windows platform. Furthermore, in DCOM the messages that are sent between a client and a server have

a format defined by the DCOM Object RPC (ORPC) protocol. By this reason is necessary to use mechanisms for translating the messages in order to a different system can interpret and to act in the request/responses of involved participants. Although DCOM solves some issues of interoperability caused by the incompatibilities among the implementations developed by different technology suppliers, these still persist when diverse operating system platforms are involved. The Java programming language was designed with the purpose of solving these issues of interoperability.

- **Remote Method Invocation (RMI):** Java Remote Method Invocation (Java RMI) enables the programmer to create distributed Java technology-based to Java technology-based applications, in which the methods of remote Java objects can be invoked from other Java virtual machines, possibly on different hosts (Hughes et. al, 1999). Java RMI is a mechanism that allows one to invoke a method on an object that exists in another address space. The RMI mechanism is basically an object-oriented RPC mechanism. Java RMI has recently been evolving toward becoming more compatible with CORBA. In particular, there is now a form of RMI called RMI/IIOP ("RMI over IIOP") that uses the Internet Inter-ORB Protocol (IIOP) of CORBA as the underlying protocol for RMI communication. Java/RMI presents difficulties of interoperability. These difficulties reside in the use of the marshalling/unmarshalling of objects which is specific of the Java programming language. In the context of the supply chain, this means the business processes should be written in Java. In order to solve this issue, the World Wide Web Consortium (W3C) proposed a platform-independent description language well-known as XML
- **XML (eXtensible Markup Language):** XML was developed as a way to tag or identify pieces of data within a file or Web page. It is a subset of a 20-year old language called the Standard Generalized Mark-Up Language (SGML). XML is similar in form to HTML (Hypertext markup Language) which describes the content of a Web page in terms of how it is to be displayed (text and graphics) and interacted with. XML is called extensible because it defines only the techniques of tagging (Bray et. al, 2008). However, XML's flexibility has given rise to many industry-specific and proprietary vocabularies. These now threaten its potential to serve as a single, global standard for exchanging business-to-business electronic transactions. Just as different companies and industries use a variety of different documents and terms to accomplish the same transactions, so must XML be adapted to the specifics of a company or industry practice (Chen, 2003). By some estimates, more than 30 industry-specific initiatives are underway. RosettaNet is a good example of industry-specific standards being developed upon XML. This consortium of 40 companies in the computer industry have published XML dictionaries for 50 partner interface processes (PIPs) related to catalog updates, pricing, order management, purchasing, and inventory availability. Another 100 PIPs are planned. Another consortium, The Open Applications Group, Inc., has developed PaperXML for paper industry transactions, and SMDX for semiconductor manufacturing. The Chemical Industry Data Exchange (CIDX) has defined more than 700 data elements and 50 transactions based upon XML. Proprietary versions of XML abound -- for example, Ariba's cXML and CommerceOne's xCBL, both for procurement, and Microsoft's BizTalk, a gen-

eral purpose development tool for XML-based applications. With the proliferation of XML implementations and versions has come the need for translation software and services. These generally employ schema libraries and dictionaries that translate tag and data meanings, and templates that map one XML document to another (Savoie & Lee, 2001).

- **Web Services:** A Web service is a software component that is accessible by means of messages sent using standard web protocols, notations and naming conventions, including the XML protocol (Vinoski, 2003). The notorious success that the application of the Web service technology has achieved in B2B e-Commerce has also lead it to be viewed as a promising technology for designing and building effective business collaboration in supply chains. Deploying Web services reduces the integration costs and brings in the required infrastructure for business automation, obtaining a quality of service that could not be achieved otherwise (Adams et. al, 2003), (Samtani & Sadhwani, 2002). Service-Oriented Architecture (SOA) is an architectural paradigm for creating and managing "business services" that can access these functions, assets, and pieces of information with a common interface regardless of the location or technical makeup of the function or piece of data (Papazoglou, 2003). This interface must be agreed upon within the environment of systems that are expected to access or invoke that service. With a SOA infrastructure, we can represent software functionality as discoverable services on the network. SOAs have been around for many years, but the distinctive feature of the SOAs we address is that they are based on Internet and Web standards, in particular, Web services.
- **Business Process Execution Language for Web Services (BPEL):** BPEL is a process modeling language for the representation of compositional workflow structures to coordinate elementary Web service invocations. BPEL builds on Microsoft's XLANG (Web Services for Business Process Design) (Thatte, 2001) and IBM's WSFL (Web Services Flow Language) (Leymann, 2001) combining block structured language constructs borrowed from XLANG with a graph-oriented notation originated from WSDL. BPEL closely follows the WS/Coordination and WS/Transaction specifications. The former describes how Web services may use predefined coordination contexts to be associated to a particular role in a collaboration activity (Cabrera et. al, 2005b). The latter provides an infrastructure that provides transaction semantics to the coordinated activities (Cabrera et. al, 2005a). A BPEL document consists of three parts describing data, coordination activities and communication activities (Little & Webber, 2003). Data tags are used to define a set of external partners and the state of the workflow. Coordination activity tags define the process behavior by means of traditional control flow structures. Finally, communication activity tags define communication with other Web services through coordination activities by sending and receiving information.

BEST PRACTICES IN E-PROCUREMENT

Best-in-class e-procurement performers have long-term, well-thought-out strategies for e-procurement implementation. Many such systems have been implemented in phases, with each new phase building off the successes – and lesson learned–of prior phases. However, all examples of Best Practices in e-Procurement have many things in common. AberdeenGroup, Inc. (2005) identified key strategies used by companies that have achieved best practice status in e-procurement:

- Solicit top management support to help drive system compliance and ensure sufficient funding and resources are made available.
- Focus on ease of use to improve end users' acceptance of the system.
- Don't underestimate change management. Insufficient focus on change management has held back acceptance of many e-procurement systems.
- Make sure processes are efficient before applying automated solutions.
- Clearly define and reinforce metrics for measuring costs, process efficiency, and performance of e-procurement technologies and processes. Where possible link incentives for both procurement and business units to these metrics.

Though much progress has been made, significant challenges to successful e-procurement implementation remain. Specifically:

- **Supplier Enablement**: In the early days of e-procurement, buying enterprises and solution providers underestimated the time, effort, and resources required to enable suppliers to transaction business electronically. Leading enterprises typically use a combination of supplier-enablement approaches. Though tremendous progress has been made in supplier enablement, all involved parties – end users, suppliers, and solution providers – continue to work to make enablement as simple and cost effective as possible.
- **User Adoption:** Individual end users and entire business units will naturally resist any change in business processes that takes away buying power and buying flexibility. Over the past few years, user adoption has increased at essentially the same pace as the increase in suppliers enabled. With more products and suppliers on the e-procurement system, users have less reason to try to circumvent the system. Still, end users report that several factors continue to hold back user adoption, including inadequate representation of spending categories within the system, inconsistent purchase requirements, procedures, and supply bases by site or region, and a lack of executive mandates or policies to drive adoption and system compliance. Best Practice enterprises have worked on user adoption for years, and many supply executives at these enterprises have become leading "sellers" of the e-procurement system to end users.
- **Budget and Policy Support**: In AberdeenGroup, Inc. (2005) e-procurement benchmark research late last year, more than half of research respondents reported that securing budget/policy support for their e-procurement initiative was a challenge that delayed or muted the benefits of e-procurement.

In contrast, the best practice enterprises depicted in AberdeenGroup, Inc. (2005) received top management support and a level of investment needed to gain cost savings, process efficiencies, and the other benefits of e-procurement. However, even supply executives at best practice enterprises would like to see more investment and support of their e-procurement systems.

Research and new trends for e-procurement is presented below in order to provide a guide for designing effective and well-planed process models in e-procurement which is an important prerequisite for implementation success.

Research and New Trends for E-Procurement

Today businesses need to constantly adapt and reconfigure their IT assets, systems, and business operations to meet changing customer demands; compress business cycles; and differentiate from competition. New trends for developing e-procurement system are addressed in adopting different architectural styles. For instance, when an enterprise uses the SOA architectural style, it does not address all the capabilities needed in a typical supply chain management scenario. SOA does not have the ability to monitor, filter, analyze, correlate, and respond in real time to events. These limitations are addressed with an Event-Driven Architecture (EDA).

An EDA combined with SOA, provides that ability to create a supply chain management architecture that enables business. An EDA is an architectural paradigm based on using events that initiate the immediate delivery of a message that informs to numerous recipients about the event so they can take appropriate action (Sriraman & Radhakrishnan, 2005). In this context, an event is a trigger that typically corresponds to the occurrence of some business activities, for instance, the receipt of an order. An EDA comprises event consumers and event producers. Event consumers subscribe to an intermediary event manager, and event producers publish to this manager. When the event manager receives an event from a producer, the manager forwards the event to the consumer. If the consumer is unavailable, the manager can store the event and try to forward it later. Then, the primary value of EDA is that it allows companies to identify and respond to events coming from supply chain management collaborations that need to be addressed by one or more systems through event management. The events, collected via an EDA, can be analysed and correlated to identify relevant patterns, and then aggregated to build up information that is needed to solve the procurement problem. With this process, companies can proactively address and respond to real-world scenarios in real time.

A commercial toolkit is provided by TIBCO™ in order to enabling real-time business through a Service-Oriented and Event-Driven Architecture. TIBCO™ developed a set of applications in order to provide the following benefits where an enterprise can: 1) Improve ability to support new and changing business objectives, 2) Expand and extend the value of existing applications, and 3) Reduce the cost and risk of deploying new business services.

Another trend is to simplify the enterprise integration and middleware problem. As a solution, the Enterprise Service Bus (ESB) has emerged as software architecture in order to provide fundamental services for complex architectures via an event-driven and standards-based messaging engine (the bus). The ESB is an enterprise platform that implements standardized interfaces for communication, connectivity, transformation, portability, and security. An ESB implementation must cover: 1) Standards-based communication infrastructure, 2) Standards-based connectivity, 3) Standards-based transformation engines, 4) SOA for application composition and deployment, and 5) Standards-based security. Unlike the enterprise application integration (EAI) approach, an enterprise service bus builds on base functions broken up into their constituent parts, with distributed deployment where needed, working in harmony as necessary. An example of an ESB implementation is the Fiorano ESB™ (Fiorano Enterprise Service Bus™) that incorporates tools and infrastructure enabling businesses to easily integrate existing systems both within and across enterprises with standards-based technology.

CONCLUSION

Supply Chain Management has proved important strategic in the business models and decision making in the organizations, because considered the key processes as sourcing and procurement and all logistics management activities. It also help to coordinate the inter-relations of the key elements of the supply chain, such are suppliers, producers and customers. One tool that has helped to development the supply chains is the e-procurement, that is a system that allow multiple access levels and permissions help managers organize administrative users by roles, groups, or tasks in the procurement process.

We covered the basic concepts and the participants in e-procurement for supply chain management. Next, we reviewed in depth the main e-procurement system reported in the literature. We presented some experiences and success stories. Furthermore, we identified the main information technologies for developing Web-based systems for e-procurement. In this sense, we addressed web services technologies. We have presented some selection criteria, implementation strategies, and process redesign initiatives for successful e-procurement deployment. Research and new trends for e-procurement were also presented in this book chapter in order to provide a guide for designing effective and well-planed process models in e-procurement which is an important prerequisite for implementation success.

We believe this book chapter will provide a guide for selecting emergent approaches based on internet standards in order to achieve interoperability in the e-procurement process among different participants in the Supply Chain Management.

ACKNOWLEDGMENT

This work was supported by the General Council of Superior Technological Education of Mexico (DGEST). Additionally, this work was sponsored by the National Council of Science and Technology (CONACYT) and the Public Education Secretary (SEP) through PROMEP.

REFERENCES

AberdeenGroup, Inc. (2005). *Best practices in e-procurement: Reducing costs and increasing value through online buying*. Boston, MA: Author.

Adams, H., Gisolfi, D., Snell, J., & Varadan, R. (2003). *Custom extended enterprise exposed business services application pattern scenario*. Retrieved from http://www-106.ibm.com/developerworks/webservices/library/ws-best5/

Atkins, D., & Liang, L. (2010). A note on competitive supply chains with generalised supply costs. *European Journal of Operational Research*, *207*(3), 1316–1320. doi:10.1016/j.ejor.2010.07.012

Bailey, K., & Francis, M. (2008). Managing information flows for improved value chain performance. *International Journal of Production Economics*, *111*(1), 2–12. doi:10.1016/j.ijpe.2006.11.017

Baily, P. J. H. (2008). *Procurement principles and management* (p. 394). Harlow, UK: Prentice Hall Financial Times. ISBN-13: 978-0273713791

Blanc, S., Ducq, Y., & Vallespir, B. (2006). Interoperability problems in supply chains context. *Information Control Problems in Manufacturing Conference,* (pp. 621-626).

Boldt, J. (1995). *Common object request broker architecture* (CORBA/IIOP) specification version 2.0. Object Management Group, Final Report.

Bowersox, D. J., & Daugherty, P. J. (1995). Logistics paradigm: the impact of information technology. *Journal of Business Logistics*, *16*(1), 65–80.

Bray, T., Paoli, J., Sperberg-McQueen, C. M., Maler, E., & Yergeau, F. (2008). *Extensible markup language* (XML) 1.0 (Fifth Edition). W3C Recommendation. Retrieved from http://www.w3.org/TR/REC-xml

Burns, T., & Stalker, G. M. (1961). *The management of innovation*. London, UK: Tavistock.

Cabrera, L. F., et al. (2005a). *Web services atomic transaction* (WS-AtomicTransaction), Version 1.0. Cabrera, L. F., et. al (2005b). *Web services coordination* (WS-Coordination), Version 1.0.

Cellarius, P. (1998). Interoperability: The key to competitive supply in the Global Information Society (GIS). *Computer Standards & Interfaces*, *20*(2-3), 123–128. doi:10.1016/S0920-5489(98)00046-4

Chen, M. (2003). Factors affecting the adoption and diffusion of XML and Web services standards for e-business systems. *International Journal of Human-Computer Studies*, *58*(3), 259–279. doi:10.1016/S1071-5819(02)00140-4

Chopra, S., & Meindl, P. (2001). Supply chain management: Strategy, planning and operation. *Pearson Education Asia.*, *ISBN-13*, 978–0130264657.

Christopher, M. (1998). *Logistics and supply chain management. Strategies for reducing cost and improving service*. London, UK: Financial Time Management. doi:10.1080/13675569908901575

Cooper, M. C., Lambert, D. M., & Pagh, J. D. (1997). Supply chain management: More than a new name for logistics. *The International Journal of Logistics Management*, *8*(1), 1–14. doi:10.1108/09574099710805556

Corbett, C., & Van Wassenhove, L. (1993). Trade-offs? What trade-offs? Competence and competitiveness in manufacturing strategy. *California Management Review*, *35*(4), 107–122.

Council of Supply Chain Management Professionals (CSCMP). (2006). *Home page*. Retrieved from www.cscmp.org

Craighead, C., Hult, G., & Ketchen, D. (2009). The effects of innovation–Cost strategy, knowledge, and action in the supply chain on firm performance. *Journal of Operations Management*, *27*(5), 405–421. doi:10.1016/j.jom.2009.01.002

Dewsnap, B., & Jobber, D. (2000). The sales-marketing interface in consumer packaged goods companies: A conceptual framework. *Journal of Personal Selling & Sales Management*, *20*(2), 109–119.

Dirickx, Y. M., & Jennergren, L. P. (1979). *Systems analysis by multilevel methods*. Chichester, UK: John Wiley.

Dobler, D. W., & Burt, D. N. (1996). *Purchasing and supply management* (p. 9). New York, NY: McGraw-Hill.

Droge, C., Germain, R., & Daugherty, P. J. (1989). *Servicing the exchange relationship: organizational configuration and its effects on intra-firm and buyer-seller communications*. In Annual Conference of Council of Logistics Management, St. Louis, MO.

Forrester, J. W. (1961). Industrial dynamics. *Editorial Pegasus.*, *ISBN-10*, 1883823366.

Galunic, C. D., & Eisenhardt, K. M. (1994). Renewing the strategy-structure-performance paradigm. In B. M. Staw & L. L. Cummings (Eds.), *Research in Organizational Behaviour, 16*, 215-255.

Ghoshal, S., Korine, H., & Szulansi, G. (1994). Interunit communication in multinational corporations. *Management Science*, *40*(1), 96–110. doi:10.1287/mnsc.40.1.96

Griffith, D. (2006). Human capital in the supply chain of global firms. *Organizational Dynamics*, *35*(3), 251–263. doi:10.1016/j.orgdyn.2006.05.004

Gunasekaran, A., & Ngai, M. (2004). Information systems in supply chain integration and management. *European Journal of Operational Research*, *159*(2), 269–295. doi:10.1016/j.ejor.2003.08.016

Handfield, R. B., & Nichols, E. L. Jr. (1999). *Introduction to supply chain management* (p. 2). Upper Saddle River, NJ: Prentice-Hall.

Horstmann, M., & Kritland, M. (1997). *DCOM architecture. MSDN Library, Specifications*. Microsoft Corp.

Huang, C., & Lin, S. C. (2010). Sharing knowledge in a supply chain using the semantic web. *Expert Systems with Applications*, *37*(4), 3145–3161. doi:10.1016/j.eswa.2009.09.067

Hughes, M., Shoffner, M., Hamner, D., Winslow, M., & Hughes, C. (1999). Java network programming. *Manning Publications., ISBN-10*, 188477749X.

Hult, G., Ketchen, D., Cavusgil, T., & Calantone, R. (2006). Knowledge as a strategic resource in supply chains. *Journal of Operations Management*, *24*(5), 458–475. doi:10.1016/j.jom.2005.11.009

Jennergren, L. P., & Muller, W. (1973). Simulation experiments of resource-allocation decisions in two-level organizations. *Social Science Research*, *2*(4), 333–352. doi:10.1016/0049-089X(73)90008-2

Johnson, P. F., & Leenders, M. R. (2006). A longitudinal study of supply organizational change. *Journal of Purchasing and Supply Management*, *12*, 332–342. doi:10.1016/j.pursup.2007.01.007

Kalakota, R., & Robison, M. (1999). *E-business, roadmap for success*. Addison-Wesley Longman.

Katz, R., & Allen, T. J. (1985). Project performance and the locus of influence in the R&D matrix. *Academy of Management Journal*, *28*(1), 67–87. doi:10.2307/256062

Kim, D. (2006). Process chain: A new paradigm of collaborative commerce and synchronized supply chain. *Business Horizons*, *49*(5), 359–367. doi:10.1016/j.bushor.2005.11.004

Kim, S. W. (2007). Organizational structures and the performance of supply chain management. *International Journal of Production Economics*, *106*(2), 323–345. doi:10.1016/j.ijpe.2006.07.010

Kothari, T., Hu, C., & Roehl, W. (2005). E-procurement: An emerging tool for the hotel supply chain management. *International Journal of Hospitality Management*, *24*(3), 369–389. doi:10.1016/j.ijhm.2004.09.004

Laínez, J., Bojarski, A., Espuña, A., & Puigjaner, L. (2008). Mapping environmental issues within supply chains: a LCA based approach. *Computer Aided Chemical Engineering*, *25*, 1131–1136. doi:10.1016/S1570-7946(08)80195-2

Lawrence, P. R., Kolodny, H. F., & Davis, S. M. (1982). The human side of matrix: Readings in the management of innovation, (pp. 504-519).

Lee, H., Padmanabhan, V., & Whang, S. (1997). The bullwhip effect in supply chains. *Sloan Management Review*, *38*(3), 93–102.

Leenders, M. R., Fearson, H. E., Flynn, A. E., & Johnson, P. F. (2002). *Purchasing and supply management*. New York, NY. *McGraw-Hill Companies Inc., ISBN-13*, 978–0072370607.

Leenders, M. R., & Johnson, P. F. (2000). *Major structural changes in supply organizations*. Tempe, AZ: Center for Advanced Purchasing Studies.

Leymann, F. (2001). *Web services flow language (WSFL) version 1.0*. IBM Software Group.

Little, M., & Webber, J. (2003, August 1). Introducing BPEL4WS 1.0: Building on WS-transaction and WS-coordination. *Web Services Journal*, 28-33.

Manolis, C., Gassenheimer, B., & Winsor, R. D. (2004). The moderating effect of solidarity as conduct: A theoretical and empirical perspective. *Journal of Marketing & Practice*, *12*(3), 48–60.

Miles, R. E., & Snow, C. C. (1978). *Organizational strategy, structure and process*. New York, NY: McGraw Hill.

Milgrom, P., & Roberts, J. (1992). *Economics, organization and management*. Upper Saddle River, NJ: Prentice Hall.

Min, H., & Zhou, G. (2002). Supply chain modeling: Past, present and future. *Computers & Industrial Engineering*, *43*, 231–249. doi:10.1016/S0360-8352(02)00066-9

Minor, E. D., Hensley, R. L., & Wood, D. R. (1994). A review of empirical manufacturing strategy studies. *International Journal of Operations & Production Management*, *14*(1), 5–25. doi:10.1108/01443579410049252

Mollenkopf, D., Gibson, A., & Ozanne, L. (2000). The integration of marketing and logistics: An empirical examination of New Zealand firms. *Journal of Business Logistics*, *21*(2), 89–112.

Moreno-Luzon, M. D., & Peris, F. J. (1998). Strategic approaches, organizational design and quality management-integration in a fit and contingency model. *International Journal of Quality Science*, *3*(4), 328–347. doi:10.1108/13598539810243667

Nelson, D., Moody, P., & Stegner, J. (2002). *The purchasing machine: How the top ten companies use best practices to manage their supply chains* (p. 184). New York, NY: The Free Press.

Panayiotou, N., Gayialis, P., & Tatsiopoulos, P. (2004). An e-procurement system for governmental purchasing. *International Journal of Production Economics*, *90*(1), 79–102. doi:10.1016/S0925-5273(03)00103-8

Papazoglou, M. P. (2003). Service-oriented computing: Concepts, characteristics and directions. In *Proceedings of the Fourth International Conference on Web Information Systems Engineering*. Los Alamitos, NM: IEEE Press.

Perona, M., & Miragliotta, G. (2004). Complexity management and supply chain performance assessment: A field study and a conceptual framework. *International Journal of Production Economics*, *90*(1), 103–115. doi:10.1016/S0925-5273(02)00482-6

Perrone, G., Roma, P., & Lo Nigro, G. (2010). Designing multi-attribute auctions for engineering services procurement in new product development in the automotive context. *International Journal of Production Economics*, *124*(1), 20–31. doi:10.1016/j.ijpe.2009.10.003

Podlogar, M. (2007). E-procurement success factors: Challenges and opportunities for a small developing country. In Pani, A. K., & Agrahari, A. (Eds.), *E-procurement in emerging economies: Theory and cases*. Hershey, PA: IDEA Group Publishing. doi:10.4018/978-1-59904-153-7.ch003

Porter, M. E. (1980). *Competitive strategy: Techniques for analyzing industries and competitors*. New York, NY: The Free Press.

Presutti, W. D. (2003). Supply management and e-procurement: Creating value in the supply chain. *Industrial Marketing Management*, *32*(3), 219–226. doi:10.1016/S0019-8501(02)00265-1

Rayport, J. F., & Jaworski, B. J. (2002). *Introduction to electronic commerce*. New York, NY: McGraw – Hill Publishers.

Ronchi, S., Brun, A., Golini, R., & Fan, X. (2010). What is the value of an IT e-procurement system? *Journal of Purchasing and Supply Management*, *16*(2), 131–140. doi:10.1016/j.pursup.2010.03.013

Rushton, A., Croucher, P., & Baker, P. (2010). *The handbook of logistics & distribution management*. London, UK: Kogan Page. ISBN 978 0 7494 5714 3

Samtani, G., & Sadhwani, D. (2002). Enterprise application integration and Web services. In Fletcher, P., & Waterhouse, M. (Eds.), *Web services business strategies and architectures* (pp. 39–54). Expert Press, Ltd.

Savoie, B. J., & Lee, H. (2001). *Key technologies & concepts for supply chain systems & integration*. Marietta, GA: High Performance Concepts, Inc.

Sriraman, B., & Radhakrishnan, R. (2005). *Event-driven architecture augmenting service-oriented architecture*. Sun Microsystems.

Thatte, S. (2001). *Web services for business process design (XLANG)*. Microsoft Corporation.

Thomas, D. J., & Griffin, P. M. (1996). Coordinated supply chain management. *European Journal of Operational Research, 94*(1), 1–15. doi:10.1016/0377-2217(96)00098-7

Tsai, W. (2002). Social structure of "cooperation" within a multiunit organization: Coordination, competition, and intraorganizational knowledge sharing. *Organization Science, 13*(2), 179–191. doi:10.1287/orsc.13.2.179.536

Türkay, M., Oruç, C., Fujita, K., & Tatsuyuki, A. (2004). Multi-company collaborative supply chain management with economical and environmental considerations. *Computers & Chemical Engineering, 28*(6-7), 985–992. doi:10.1016/j.compchemeng.2003.09.005

Verissimo, P. J. (2009). The new supply chain's frontier: Information management. *International Journal of Information Management, 29*(5), 372–379. doi:10.1016/j.ijinfomgt.2009.02.001

Vickery, S. K. (1991). A theory of production competence revisited. *Decision Sciences, 22*, 635–643. doi:10.1111/j.1540-5915.1991.tb01286.x

Vinoski, S. (2003). Integration with Web services. *IEEE Internet Computing*, (November-December): 75–77. doi:10.1109/MIC.2003.1250587

Volberda, H. W. (1998). *Building the flexible firm, how to remain competitive*. Oxford, UK: Oxford University Press.

Waters, D. (2003). Logistics: An introduction to supply chain management. New York, NY. *Palgrave McMillan., ISBN-10*, 0333963695.

Whyte, C. K. (2000, April). E-procurement: The new competitive weapon. *Purchasing Today*, p. 25.

Yu, Y., Yu, H., Itoga, H., & Lin, T. (2008). Decision-making factors for effective industrial e-procurement. *Technology in Society, 30*(2), 163–169. doi:10.1016/j.techsoc.2007.12.004

Zilbert, A. B. (2000). A comparative study of traditional electronic data interchange versus internet electronic data interchange. In D. Colton, J. Caouette, & B. Raggad (Eds.), *Proceedings ISECON*, Vol. 17. Philadelphia, PA: 501 AITP Foundation for Information Technology Education.

ADDITIONAL READING

Alor, G., Aguilar, A., Juarez, U., Posada, R., Cortes, G., & Garcia, M. ... Rodriguez, A. (2010). HYDRA: A middleware-oriented integrated architecture for e-procurement in supply chains. In N. T. Nguyen & R. Kowalczyk (Eds.), *Transactions on CCI I, LNCS 6220*, (pp. 1–20). Berlin, Germany: Springer-Verlag.

Alor, G., Aguilar, A., Juárez, U., Posada, R., Robles, G., & Martinez, M. ... González, A. (2009). A hybrid architecture for e-procurement. In N. T. Nguyen, R. Kowalczyk & S.-M. Chen (Eds.), *ICCCI 2009, LNCS, Vol. 5796*, (pp. 685–696). Heidelberg, Germany: Springer.

Dimitri, N., Piga, G., & Spagnolo, G. (2006). *Handbook of procurement*. Cambridge University Press. ISBN 10 0-521-87073-9

Oracle. (2012). *Peoplesoft enterprise eprocurement*. Retrieved January 22, 2012, http://www.oracle.com/us/products/applications/peoplesoft-enterprise/srm/053359.html

Pani, A., & Agrahari, A. (2007). *E-procurement in emerging economies*. Hershey, PA: IDEA Group Publishing. doi:10.4018/978-1-59904-153-7

SAP. (2012). *SAP supply chain management*. Retrieved January 19, 2012, http://www.sap.com/mexico/solutions/business-suite/scm/index.epx

Supply Chain Council. (2012). *The supply chain operations reference* (SCOR Model). Retrieved January 15, 2012, from http://supply-chain.org/

Compilation of References

10 *ders Information Services Project*. (2012). Reviewed http://rd.10ders.net/

Abdullah, A. B. (2004). *Keynote address – Managing the national economy in challenging times: Enhancing the delivery systems and mechanism*. Kuala Lumpur, Malaysia: National Institute of Public Administration (INTAN).

Aberdeen Group. (1999). *Internet procurement: The importance of maintenance and repair*. Executive White Paper. Boston, MA: Aberdeen Group, Inc. Retrieved from http://www.aberdeen.com

Aberdeen Group. (2001). *Commerce networks: Extending the value of e-commerce*. Executive White Paper. Boston, MA: Aberdeen Group, Inc. Retrieved from http://www.aberdeen.com

Aberdeen Group. (2005). *Best practices in e-procurement: Reducing costs and increasing value through online buying*. Boston, MA: Author.

Adams, H., Gisolfi, D., Snell, J., & Varadan, R. (2003). *Custom extended enterprise exposed business services application pattern scenario*. Retrieved from http://www-106.ibm.com/developerworks/webservices/library/ws-best5/

Adams, C., & Lioyd, S. (2002). *Understanding PKI: Concepts, standards, and deployment considerations* (2nd ed.). The Addison-Wesley Professional.

Adams, D. A., Nelson, R. R., & Todd, P. A. (1992). Perceived usefulness, ease of use, and usage of information technology: A replication. *Management Information Systems Quarterly*, *16*(2), 227–247. doi:10.2307/249577

Adeces & Asociación de Internautas. (2009). *E-administración autonómica. Se buscan ciudadanos que usen los servicios electrónicos*. Madrid, Spain: Adeces. Retrieved February 4, 2012, from http://www.adeces.org/administracion%20electronica%202009.pdf

Adobor, H., & McMullen, R. (2007). Supplier diversity and supply chain management: A strategic approach. *Business Horizons*, *50*(3), 219–229. doi:10.1016/j.bushor.2006.10.003

Agarwal, R., Lewis, W., & Sambamurthy, V. (2003). Sources of influence on beliefs about information technology use: An empirical study of knowledge workers. *Management Information Systems Quarterly*, *27*(4), 657–678.

Agarwal, R., & Prasad, J. (1998). The antecedents and consequences of user perceptions in information technology adoption. *Decision Support Systems*, *22*(1), 15–29. doi:10.1016/S0167-9236(97)00006-7

Agarwal, R., Sambamurthy, V., & Stair, R. M. (2000). Research report: The evolving relationship between general and specific computer self-efficacy – An empirical assessment. *Information Systems Research*, *11*(4), 418–430. doi:10.1287/isre.11.4.418.11876

Akkaynak, O. S. (2004). *In PPA, 2003 Yılı Faaliyet Raporu* [2003 Activity Report]. (pp. 3–5). Ankara: Sunuş.

Akyer, M. (2011). *E-İhale ve EKAP Uygulamaları*. Retrieved July 14, 2011, from http://www.diskapieah.gov.tr/dokumanlar/ekap.ppt

Allen, B. A., Juillet, L., Paquet, G., & Roy, J. (2001). E-Governance & government on-line in Canada: Partnerships, people & prospects. *Government Information Quarterly*, *18*(2), 93–104. doi:10.1016/S0740-624X(01)00063-6

Allen, E. (2002). *Managing strategic service delivery partnerships: From governance to delivery*. London, UK: New Local Government Network.

Aman, A., & Kasimin, H. (2011). E-procurement implementation: A case of Malaysia government. *Transforming Government: People. Process and Policy, 5*(4), 330–344.

Amelinckx, I., Muylle, S., & Lievens, A. (2008). Extending electronic sourcing theory: An exploratory study of electronic reverse auction outcomes. *Electronic Commerce Research and Applications, 7*(1), 119–133. doi:10.1016/j.elerap.2007.11.003

Andersen, K. V. (2004). *E-government and public sector process rebuilding (PPR): Dilettantes, wheelbarrows, and diamonds*. Boston, MA: Kluwer Academic Publishers.

Angeles, R., & Nath, R. (2007). Business-to-business e-procurement: Success factors and challenges to implementation. *Supply Chain Management: An International Journal, 12*(2), 104–115. doi:10.1108/13598540710737299

Ariely, D. (2009). *Predictably irrational*. London, UK: Harper Collins Publishers.

Atkins, D., & Liang, L. (2010). A note on competitive supply chains with generalised supply costs. *European Journal of Operational Research, 207*(3), 1316–1320. doi:10.1016/j.ejor.2010.07.012

Bache, I. (2001). Different seeds in the same plot? Competing models of capitalism and the incomplete contracts of partnership design. *Public Administration, 79*(2), 337–359. doi:10.1111/1467-9299.00259

Baião, J., & Seco, A. (2000). *Gestión de los recursos de tecnología de la información en el contexto de la modernización gobernamental*. BID.

Baier, C., Hartmann, E., & Moser, R. (2008). Strategic alignment and purchasing efficacy: An exploratory analysis of their impact on financial performance. *Journal of Supply Chain Management, 44*(4), 36–52. doi:10.1111/j.1745-493X.2008.00071.x

Bailey, K., & Francis, M. (2008). Managing information flows for improved value chain performance. *International Journal of Production Economics, 111*(1), 2–12. doi:10.1016/j.ijpe.2006.11.017

Baily, P. J. H. (2008). *Procurement principles and management* (p. 394). Harlow, UK: Prentice Hall Financial Times. ISBN-13: 978-0273713791

Baily, P., Farmer, D., Jessop, D., & Jones, D. (2008). *Procurement principles and management* (10th ed.). London, UK: Prentice Hall.

Bajari, P., & Hortacsu, A. (2003). Winner's curse, reserve prices, and endogenous entry: Empirical insights from Ebay auctions. *The Rand Journal of Economics, 3*(2), 329–355. doi:10.2307/1593721

Ball, R., Heafey, M., & King, D. (2001). The private finance initiative: A good deal for the public purse or a drain on future generations? *Policy and Politics, 29*, 95–108. doi:10.1332/0305573012501224

Bapna, R., Goes, P., Gupta, A., & Jin, Y. (2004). User heterogeneity and its impact on electronic auction market design: An empirical explanation. *Management Information Systems Quarterly, 28*(1), 21–43.

Barak Obama. (2009). *Transparency and Open Government. Memorandum for the Heads of Executive Departments and Agencies.* Government of the United States. The White House. Retrieved from http://www.whitehouse.gov/the_press_office/TransparencyandOpenGovernment

Barnaby, T. (2002). *Distributed. NET programming in C.* Berkely, CA: Apress.

Bartezzaghi, E., & Ronchi, S. (2005). E-Sourcing in a buyer–operator–seller perspective: Benefits and criticalities. *Production Planning and Control, 16*(4), 405–412. doi:10.1080/09537280500063459

Bartonitz, M. (2011). *Vom Status Quo der Standards im Geschäftsprozessmanagement*. SAPERION. Retrieved from http://www.saperionblog.com/lang/de/vom-status-quo-der-standards-im-geschaftsprozessmanagement-und-der-wende-in-deutschland/5428/

Bates, T. (2001). Minority business access to mainstream markets. *Journal of Urban Affairs, 23*(1), 41–56. doi:10.1111/0735-2166.00074

Battle, S., Bernstein, A., Boley, H., Grosof, B., Gruninger, M., & Hull, R. ... Tabet, S. (2005). *Semantic Web services framework (SWSF) overview.* Retrieved from http://www.w3.org/Submission/SWSF/

Beall, S., Carter, C., Carter, P. L., Germer, T., Hendrick, T., & Jap, S. L. ... Petersen, K. (2003). *The role of reverse auctions in strategic sourcing.* Retrieved from www.capsresearch.org

Beardsley, C. T. (1972). Is your computer insecure? *IEEE Spectrum*, *9*(1), 67–78. doi:10.1109/MSPEC.1972.5218476

Beaumaster, S. (1999). *IT implementation issues in local government: An analysis.* Unpublished doctoral dissertation, Blacksburg, Virginia, USA.

Bennett, D., & Harvey, A. (2009). *Publishing open government data.* W3C Working Draft 8 September 2009. Retrieved http://www.w3.org/TR/gov-data/

Berman, S. J. (2012). Digital transformation: Opportunities to create new business models. *Strategy and Leadership*, *40*(2), 16–24. doi:10.1108/10878571211209314

BERNAMA. (n.d.). *2006Budget underscores govt continued commitment for ICT.* Retrieved March 19, 2007, from http://www.e-government research/msc/BUDGET 2006.com/

Bernard, H. (1976). *Totale Oorlog en Revolutionaire Oorlog* (*Vol. I*). Brussels, Belgium: Royal Military Academy.

Berners-Lee, T., Hendler, J., & Lassila, O. (2001). The Semantic Web. *Scientific American*, *284*(6), 34–35. doi:10.1038/scientificamerican0501-34

Berryman, J. M. (2007). Judgments during information seeking: A naturalistic approach to understanding of enough information. *Journal of Information Science*, *20*(10), 1–11.

Bettis, R., Bradley, S., & Hamel, G. (1992). Outsourcing and industrial decline. *The Academy of Management Executive*, *6*(1), 7–22.

Bharadwaj, S. G., Varadarajan, P. R., & Fahy, J. (1993). Sustainable competitive advantage in service industries: A conceptual model and research propositions. *Journal of Marketing*, *57*(4), 83–99. doi:10.2307/1252221

Bhimani, A. (1996). Securing the commercial internet. *Communications of the ACM*, *39*(6), 29–35. doi:10.1145/228503.228509

Bing, H., Zheng-Ding, Q., & Dong-Mei, S. (2002). Secure authentication system incorporating hand shapes verification and cryptography techniques. *Proceedings of IEEE Region 10 Conference on Computers, Communications, Control and Power Engineering*, Vol. 1, (pp. 156-159).

Blake, J. (2007). Caring for the bottom line. *Human Resource Planning*, *30*(1), 36–44.

Blanc, S., Ducq, Y., & Vallespir, B. (2006). Interoperability problems in supply chains context. *Information Control Problems in Manufacturing Conference,* (pp. 621-626).

Bobbitt, M. L., & Dabholkar, P. A. (2001). Integrating attitudinal theories to understand and predict use of technology-based self-service. *International Journal of Science Industry Management*, *12*(5), 423–450.

Bof, F., & Previtali, P. (2007). Organisational pre-conditions for e-procurement in governments: The Italian experience in the public health care sector. *The Electronic Journal of E-Government*, *5*(1), 1–10.

Boldt, J. (1995). *Common object request broker architecture* (CORBA/IIOP) specification version 2.0. Object Management Group, Final Report.

Booch, G., Rumbaugh, J., & Jacobson, I. (2005). *Unified modeling language user guide* (2nd ed.). New York, NY: The Addison-Wesley.

Booth, D., Champion, I. M., Ferris, C., Haas, H., McCabe, F., Newcomer, E., & Orchard, D. (2004). *Web services architecture.* Retrieved from http://www.w3.org/TR/ws-arch/

Bovaird, T. (2007). *Strategic management in the public sector.* Oxford, UK: Oxford University Press.

Bowersox, D. J., & Daugherty, P. J. (1995). Logistics paradigm: the impact of information technology. *Journal of Business Logistics*, *16*(1), 65–80.

Bowser, M., Cantle, N., & Allan, N. (2011). *Unraveling the complexity of risk.* Presented at Open Forum of The Actuarial Profession (January 21, 2011). London.

Boyne, G. A. (1998). Competitive tendering in local government: A review of theory and evidence. *Public Administration*, *76*(4), 695–712. doi:10.1111/1467-9299.00132

Bray, T., Paoli, J., Sperberg-McQueen, C. M., Maler, E., & Yergeau, F. (2008). *Extensible markup language* (XML) 1.0 (Fifth Edition). W3C Recommendation. Retrieved from http://www.w3.org/TR/REC-xml

Bressler, S., & Grantham, C. (2000). *Communities of commerce: Building internet business communities to accelerate growth, minimize risk, and increase customer loyalty*. New York, NY: McGraw Hill.

Brooks, B. (2007). The pulley model: A descriptive model of risky decision-making. *Safety Science Monitor, 11*(1), 1–14.

Bruch, J., & Bellgran, M. (2012). Design information for efficient equipment supplier/buyer integration.

Brunelli, M. (2000). E-auctions online save millions for Quaker Oats and SmithKlineBeecham. *Purchasing, 128*(4), S22.

Burke, L. A., & Miller, M. K. (1999). Taking the mystery out of intuitive decision making. *The Academy of Management Executive, 13*(4), 91–99. doi:10.5465/AME.1999.2570557

Burns, T., & Stalker, G. M. (1961). *The management of innovation*. London, UK: Tavistock.

Business Dictionary. (2012). *Definition of e-procurement*. Retrieved April 22, 2012, from http://www.business-dictionary.com/definition/electronic-procurement-e-procurement.html

Byatt, I. (2002). *Delivering better services for citizens: A review of local government procurement in England*. London, UK: Department for Transport, Local Government and the Regions/The Local Government Association.

Cabrera, L. F., et al. (2005a). *Web services atomic transaction* (WS-AtomicTransaction), Version 1.0. Cabrera, L. F., et. al (2005b). *Web services coordination* (WS-Coordination), Version 1.0.

Cáceres, S. (2004). *Observatorio de la sociedad de la información. Un mundo de brechas y puentes digitales.* Retrieved February 5, 2012, from http://fundacionorange.es/areas/28_observatorio/pdfs/DEF_20.pdf

Calista, D., & Melitski, J. (2007). E-government and e-governance: Converging constructs of public sector information and communications technologies. *Public Administration Quarterly, 31*(1).

Caño, M. J., & Folgueras, A. (2011, May 25). *IT governance for e-procurement. Applicability of the norm ISO/IEC to reach the interoperability and generalization.* Retrieved May 31, 2011, from http://es.scribd.com/doc/56447197/iT-Governance-for-E-Procurement-6

Capgemini Consulting. (2011). *Estudio comparativo 2011 de los servicios públicos online en las comunidades autónomas.* Resultados 5ª Medición, Abril 2011. Madrid, Spain: Fundación Orange. Retrieved February 7, 2012, from http://www.informeeespana.es/docs/Estudio_Comparativo_2011_Servicios_on_line.pdf

Carlsson, C., Hyvonen, K., Repo, P., & Walden, P. (2005). *Adoption of mobile services across different technologies.* Retrieved October 13, 2006, from http://www.bledconference.org/

Carter, C. R., Auskalnis, R. J., & Ketchum, C. L. (1999). Purchasing from minority business enterprises: Key success factors. *Journal of Supply Chain Management, 35*(1), 28–32. doi:10.1111/j.1745-493X.1999.tb00053.x

Carter, C. R., Kaufmann, L., Beall, S., Carter, P. L., Hendrick, T. E., & Peterson, K. J. (2004). Reverse auctions-grounded theory from the buyer and supplier perspective. *Transportation Research Part E, Logistics and Transportation Review, 40*, 229–254. doi:10.1016/j.tre.2003.08.004

Carter, C. R., & Stevens, C. K. (2007). Electronic reverse auction configuration and its impact on buyer price and supplier perceptions of opportunism: A laboratory experiment. *Journal of Operations Management, 25*(5), 1035–1054. doi:10.1016/j.jom.2006.10.005

Cavanha Filho, A. O. (2001). Logística: Novos modelos. *Qualitymark, 167.*

Celino, I., Karla, A., De Medeiros, A., Zeissler, G., Oppitz, M., Facca, F., & Zoeller, S. (2007). Semantic business process analysis. *Business, 251*, 1–4.

Cellarius, P. (1998). Interoperability: The key to competitive supply in the Global Information Society (GIS). *Computer Standards & Interfaces*, *20*(2-3), 123–128. doi:10.1016/S0920-5489(98)00046-4

CERES. (2012). *Entidad pública de certificación que permite autentificar y garantizar la confidencialidad de las comunicaciones*. Retrieved February 8, 2012, from http://www.cert.fnmt.es

Cerrillo, A. (2008). *E-administración*. Barcelona, Spain: UOC.

CHANGE. (2012). *Change.org*. Retrieved February 5, 2012, from http://www.change.org

Chan, S. C., & Lu, M. T. (2004). Understanding Internet banking adoption and use behavior: A Hong Kong perspective. *Journal of Global Information Management*, *12*(3), 21–43. doi:10.4018/jgim.2004070102

Chen, S., & Ravallion, M. (2008). The developing world is poorer than we thought, but no less successful in the fight against poverty. *The World Bank Development Research Group*. Retrieved from http://elibrary.worldbank.org/docserver/download/4703.pdf?expires=1328136769&id=id&accname=guest&checksum=13842B7AFFC09192E20FCFBA7D547269

Chen, M. (2003). Factors affecting the adoption and diffusion of XML and Web services standards for e-business systems. *International Journal of Human-Computer Studies*, *58*(3), 259–279. doi:10.1016/S1071-5819(02)00140-4

Cheung, W., & Chang, M. K. (2000). Prediction of Internet and World Wide Web usage at work: A test of an extended Triandis model. *Decision Support Systems*, *30*(1), 83–100. doi:10.1016/S0167-9236(00)00125-1

Choi, T. Y. (1996). An exploration of supplier selection practices across the supply chain. *Journal of Operations Management*, *14*(4), 333–343. doi:10.1016/S0272-6963(96)00091-5

Chopra, S., & Meindl, P. (2001). Supply chain management: Strategy, planning and operation. *Pearson Education Asia., ISBN-13*, 978–0130264657.

Christopher, M. (1998). *Logistics and supply chain management. Strategies for reducing cost and improving service*. London, UK: Financial Time Management. doi:10.1080/13675569908901575

Christopher, M., Lowson, R., & Peck, H. (2004). Creating agile supply chains in the fashion industry. *International Journal of Retail & Distribution Management*, *32*(8), 367–376. doi:10.1108/09590550410546188

Clement, L., Hately, A., von Riegen, C., & Rogers, T. (2004). *UDDI version 3.0.2*. UDDI Spec Technical Committee Draft. Retrieved March 24, 2012, from http://uddi.org/pubs/uddi-v3.0.2-20041019.htm

Cockburn, C., & Wilson, T. D. (1996). Business use of the World-Wide Web. *International Journal of Information Management*, *16*(2), 83–102. doi:10.1016/0268-4012(95)00071-2

Commission of the European Communities. (2008). *Communication from the Commission to the Council, the European Parliament, the European Economic and Social Committee and the Committee of the Regions: "Think Small First". A "small business act"*. COM. 394.

Cooper, M. C., Lambert, D. M., & Pagh, J. D. (1997). Supply chain management: More than a new name for logistics. *The International Journal of Logistics Management*, *8*(1), 1–14. doi:10.1108/09574099710805556

Cooper, R. G. (1997). Examining some myths about new product winners. In Katz, R. (Ed.), *The human side of managing technological innovation* (pp. 550–560).

Corbett, C., & Van Wassenhove, L. (1993). Trade-offs? What trade-offs? Competence and competitiveness in manufacturing strategy. *California Management Review*, *35*(4), 107–122.

Costello, A. B., & Osborne, J. W. (2005). Best practices in exploratory factor analysis: Four recommendations for getting the most from your analysis. *Practical Assessment, Research & Evaluation*, *10*(7).

Coulson, A., Darwin, J., Davis, H., et al. (1998). *Client-contractor relationships in ten local authorities*. Occasional Paper 18. Birmingham, UK: School of Public Policy.

Council of Supply Chain Management Professionals (CSCMP). (2006). *Home page*. Retrieved from www.cscmp.org

Craighead, C., Hult, G., & Ketchen, D. (2009). The effects of innovation–Cost strategy, knowledge, and action in the supply chain on firm performance. *Journal of Operations Management*, *27*(5), 405–421. doi:10.1016/j.jom.2009.01.002

Cromm, S., & Brandon-Jones, A. (2007). Impact of e-procurement: Experiences from ımplementation in the UK public sector. *Journal of Purchasing and Supply Management*, *13*(4), 294–303. doi:10.1016/j.pursup.2007.09.015

CTIC. (2009). *Polílticas de uso de servicios de participación ciudadana en el contexto de las administraciones públicas*. Gijón, Spain: CTIC Centro Tecnológico. Retrieved January 25, 2012, from http://ct.ctic.es/web/export/sites/default/es/documentos/864-2009.pdf

Dai, Q., & Kauffman, R. J. (2000). *Business models for internet-based e-procurement systems and b2b electronic markets: An exploratory assessment*. Minneapolis, MN: University of Minnesota.

Daniel, E. (1999). Provision of electronic banking in the UK and Republic of Ireland. *International Journal of Bank Marketing*, *17*(2), 72–83. doi:10.1108/02652329910258934

Dasgupta, M. (2012). Conceptual paper: Organizational learning and its practices. *Sage Open*, 1-11. DOI: 10.1177/2158244011432198

Davila, A., Gupta, M., & Palmer, R. J. (2002). *Moving procurement systems to the Internet: The adoption and use of e-procurement technology models*. Stanford GSB Research Paper No. 1742. Retrieved, March 22, 2003, at http://ssrn.com/abstract=323923

Davis, F. D. (1986). *A technology acceptance model empirical testing new end-user information systems: Theory and results*. Doctoral dissertation, Sloan School of Management, Massachusetts Institute of Technology.

Davis, D. F., Bagozzi., P, R., & Warsaw, R. P. (1989). User acceptance of computer technology: A comparison of two theoretical models. *Management Science*, *35*(8), 982–1003. doi:10.1287/mnsc.35.8.982

Davis, F. D. (1989). Perceived usefulness, perceived ease of use and user acceptance of information technology. *Management Information Systems Quarterly*, *13*(3), 319–340. doi:10.2307/249008

Dewsnap, B., & Jobber, D. (2000). The sales-marketing interface in consumer packaged goods companies: A conceptual framework. *Journal of Personal Selling & Sales Management*, *20*(2), 109–119.

DIGIT. Directorate-General for Informatics. (2010, February 9). *The value of e-PRIOR, the European e-Procurement platform offered by the European Commission*. Retrieve June 10, 2011, from www.epractice.eu/files/e-PRIOR%20v1.0.ppt

Dirickx, Y. M., & Jennergren, L. P. (1979). *Systems analysis by multilevel methods*. Chichester, UK: John Wiley.

DNIElectronico. (2012). *Portal oficial sobre el DNI electrónico*. Retrieved January 20, 2012, from http:// http://www.dnielectronico.es/

Dobler, D. W., & Burt, D. N. (1996). *Purchasing and supply management* (p. 9). New York, NY: McGraw-Hill.

Dollinger, M. J., Enz, C. A., & Daily, C. M. (1991). Purchasing from minority small businesses. *International Journal of Purchasing and Materials Management*, *27*(2), 9–14.

Domingue, J., Roman, D., & Stollberg, M. (2005). Web service modeling ontology (WSMO): An ontology for Semantic Web services. *Architecture (Washington, D.C.)*, (n.d), 776–784.

Dover, P. A. (1998). The effect of technology selection on consumer adoption of in home computerized banking. *International Journal of Marketing*, *2*, 31–37.

Downs, G. W. Jr, & Mohr, L. B. (1976). Conceptual issues in the study of innovation. *Administrative Science Quarterly*, *21*, 700–714. doi:10.2307/2391725

Drapeau, M. (2009). Government 2.0: The rise of the Goverati. Retrieved January 31, 2012, from http://www.readwriteweb.com/archives/government_20_rise_of_the_goverati.php

Droge, C., Germain, R., & Daugherty, P. J. (1989). *Servicing the exchange relationship: organizational configuration and its effects on intra-firm and buyer-seller communications*. In Annual Conference of Council of Logistics Management, St. Louis, MO.

Dror, Y., & Hamel, G. (1998). *Alliance advantage*. Cambridge, MA: Harvard Business School Press.

Drucker, P. F. (1992). Sell the mailroom: Unbundling in the 1990s. In *Managing for the future: The 1990s and beyond* (pp. 220–223). Oxford, UK: Butterworth-Heinemann.

DTLR. (2001). *Local authority procurement: A research report*. Department for Transport, Local Government andthe Regions, London.

Dutta, S., Kwan, S., & Segev, A. (1997). *Transforming business in the marketspace: Strategic marketing and customer relationships*. Fontainebleau, France: INSEAD.

Dutton, W. H., & Eynon, R. (2010). Networked individuals and institutions: A cross-sector comparative perspective on patterns and strategies in government and research. *The Information Society*, *25*(3), 207.

Edmondson, V. C., Suh, W. S., & Munchus, G. (2008). Exceeding government-mandated social programs: Minority supplier development programs. *Management Research News*, *31*(2), 111–124. doi:10.1108/01409170810846830

eEspaña. (2011). *Informe anual sobre el desarrollo de la sociedad de la información en España*. Fundación Orange. Retrieved February 10, 2012, from http://www.informeeespana.es/docs/eE2011.pdf

E-Government Advisory Group. (2008). *Öncelikli 11 E-Devlet Projesi*. 12 Haziran, Ankara.

Eisenhardt, K. M. (1989). Building theories from case study. *Academy of Management Review*, *14*(4), 532–550.

Eisenhardt, K.M., & Sull, D. (2001). Strategy as simple rules. *Harvard Business Review*, (1): 106–116.

Ellram, L. M. (1990). The supplier selection decision in strategic partnerships. *Journal of Purchasing & Materials Management*, *26*(4), 8–14.

Emiliani, M. L. (2000). Business-to-business online auctions: Key issues for purchasing process improvement. *Supply Chain Management: An International Journal*, *5*(4), 176–186. doi:10.1108/13598540010347299

Emiliani, M. L. (2004). Sourcing in the global aerospace supply chain using online reverse auctions. *Industrial Marketing Management*, *33*(1), 65–73. doi:10.1016/j.indmarman.2003.08.012

Emiliani, M. L., & Stec, D. J. (2002). Realizing savings from online reverse auctions. *Supply Chain Management: An International Journal*, *7*(1), 12–23. doi:10.1108/13598540210414355

Emiliani, M. L., & Stec, D. J. (2005). Wood pallet suppliers' reaction to online reverse auctions. *Supply Chain Management: An International Journal*, *10*(4), 278–287. doi:10.1108/13598540510612758

Engström, A., Wallström, A., & Salehi-Sangari, E. (2009). Implementation of public e-procurement in Swedish government entities. In *Proceedings of the International Multiconference on Computer Science and Information Technology* (pp. 315-319). Retrieved July 14, 2011, from http://www.e-procurement.nu/eprocurement/download/publicatiesoverig/implementatie-e-procurement-in-zweedse-overheid.pdf

Enterprise Europe Network Flanders. (2009). *Tender alerting service*. Reviewed http://www.enterpriseeuropevlaanderen.be/nl/home/overheidsopdrachten/tender-alert-service.html

Erridge, A., & Greer, J. (2000). Policy network analysis of UK Central Government civil procurement. *Public Policy and Administration*, *15*(4), 25–49. doi:10.1177/095207670001500403

Erridge, A., & Greer, J. (2002). Partnerships and public procurement: Building social capital through supply relations. *Public Administration*, *80*(3), 503–522. doi:10.1111/1467-9299.00315

Erridge, A., & Nondi, R. (1994). Public procurement, competition and partnership. *European Journal of Purchasing and Supply Management*, *1*(3), 169–179. doi:10.1016/0969-7012(94)90006-X

Essig, M. (2000). Purchasing consortia as symbiotic relationships: Developing the concept of "consortium sourcing". *European Journal of Purchasing & Supply Management*, *6*(1), 13–22. doi:10.1016/S0969-7012(99)00031-3

Etzion, H., Pinker, E., & Seidmann, A. (2003). *Analyzing the simultaneous use of auctions and posted prices for online selling*. Working paper CIS-03-01. University of Rochester.

Euroalert.net. (2012). Retrieved from http://euroalert.net/

Euroalert.net. (2012b). *On-line store web site*. Reviewed http://euroalert.net/en/buy.aspx

Euroalert.net. (2012c). *On-line store, 10ders alerts page*. Reviewed http://euroalert.net/en/tenders-alerts

Euroalert.net. (2012d). *On-line store, 10ders reports page*. Reviewed http://euroalert.net/en/Tenders-Reports

Euroalert.net. (2012e). *On-line store, 10ders lists sample*. Reviewed http://euroalert.net/dl/docs/10dersLists/Euroalert-10dersLists-Winners-Demo-Construction-Romania-2008-2011.xls

Euroalert.net. (2012f). *On-line store: Widgets services page*. Reviewed http://euroalert.net/en/widgets_service_options.aspx

Euroalert.net. (2012g). *Client portfolio*. Reviewed http://euroalert.net/en/clients-portfolio.aspx.

Euroalert.net. (2012h). *Euroalert presents its experience at the Open Software World Conference 2012 and the W3C Day in Spain*. Retrieved from http://en.blog.euroalert.net/search/label/Open%20data

European Commission & DG Information Society. (2010). *A digital agenda for Europe*. Retrieved http://ec.europa.eu/information_society/digital-agenda/index_en.htm

European Commission & DG Information Society. (2010b). *Beyond raw data: public sector information, done well*. Retrieved http://ec.europa.eu/information_society/events/cf/dae1009/item-display.cfm?id=5257

European Commission. (2000). *Lisbon strategy for growth and jobs*. Retrieved May 30, 2011, from http://ec.europa.eu/archives/growthandjobs_2009/

European Commission. (2002). *e-Europe 2002 action plan*. Retrieved May 30, 2011, from http://ec.europa.eu/information_society/eeurope/2002/index_en.htm

European Commission. (2005). *e-Europe 2005 action plan*. Retrieved May 30, 2011, from http://ec.europa.eu/information_society/eeurope/2005/index_en.htm

European Commission. (2005, January). *Functional requirements for e-procurement (Volume I, main requirements)*. Retrieved June 8, 2011 from http://ec.europa.eu/idabc/servlets/Doc1ad3.pdf?id=22191

European Commission. (2005, July 8). *Requirements for conducting public procurement using electronic means under the new public procurement directives 2007/18/CE and 2004/17/CE*. Retrieved June 3, 2011, from the http://ec.europa.eu/internal_market/publicprocurement/docs/eprocurement/sec2005-959_en.pdf

European Commission. (2006, April 25). *i2010 eGovernment action plan: Accelerating eGovernment in Europe for the benefit of all*. Retrieved May 30, 2011, from http://ec.europa.eu/information_society/activities/egovernment/policy/action_plan/index_en.htm

European Commission. (2008). *European code of best practices facilitating access by SMEs to public procurement contracts*. SEC. 2193

European Commission. (2009, December 1). *Commission regulation (EC) No 1177/2009, of 30 November 2009, amending Directives 2004/17/EC, 2004/18/EC and 2009/81/EC of the European Parliament and of the Council in respect of their application thresholds for the procedures for the award of contracts*. Retrieved June 4, 2011, from http://eur-lex.europa.eu/LexUriServ/LexUriServ.do?uri=OJ:L:2009:314:0064:0065:EN:PDF

European Commission. (2010). *e-Europe 2010 action plan*. Retrieved May 30, 2011, from http://ec.europa.eu/information_society/eeurope/i2010/index_en.htm

European Commission. (2010). *Green Paper on expanding the use of e-Procurement in the EU*. Retrieved July 14, 2011, from http://ec.europa.eu/internal_market/consultations/docs/2010/e-procurement/green-paper_en.pdf

European Commission. (2010). *Public procurement indicators 2009*. Retrieved from http://ec.europa.eu/internal_market/publicprocurement/docs/indicators2010_en.pdf

European Commission. (2010, August 26). *A digital agenda for Europe*. Retrieved 30 May, 2011, from http://eur-lex.europa.eu/LexUriServ/LexUriServ.do?uri=COM:2010:0245:FIN:EN:PDF

European Commission. (2010, December 15). *The European eGovernment action plan 2011-2015. Harnessing ICT to promote smart, sustainable & innovative Government*. Retrieved May 30, 2011, from http://ec.europa.eu/information_society/activities/egovernment/action_plan_2011_2015/docs/action_plan_en_act_part1_v2.pdf

European Commission. (2010, February 2). *Lisbon strategy evaluation document*. Retrieved May 30, 2011, from http://ec.europa.eu/archives/growthandjobs_2009/pdf/lisbon_strategy_evaluation_en.pdf

European Commission. (2010, October 18). *Green paper on expanding the use of e-Procurement in the EU.* Retrieved June 1, 2011 from http://ec.europa.eu/internal_market/consultations/docs/2010/e-Procurement/green-paper_en.pdf

European Commission. (2011). *Europe 2020*. Retrieved May 30, 2011, from http://ec.europa.eu/europe2020/index_en.htm

European Commission. (2011). *Modernising European public procurement to support growth and employment*. Press release. Retrieved http://europa.eu/rapid/pressReleasesAction.do?reference=IP/11/1580

European Commission. (2011b). *Digital agenda: Turning government data into gold.* Press release. Retrieved from http://europa.eu/rapid/pressReleasesAction.do?reference=IP/11/1524

European Commission. (2011c). *Final report. Cross-border procurement above EU-thresholds.* Rambøll Management. Retrieved http://ec.europa.eu/internal_market/publicprocurement/docs/modernising_rules/cross-border-procurement_en.pdf

European Commission. (2011d). *Public procurement. Modernising the rules: News legislative proposals.* Retrieved from http://ec.europa.eu/internal_market/publicprocurement/modernising_rules/reform_proposals_en.htm

European Commission. (2012). *TED: Tenders electronic daily*. Reviewed http://ted.europa.eu/

European Commission. (2012b). *Simap: Information about European public procurement*. Reviewed http://simap.europa.eu/supplier/opportunities-in-europe/index_en.htm

European Parliament. (2003). *Directive 2003/98/EC of the European Parliament and of the Council on the re-use of public sector information*, 345/90. Retrieved from http://eur-lex.europa.eu/LexUriServ/LexUriServ.do?uri=OJ:L:2003:345:0090:0096:EN:PDF

European Parliament. Council. (2004a, March 31). *Directive 2004/17/EC of the European Parliament and of the Council of 31 March 2004 coordinating the procurement procedures of entities operating in the water, energy, transport and postal services sectors*. Retrieved June 2, 2011 from http://eur-lex.europa.eu/LexUriServ/LexUriServ.do?uri=CELEX:32004L0017:EN:NOT

European Parliament. Council. (2004b, March 31). *Directive 2004/18/EC of the European Parliament and of the Council of 31 March 2004 on the coordination of procedures for the award of public works contracts, public supply contracts and public service contracts*. Retrieved June 2, 2011 from http://eur-lex.europa.eu/LexUriServ/LexUriServ.do?uri=CELEX:32004L0018:EN:NOT

European Union. (2010a, December 15). *Digital agenda: E-government action plan - What would it do for me?* Retrieved May 31, 2011, from the http://europa.eu/rapid/pressReleasesAction.do?reference=MEMO/10/681

European Union. (2010b, December 15). *Digital agenda: Pilot projects show the way in easy access to online public services across the EU*. Retrieved June 10, 2011, from http://europa.eu/rapid/pressReleasesAction.do?reference=MEMO/10/680

European Union. (2011). *Summaries of EU legislation: Common procurement vocabulary.* Retrieved from http://europa.eu/legislation_summaries/internal_market/businesses/public_procurement/l22008_en.htm

Eurostat. (2011). *Value of public procurement which is openly advertised, as a percentage of GDP*. Retrieved from http://epp.eurostat.ec.europa.eu/tgm/table.do?tab=table&init=1&plugin=1&language=en&pcode=tsier090

Eurovoc. (2010). *Multilingual thesaurus of the European Union.* Reviewed http://eurovoc.europa.eu/.

EVERY. (2012). *Everyone counts*. Retrieved February 5, 2012, from http://www.everyonecounts.com

EXIS-TI. (2011). Retrieved from http://www.exis-ti.com/

Faris, C. W., Robinson, P. J., & Wind, Y. (1967). *Industrial buying and creative marketing*. Boston, MA: Allyn & Bacon.

Featherman, M. S. (2001). Extending the technology acceptance model by inclusion of perceived risk. *Proceedings of the Seventh Americans Conference on Information Systems,* (pp. 758-760).

Fensel, D., Kopecký, J., & Vitvar, T. (2008). MICROWSMO: Semantic description of restful services. WSMO Deliverable. Retrieved from http://wsmo.org/TR/d38/v0.1/20080219/d38v01_20080219.pdf

Fernández-i-Marín, X. (2010). *The impact of e-government promotion in Europe: Internet dependence and critical mass*. Communication at the Internet, Politics, Policy 2010: An Impact Assessment Conference, 16-17 September 2010. Oxford, UK: Oxford Internet Institute. Retrieved February 13, 2012, from http://fundacionorange.es/areas/28_observatorio/pdfs/DEF_26.pdf

Filkin, G., Bassam, G., & Corrigan, P. (1999). *Starting to modernize*. London, UK: New Local Government Network.

Finch, B. J. (2007). Customer expectations in online auction environments: An exploratory study of customer feedback and risk. *Journal of Operations Management, 25*(5), 985–997. doi:10.1016/j.jom.2006.10.007

Fleury, P. F., Wanke, P., & Figueiredo, K. F. (2000). *Logística empresarial: A perspectiva Brasileira. Collection COPPEAD DE Administração*. São Paulo, Brazil: Atlas.

Forrester Research Inc. (2001, April). *eFiling kick-starts government*.

Forrester. (2002). ISM/*Forrester research report on ebusiness*. Institute for Supply Management, April.

Forrester. (2003). *ISM/Forrester research report on ebusiness*. Institute for supply management, April.

Forrester, J. W. (1961). Industrial dynamics. *Editorial Pegasus., ISBN-10*, 1883823366.

Frambach, R. T. (1995). Diffusion of innovations in business –to-business markets. In M. Bruce & W. G. Biemans (Eds.), *Product development: Meeting the challenge of the design-marketing interface*, (pp. 249-245). John Wiley and Sons Ltd.

Frambach, R. T. (1993). An integrated model of organizational adoption and diffusion of innovations. *European Journal of Marketing, 27*(5), 22–41. doi:10.1108/03090569310039705

Franco, C. F. Jr. (2001). *E-business: Tecnologia da informação e negócios na Internet*. São Paulo, Brazil: Atlas.

Fu, J. R., Fan, C. K., & Chao, W. P. (2006). Acceptance of electronic tax filing: A study of tax payers intentions. *Journal of International Management, 43*(1), 109–126.

Fundación, C. T. I. C. (2012). *Public dataset catalogs faceted browser*. Retrieved ttp://datos.fundacionctic.org/sandbox/catalog/faceted/

Fung, P. (1999). Managing purchasing in a supply chain context evolution and resolution. *Logistics Information Management, 12*(5), 362–367. doi:10.1108/09576059910295788

Funston, F., & Wagner, S. (2010). *Surviving and thriving in uncertainty: Creating the risk intelligent enterprise*. Hoboken, NJ: John Wiley & Sons.

Galunic, C. D., & Eisenhardt, K. M. (1994). Renewing the strategy-structure-performance paradigm. In B. M. Staw & L. L. Cummings (Eds.), *Research in Organizational Behaviour, 16*, 215-255.

Gansler, J. S., Lucyshyn, W., & Ross, K. M. (2003). *Digitally integrating the government supply chain: E-procurement, e-finance, and e-logistics. E-University of Maryland*. USA: Government Series.

Gardenal, F. (2010, August 26-28). *Public e-procurement define, measure and optimize organizational benefits*. Paper presented at the 4th International Public Procurement Conference, Seoul, South Korea. Retrieved July 14, 2011, from http://www.ippa.org/IPPC4/Proceedings/05e-Procurement/Paper5-1.pdf

Garson, G. D. (2008). *Topics in multivariate analysis*. Retrieved from http://www2.chass.ncsu.edu

Gartner Group. (2000). *E-government strategy: Cubing the circle*. Research Notes, Strategic Planning Assumption.

Gateway Strategic Consultancy Services. S.L. (2012). *Company web site*. Retrieved from http://gateway-scs.es/en/

Gattiker, T., Huang, X., & Schwarz, J. (2007). Negotiation, email, and internet reverse auctions: how sourcing mechanisms deployed by buyers affect suppliers' trust. *Journal of Operations Management*, *25*(1), 184–202. doi:10.1016/j.jom.2006.02.007

Gebauer, J. & Segev. A. (2001). *Changing shapes of supply chains – How the internet could lead to a more integrated procurement function*. University of California, Berkeley, Haas School of Business. Fisher Center for Information Technology and Marketplace transformation - Working Paper 01 – WP – 1041.

Gefen, D., Straub, D. W., & Karahana, E. (2003). Trust and TAM in online shopping: An integrated model. *Management Information Systems Quarterly*, *27*(1), 51–90.

Gharajedaghi, J. (2011). *Systems thinking: Managing chaos and complexity – A platform for designing business architecture*. Amsterdam, The Netherlands: Morgan Kaufmann.

Ghoshal, S., Korine, H., & Szulansi, G. (1994). Interunit communication in multinational corporations. *Management Science*, *40*(1), 96–110. doi:10.1287/mnsc.40.1.96

Gichoya, D. (2005). Factors affecting the successful implementation of ICT projects in government. *The Electronic. Journal of E-Government*, *3*(4), 175–184.

Giunipero, L. G., & Sawchuk, C. (2000). *E-purchasing plus – Changing the way corporations buy*. ShareMax.com.

Godoy, A. S. (1995). Introdução à pesquisa qualitativa e suas possibilidades. *Revista de Administração de Empresas, 35*(3).

Golder, A. (2004). Buyers prefer web to find suppliers. *Supply Management*, *9*(10), 8–10.

Gore, J. (1996). *Chaos, complexity, and the military*. National Defense University.

Government of United Kingdom & Transparency Board. (2010). *New public sector transparency board and public data transparency principles*. Retrieved http://data.gov.uk/blog/new-public-sector-transparency-board-and-public-data-transparency-principles

Graham, I. (2006). *Business rules management and service oriented architecture*. John Wiley & Sons.

Griffith, D. (2006). Human capital in the supply chain of global firms. *Organizational Dynamics*, *35*(3), 251–263. doi:10.1016/j.orgdyn.2006.05.004

Guida, G., & Tasso, C. (1994). *Design and development of knowledge-based systems: From life cycle to development methodology*. Chichester, UK: John Wiley & Sons.

Gül, H. (2010). Kamu İhale Kurumu Başkanı Hasan Gül'ün Bilişim Ajandası Dergisine verdiği bilgi, *Bilişim Dergisi, 127*. Retrieved July 14, 2011, from http://www.bilisimdergisi.org/s127

Gül, H. (2011, April 4). *Kamu İhale Kurumu Başkanı Hasan Gül'ün Telekom Dünyasına verdiği bilgi*. Retrieved July 14, 2011, from http://www.telekomdunyasi.com/?action=haber_detay&id=78

Gunasekaran, A., & Ngai, E. W. T. (2008). Adoption of e-procurement in Hong Kong: An empirical research. *International Journal of Production Economics*, *113*, 159–175. doi:10.1016/j.ijpe.2007.04.012

Gunasekaran, A., & Ngai, M. (2004). Information systems in supply chain integration and management. *European Journal of Operational Research*, *159*(2), 269–295. doi:10.1016/j.ejor.2003.08.016

Guttman, R. H., & Maes, P. (1998). Agent-mediated integrative negotiation for retail electronic commerce. In *Proceedings of the Workshop on Agent Mediated Electronic Trading* (AMET'98).

Hagel, J., & Singer, M. (1999). Unbundling the corporation. *Harvard Business Review*, (2): 133.

Hair, J. F., Black, W. C., Babin, B. J., & Anderson, R. E. (2010). *Multivariate data analysis*. Upper Saddle River, NJ: Prentice-Hall.

Hambleton, R. (1998). Competition and contracting in UK local government. In Oatley, N. (Ed.), *Cities, economic competition and urban policy*. London, UK: Paul Chapman.

Handfield, R.B., Straight, S. L., & Stirling, W. A. (2002). Reverse auctions: how do supply managers really feel about them. *Inside Supply Management, 13*(11), 56–61.

Handfield, R. B., & Nichols, E. L. Jr. (1999). *Introduction to supply chain management* (p. 2). Upper Saddle River, NJ: Prentice-Hall.

Hannon, D. (2003, August 14). Purchasing survey shows e-sourcing adoption stalls. *Purchasing.*

Hannon, D., Hartley, J., & Lane, M. D. (2004, June 3). GSK closes the loop using e-sourcing tools. Purchasing.

Hannon, D. (2006). E-Sourcing finds its place. *Purchasing, 135*(16), 51–52.

Harland, C., Gibbs, J., & Sutton, R. (2000). Supply strategy for the public sector: Framing the issues. *Proceedings of the International Purchasing & Supply Research and Education Association* (IPSERA) Annual Conference, London, Western Ontario.

Harland, C., Graves, A., Knight, L., & Lamming, R. (2002). *The future of public sector supply: Developing a research agenda.* UK: Centre for Research in Strategic Purchasing and Supply. University of Bath.

Hartley, J., Lane, M. D., & Hong, Y. (2004). An exploration of the adoption of e-auctions in supply management. *IEEE Transactions on Engineering Management, 51*(2), 153–161. doi:10.1109/TEM.2004.826010

Hashim, R. (2006). Electronic procurement (e-procurement) implementation issues in the Selangor local government. *Proceedings of the 6th European Conference on e-Government*, Pilipps-Universitat, Marburg, Germany.

Hatch, J. A. (2002). *Doing qualitative research in education settings.* Albany, NY: State University of New York Press.

Hawking, P., Stein, A., Wyld, D. C., & Foster, S. (2004). E-procurement: Is the ugly duckling actually a swan down under? *Asia Pacific Journal of Marketing and Logistics, 16*(1), 3–26. doi:10.1108/13555850410765140

Head of State of Spain. (2007, June 22). *Law 11/2007, of 22 June, on citizen's electronic access to public services.* Retrieved May 31, 2011, from http://www.boe.es/boe/dias/2007/06/23/pdfs/A27150-27166.pdf

Head of State of Spain. (2007, October 30). *Law 30/2007 of 30th October, on public sector contracts.* Retrieved May 31, 2011, from http://www.boe.es/boe/dias/2007/10/31/pdfs/A44336-44436.pdf

Head of State of Spain. (2011, March 4). *Law 2/2011, of March 4, sustainable economy.* Retrieved May 31, 2011, from www.boe.es/boe/dias/2011/03/05/pdfs/BOE-A-2011-4117.pdf

Heeks, R. (2008). Benchmarking e-government: Improving the national and international measurement evaluation and comparison of e-government. In Irani, Z., & Love, P. (Eds.), *Evaluation of information systems.* Butterworth-Heinemann. doi:10.1016/B978-0-7506-8587-0.50017-2

Heijden, H., Verhage, T., & Creemers, M. (2003). Understanding online purchase intentions. Contributions from technology and trust perspective. *European Journal of Information Systems, 12*(1), 41–48. doi:10.1057/palgrave.ejis.3000445

Henriksen, H. Z., Mahnke, V., & Hansen, J. M. (2004). Public e-Procurement adoption: Economic and political rationality. *Proceedings of the 37th Hawaii International Conference on System Sciences* (HICSS-37). IEEE Computer Society.

Heywood, J. B., Barton, M., & Heywood, C. (2001). *E-procurement: A guide to successful e-procurement implementation.* Financial Times Prentice Hall.

Holloway, R. E. (1977). *Perception of an innovation.* Syracuse University Project Advance, Unpublished Doctoral Dissertation, Syracuse University.

Hong, W., Thong, J., Wong, W., & Tam, K. Y. (2001). Determinants of user acceptance of digital libraries: An empirical examination of individual differences and system characteristics. *Journal of Management Information Systems, 18*(3), 97–124.

Horstmann, M., & Kritland, M. (1997). *DCOM architecture. MSDN Library, Specifications.* Microsoft Corp.

Hovhannisian, K. (2001). *Exploring on the technology landscapes: Real options thinking in the context of the complexity theory.* Paper presented at the DRUID Winter Conference (January 17-19, 2002), Aalborg, Denmark.

Hu, Y., Yang, Q. P., Sun, X., & Wei, P. (2008). Applying Semantic Web services to enterprise Web. *Engineering, September,* 9–11.

Huang, X.-G., Shen, L., & Feng, Y.-H. (2008). A user authentication scheme based on fingerprint and USIM card. *International Conference on Intelligent Information Hiding and Multimedia Signal Processing*, (pp. 1261-1264).

Huang, C., & Lin, S. C. (2010). Sharing knowledge in a supply chain using the semantic web. *Expert Systems with Applications*, *37*(4), 3145–3161. doi:10.1016/j.eswa.2009.09.067

Hughes, M., Shoffner, M., Hamner, D., Winslow, M., & Hughes, C. (1999). Java network programming. *Manning Publications.*, *ISBN-10*, 188477749X.

Hui, E. Y. Y., & Tsang, A. H. C. (2004). Sourcing strategies of facilities management. *Journal of Quality in Maintenance Engineering*, *10*(2), 85–92. doi:10.1108/13552510410539169

Hult, G., Ketchen, D., Cavusgil, T., & Calantone, R. (2006). Knowledge as a strategic resource in supply chains. *Journal of Operations Management*, *24*(5), 458–475. doi:10.1016/j.jom.2005.11.009

Hur, D., Hartley, J., Lane, M. D., & Duplaga, E. (2006). Exploring the barriers to the adoption of e-auctions for sourcing. *International Journal of Operations & Production Management*, *26*(2), 202–221. doi:10.1108/01443570610641675

Hur, D., & Mabert, V. (2006). Implementing reverse e-auctions: A learning process. *Business Horizons*, *49*(1), 21–29. doi:10.1016/j.bushor.2005.05.001

Hur, D., Mabert, V., & Hartley, J. (2007). Getting the most out of reverse e-auction investment. *Omega*, *35*(4), 403–416. doi:10.1016/j.omega.2005.08.003

Huxham, C. (Ed.). (1995). *Creating collaborative advantage*. London, UK: Sage.

ICMA. (October 2002). *Electronic government survey findings*. Retrieved March 20, 2003, from http://egov.e21corp.com/site/html/eNewsletter/oct2002/survey.html

Igbaria, M., Guimaraes, T., & Davis, G. B. (1995). Testing the determinants of microcomputer usage via a structural equation model. *Journal of Management Information Systems*, *11*(4), 87–114.

Igbaria, M., Parasuraman, S., & Baroudi, J. J. (1996). A motivational model of computer usage. *Journal of Management Information Systems*, *13*(1), 127–143.

Igbaria, M., Zinatelli, N., Cragg, P., & Cavaye, A. (1997). Personal computing acceptance factors in small firms: A structural equation model. *Management Information Systems Quarterly*, *21*(3), 279–302. doi:10.2307/249498

ILBS – International Law Book Series. Laws of Malaysia. (2003). *Local Government Act 1976 (Act 171) & Subsidiary Legislation: As at 25th July 2003*. Kuala Lumpur, Malaysia: Direct Art Company.

James, G. (2000). Empowering bureaucrats. *MC Technology Marketing Intelligence*, *20*(12), 62–68.

Janssen, M., & Kuk, G. (2006). *A complex adaptive system perspective of enterprise architecture in electronic government*. Paper presented at the 39th Hawaii International Conference on System Sciences, Hawaii

Jantan, M., Ramayah, T., & Chin, W. W. (2001). Personal computer acceptance by small and medium sized companies evidence from Malaysia. *Journal Management & Business*, *3*(1), 1–14.

Jap, S. (2002). Online reverse auctions: Issues, themes and prospects for the future. *Journal of the Academy of Marketing Science*, *30*(4), 506–525. doi:10.1177/009207002236925

Jap, S. (2003). An exploratory study of the introduction of online reverse auctions. *Journal of Marketing*, *67*, 96–107. doi:10.1509/jmkg.67.3.96.18651

Jap, S. (2007). The impact of online reverse auction design on buyer–supplier relationships. *Journal of Marketing*, *71*(1), 146–159. doi:10.1509/jmkg.71.1.146

Jarvenpaa, S. L., & Todd, P. A. (1997). Consumer reactions to electronic shopping in the World Wide Web. *International Journal of Electronic Commerce*, *1*(2), 59–88.

Jaworski, B. J., & Kohli, A. K. (1993). Market orientation: antecedents and consequences. *Journal of Marketing*, *57*, 53–70. doi:10.2307/1251854

Jeeva, A. (2011). *Poverty reduction strategies via procurement policies.* Paper presented at the The 20th Annual IPSERA Conference International Purchasing and Supply Education and Research Association, Maastricht, The Netherlands: Maastricht University.

Jennergren, L. P., & Muller, W. (1973). Simulation experiments of resource-allocation decisions in two-level organizations. *Social Science Research*, *2*(4), 333–352. doi:10.1016/0049-089X(73)90008-2

Johnson, F. P., & Leenders, M. R. (2003). Gaining and losing pieces of the supply chain. *Journal of Supply Chain Management*, *39*(1). doi:10.1111/j.1745-493X.2003.tb00147.x

Johnson, P. F., & Leenders, M. R. (2006). A longitudinal study of supply organizational change. *Journal of Purchasing and Supply Management*, *12*, 332–342. doi:10.1016/j.pursup.2007.01.007

Joia, L. A., & Zamot, F. (2002). Reverse auctions in the Brazilian government: A case study. Retrieved December 4, 2008, from www.ebape.fgv.br/academico/asp/dsp_opb_artigos.asp

Joia, L. A., & Zamot, F. (2002, June 17-19). *Eprocurement by the Brazilian government some findings from a case study.* Paper presented at the 15th Bled Electronic Commerce Conference eReality: Constructing the eEconomy, Bled, Slovenia. Retrieved July 14, 2011, from http://ecom.fov.uni-mb.si/proceedings.nsf/Proceedings/6C6F126D51DD7065C1256E9F00354995/$File/joia.pdf

Jones, E., Sundaram, S., & Chin, W. (2002). Factors leading to sales force automation use: A longitudinal analysis. *Journal of Personal Selling & Sales Management*, *22*(3), 145–157.

Kagel, J. H., & Levin, D. (1986). The winner's curse and public information in common value auctions. *The American Economic Review*, *76*(5), 894–920.

Kagel, J. H., Levin, D., Battalio, R., & Meyer, D. J. (1989). First-price common value auctions: Bidder behavior and the winner's curse. *Economic Inquiry*, *27*(2), 241–258. doi:10.1111/j.1465-7295.1989.tb00780.x

Kagel, J. H., & Roth, A. E. (1995). *Auctions: A survey of experimental research. The handbook of experimental economics*. New York, NY: Princeton University Press.

Kakabadse, A., & Kakabadse, N. (2005). Outsourcing: current and future trends. *Thunderbird International Business Review*, *47*(2), 183–204. doi:10.1002/tie.20048

Kalakota, R., & Robison, M. (1999). *E-business, roadmap for success*. Addison-Wesley Longman.

Kamann, D. J., et al. (2004). Joint purchasing: Theory and practice. *International Purchasing and Supply Education and Research Association Conference*, Catania, (pp. 511-520).

Kamu İhale Kurumu ile Sağlık Bakanlığı Arasında İmzalanan İşbirliği Protokolü. (2005, November 11). Retrieved July 14, 2011, from http://www.ihale.gov.tr/e_zirve/3_program.pps

Kanishka, K., & Hepu, D. (2010). *Exploring the public value of e-government.* 23rd Bled eConference, June 20–23, 2010; Bled, Slovenia.

Kanter, R. M. (1994). Collaborative advantage: The art of alliances. *Harvard Business Review*, (July): 96–108.

Karahanna, E., Straub, D., & Chervany, N. (1999). Information technology adoption across time: A cross-sectional comparison of pre-adoption beliefs. *Management Information Systems Quarterly*, *23*(2), 183–213. doi:10.2307/249751

Karim, M. R. A. (1999). *Reengineering the public service: Leadership and change in an electronic age*. Kuala Lumpur, Malaysia: Pelanduk Publications.

Karim, M. R. A. (2003). Technology and improved service delivery: Learning points from the malaysian experience. *International Review of Administrative Sciences: Creating Self-Confident Government*, *69*, 191–201. doi:10.1177/0020852303069002005

Karim, M. R. A., & Khalid, N. M. (2003). *E-government in Malaysia: Improving responsiveness and capacity to serve*. Selangor, Malaysia: MAMPU and Pelanduk Publications.

Katz, R., & Allen, T. J. (1985). Project performance and the locus of influence in the R&D matrix. *Academy of Management Journal*, *28*(1), 67–87. doi:10.2307/256062

Kaufmann, L., & Carter, C. R. (2003). Deciding on the mode of negotiation: To auction or not auction electronically. *Proceedings of the 14th ANARSPSCM*, (pp. 191-226).

Kelliher, F. (2007). Small firm cooperative constructs: Addressing industry power relationships. *Journal of Small Business and Enterprise Development*, *14*(3), 501–513. doi:10.1108/14626000710773574

Kelly, F., & Steinberg, R. (2000). A combinatorial auction with multiple winners for universal service. *Management Science*, *46*(4), 586–596. doi:10.1287/mnsc.46.4.586.12054

Kerr, J. (2006). The changing complexion of supplier diversity. *Supply Chain Management Review*, *10*(2), 38–45.

Kettl, D. F. (1993). *Sharing power: Public governance and private markets*. Washington, DC: The Brookings Institution.

Kim, D. (2006). Process chain: A new paradigm of collaborative commerce and synchronized supply chain. *Business Horizons*, *49*(5), 359–367. doi:10.1016/j.bushor.2005.11.004

Kim, S. W. (2007). Organizational structures and the performance of supply chain management. *International Journal of Production Economics*, *106*(2), 323–345. doi:10.1016/j.ijpe.2006.07.010

Kirkpatrick, I. (2001). Out of sight - Out of mind: Assessing the impact of markets for children's residential care. *Public Administration*, *79*(1), 49–71. doi:10.1111/1467-9299.00245

Kivisto, T. (2003). *Consortia purchasing and logistics in Kuopio area – Lessons learned from a 4 year project*. Budapest, Hungary: IRSPP Proceedings.

Klein, S. (1997). Introduction to electronic auctions. *Electronic Markets*, *7*, 3–6. doi:10.1080/10196789700000041

Klemperer, P. (1999). Auction theory: A guide to the literature. *Journal of Economic Surveys*, *13*(3), 227–286. doi:10.1111/1467-6419.00083

Klijn, E., & Teisman, G. R. (2004). Public-private partnerships: The right form at the wrong moment? An analysis of institutional and strategic obstacles. In Ghobadian, A. (Eds.), *Public-private partnerships: Policy and experience*. Basingstoke, UK: Palgrave Macmillan.

Knight, L. (2003). *Academic report from the 1st International Research Study on Public Procurement*. UK: Centre for Research in Strategic Purchasing and Supply, University of Bath.

Kopecký, J., & Vitvar, T. (2008). WSMO-Lite: Lowering the Semantic Web services barrier with modular and light-weight annotations. In *Proceedings of the 2008 IEEE International Conference on Semantic Computing*, (pp. 238–244). Washington, DC: IEEE Computer Society.

Kopecký, J., Vitvar, T., Bournez, C., & Farrell, J. (2007). SAWSDL: Semantic annotations for WSDL and XML schema. *IEEE Internet Computing*, *11*, 60–67. doi:10.1109/MIC.2007.134

Kopits, G., & Craig, J. (1998). *Transparency in government operations*. Occasional Paper. Washington, DC: IMF.

Kothari, T., Hu, C., & Roehl, W. (2005). E-procurement: An emerging tool for the hotel supply chain management. *International Journal of Hospitality Management*, *24*(3), 369–389. doi:10.1016/j.ijhm.2004.09.004

Kraljic, P. (1983). Purchasing must become supply management. *Harvard Business Review*, *61*, 109–117.

Krause, D. R., Ragatz, G. L., & Hughley, S. (1999). Supplier development from the minority supplier's perspective. *Journal of Supply Chain Management*, *35*(4), 33–41. doi:10.1111/j.1745-493X.1999.tb00242.x

Laínez, J., Bojarski, A., Espuña, A., & Puigjaner, L. (2008). Mapping environmental issues within supply chains: a LCA based approach. *Computer Aided Chemical Engineering*, *25*, 1131–1136. doi:10.1016/S1570-7946(08)80195-2

Lance, C. E., Butts, M., & Michels, L. (2006). The sources of four commonly reported cutoff criteria: What did they really say? *Organizational Research Methods*, *9*, 202–220. doi:10.1177/1094428105284919

Lanzola, G., & Suarez, F. F. (2012). Closing the technology adoption-use divide: The role of contiguous user bandwagon. *Journal of Management*, *38*(3), 836–859. doi:10.1177/0149206310369938

LAPSI Project. (2012). *The European thematic network on legal aspects of public sector information*. Reviewed http://www.lapsi-project.eu/

Larman, C. (2001). *Applying UML and patterns: An introduction to object-oriented analysis and design and the unified process* (2nd ed.). NJ: Prentice Hall.

Laudon, K. C., & Traver, C. G. (2007). *E-commerce: Business, technology, society* (3rd ed.). Upper Saddle River, NJ: Prentice Hall.

Lawrence, P. R., Kolodny, H. F., & Davis, S. M. (1982). The human side of matrix: Readings in the management of innovation, (pp. 504-519).

Lawther, W. C. (2003). Contracting for the 21st century: A partnership model. In Abramson, M. A., & Harris, R. S. III, (Eds.), *The procurement revolution* (pp. 167–216). Lanham, MD: Rowan and Littlefield.

Lee, D., Park, J., & Ahn, J. (2001). On the explanation of factors affecting e-commerce adoption. *Twenty-Second International Conference on Information Systems,* (pp. 109-120).

Lee, J. E., & Ho, P. S. (2002). A retail investor's perspective on the acceptance if Internet stock trading. *Proceedings of the 36th HICSS,* (pp. 1-11).

Lee, C. W., Kwon, I.-W. G., & Severance, D. (2007). Relationship between supply chain performance and degree of linkage among supplier, internal integration, and customer. *Supply Chain Management, 12*(6), 444–452. doi:10.1108/13598540710826371

Lee, G. G., & Lin, H. F. (2005). Customer perceptions of e-service quality in online shopping. *International Journal of Retail and Distribution Management, 33*(2), 161–176. doi:10.1108/09590550510581485

Lee, H., Padmanabhan, V., & Whang, S. (1997). The bullwhip effect in supply chains. *Sloan Management Review, 38*(3), 93–102.

Leenders, M. R., Fearson, H. E., Flynn, A. E., & Johnson, P. F. (2002). *Purchasing and supply management.* New York, NY. *McGraw-Hill Companies Inc., ISBN-13,* 978–0072370607.

Leenders, M. R., & Johnson, P. F. (2000). *Major structural changes in supply organizations*. Tempe, AZ: Center for Advanced Purchasing Studies.

Levi, M., Kleindorfer, P., & Wu, D. (2003). Codifiability, relationship-specific IT investment, and optimal contracting. *Journal of Management Information Systems, 20*(2), 77–98.

Leymann, F. (2001). *Web services flow language (WSFL) version 1.0.* IBM Software Group.

Liao, S. H., Cheng, C. H., Liao, W. B., & Chen, I. L. (2003). A Web-based architecture for implementing electronic procurement in military organizations. *Technovation, 23*(6), 521–533. doi:10.1016/S0166-4972(02)00006-8

Li, B., Akintoye, A., Edwards, P. J., & Hardcastle, C. (2005a). The allocation of risk in PPP/PFI construction projects in the UK. *International Journal of Project Management, 23*(1), 25–35. doi:10.1016/j.ijproman.2004.04.006

Li, B., Akintoye, A., Edwards, P. J., & Hardcastle, C. (2005b). Critical success factors for PPP/PFI projects in the UK construction industry. *Construction Management and Economics, 23*(5), 459–471. doi:10.1080/01446190500041537

Libet, B. (2011). Do we have free will? In Sinnott-Armstrong, W., & Nadel, L. (Eds.), *Conscious will and responsibility* (pp. 1–10). Oxford, UK: Oxford Press.

Lienhard, A. (2006). Public private partnerships (PPPs) in Switzerland: Experiences—risks—potentials. *International Review of Administrative Sciences, 72*(4), 547–563. doi:10.1177/0020852306070083

Little, M., & Webber, J. (2003, August 1). Introducing BPEL4WS 1.0: Building on WS-transaction and WS-coordination. *Web Services Journal*, 28-33.

Liu, J., Derzsi, Z., Raus, M., & Kipp, A. (2008). E-government project evaluation: An integrated framework. In Wimmer, M. A., Scholl, H. J., & Ferro, E. (Eds.), *Electronic government* (*Vol. 5184*, pp. 85–97). Berlin, Germany: Springer-Verlag. doi:10.1007/978-3-540-85204-9_8

LOD2 Project. (2012). *Creating knowledge out of interlinked data.* Retrieved from http://lod2.eu/

Lohse, G. L., & Spiller, P. (1998). Electronic shopping. *Communications of the ACM, 41*(7), 81–87. doi:10.1145/278476.278491

Lopes, E., & Santos, L. (2006). *Estratégias de e-procurement na administração pública: Uma revisão de literatura. Conferência Ibérica de Sistemas e Tecnologias de Informação*. CISTI.

Lorange, P., & Roos, J. (1992). *Strategic alliances: Formation, implementation and evolution*. Oxford, UK: Blackwell.

Lösch, A., & Lambert, J. S. (2007). E-reverse auctions revisited: An analysis of context, buyer-supplier relations and information behavior. *The Journal of Supply Chain Management*, *43*(4), 47–63. doi:10.1111/j.1745-493X.2007.00040.x

Lowe, D., & Ng, S. (2006). *The implications of complex adaptive systems thinking for future command and control*. Paper presented at 11th International Command and Control Research and Technology Symposium (September, 2006). Cambridge, UK.

Lucking-Reiley, D. (1999). Using field experiments to test equivalence between auction formats: Magic on the Internet. *The American Economic Review*, *89*(5), 1063–1080. doi:10.1257/aer.89.5.1063

Lucking-Reiley, D., Bryan, D., Prasad, N., & Reeves, D. (2007). Pennies from eBay: The determinants of price in online auctions. *The Journal of Industrial Economics*, *55*(2). doi:10.1111/j.1467-6451.2007.00309.x

Lynette, I. M., & Stephen, H. H. (2003). *Authentication and its privacy effects*. IEEE Computer Society, National Academy of Sciences.

Lysons, K., & Farrington, B. (2006). *Purchasing and supply chain management* (7th ed.). Essex, UK: Pearson Education.

Mabert, V., & Schoenherr, T. (2001). Evolution of online auctions in B2B procurement. *PRACTIX*, *5*(1), 15–19.

Mabert, V., & Skeels, J. (2002). Internet reverse auctions: Valuable tool in experienced hands. *Business Horizons*, *45*(4), 70–76. doi:10.1016/S0007-6813(02)00229-X

MacKenzie, C. M., Laskey, K., McCabe, F., Brown, P. F., & Metz, R. (2006). *Reference model for service oriented architecture 1.0* (pp. 1–31). OASIS Open.

Mahadeo, J. D. (2009). Towards an understanding of the factors influencing the acceptance and diffusion of e-government services. *Electronic. Journal of E-Government*, *7*(4), 391–402.

Mahmoud, T. (2009). Semantic SOA-based model to be applied in business environments. *CENTERIS 2009 Conference on ENTERprise Information Systems Proceedings*, (pp. 473-482). Ofir, Portugal.

Maira, A. N., & Taylor, M. R. (1999). *The big picture: An overview of eletronic commerce. Prism. First Quarter. Arthur D.* Little.

Malhotra, N. K. (2001). *Pesquisa de marketing: Uma orientação aplicada*. Porto Alegre, Brazil: Bookman.

Manchester Declaration. (2005, November 24). Retrieved July 14, 2011, from http://ec.europa.eu/information_society/activities/egovernment/docs/pdf/manchester_declaration.pdf

Maniatopoulos, G. (2004). Enacting e-procurement technologies within UK local authorities. *Proceedings of the IADIS International Conference e-Society*, Vol. 2, (pp. 850–854).

Manly, B. F. J. (2000). *Multivariate statistical methods: A primer*. New York, NY: CRC Press.

Manolis, C., Gassenheimer, B., & Winsor, R. D. (2004). The moderating effect of solidarity as conduct: A theoretical and empirical perspective. *Journal of Marketing & Practice*, *12*(3), 48–60.

Marcoulides, G. A., & Hershberger, S. L. (1997). *Multivariate statistical methods: A first course*. Mahwah, NJ: L Erbaum.

Marín, J. L. (2011). *Euroalert.net: Building a pan-European platform to aggregate public procurement data and deliver commercial services for SMEs powered by open data*. Presented at the Digital Agenda Assembly.

Martin, D., Burstein, M., Mcdermott, D., Mcilraith, S., Paolucci, M., & Sycara, K. (2007). Bringing semantics to Web services with OWL-S. *World Wide Web (Bussum)*, *10*, 243–277. doi:10.1007/s11280-007-0033-x

Martin, S. (2002). Best value: New public management or new direction? In Mclaughlin, K., Osborne, S. P., & Ferlie, E. (Eds.), *New public management: Current trends and future prospects*. London, UK: Routledge.

Mathieson, K. (1991). Predicting user intention: Comparing the technology acceptance model with theory of planned behavior. *Information Systems Research*, *2*(3), 173–191. doi:10.1287/isre.2.3.173

Mauboussin, M. (2011). Embracing complexity. *Harvard Business Review*, (September): 89–92.

McAfee, P. R., & McMillan, J. (1987). Auctions and bidding. *Journal of Economic Literature*, *25*(2), 699–738.

Meier, R., Williams, M., & Singley, R. (2002). The strategic role of reverse auctions in the quotation and selection process. *PRACTIX*, *5*(3), 13–17.

Mell, P., & Grance, T. (2011). *The NIST definition of cloud computing*. Gaithersburg, MD: National Institute of Standards and Technology.

Meyer, T. (2011, February). *E-procurement: Public procurement worth two trillion euros needs smarter spending*. Deutsche Bank Research, Germany. Retrieved July 14, 2011, from http://www.dbresearch.de/PROD/DBR_INTERNET_DE-PROD/PROD0000000000269867.PDF

Miles, M. B., & Huberman, A. M. (1994). *Qualitative data analysis: An expanded source book* (2nd ed.). Thousand Oaks, CA: Sage.

Miles, R. E., & Snow, C. C. (1978). *Organizational strategy, structure and process*. New York, NY: McGraw Hill.

Milgrom, P. (1989). Auctions and bidding: A primer. *The Journal of Economic Perspectives*, *3*(3), 3–22.

Milgrom, P., & Roberts, J. (1992). *Economics, organization and management*. Upper Saddle River, NJ: Prentice Hall.

Millet, I., Parente, D., Fizel, J., & Venkatraman, R. (2004). Metrics for managing online procurement auctions. *Interfaces*, *34*(3), 171–179. doi:10.1287/inte.1040.0073

Min, H. (1994). International supplier selection: a multi-attribute utility approach. *International Journal of Physical Distribution & Logistics Management*, *24*(5), 24–33. doi:10.1108/09600039410064008

Min, H. (2009). The best-practice supplier diversity program at Caterpillar. *Supply Chain Management*, *14*(3), 167–170. doi:10.1108/13598540910954502

Min, H., & Zhou, G. (2002). Supply chain modeling: Past, present and future. *Computers & Industrial Engineering*, *43*, 231–249. doi:10.1016/S0360-8352(02)00066-9

Ministers of European Union (EU) Member States, Accession States and Candidate Countries and Ministers of the European Free Trade Area (EFTA) Countries. (2005, November 24). *Ministerial declaration approved unanimously on 24 November 2005, Manchester, United Kingdom*. Retrieved May 30, 2011, from http://ec.europa.eu/information_society/activities/e-Government/docs/pdf/manchester_declaration.pdf

Ministers responsible for eGovernment policy of the European Union (EU) Member States, the Candidate Countries and the European Free Trade Area (EFTA). (2009, November 18). *Ministerial declaration on eGoverment*. Malmö, Sweden Retrieved May 30, 2011, from http://ec.europa.eu/information_society/activities/e-Government/events/past/malmo_2009/press/ministerial-declaration-on-e-Government.pdf

Minor, E. D., Hensley, R. L., & Wood, D. R. (1994). A review of empirical manufacturing strategy studies. *International Journal of Operations & Production Management*, *14*(1), 5–25. doi:10.1108/01443579410049252

Mollenkopf, D., Gibson, A., & Ozanne, L. (2000). The integration of marketing and logistics: An empirical examination of New Zealand firms. *Journal of Business Logistics*, *21*(2), 89–112.

Monteiro, J. C. (2002). *Logistica S/A - A logística corporativa auto suficiente*. Monograph at Instituto de Ciências Sociais (ICS) of AEUDF, Brasília.

Monti, M. (2010). *A new strategy for the single market – At the service of Europe's economy and society*. Retrieved from http://ec.europa.eu/bepa/pdf/monti_report_final_10_05_2010_en.pdf

Montier, J. (2010). *The little book of behavioral investing*. Hoboken, NJ: John Wiley & Sons.

Moon, J. M., & Kim, Y. G. (2001). Extending the TAM for a World-Wide-Web context. *Information & Management*, *38*, 217–230. doi:10.1016/S0378-7206(00)00061-6

Moon, M. J. (2005). E-procurement management in state governments: Diffusion of e-procurement practices and its determinants. *Journal of Public Procurement*, *5*(1), 54–72.

Moore, G. C. (1987). End user computing and office automation: A diffusion of innovations perspective. *INFOR*, *25*(3), 214–235.

Moore, G. C., & Benbasat, I. (1991). Development of an instrument to measures the perceptions of adopting an information technology innovation. *Information Systems Research*, *2*(3), 173–199. doi:10.1287/isre.2.3.192

Moreno-Luzon, M. D., & Peris, F. J. (1998). Strategic approaches, organizational design and quality management-integration in a fit and contingency model. *International Journal of Quality Science*, *3*(4), 328–347. doi:10.1108/13598539810243667

Mortensen, M., & Arlbjorn, J. (2012). Inter-organizational supplier development: The case of customer attractiveness and strategic fit. *Supply Chain Management: An International Journal*, *17*(2), 152–171. doi:10.1108/13598541211212898

Mukhopadhyay, B. (2011). Evaluating public procurement. *Review of Market Integration*, *3*(1), 21–68. doi:10.1177/097492921100300103

Multimedia Development Corporation. (n.d.). *The MSC Malaysia flagship applications*. Retrieved from http://www.MSCMalaysia.com

Murray, J. G., Rentell, P. G., & Geere, D. (2008). Procurement as a shared service in English local government. *International Journal of Public Sector Management*, *21*(5), 540–555. doi:10.1108/09513550810885822

Muse, (2000). *The role of group purchasing organizations in the US health care system*. Washington, DC: HIGPA.

MyGovernment. *The Malaysia Government's official portal*. Retrieved March 19, 2007, from http://www.myGoverment.com/

Nazário, P. (2002). *A importância de sistemas de informação para a competitividade logística*. Centro de Estudos Logística – COPPEAD/UFRJ. Rio de Janeiro. Retrieved December 14, 2008, from http://www.cel.coppead.ufrj.br/fr- bench2.htm

Ndubisi, N. O., Gupta, O. K., & Ndubisi, G. C. (2005). The moguls' model of computing: Integrating the moderating impact of users' persona into the technology acceptance model. *Journal of Global Information Technology Management*, *8*(1), 27–47.

Ndubisi, N., Jantan, M., & Richardson, S. (2001). Is the technology acceptance model valid for entrepreneurs? Model testing and examining usage determinants. *Asian Academy of Management Journal*, *6*(2), 31–54.

Neale, P., Thapa, S., & Boyce, C. (2006). *Preparing a case study: A guide for designing and conducting a case study for evaluation input.* Pathfinder International. Retrieved July 15, 2011, from http://www.pathfind.org/site/DocServer/m_e_tool_series_case_study.pdf

Neef, D. (2001). *E-procurement: From strategy to implementation*. Upper Saddle River, NJ: Prentice Hall.

Nelson, D., Moody, P., & Stegner, J. (2002). *The purchasing machine: How the top ten companies use best practices to manage their supply chains* (p. 184). New York, NY: The Free Press.

Nelson, K. L., & Svara, J. H. (2012). Form of government still matters: Fostering innovation in U.S. municipal governments. *American Review of Public Administration*, *42*(3), 257–281. doi:10.1177/0275074011399898

Neuman, W. L. (2003). *Social research methods: Qualitative and quantitative approaches* (5th ed.). Boston, MA: Allyn and Bacon.

Nielsen, J., Molich, R., Snyder, C., & Farrell, S. (2000). *E-commerce user experience: Trust*. Fremont, CA: Nielsen Norman Group. Retrieved March 1, 2001, from http://www.nngroup.com/reports/ecommerce/

Nollet, J., & Beaulieu, M. (2003). The development of group purchasing: An empirical study in the healthcare sector. *Journal of Purchasing and Supply Management*, *9*, 3–10. doi:10.1016/S0969-7012(02)00034-5

Novaes, A. G. (2001). *Logística e gerenciamento da cadeia de distribuição: Estratégia, operação e avaliação*. Rio de Janeiro, Brazil: Campus.

Office of the Prime Minister. (2002). *e-Türkiye Girişimi I. Ara Rapor*, Mayıs.

Office of the Prime Minister. (2003). *e-Dönüşüm Türkiye Projesi*. 27 Şubat 2003 tarihli genelge.

Official e-Government Website of the Ministry of Territorial Policy and Public Administration of Spain. (n.d.). Retrieved May 31, 2011, from http://administracionelectronica.gob.es

Özbilgin, I. G., & Imamalu, M. Y. (2011). The impact of dynamic purchasing systems in the electronic public procurement processes. *Procedia Computer Sciences*, *3*, 1571–1575. doi:10.1016/j.procs.2011.01.051

Paine, von S., Atreya, M., & Hammond, B. (2002). *Digital signatures*. McGraw-Hill Professional.

Panayiotou, N. A., Gayialis, S. P., & Tatsiopoulos, I. P. (2004). An e-procurement system for governmental purchasing. *International Journal of Production Economics*, *90*(1), 79–102. doi:10.1016/S0925-5273(03)00103-8

Panayiotou, N., Gayialis, P., & Tatsiopoulos, P. (2004). An e-procurement system for governmental purchasing. *International Journal of Production Economics*, *90*(1), 79–102. doi:10.1016/S0925-5273(03)00103-8

Papazoglou, M. P. (2003). Service-oriented computing: Concepts, characteristics and directions. In *Proceedings of the Fourth International Conference on Web Information Systems Engineering*. Los Alamitos, NM: IEEE Press.

Parente, D. H. (1998). Across the manufacturing-marketing interface: classification of significant research. *International Journal of Operations & Production Management*, *18*(12), 1205–1222. doi:10.1108/01443579810236638

Parente, D. H., Venkataraman, R., Fizel, J., & Millet, I. (2004). A conceptual research framework for analyzing online auctions in a B2B environment. *Supply Chain Management: An International Journal*, *9*(4), 287–294. doi:10.1108/13598540410550037

Parker, D., & Vaidya, K. (2000). An economic perspective on innovation networks. In Conway, S., & Jones, O. (Eds.), *Social interaction and organisational change*. London, UK: Imperial College Press.

Parycek, P., & Prosser, A. (Eds.). (2010). *EDem2010, Proceedings of the 4th International Conference on E-Democracy*. Wien, Austria: Österreichische Computer Gesellschaft.

Patterson, A., & Pinch, P. (1995). Hollowing out the local state: Compulsory competitive tendering and the restructuring of British public sector service. *Environment & Planning A*, *27*, 1437–1461. doi:10.1068/a271437

Pavlou, P. A. (2003). Consumer acceptance of electronic commerce: Integrating trust and risk with the technology acceptance model. *International Journal of Electronic Commerce*, *7*(3), 69–103.

Pearcy, D. H., & Giunipero, L. C. (2006). The impact of electronic reverse auctions on purchase price reduction and governance structure: An empirical investigation. *International Journal of Services Technology and Management*, *7*(3), 215–236.

Pearson, J. N., Fawcett, S. E., & Cooper, A. (1993). Challenges and approaches to purchasing from minority-owned firms: A longitudinal examination. *Entrepreneurship: Theory & Practice*, *18*(2), 71–88.

Pedersen, J. (1996). Product standardization playing to win. *In Vivo (Athens, Greece)*, (June): 15–20.

Peffers, K., Tuunanen, T., Rothenberger, M., & Chatterjee, S. (2008). A design science research methodology for information systems research. *Journal of Management Information Systems*, *24*(3), 45–77. doi:10.2753/MIS0742-1222240302

Peña-López, I. (2011). *Empowerment and governance in the information society*. Position paper for the Democracy and the power of the individual conference, The Ditchley Foundation, 03-05 February 2011, Enstone. Retrieved February 14, 2012, from http://ictlogy.net/articles/20110204_ismael_pena-lopez_-_empowerment_governance_information_society.pdf

Perona, M., & Miragliotta, G. (2004). Complexity management and supply chain performance assessment: A field study and a conceptual framework. *International Journal of Production Economics*, *90*(1), 103–115. doi:10.1016/S0925-5273(02)00482-6

Perri, D. (2002). *Towards holistic governance: The new reform agenda*. Basingstoke, UK: Palgrave Macmillan.

Perrone, G., Roma, P., & Lo Nigro, G. (2010). Designing multi-attribute auctions for engineering services procurement in new product development in the automotive context. *International Journal of Production Economics*, *124*(1), 20–31. doi:10.1016/j.ijpe.2009.10.003

Phillips, W., Knight, L., Caldwell, N., & Warrington, J. (2007). Policy through procurement - The introduction of digital signal process (DSP) hearing aids into the English NHS. *Health Policy (Amsterdam)*, *80*(1), 77–85. doi:10.1016/j.healthpol.2006.03.008

Pinker, J., Seidmann, A., & Vakrat, Y. (2003). Managing online auctions: Current business and research issues. *Management Science*, *49*(11), 1457–1484. doi:10.1287/mnsc.49.11.1457.20584

Piore, M., & Sabel, C. (1984). *The second industrial order: Possibilities for prosperity*. New York, NY: Basic Books.

Plouffe, C. R., Hulland, J., & Vandenbosch, M. (2001). Research report: Richness versus parsimony in modeling technology adoption decisions – Understanding merchant adoption of a smart card-based payment system. *Information Systems Research*, *12*(2), 208–222. doi:10.1287/isre.12.2.208.9697

PLS-Ramboll. (2000). *Analysis of electronic public procurement pilot projects in the European Union*. Retrieved July 10, 2011, from http://www.eproc.org/site/guides/analysisofeprocurement.pdf

Podlogar, M. (2007). E-procurement success factors: Challenges and opportunities for a small developing country. In Pani, A. K., & Agrahari, A. (Eds.), *E-procurement in emerging economies: Theory and cases*. Hershey, PA: IDEA Group Publishing. doi:10.4018/978-1-59904-153-7.ch003

Porter, M. E. (1980). *Competitive strategy: Techniques for analyzing industries and competitors*. New York, NY: The Free Press.

Postner, H. (1990). The contracting-out problem in service sector analysis: choice of statistical unit. *Review of Income and Wealth*, *36*(2), 177–186. doi:10.1111/j.1475-4991.1990.tb00279.x

PPA. (2003). *2002 Yılı Mali Raporu* [2002 Financial Report]. Ankara.

PPA. (2004). *2003 Yılı Faaliyet Raporu* [2003 Activity Report]. Ankara.

PPA. (2005a). *2004 Yılı Faaliyet Raporu* [2004 Activity Report]. Ankara.

PPA. (2005b). *Elektronik Kamu Satınalma Sistemi Bilgi Notu, Ankara*. Retrieved July 14, 2011, from http://www.ihale.gov.tr/eihalecs/EKSAS_bilgi_notu.pdf

PPA. (2005c, June 13). *E-İhale Forumu, Ankara*. Retrieved July 14, 2011, from http://www.ihale.gov.tr/Elektronik_Ihale/Elektronik_Ihale.htm

PPA. (2005d, November 16). *E-İhale Zirvesi, İstanbul*. Retrieved July 14, 2011, from http://www.ihale.gov.tr/Elektronik_Ihale/Elektronik_Ihale.htm

PPA. (2006). *2005 Yılı Faaliyet Raporu* [2005 Activity Report]. Ankara.

PPA. (2007). *2006 Yılı Faaliyet Raporu* [2006 Activity Report]. Ankara.

PPA. (2008). *2007 Yılı Faaliyet Raporu* [2007 Activity Report]. Ankara.

PPA. (2009). *E-İhale: EKAP-Elektronik Kamu Alımları Platformu*. 14 Aralık 2009 Sunum.

PPA. (2010). *2009 Yılı Faaliyet Raporu* [2009 Activity Report]. Ankara.

PPA. (2011a). *EKAP Nedir? Eğitim Sunusu*. Retrieved July 14, 2011, from http://www.dmo.gov.tr/Duyurular/egitim/KİKEĞİTİMi2011SUNUMLARI/EkapNedir.pptx

PPA. (2011b). *EKAP statistics*. Retrieved July, 20, from https://ekap.kik.gov.tr/EKAP/Default.aspx

Presutti, W. D. (2003). Supply management and e-procurement: Creating value in the supply chain. *Industrial Marketing Management*, *32*(3), 219–226. doi:10.1016/S0019-8501(02)00265-1

PricewaterhouseCoopers. (2001). *Como implanter um E-Procurement na Internet*. Webb Fácil 3. Retrieved December 12, 2008, from http://www.webb.com.br

Prud'Hommeaux. E., & Seaborne, A. (2008). SPARQL query language for RDF. W3C Recommendation. Retrieved March 24, 2012, from http://www.w3.org/TR/rdf-sparql-query/

Public Procurement Law. *Laws of Turkish Republic*, No 4734 of 2002. Retrieved July 14, 2011, from http://www.mevzuat.gov.tr

Pucket, S., & Purdy, S. C. (2011). Are voluntary movements initiated preconsciously? The relationships between readiness potentials, urges, and decisions. In Sinnott-Armstrong, W., & Nadel, L. (Eds.), *Conscious will and responsibility* (pp. 1–10). Oxford, UK: Oxford Press. doi:10.1093/acprof:oso/9780195381641.003.0005

Quayle, M., et al. (2000). Comparative study of purchasing in UK and Canadian government. In *Proceedings of the 9th International Annual IPSERA Conference*, University of Western Ontario, Canada. 24–27 May.

Quayle, M. (1998). The impact of strategic procurement in the UK government sector. *International Journal of Public Sector Management, 11*(5), 397–413. doi:10.1108/09513559810226860

Quesada, G., Gonzalez, M. E., Mueller, J., & Mueller, R. (2010). Impact of e-procurement on procurement practices and performance. *Benchmarking: An International Journal, 17*(4), 516–538. doi:10.1108/14635771011060576

Rabaey, M. (2011, May 10-12). *Game theoretic real option approach of the procurement of department of defense: Competition or collaboration.* Paper presented at the 8th Annual Acquisition Research Symposium. Montery CA, USA.

Rabaey, M. (2012). A public economics approach to enabling enterprise architecture with the government cloud in Belgium. In Saha, P. (Ed.), *Enterprise architecture for connected e-government: Practices and innovations.* Hershey, PA: IGI Global.

Rabaey, M. (2012a). Holistic investment framework for cloud computing: A management-philosophical approach based on complex adaptive systems. In Bento, A., & Aggarwal, A. (Eds.), *Cloud computing service and deployment models: Layers and management.* Hershey, PA: IGI Global.

Rabaey, M., & Mercken, R. (2012). Framework of knowledge and intelligence base: From intelligence to service. In Ordoñez de Pablos, P., & Lytras, M. D. (Eds.), *Knowledge management and drivers of innovation in services industries.* Hershey, PA: IGI Global. doi:10.4018/978-1-4666-0948-8.ch017

Rabaey, M., Tromp, H., & Vandenborre, K. (2007). Holistic approach to align ICT capabilities with business integration. In Cunha, M., Cortes, B., & Putnik, G. (Eds.), *Adaptive technologies and business integration: Social, managerial, and organizational dimensions* (pp. 160–173). Hershey, PA: Idea Group Publishing.

Rabaey, M., Vandenborre, K., Vandijck, E., Timmerman, M., & Tromp, H. (2007a). Semantic web services and BPEL: Semantic service oriented architecture - Economical and philosophical issues. In Salam, A., & Stevens, J. (Eds.), *Semantic Web technologies and ebusiness: Toward the integrated virtual organization and business process automation* (pp. 127–153). Hershey, PA: Idea Group Publishing. doi:10.4018/978-1-59904-192-6.ch005

Ramayah, T., Dahlan, N., Teck, T. K., & Aafaqi, B. (2003a). Perceived web security and web-based online transaction intent. *Multimedia Cyberspace Journal (MMCJ), 1.*

Ramayah, T., Jantan, M., & Bushra, A. (2003a). Internet usage among students of institutions of higher learning: The role of motivational variables. *The Proceedings of the 1st International Conference on Asian Academy of Applied Business Conference*, Sabah, Malaysia, 10 – 12th July, 2003.

Ramayah, T., Siron, R., Dahlan, N., & Mohamad, O. (2002). Technology usage among owners/managers of SMe's: The role of demographic and motivational variables. *The Proceedings of the 6th Annual Asian-Pacific Forum for Small Business on "Small and Medium Enterprises Linkages, Networking and Clustering,* Kuala Lumpur, Malaysia.

Ramayah, T. (2006a). Doing e-research with e-library. *The International Journal of Technology Knowledge & Society, 1*(4), 71–82.

Ramayah, T. (2006b). Interface characteristics, perceived ease of use and intention to use an online library in Malaysia. *Information Development, 22*(2), 123–133. doi:10.1177/0266666906065575

Ramayah, T., & Aafaqi, B. (2004). Role of self- efficacy in e-library usage among students of a public university in Malaysia. *Malaysian Journal of Library & Information Science, 9*(1), 39–57.

Ramayah, T., Ignatius, J., & Aafaqi, B. (2005). PC usage among students in a private institution of higher learning: The moderating role of prior experience. *Educators and Education Journal*, *20*, 131–152.

Ramayah, T., Jantan, M., Mohd Noor, M. N., Razak, R. C., & Koay, P. L. (2003b). Receptiveness of Internet banking by Malaysian consumers: The case of Penang. *Asian Academy of Management Journal*, *8*(2), 1–29.

Ramayah, T., Zainudin, Y., & Youn, F. C. (2003b). The effect of self-efficacy on internet usage in the organization. *Jurnal ANALISIS*, *10*(2), 187–220.

Ram, M., & Smallbone, D. (2003). Supplier diversity initiatives and the diversification of ethnic minority businesses in the UK. *Policy Studies*, *24*(4), 187–204. doi:10.1080/0144287042000216117

Raubenheimer, J. E. (2004). An item selection procedure to maximize scale reliability and validity. *South African Journal of Industrial Psychology*, *30*(4), 59–64.

Rayport, J. F., & Jaworski, B. J. (2002). *Introduction to electronic commerce*. New York, NY: McGraw – Hill Publishers.

Ren, Z., Kwaw, P., & Yang, F. (2012). Ghana's public procurement reform and the continuous use of the traditional procurement system: The way forward. *Built Environment Project and Asset Management*, *2*(1), 4–4. doi:10.1108/20441241211235053

Richardson, L., & Ruby, S. (2007). *RESTful Web services*. O'Reilly Media.

Rigg, J., & Nattapoolwat, S. (2001). Embracing the global in Thailand: Activism and pragmatism in an era of deagrarianization. *World Development*, *29*(6), 945–960. doi:10.1016/S0305-750X(01)00021-3

Rogers, E. M. (1983). *Diffusion of innovation* (3rd ed.). New York, NY: The Free Press.

Rogers, E. M. (1995). *Diffusion of innovations*. New York, NY: The Free Press.

Rolfstam, M. (2009). Public procurement as an innovation policy tool: The role of institutions. *Science & Public Policy*, *36*(5), 349–360. doi:10.3152/030234209X442025

Ronchi, S., Brun, A., Golini, R., & Fan, X. (2010). What is the value of an IT e-procurement system? *Journal of Purchasing and Supply Management*, *16*(2), 131–140. doi:10.1016/j.pursup.2010.03.013

Rosenau, J. (2004). Strong demand, huge supply: Governance in an emerging epoch. In Bache, I., & Flinders, M. (Eds.), *Multi-level governance*. Oxford, UK: Oxford University Press. doi:10.1093/0199259259.003.0003

Rothkopf, M. H., Pekec, A., & Harstad, R. M. (1998). Computationally manageable combinational auctions. *Management Science*, *44*, 1131–1147. doi:10.1287/mnsc.44.8.1131

Rozemeijer, F. (2000). *Creating corporate advantage in purchasing*. Eindhoven, The Netherlands: Eindhoven University of Technology.

Rushton, A., Croucher, P., & Baker, P. (2010). *The handbook of logistics & distribution management*. London, UK: Kogan Page. ISBN 978 0 7494 5714 3

Saha, P. (2010). *As platform for connected government (Phase 1 Report)*.

Samtani, G., & Sadhwani, D. (2002). Enterprise application integration and Web services. In Fletcher, P., & Waterhouse, M. (Eds.), *Web services business strategies and architectures* (pp. 39–54). Expert Press, Ltd.

Satizábal, C., Páez, R., & Forné, J. (2006). *PKI trust relationships: From a hybrid architecture to a hierarchical model*. International Conference on Availability, Reliability and Security (ARES'06).

Satterthwaite, D. (2001). Reducing urban poverty: Constraints on the effectiveness of aid agencies and development banks and some suggestions for change. *Environment and Urbanization*, *13*(1), 137–157. doi:10.1177/095624780101300111

Savoie, B. J., & Lee, H. (2001). *Key technologies & concepts for supply chain systems & integration*. Marietta, GA: High Performance Concepts, Inc.

Schichtenberg, H. (2007). *Microsoft. NET 3.0 - Crashkurs*. Microsoft Press.

Schoenherr, T., & Tummala, V. (2007). Electronic procurement: A structured literature review and directions for future research. *International Journal of Procurement Management, 1*(1/2). doi:10.1504/IJPM.2007.015353

Schotanus, F., & Telgen, J. (2005). Implications of a classification of forms of cooperative purchasing. *Proceedings of the 21st IMP Conference,* 1-3 September 2005, RSM Erasmus University, The Netherlands.

Schwester, R. W. (2009). Examining the barriers to e-government adoption. *Electronic. Journal of E-Government, 7*(1), 113–122.

Scribner, K. (2007). *Microsoft Windows workflow foundation*. Microsoft Press.

Segars, A. H., & Grover, V. (1993). Re-examining perceived ease of use and usefulness: A confirmatory factor analysis. *Management Information Systems Quarterly, 17*(4), 517–525. doi:10.2307/249590

Seneviratne, S. J., & Garson, G. D. (Eds.). (1999). *Information technology and organizational change in the public sector*. Hershey, PA: Idea Group Publishing.

Shackleton, P., & Dawson, L. (2007). *Doing it tough: Factors impacting on local e-government maturity*. 20th Bled eConference, June 4–6, Bled, Slovenia.

Shah, M., & Ram, M. (2006). Supplier diversity and minority business enterprise development: Case study experience of three US multinationals. *Supply Chain Management, 11*(1), 75–81. doi:10.1108/13598540610642493

Sharma, A., & Loh, P. (2009). Emerging trends in sourcing of business services. *Business Process Management Journal, 15*(2), 149–165. doi:10.1108/14637150910949425

Shattuck, L. G., & Miller, N. L. (2006). Naturalistic decision making in complex systems: A dynamic model of situated cognition combining technological and human agents. *Organizational Behavior: Special Issue on Naturalistic Decision Making in Organizations, 27*(7), 989–1009.

SIMPLY. (2012). *Simply voting online election system*. Retrieved February 5, 2012, from http://www.simplyvoting.com

Singer, M., Konstantinidis, G., Roubik, E., & Beffermann, E. (2009). Does e-procurement save the state money? *Journal of Public Procurement, 9*(1), 58–78.

Skelcher, C. (2005). Jurisdictional integrity, polycentrism and the design of democratic governance. *Governance: An International Journal of Policy, Administration and Institutions, 18*(1), 89–110. doi:10.1111/j.1468-0491.2004.00267.x

Skjøtt-Larsen, T., Kotzab, H., & Grieger, M. (2003). Electronic marketplaces and supply chain relationships. *Industrial Marketing Management, 32*(3), 199–210. doi:10.1016/S0019-8501(02)00263-8

Slater, S. F., Weigand, R. A., & Zwirlein, T. J. (2008). The business case for commitment to diversity. *Business Horizons, 51*(3), 201–209. doi:10.1016/j.bushor.2008.01.003

Smart, A. (2009). Exploring the business for e-procurement. *International Journal of Physical Distribution & Logistics Management, 40*(3), 181–201. doi:10.1108/09600031011035083

Smeltzer, L., & Carr, A. (2003). Electronic reverse auctions: promises, risks and conditions for success. *Industrial Marketing Management, 32*(6), 481–488. doi:10.1016/S0019-8501(02)00257-2

Smeltzer, L., & Ruzicka, M. (2000). Electronic reverse auctions: integrating the tool with the strategic sourcing process. *PRACTIX, 3*(4), 1–6.

Snowden, D., & Boone, M. (2007). A leader's framework for decision making: Wise executives tailor their approach to fit the complexity of the circumstances they face. *Harvard Business Review*, (November): 68–76.

Social Security Institution. (2011). *2010 Yılı Faaliyet Raporu* [2010 Activity Report]. Ankara.

Solak, F. (2010). *Elektronik İhale Projesi*. 7. Ulusal Tıp Bilişimi Kongresi Sunusu. Retrieved July 14, 2011, from http://www.turkmia.org/files/konusma2010/solak.pptx

Solak, F. (2011). E-İhale ve Ayrıntıları. *Röportaj*, 44-46.

Somasundaram, R. (2008). Challenges in implementation of e-procurement in the Indian government. In Anttiroiko, A.-V. (Ed.), *Electronic government: Concepts, methodologies, tools, and applications* (pp. 2106–2121). New York, NY: Information Science Reference. doi:10.4018/978-1-59904-947-2.ch159

Somasundaram, R., & Damsgaard, J. (2005). Policy recommendations for electronic public procurement. *The Electronic. Journal of E-Government, 3*(3), 147–156.

SPOTME. (2012). *Make your meetings matter – SpotMe*. Retrieved February 5, 2012, from http://www.spotme.com

Sriraman, B., & Radhakrishnan, R. (2005). *Event-driven architecture augmenting service-oriented architecture*. Sun Microsystems.

Stangor, C. (2004). *Research methods for the behavioral sciences* (2nd ed.). New York, NY: Houghton Mifflin.

Starcevic, D., et al. (2008). *Inception project for e-procurement web portal*. Belgrade, Serbia: Faculty of Organizational Sciences.

State Planning Organization. (2004). *e-Dönüşüm Türkiye Projesi Kısa Dönem Eylem Planı (2003-2004)*. Ankara.

State Planning Organization. (2005). *e-Dönüşüm Türkiye Projesi 2003-2004 Kısa Dönem Eylem Planı Uygulama Sonuçları ve 2005 Eylem Planı*. Ankara.

Steane, P. D., & Walker, D. H. T. (2000). Competitive tendering and contracting public sector services in Australia—A facilities management issue. *Facilities, 18*(5), 245–255. doi:10.1108/02632770010328144

Stefan, J. P., & Santiago, R. E. (1989). The benefits of group purchasing. *Journal of Property Management, 54*(5), 50–52.

Sterman, J. D. (2010). *Business dynamics – Systems thinking and modelling for a complex world*. India: Tata McGraw-Hill.

Suarez, G., & Laguado, R. (2007, April). *Public e-procurement manual for Latin America: Conceptual and legal model, indicators, interoperability*. United Nations Publication. Retrieve May 31, 2011 from http://www.eclac.org/publicaciones/xml/8/28648/DocW130.pdf

Suchman, M. C. (1995). Managing legitimacy: Strategic and institutional approaches. *Academy of Management Review, 20*(3), 571–610.

Tanner, C., et al. (2007). *Current trends and challenges in electronic procurement: An empirical study*. 20th Bled eConference, June 4–6, Bled, Slovenia.

Tatnall, A. (2005). *Web portals: The new gateways to internet information and services*. Hershey, PA: Idea Group Publishing.

Taylor, S., & Todd, P. (1995). Understanding the information technology usage: A test of competing models. *Information Systems Research, 6*(2), 144–176. doi:10.1287/isre.6.2.144

Thai, K. V. (2004). Challenges in public procurement. In K. V. Thai, et al., (Eds.), *Challenges in public procurement: An international perspective* (Vol. 3). Boca Raton, FL: Academics Press. Retrieved July 14, 2011, from http://www.ippa.ws/ippc1_book.html

Thatte, S. (2001). *Web services for business process design (XLANG)*. Microsoft Corporation.

The Star. (2002a, 12 November). Malaysia sees growth in e-government usage. *The Star, Business*, p.11

The Star. (2006a, May 1). IRB won't send out the tax forms from next year. *The Star. Nation (New York, N.Y.)*, (n.d.), 1.

The Sun. (2006a, 19 April). eFiling digital certificate. *The Star*, p.5

Thomas, D. J., & Griffin, P. M. (1996). Coordinated supply chain management. *European Journal of Operational Research, 94*(1), 1–15. doi:10.1016/0377-2217(96)00098-7

Thomson, J. T. (2009). Remodelled and restyled e-procurement – New power relationships down under. *Electronic. Journal of E-Government, 7*(2), 183–194.

Tonkin, C. (2003). *E-procurement in the public sector: Story, myth and legend*. Dublin, Ireland: The Policy Institute, Trinity College.

Tornatzky, L. G., & Klein, J. K. (1982). Innovation characteristics and innovation adoption-implementation: A meta analysis of findings. *IEEE Transactions on Engineering Management, 29*(1), 28–45.

Torrejón, A. (2005). *Algunas reflexiones sobre las ciudades del siglo XXII*. Observatorio de la Sociedad de la Información. Retrieved February 5, 2012, from http://microsites.oii.ox.ac.uk/ipp2010/system/files/IPP2010_Fernandez-i-Marin_Paper.pdf

Triandis, H. C. (1977). *Interpersonal behavior*. Monetary, CA: Brooks/Cole.

Triviños, A. N. S. (1992). *Introdução à pesquisa em ciências sociais*. São Paulo, Brazil: Atlas.

Tsai, W. (2002). Social structure of "cooperation" within a multiunit organization: Coordination, competition, and intraorganizational knowledge sharing. *Organization Science*, *13*(2), 179–191. doi:10.1287/orsc.13.2.179.536

Turban, E. (1997). Auctions and bidding on the Internet: An assessment. *EM–Electronic Auctions, EM–Eletronic Markets, 7*(4).

Turban, E., Chung, H. M., Chung, M., & Lee, J. K. (1999). *Electronic commerce: A managerial perspective*. Upper Saddle River, NJ: Prentice Hall.

Türkay, M., Oruç, C., Fujita, K., & Tatsuyuki, A. (2004). Multi-company collaborative supply chain management with economical and environmental considerations. *Computers & Chemical Engineering*, *28*(6-7), 985–992. doi:10.1016/j.compchemeng.2003.09.005

Turner, D. N., & Martin, S. (2004). Managerialism meets community development: Contracting for social outcomes. *Policy and Politics*, *32*(1), 21–32. doi:10.1332/030557304772860021

UNPAN. (2010). *UN e-government survey 2010: Leveraging e-government at a time of financial and economic crisis*. New York, NY: UNPAN. Retrieved January 30, 2012, from http://unpan1.un.org/intradoc/groups/public/documents/un-dpadm/unpan038851.pdf

UNU-IIST-SP. (2008). *15th UNeGov.net school on foundations of electronic governance*. Retrieved April 11, 2011, from http://www.egov.iist.unu.edu/

Urquhart, J. (2010). *What cloud computing can learn from 'flash crash'*. Retrieved April 20, 2012, from http://news.cnet.com/8301-19413_3-20004757-240.html

Vaidya, K., Sajeev, A. S. M., & Callender, G. (2006). Critical factors that influence eprocurement implementation success in the public sector. *Journal of Public Procurement*, *6*(2), 70–99.

Van Der Aalst, W. M. P., Aldred, L., Dumas, M., & Ter Hofstede, A. H. M. (2004). Design and implementation of the YAWL system. *Proceedings of the 16th International Conference on Advanced Information Systems Engineering CAiSE04, 3084,* (pp. 281–305).

Van Der Aalst, W. M. P. (2008). *Challenges in business process analysis* (pp. 27–42). Springer-Verlag.

van der Hof, S., & Groothuis, M. (Eds.). (2011). *Innovating government: Normative, policy and technological dimensions of modern government*. The Hague, The Netherlands: TMC Asser Press.

Van Heck, E. (1998). How should CIOs deal with Web-based auctions? *Communications of the ACM*, *41*, 99–100. doi:10.1145/278476.278495

Van Slyke, C., Belanger, F., & Communale, C. L. (2004). Factors influencing the adoption of Web-based shopping: The impact of trust. *The Data Base for Advances in Information Systems*, *35*(2), 32–49. doi:10.1145/1007965.1007969

van Weele, A. J. (2005). *Purchasing & supply chain management: Analysis, strategy, planning and practice* (4th ed.). Australia: Thomson.

Vargas, L., & Maldonado, G. (2001). *Guia para a apresentação de trabalhos científicos*. Rio Grande do Sul, Brazil: UFRGS.

Venetianer, T. (1999). *Como vender seu peixe na Internet: Um guia prático de marketing e comércio eletrônicos*. Rio de Janeiro, Brazil: Campus.

Venkatesh, V. (2000). Determinants of perceived ease of use: Integrating control, intrinsic motivation, and emotion into the technology acceptance model. *Information Systems Research*, *11*(4), 342–365. doi:10.1287/isre.11.4.342.11872

Venkatesh, V., & Davis, F. D. (1996). A model of the antecedents of perceived ease of use: Development and test. *Decision Sciences*, *27*(3), 451–481. doi:10.1111/j.1540-5915.1996.tb01822.x

Venkatesh, V., & Davis, F. D. (2000). A theoretical expansion of the technology acceptance model: four longitudinal field studies. *Management Science*, *46*(2), 186–204. doi:10.1287/mnsc.46.2.186.11926

Venkatesh, V., Morris, G. M., Davis, B. G., & Davis, D. F. (2003). User acceptance of information technology: Toward a unified view. *Management Information Systems Quarterly*, *27*(3), 425–478.

Vergara, S. C. (1998). *Projetos e relatórios de pesquisa em administração* (2nd ed.). São Paulo, Brazil: Atlas.

Verhoef, P. C., & Langerak, F. (2001). Possible determinants of consumers' adoption of electronic grocery shopping in the Netherlands. *Journal of Retailing and Consumer Services, 8*(5), 275–285. Wikipedia. (n.d.). *Multimedia super corridor*. Retrieved December 23, 2006, from http://www.wikipedia.com/

Verissimo, P. J. (2009). The new supply chain's frontier: Information management. *International Journal of Information Management*, *29*(5), 372–379. doi:10.1016/j.ijinfomgt.2009.02.001

Vickery, S. K. (1991). A theory of production competence revisited. *Decision Sciences*, *22*, 635–643. doi:10.1111/j.1540-5915.1991.tb01286.x

Vigoroso, M. (1999). Are Internet auctions ready to gear up? *Purchasing*, *126*(2), 85–86.

Vinoski, S. (2003). Integration with Web services. *IEEE Internet Computing*, (November-December): 75–77. doi:10.1109/MIC.2003.1250587

Volberda, H. W. (1998). *Building the flexible firm, how to remain competitive*. Oxford, UK: Oxford University Press.

W3C SWEO. (2012). *Community project. Linking open data*. Retrieved http://www.w3.org/wiki/SweoIG/TaskForces/CommunityProjects/LinkingOpenData

Wagner, S. M., & Schwab, A. P. (2004). Setting the stage for successful electronic reverse auctions. *Journal of Purchasing and Supply Management*, *10*(1), 11–26. doi:10.1016/j.pursup.2003.11.001

Walker, H., et al. (2003). *The developing role of purchasing confederations in complex supply networks.* Paper presented at British Academy of Management Annual Conference 2003.

Walker, A. (2001). Value creation in buyer–seller relationships. *Industrial Marketing Management*, *30*, 365–377. doi:10.1016/S0019-8501(01)00156-0

Walley, M. J. C., & Fortin, D. R. (2005). Behavioral outcomes from online auctions: Reserve price, reserve disclosure, and initial bidding influences in the decision process. *Journal of Business Research*, *58*, 1409–1418. doi:10.1016/j.jbusres.2003.10.014

Walsh, K. (1995). *Public services and market mechanisms: Competition, contracting and the new public management.* London, UK: Macmillan.

Walsh, K., & Davis, H. (1993). *Competition and service: The impact of the Local Government Act 1988.* London, UK: HMSO.

Ward, J. (1995). *Principles of information systems management*. New York, NY: Routledge.

Waters, D. (2003). Logistics: An introduction to supply chain management. New York, NY. *Palgrave McMillan., ISBN-10*, 0333963695.

Weeds, H. (2006). *Applying option games: When should real options valuation be used?* Colchester, UK: University of Essex. Retrieved from http://privatewww.essex.ac.uk/~hfweeds/

Weigold, T., Kramp, T., & Baentsch, M. (2008). Remote client authentication. *IEEE Security & Privacy*, *6*(4), 36–43. doi:10.1109/MSP.2008.93

Weijnen, M. P. C., Herder, P. M., & Bouwmans, I. (2008). Designing complex systems: A contradiction in terms. In M. Eekhout, R. Visser, & T. Tomiyama (Eds.), *Delft science in design: A Congress on interdisciplinary design*, (pp. 235-254). Delft, The Netherlands: IOS Press.

Wellman, M. P., Reeves, D. M., Lochner, K. M., & Vorobeychik, Y. (2002). *Price prediction in a trading agent competition. Technical report*. University of Michigan.

Weske, M. (2010). *Business process management: Concepts, languages, architectures*. Springer Publishing Company, Incorporated.

WESO (Oviedo Semantic Web). (2012). *MOLDEAS-Methods on linked data for e-procurement applying semantics*. Reviewed http://purl.org/weso/moldeas/

WESO (Oviedo Semantic Web). (2012b). Retrieved from http://www.weso.es/

Whitfield, G., & Landeros, R. (2006). Supplier diversity effectiveness: Does organizational culture really matter? *Journal of Supply Chain Management*, *42*(4), 16–28. doi:10.1111/j.1745-493X.2006.00019.x

Whyte, C. K. (2000, April). E-procurement: The new competitive weapon. *Purchasing Today*, p. 25.

Wikipedia. (n.d.). *E-procurement*. Retrieved April 20, 2012, from http://en.wikipedia.org/wiki/E-procurement

Wikipedia. (n.d.). *Public eProcurement*. Retrieved April 20, 2012, from http://en.wikipedia.org/wiki/Public_eProcurement

Williamson, J. E. (2000). Many purchasers want more from GPOS. *Healthcare Purchasing News, 18*.

Williamson, O. E. (1975). *Markets and hierarchies: Analysis and anti-trust implications*. New York, NY: Free Press.

World Trade Organization. (2011). *Historic deal reached on government procurement*. Government Procurement Agreement. Retrieved from http://www.wto.org/english/news_e/news11_e/gpro_15dec11_e.htm

Worthington, I., Ram, M., Boyal, H., & Shah, M. (2008). Researching the drivers of socially responsible purchasing: A cross-national study of supplier diversity initiatives. *Journal of Business Ethics*, *79*(3), 319–331. doi:10.1007/s10551-007-9400-x

Wurman, P. R., et al. (1998). *Flexible double auctions for electronic commerce: Theory and implementation*. University of Michigan, Artificial Intelligence Laboratory. Retrieved April 2, 2011, from http://citeseerx.ist.psu.edu/viewdoc/download?doi=10.1.1.35.1798&rep=rep1&type=pdf

Wyld, D. (2000). *The auction model: How the public sector can leverage the power of e-commerce through dynamic pricing*. Southeastern Louisiana University. Hammond.

Xiaoming, M. (2008). *Study on the model of e-commerce identity authentication based on multi-biometric features identification*. International Colloquium on Computing, Communication, Control, and Management ISECS 2008.

Yin, R. E. (2001). *Estudo de caso – Planejamento e métodos* (2nd ed.). Porto Alegre, Brazil: Bookman.

Yoichi, S. (2002). Development of personal authentication systems using fingerprint with smart cards and digital signature technologies control. *Proceedings of the Conference ICARCV 2002*, Vol. 2, (pp. 996-1001).

Yoshiaki, I., Yoichi, S., & Masanori, K. (2001). Development of personal authentication system using fingerprint with digital signature technologies. *Proceedings of the Hawaii International Conference HICSS-34*, Island of Maui, Hawaii, (pp. 1-9).

Yu, Y., Yu, H., Itoga, H., & Lin, T. (2008). Decision-making factors for effective industrial e-procurement. *Technology in Society*, *30*(2), 163–169. doi:10.1016/j.techsoc.2007.12.004

Zhenhua, W. (2008). Biometrics authentication system on open network and security analysis. *Proceedings of ISECS 2008*.

Zhou, H.-G., & Dai, S.-H. (2008). PKI-based e-business security system. *Proceedings of 3rd International Conference on Innovative Computing Information and Control*, June 18 - 20, 2008, Dalian, China.

Zilbert, A. B. (2000). A comparative study of traditional electronic data interchange versus internet electronic data interchange. In D. Colton, J. Caouette, & B. Raggad (Eds.), *Proceedings ISECON*, Vol. 17. Philadelphia, PA: 501 AITP Foundation for Information Technology Education.

About the Contributors

Patricia Ordóñez de Pablos is a Professor in the Department of Business Administration in the Faculty of Economics and Business of the University of Oviedo, Spain. Her teaching and research interests focus on the areas of strategic management, knowledge management, intellectual capital measuring and reporting, organizational learning, human resources management and IT. She serves as Executive Editor of the *International Journal of Learning and Intellectual* and the *International Journal of Strategic Change Management*. She also serves as Associate Editor of *Behaviour and Information Technology*.

Juan Manuel Cueva Lovelle is a Mining Engineer from Oviedo Mining Engineers Technical School in 1983 (Oviedo University, Spain). Ph. D. from Madrid Polytechnic University, Spain (1990). Since 1985 he is a Professor at the Languages and Computers Systems Area in Oviedo University (Spain). ACM and IEEE voting member. His research interests include object-oriented technology, language processors, human-computer interface, Web engineering, modeling software with BPM, DSL, and MDA.

Jose Emilio Labra Gayo obtained his PhD. in Computer Science Engineering in 2001 at the University of Oviedo with distinction. Since 2004, he is the Dean of the School of Computer Science Engineering at the University of Oviedo and he is also the main researcher of the Semantic Web research group WESO. The group collaborates is focused on practical applications of semantic web and linked open data and has been involved in several projects with industrial partners and public administrations. Apart of teaching in the University of Oviedo, He has been regularly invited to teach in several doctorate or postgraduate courses in the Universidad Técnica Federico Santa María, in Chile, or the Universidad Pontificia de Salamanca, in Madrid, Spain. His research interests are Semantic Web technologies, programming languages, and Web engineering, where he has published a number of papers in selected conferences and journals. He participates in several committees like the European Semantic Web Conference, the International Conference on Web Engineering, or the International Workshop on Social Data on the Web.

Robert D. Tennyson is Professor of Educational Psychology at the University of Minnesota. He is Editor of a professional journal, *Computers in Human Behavior*. He also serves on editorial boards for seven other peer reviewed journals. His research and publications include topics on problem solving, concept learning, intelligent systems, testing and measurement, instructional design, and advanced learning technologies. He has directed sponsored workshops and advanced study institutes in Germany, Greece, Norway, Spain, and Taiwan. He has authored over 300 journal articles, books, and book chapters.

***

Davide Aloini is Assistant Professor at the Faculty of Engineering, University of Pisa (Department of Energy and System Engineering). He got his master degree in Management Engineering with honours at the University of Pisa in 2005. In December 2008 Davide got his PhD degree concluding the Doctoral Program in Management Engineering at the University of Rome 'Tor Vergata'. He discussed the results of a research project on the Risk Management application to ERP projects. He his member of the Italian Management Engineering Association (AiIG), the Continuous Innovation Network (CiNET) and the International Purchasing and Supply Education and Research Association (IPSERA). His research interests include: Supply Chain Management, Information Management (ERP and E-procurement systems), Risk Management, Innovation Management.

Giner Alor-Hernandez is a full-time researcher of the Division of Research and Postgraduate Studies of the Instituto Tecnologico de Orizaba. He received a MSc and a PhD in Computer Science of the Center for Research and Advanced Studies of the National Polytechnic Institute (CINVESTAV), Mexico. He is involved in several Mexican research projects and he has been a committee program member of several international conferences in computer science. His research interests include Web services, e-commerce, Semantic Web, Web 2.0, service-oriented and event-driven architectures and enterprise application integration. He is an IEEE and ACM Member.

Jose Manuel Saiz Alvarez is Lecturer at Universidad Antonio de Nebrija (2003-), Universidad Pontificia de Salamanca (1998-), Centro de Estudios Universitarios "Ramón Areces" (2003-), EBP-Madrid Chamber of Commerce & Industry (2004-) and Director of the "Economic and Law Analysis Group" (GRAEJ), Faculty of Law, Economics and Business Sciences, Universidad Antonio de Nebrija (2003-). Researcher and co-founder of the Institute to Foster Economic Research (FIEC Institute) (2004-). He collaborates in journals (*Economista Digital*)(2003-) and in radio (Onda Sierra)(2004-). Author of three books, and director of a project with Vision Net, 2004, and co-director of a project with Libros en Red, 2004. He earned his Ph.D. (summa cum laude), Economics and Business Sciences, Universidad Autónoma de Madrid, Spain, 1998. Ph.D. (summa cum laude) Sociology, Universidad Pontificia de Salamanca, Spain, 2002.

Jose María Alvarez (PhD ABD) is Master of Computer Science (2007) and Bachelor of Computer Science (2005) by the University of Oviedo. In June 2008 he was rewarded with the "Best Final Degree Project in Computer Science" by the Official Association of Computer Engineers of Asturias (Spain) thanks to this project "Activation of concepts in ontologies through the Spreading Activation Technique." From 2005 to 2010 he worked at the R\&D Department in the Semantic Technologies area within CTIC Foundation, more specifically he worked in projects related to semantic web services, rule based systems, search systems, linked data, etc. During this stage he participated in several research projects in different research programmes: PRAVIA project-PCTI Asturias cod. IE05-172 (Regional scope), PRIMA-Plan Avanza-cod. TSI-020302-2008-32 (National scope) and ONTORULE-FP7 cod. 231875 (European scope). Now he holds a position as Assistant Professor at the Department of Computer Science within the University of Oviedo and he is also senior researcher at WESO Research Group (University of Oviedo). He is waiting for defending his PhD dissertation about e-Procurement and Linked Data supervised by Dr. José Emilio Labra Gayo.

Ng Yee Boon finished her Bachelor of Management with Honours at the School of Management in USM. Currently she is employed in a multinational Malaysia. Her research focused on technology adoption by student users.

Ramón Calmeau is Master of Computer Science by the University of Basque Country. He holds a grant by the Spanish National Research Council (CSIC) finishing his research stage in the Department of Signal Detection Theory and Communications at the University of Valladolid. He is also member of ACM and is the author of several international research publications in the areas of groupware and security. He currently works at EXIS TI as Technical Manger and holds responsibility over the Software Engineering policies of the company.

Özhan Çetinkaya is an Associate Professor at Uludağ University, Faculty of Economics and Administrative Sciences in Bursa, Turkey. He received his PhD in public budgeting and fiscal planning from the Institute of Social Sciences, Uludağ University in 1996. His research interests concern public budgeting reforms, public procurement, local government, and privatization.

Guillermo Cortes-Robles obtained his Master in Science of Industrial Engineering from the Instituto Tecnológico de Orizaba and a PhD in Industrial Systems from the Institut National Polytechnique de Toulouse in France. He is today Professor of Engineering Science at the Instituto Tecnológico de Orizaba in the postgraduate school, specifically in the Engineering Management Master and the Industrial Engineering PhD. His research interests are application of TRIZ theory combined with several approaches: knowledge management, decision support systems, genetic algorithms, creativity techniques, among other approaches with the aim of accelerating the innovation process. He is today an active member of the board of the Mexican TRIZ association (AMETRIZ).

Rubén González Crespo is a Research Manager in Accessibility and Usability in Web Environments for people with severe disabilities. He has BS in Computer Management from the Politechnical University of Madrid and Computer Engineering from the Pontifical University of Salamanca, and Master in Project Management from the same university. PhD from the Pontifical University of Salamanca in 2008 and PhD Extraordinary Award given by the UPSA where he is Professor at the School of Computing (Madrid Campus) since 2005. Currently, he is the Director of the Master in Project Management, Professor of Doctoral programs organized by the University and Master's programs in GIS, Software Engineering, and Security.

Tolga Demirbaş is an Assistant Professor at Uludağ University, Faculty of Economics and Administrative Sciences in Bursa, Turkey. He received his PhD in Public Budgeting and Fiscal Planning from the Institute of Social Sciences, Uludağ University in 2006. His research interests concern public budgeting reforms, performance budgeting and auditing, fiscal transparency, and e-government.

Riccardo Dulmin was born in Piombino (LI). He graduated in Electronic Engineering from the University of Pisa and has been working with the Economics and Logistic Section of the Department of Energy and System Engineering since 1996; from 1999 to 2006 he was a Researcher and Assistant Professor in Economics and Managerial Engineering; since 2006 he has been an Associate Professor of Information Technologies for Enterprises management. His research interests include supply chain management, study, the development and applications of decision analysis, artificial intelligence tools and techniques in operations management, and informative systems.

Mai Rodríguez Entem is Graduate in Law by the University of Salamanca, Spain (1998), with specialized training in EU Law and EU Economics in the same University. In addition to her university education, she holds a Diploma as Specialist in Foreign Trade by the Spanish Foreign Trade Institute, ICEX (1999) and is a certified advisor within the International Tenders Programme, ILI, developed by the Spanish High Council of the Chambers of Commerce to promote International tendering within SMEs. From 1998 until now she held positions as junior market analyst at the Commercial Section of the Spanish Embassy in Lisbon – Portugal (2000-2001), Export Manager Assistant at the medicinal supplements company Biodes (2001-2004) and head of the Studies Department at the Latin-American Association of Underground Networks and Subways, ALAMYS within Metro de Madrid, Spain (2004-2008). She currently holds a position as head of the International Department at Gateway Strategic Consultancy Services, owner of the brand EUROALERT.NET, and is in charge for the International activities related to its commercialization, monitoring new developments in EU public procurement environment, and the legal and administrative issues related to the collection of new sources of information in public procurement in different Member States.

Erdal Eroğlu is a Researcher Assistant at Uludağ University, Faculty of Economics and Administrative Sciences in Bursa, Turkey. Getting his Master's degree in the Department of Public Finance at Uludağ University in 2009, he is still a PhD student in the same department at Uludağ University. His research interests concern public budgeting reforms, budget policy, public finance, and social and transfer expenditure.

Jorge Luis García-Alcaraz, he received the Ph. D. degree in Industrial Engineering from the Institute of Technology of Ciudad Juarez. He is currently a Professor in the department of Industrial Engineering and Manufacturing of the Autonomous University of Ciudad Juarez. His research interests are technology transfer, multivariate data analysis applied to production processes, mathematical modeling of processes and ergonomic design. He is part of doctoral committees at several universities, such as the National Autonomous University of Mexico, Autonomous University of Baja California, University of La Rioja, Zaragoza University, among others.

B. Cristina Pelayo Garcia-Bustelo is a Lecturer in the Computer Science Department of the University of Oviedo. Dr. Garcia-Bustelo has a Ph.D. from the University of Oviedo in Computer Engineering. Her research interests include object-oriented technology, Web engineering, eGovernment, and modeling software with BPM, DSL, and MDA.

Rugayah (Gy) Hashim is an Associate Professor of Management Information Systems at the Faculty of Administrative Science and Policy Studies, Universiti Teknologi MARA (UiTM), Shah Alam, Selangor, Malaysia. Currently, Dr. Hashim is seconded to the Research Management Institute, Universiti Teknologi MARA as the Head of Research Impact Unit. Her research interests include infonomics, e-government, social capital, environmental sustainability, public administration, and political science.

Ananda Jeeva is a Senior Lecturer and Researcher in procurement, supply, and logistics management with 25 years industry experience in business process improvements, operations management, work flow, customer relations management, project management, and telecommunications network planning. He has also implemented ISO9000 quality assurance projects. He holds a Bachelor of Commerce (Marketing & Management) and a Master of Business Administration. He is also an Electronics Engineer. He completed his PhD in Procurement Flexibility with a Supply Chain Management perspective at Curtin University. Ananda has published in international journals and presented in international conferences.

Luiz Antonio Joia is an Associate Professor and Principal of the *e:lab* – Research Laboratory on e-Government and e-Business at the Brazilian School of Public and Business Administration of Getulio Vargas Foundation. He is also an Adjunct Professor at Rio de Janeiro State University. He holds a B.Sc. in Civil Engineering from the Military Institute of Engineering, Brazil, and an M.Sc. in Civil Engineering and a D.Sc. in Production Engineering from the Federal University of Rio de Janeiro. He also holds an M.Sc. in Management Studies from the Oxford University, U.K. He was a World Bank consultant in Educational Technology and is an invited member of the Technical Board of the Working Group WG 8.5 (Informatics in the Public Administration) of the IFIP (International Federation for Information Processing). His research interests lie on IT for development, e-Government, e-Business, strategic use of IT, and actor-network theory.

José Emilio Labra is Associate Professor at the Department of Computer Science, (University of Oviedo) from 1992. In 2001 he obtained the degree in Doctor of Philosophy in Information and Computer Science with the dissertation "Developing Modular Language Processors through Reusable Semantic Specifications." This research work was awarded with the "Extraordinary Doctorate Award." Since 2004 he holds the position as Dean of Computer Engineering School at the University of Oviedo. From a research point view he is focused on (but not restricted to) the application and development of innovative solutions with semantic technologies. In this context he is the main researcher of the WESO Research Group at the Department of Computer Science, and he is involved in several research projects at different scopes: regional, national, and European. Finally, he is the author of more than 50 scientific publications and member, reviewer, and part of the program committee of the main conferences and journals in his research area like International Conference on Web Engineering, Social Data on The Web, Workshop on Web Services, and ACM Conferences. He is currently editor of different special issues of the IGI Global journals.

May-Chiun Lo is currently the Head of Research Capacity Enhancement Unit at Research Innovation Management Centre and a Senior Lecturer with the Faculty of Economics & Business, University of Malaysia Sarawak (UNIMAS). She graduated with First Class Honours in Finance from Universiti Kebangsaan Malaysia and holds a Master of Business Administration from Herriot-Watt University, United Kingdom, while her Ph.D in Management was awarded by Universiti Sains Malaysia. Her professional career began with Malayan Banking Berhad and she subsequently progressed to join UNIMAS. Dr. Lo's areas of expertise include corporate leadership, strategic management, entrepreneurship, banking, and financial management, and her publications have appeared in on topics such as organizational behavior, leadership in organizations, strategic planning, operational management, and ecotourism for rural destination. Dr. Lo is also active in industry consultancy, and has conducted numerous workshops and trainings on corporate leadership and financial management for industry and government agencies.

Tariq Mahmoud had studied Information Engineering at Al-Baath University (Homs, Syria) from 2000 till 2005. He was also a Research Assistant at Al-Baath University till 2007 where he started a PhD degree at Carl von Ossietzky University of Oldenburg (Germany). He is currently a Research Assistant at the working group of business information systems at the Carl von Ossietzky University of Oldenburg (Germany). His research interest include: distributed information systems, service-oriented architectures, Web services, Semantic Web services, IT for green, ontologies, and Semantic Web. His current research work focuses mainly on applying lightweight semantics to SOA-enabled enterprise solutions.

Ángel Marín is Industrial Engineer by the University of Valladolid, Spain. Between 2000 and 2002 he held a position as System Administrator and Network Administrator at the General Foundation of the University of Valladolid. In 2002, he joined Gateway Strategic consultancy Services, owner of the brand EUROALERT.NET, as Network and Systems Administrator. He currently holds a position as CTO of the company, where he is also partner and member of the board. He is responsible for the corporate policies in the areas related to R&D, software production, and exploitation and management of technological services. He developed an active work within the Open Source community, and is responsible for Gateway SCS' policy and interaction with Open Source projects. He is also co-founder of the Hoopshype.com project, which was acquired in 2008 by the media conglomerate made up by USA Today and Fantasy Sport Ventures. He is still responsible for the technological deployment and development of the site.

Jose Luis Marín is Telecommunications Engineer (2000) and holds a Business Administration Degree (2006) by the University of Valladolid, Spain. His professional career has been developed at the company Gateway Strategic Consultancy Services, owner of the brand EUROALERT.NET, of which he is one of the co-founders. He is currently one of the partners and member of the management board, as well as CEO of the company, holding the responsibility for the company's business plan implementation and R&D strategy. In his professional career he has been lead researcher in more than ten R&D projects in the field of Internet-related technologies and has taken part in the evaluation of Seventh Framework Programme projects – FP7, as independent expert in 2011 and 2012. He currently takes part in the editorial coordination of the Pocket Innova book collection focused on Innovation, and is the author of the book "Web 2.0. Una descripción muy sencilla de los cambios que estamos viviendo," Netbiblo (2010), and co-author of the blog "Open Economy." He has an active participation in the open source, open data and open knowledge communities, and has taken part as panelist in several meetings and conferences such as FICOD09 (2009), PSI Meeting (2010), Share PSI (2011), the Digital Agenda Assembly (2011), among many others.

Sergio Bravo Martín is a Computer Science Engineering from the University of Valladolid (Spain) and received the Master Diploma of Advanced Studies (2007) from the University of Salamanca, Spain. He is an active member of the research GRoup in InterAction and eLearning (GRIAL). Currently he focuses his main research areas in electronic government, Web engineering, and design patterns. He is an Associate Professor in the Computer Science Department of the University of Salamanca since 2005. Since 2000, he has worked as a member of the technical staff of the Department of Information Technologies and Communications (ITC) of the City Council of Salamanca since 2000 where he has developed his professional interests, and currently, he is Head of Division of Corporate Applications, Internet and e-Government.

Óscar Sanjuán Martínez is a Lecturer in the Computer Science Department of the University of Oviedo. He earned his Ph.D. from the Pontifical University of Salamanca in Computer Engineering. His research interests include object-oriented technology, Web engineering, software agents, and modeling software with BPM, DSL, and MDA.

Mohd Anuar Mazuki is the Chief Deputy Bursar - Accounts and Systems Unit, Bursary, Universiti Teknologi MARA (UiTM), Shah Alam, Selangor, Malaysia. Dr. Mazuki holds a PhD in Management Accounting, Master of Science-Accounting (Oklahoma, USA), and a Bachelor of Accountancy (UiTM). Other professional accreditations include, Association of Certified Chartered Accountants (ACCA), U.K., and Certified Financial Planner (CFP), U.S.A. and Malaysian Chapters. He is affiliated with several professional bodies; Malaysian Institute of Accountants (MIA), Association of Certified Chartered Accountants (ACCA), United Kingdom, American Institute of Certified Public Accountants (AICPA – Associate member), Financial Planning Association of Malaysia (FPAM), Commonwealth Association for Public Administration and Management (CAPAM), and the Malaysian Economic Association (MEA).

Miloš Milovanović is a Teaching Assistant at the University of Belgrade, School of Business Administration. He is also member of Laboratory for Multimedia Communications. Recently he acquired a Master's degree in Information Technologies and became a PhD student in the same area. His research interests include game-based learning, distributed informational systems, and multimedia.

Valeria Mininno was born in La Spezia. She graduated in Mechanical Engineering at the University of Pisa in 1993. From 1994 to 2001 she was a Researcher and Assistant Professor in Economics and Managerial Engineering; since then she has been an Associate Professor of Business Economics and Supply Chain Management. Her main research interests are in supply chain management, study, the development and applications of decision analysis, artificial intelligence tools and techniques, and their use in operations management.

Miroslav Minović is Assistant Professor of Informational Technology at University of Belgrade, School of Business Administration. He is also active member of Laboratory for Multimedia Communications. His research interests include human-computer interaction as well as the development of advanced user interfaces in education and games. Minovic received his PhD in Informational Technology from University of Belgrade in 2010.

Alexandre Ferreira Oliveira is a researcher at the *e:lab* – Research Laboratory on e-Government and e-Business - Brazilian School of Public and Business Administration of Getulio Vargas Foundation. He is also a Professor at Federal Center of Technological Education Foundation (FUNCEFET) and an invited Professor at the executive education programs at Getulio Vargas Foundation. He has held executive positions at the telecommunication industry in Brazil. He holds a B.Sc. in Electronic Engineering at the Federal University of Rio de Janeiro and an MBA at the Brazilian School of Public and Business Administration of Getulio Vargas Foundation. His research interests lie on CRM, e-Business, strategic use of IT, and logistics.

Francisco J. García Peñalvo holds a PhD in Computer Science (2000, University of Salamanca, Spain). He works as a Professor in the Computer Science Department of the University of Salamanca. He is the Research Group in Interaction and eLearning (GRIAL—http://grial.usal.es) Director. His main research interests are e-learning, computer and education, adaptive systems, web engineering, semantic web, and software reuse. He was a member of the Technological and Academic Committee of the White Book for Digital University 2010. He was Technology and Innovation Vice-Rector of the University of Salamanca from March 2007 to December 2009 and the President of the Technical Committee of the SCOPEO Observatory, an observatory for e-learning activity, innovation, and trends, from its inception until December 2009. He has more than 100 papers published in international journals and conferences.

Marc Petersen had studied Business Information Systems at Carl von Ossietzky University of Oldenburg (Germany) till 2012. He was also a research assistant at OFFIS e.V. in Oldenburg (Germany). He is currently an Enterprise Developer at open knowledge GmbH in Oldenburg (Germany) developing server-side Java applications with technologies like JSF 2.0, CDI, JAX-RS and JPA. His research interests include: adaptive applications, business intelligence and mobile cross-platform applications.

Teoh Ai Ping is a currently a Senior Lecturer with Graduate School of Business at Universiti Sains Malaysia. She graduated with a Bachelor of Accountancy (Honours), holds a Master of Science (Information Technology), and a Doctor of Business Administration. Her professional career began as a consultant in SAP R/3 enterprise resource planning system. Five years later, she progressed to join Wawasan Open University as a senior lecturer and was later appointed the Deputy Dean in School of Business and Administration. Dr. Teoh's areas of expertise include enterprise resource planning, business intelligence, technology-based service systems, enterprise risk management, and internal auditing. She is also active in industry consultancy, and has conducted numerous workshops and trainings on in her areas of expertise for industry and government agencies.

Pietro Previtali is an Assistant Professor of Business Organization at University of Pavia. He got his PhD in Management and Business Administration at Bocconi University. He teaches and conducts research on the managerial issues surrounding the introduction of information technologies in public agencies and private companies.

Marc J. A. Rabaey was IT-director in the Medical Service and CIO of the Assistant Chief of Staff Evaluation of the Belgian Ministry of Defense. He is actually System Thinking consultant in Business and Information Technology.

T. Ramayah is a Professor at the School of Management in USM. His publications appeared in *Journal of Environmental Management, Journal of Business Economics and Management, Computers in Human Behavior, Resources, Conservation and Recycling, International Journal of Information Technology & Decision Making (IJITDM), International Journal of Information Management, Lecture Notes in Computer Science, Turkish Online Journal of Education Technology, Journal of Research in Interactive Marketing, Information Development, Journal of Project Management (JoPM), IJITDM, International Journal of Services and Operations Management (IJSOM), Engineering, Construction and Architectural Management (ECAM),* and *North American Journal of Psychology,* among others. He also serves on the editorial boards and program committee of several international journals and conferences of repute.

Viveka Ramoo finished her Masters of Business Administration studies at the School of Management in USM. Currently she is running her own business in Penang, Malaysia. Her research focused on technology adoption by users.

Alejandro Rodríguez-González, PhD, is a Post-Doctoral Researcher of Bioinformatics Group at Centre for Plant Biotechnology and Genomics UPM-INIA, Polytechnic University of Madrid. His main research interests are the Semantic Web, Artificial Intelligence and Biomedical informatics field, with a particular interest on the creation of Medical Diagnosis Systems. He has a degree in Computer Science, a M.Sc in Computer Science and technology in the specialty of Artificial Intelligence, a M.Sc in Engineering Decision systems and a PhD in Computer Science. He has published several papers in international journals and edited various special issues in high quality journals. He also has participated in the organization of several workshops in top international conferences such as International Semantic Web Conference and Extended Semantic Web Conference among others.

David Rummel had studied Business Information systems at Carl von Ossietzky University of Oldenburg (Germany) till 2012. During his studies he worked as a research assistant in different departments. He currently is employed at a pharmaceutical company where he is designing and developing the company's business processes. His research interests include business process management and multi-touch technologies.

Cuauhtémoc Sánchez-Ramírez is a Professor in Supply Chain Management in the Instituto Tecnológico de Orizaba. He obtained his PhD in Industrial Engineering Science of the COMIMSA, which is a Research Center of National Council of Science and Technology of Mexico (CONACYT). He has worked as consultant on Logistics Systems in different nationals companies. His research projects have received research grants from the National Council of Science and Technology of Mexico. His research interests are the analyzed of supply chain under a system dynamics approach.

Dejan Simić Dušan Starčević is a full Professor at the School of Business Administration, University of Belgrade. He is also active member of Laboratory for Multimedia Communications. His research interests include system security and advances authentication systems that are based on biometry.

Dušan Starčević is a full Professor at the School of Business Administration, University of Belgrade, and a visiting Professor at the university's School of Electrical Engineering. He is also Vice-Dean for Scientific Research at the School of Business Administration. His main research interests include distributed information systems, multimedia, and computer graphics. He received a PhD in Information Systems from the University of Belgrade.

Lincoln C. Wood is a Senior Lecturer and Researcher in operations, logistics, and supply chain management at Curtin University of Technology in Perth, Australia. He received the CSCMP's Young Researcher Award in 2009 and later earned his PhD at the University of Auckland. In addition to his work experience in several logistics and consulting companies, Lincoln has published in journals including *Transportation Research Part B: Methodological* and the *International Journal of Operations & Production Management* and has authored many conference papers and book chapters. His research interests include strategic SCM, business cluster operations and supply chains, and service operations and supply chains.

Index

F

G

H

I

J

K

L

M

N

O

P

R

S

T

U

V

W